Reader Series
in Library and Information Science

Reader in
American Library History

edited by

Michael H. Harris

1971

Printed in the United States of America.
Published by Microcard Editions,
901 26th Street, N. W., Washington, D. C. 20037,
a part of the Industrial Products Division,
The National Cash Register Company

Foreword

Unlike many other academic disciplines, librarianship has not yet begun to exploit the contributions of the several disciplines toward the study of its own issues. Yet the literature abounds with material germane to its concerns. Too frequently the task of identifying, correlating, and bringing together material from innumerable sources is burdensome, time consuming or simply impossible. For a field whose stock in trade is organizing knowledge, it is clear that the job of synthesizing the most essential contributions from the elusive sources in which they are contained is overdue. This then is the rationale for the series, *Readers in Library and Information Science.*

The *Readers in Library and Information Science* will include books concerned with various broad aspects of the field's interests. Each volume will be prepared by a recognized student of the topic covered, and the content will embrace material from the many different sources from the traditional literature of librarianship as well as from outside the field in which the most salient contributions have appeared. The objectives of the series will be to bring together in convenient form the key elements required for a current and comprehensive view of the subject matter. In this way it is hoped that the core of knowledge, essential as the intellectual basis for study and understanding, will be drawn into focus and thereby contribute to the furtherance of professional education and professional practice in the field.

Paul Wasserman
Series Editor

v

Contents

V

Dewey, The American Library Association, and Education for Librarianship

VI

The Growth of Specialization—Into the Twentieth Century

Reader in
American Library History

INTRODUCTION

This volume is intended to contribute to the reader's understanding of the historical development of libraries and librarianship in America from the colonial period to the early twentieth century. A knowledge of American library history will surely provide an inspirational boost to the members of the profession, both young and old alike, since occupational pride is a basic characteristic of a mature profession. Librarians are often both harried by an unappreciative public and burdened with the day-to-day regimen of library administration, and sometimes lose sight of the long and honorable history of librarianship in this country.

In addition, the study of library history will broaden the perspective of the librarian in a number of ways. One of the most distressing characteristics of all the so-called "social professions" is their eventual tendency to view themselves as ends rather than means to ends, as was originally intended. An examination of American library history shows how the role of the library has been defined and redefined through the years, and will illuminate those social needs that stimulated the rise and encouraged the support of libraries over the past 300 years.

Historians point out that every age considers its own specific crises as the most significant, the most demanding, and potentially the most dangerous in the country's experience. An understanding of library history illustrates quite clearly that American librarians have faced seemingly major crises over the years; while we do not mean to suggest that we can afford the luxury of complacency at such a critical juncture in our history, it is both enlightening and encouraging to see the ways in which our predecessors perceived and overcame their most serious challenges.

The study of library history might also act as a cohesive force in an increasingly specialized profession. Perhaps an understanding of the history of the library and its unity of function will stimulate an end to the petty jealousies and antagonisms so rampant in modern librarianship. A clearer understanding of the historical definition of the function of libraries may well contribute to increased communication between librarians, the current lack of which is almost immediately obvious to people in the field.

Furthermore, the cautious use of library history will also be a significant aid in the intelligent administration of libraries. At the simplest level, an awareness of the historical development of a specific library can help an administrator effectively manage that library. At a slightly more sophisticated level, historical awareness prevents the all-too-embarrassing experience of reinventing the wheel. Of course, it is often the case that tradition is poorly suited to deal with emerging problems of the present and future. At the same time, a knowledge of library history can often dispel myths which have been so uncritically accepted by librarians in the past.

Finally, an understanding of the historical development of libraries can mitigate against the development of what the British historian J. H. Hexter once called "tunnel vision". That is, librarians often view library history as if they were looking into a tunnel through history. This would be fine if one would remember that there is earth above and around the tunnel, and that the shape and direction of the tunnel are controlled by the constitution of the substance about it. Similarly, library history, carefully researched and well written, will provide ample proof that the library is a product of a "complex of specific physical, social, and intellectual factors" and can only be understood in terms of its co-eval culture.

The papers in this book were selected with all these points in mind. It is hoped that the readings in this volume will in some small way contribute to the efficient and enlightened provision of library services, both now and in the future. The nature of the literature on American library history has in several ways influenced the content of this volume. Since there was no adequate single volume on American library history, this work attempts to be comprehensive; as a result, certain pivotal developments have had to be de-emphasized slightly, in order to connect the narrative into a meaningful whole.

A number of subfields of American library history are still basically uncharted. One specific shortcoming in the literature, for example, is in the area of school library development in the twentieth century. Unfortunately, the lack of quality research in this area means that this important subject lacks coverage in the text.

Finally, while the essays that follow are considered by the editor to be the most significant historical treatments of the American library experience available, some of them do lack up-to-date bibliographies. Consequently, a list of additional readings has been placed at the end of each section.

M. H. H.

I
THE STUDY OF AMERICAN LIBRARY HISTORY

In general, the American librarian has not been concerned with library history. The pressures of day-to-day library administration have left little time to plan for the future, let alone contemplate the past. There are those who think that this is both shortsighted and, in certain cases, costly. Pierce Butler, writing some twenty years ago in his now classic *Introduction to Librarianship*, noted that "librarianship, as we know it, can be fully apprehended only through an understanding of its historic origins." He went on to point out that many current situations in the field are "hopelessly puzzling" until one understands the history of the personal elements that went into them.

In the following essay, Jesse Shera argues convincingly in support of Butler's contention. Dean Shera analyzes a number of points in American library history where a "disregard for library history has resulted in confused thinking and much misdirected effort, consequences which eventually are professionally disastrous and socially regrettable." In doing so he also suggests the ways in which a knowledge of the historical development of libraries can contribute to an understanding of the role of the library in society, and presents some still timely suggestions relative to the future course of research in American library history.

Although Dean Shera's assessment of the research needs in American library history is now nearly twenty years old, it remains in many ways remarkably current. Since the publication of his essay, however, other important works on the subject have appeared. For a recent review of the field, the reader is directed to *A Guide to Research in American Library History*, listed as an additional reading at the end of this section.

On The Value of Library History

Jesse H. Shera

"Librarianship, as we know it, can be fully apprehended only through an understanding of its historic origins. . . . It is obvious that the librarian's
practice will be determined in part by his historical
understanding. . . . Unless the librarian has a clear
historical consciousness . . . he is quite certain at
times to serve his community badly."[1] Thus
wrote Pierce Butler almost two decades before the
Public Library Inquiry sought to assess the American public library through the application of the
most approved techniques of sociological analysis.
At first blush, Butler's insistence on the importance of historical awareness for an understanding
of the role of the library in modern society might
seem to be little more than an impassioned outcry
of a spirit in protest against an age that has rejected the values of history—against a world which
has come increasingly to believe that it, like Lot's
wife, would suffer disaster if it were to pause, even
briefly, for a retrospective glance. It is indeed true
that, when Butler so emphatically enunciated his
belief that librarianship could not fulfil its highest
social destiny if librarians remained ignorant of the
historical development of the library as a social
agency, he was contradicting the popular trend. In
the early 1930's American librarianship was striving, as it still is today, for professional respectability. There was a growing faith that librarianship
had, or could be given, an intellectual content, and
that content was sought in an ever growing corpus
of principles and techniques for the manipulation,
operation, and administration of library materials.
This was the day of glory for the technicians in
their white aprons, and everywhere attention was
concentrated on process rather than on function.

In opposition to this excessive preoccupation
with the techniques of library operations, Pierce
Butler wrote his *Introduction to Library Science.*
In this credo not only did he set forth a philosophic frame of reference within which librarianship could be seen as an integral part of the contemporary culture, but he argued strongly for a
recognition of history as basic to an understanding
of the library in relation to its coeval culture. Not
only did he reveal that a knowledge of history is

essential to the librarian's complete intellectual
equipment, but he showed history itself to be the
logical starting point for almost every inquiry into
the nature and function of the library as a social
agency.

This struggle to win for history a recognition of
its importance as a constituent element in the
emerging scholarship of library research has not
yet been won; it has, in fact, lost ground with the
increasing tendency to adopt, for research in librarianship, the methods of investigation of the
other social sciences. In the rush of librarians to
apply the form, if not the substance, of social science research to library problems, means have
often been mistaken for ends, techniques have
been employed without thought of their appropri-
ateness, results have been hastily interpreted, and
the historical method has been all but trampled
underfoot.

The purpose of the present essay is, therefore,
threefold: (1) to examine again the contribution
which history can make to an understanding of the
role of the library in society; (2) to identify and
isolate, if possible, the reasons for the decline in
the importance of history as an aid to the better
understanding of the library as a social agency; and
(3) to indicate the future course which research in
library history should take, if it is to justify the
time and effort spent in its pursuit.

THE SOCIAL VALUE OF HISTORY

Before one can make a case for the justification
of library history as an essential part of the intellectual content of librarianship, one must first attempt to determine the social utility of history itself. The writing of history is one of the oldest
major forms of human literary activity, if not the
oldest. This very fact of survival for so many centuries is in itself eloquent testimony of its social
importance. Yet it is only within the last century
or two that scholars have begun seriously to speculate about the specific values that history has to
offer. Not content with the easy assumption that
history, like virtue, is its own reward, many schol-

SOURCE: Reprinted from Jesse H. Shera, "On the Value of Library History," *Library Quarterly* 22 (July, 1952),
pp. 240-251, by permission of the publisher and the author. Copyright ©1952 by the University of Chicago Press.

ars have devoted countless hours to the reexamination of history, in the hope of extracting from it an apologia, an adequate justification, an answer to the question "What is history for?"

In the final analysis, all arguments in support of the social utility of history derive from the analogy between the memory of the individual and history as the collective memory of the group. An awareness of one's past is, for the individual, an essential part of the reasoning, or thinking, process. John Dewey, indeed, held that "thinking is a reconstructive movement of actual contents of experience in relation to each other."[2]   Admittedly, societies lack the capacity of the individual for the automatic recall of past experience, and, in the absence of an organic memory that can store experiences and reproduce them when needed, the society must create its own group memory. Thus the habit of recording in some graphic form the accounts of past experience appears even among primitive societies. As this utilitarian history was developed and refined, it gave rise to a new kind of creative narration, in which concern with accuracy was united with the pleasure of knowing the past and retelling it for the benefit of others. "The general verdict of our Western civilization," writes Crane Brinton, "has been that a knowledge of history is at the very least a kind of extension of individual experience, and therefore of value to the human intelligence that makes use of experience. And certainly the kind of knowledge we have called cumulative—natural science—is committed to the view that valid generalizations must depend on wide experience, including what is commonly called history."[3]

But the purpose of history is more than recall. Memory is not enough. The simple narration of past events is insufficient unless it is supplemented with an active understanding that can draw from this reconstruction of the past a synthesis, a series of generalizations, that not only will give the past a living reality but will make of it a medium for the better understanding of the present. Without such interpretation, history degenerates to an empty antiquarianism pursued for its own sake. The late R. G. Collingwood supplied possibly the clearest explanation of the true purpose of history, when he wrote:

> What is history for? . . . My answer is that history is "for" human self-knowledge. It is generally thought to be of importance to man that he should know himself: where knowing himself means knowing . . . his nature as man. . . . Knowing yourself means knowing what you can do; and since nobody knows what he can do until he tries, the only clue to what man can do

is what man has done. The value of history, then, is that it teaches us what man has done and thus what man is.[4]

Thus he derives his complete definition of history as

> . . . a science, or an answering of questions; concerned with human actions in the past; pursued by interpretation of evidence; for the sake of human self-knowledge.[5]

History, then, is a social science in the broadest sense, and the methods it employs are identical with the methods of the social scientists in so far as they can be practicably applied to the available historical data. The use of social science techniques in historical research is limited only by the peculiarities that inhere in the data of history itself.

But Clio is no mere stepchild of the social scientist; she is, in fact, a social scientist in her own right. The increasing attention which historians are directing toward the growth of institutional history—the history of business corporations, for example—the history of economic phenomena, and the historic impact of urbanization all testify to the historians' use of generalizations contributed by the other social sciences. The historian, in turn, contributes to the social sciences a check on such sociological generalizations. As Gottschalk has pointed out, the historian can serve the other social scientists in three ways: (1) by discovering historical cases that will illustrate and support social science generalizations, (2) by discovering cases that will contradict such generalizations, and (3) by applying social science generalizations to historical trends or series of similar or related historical events to test the validity of the former.[6] Hence "finding contradictions in and exceptions to social science generalizations is one of the ways the historian can best contribute to an understanding of society."[7]   Not only, then, does the historian provide the other social sciences with data derived from his investigations, but his work supplies a check on the validity of their concepts. The social scientist who rejects as inconsequential the findings of history is as unscientific as the historian who pretends to write about past social phenomena or social behavior without knowing the findings of the social scientists in relevant fields.

THE SOCIAL UTILITY OF
LIBRARY HISTORY

The writing of library history in the United States began, as was inevitable, with the long, tedious, and often uninspiring narration of the events, personalities, and circumstances surrounding the formation, growth, and development of individual institutions. These largely antiquarian biographies of libraries and librarians were an essential prerequisite to generalizations concerning the emergence of the library as an institutional form. Roughly three quarters of a century was devoted to this kind of minute exploration of library history, years which brought forth such notable works as Quincy's *The Boston Athenaeum,* Mason's *The Redwood Library*, Johnston's *The Library of Congress*, Wadlin's *The Boston Public Library*, Lydenberg's *The New York Public Library*, and a host of less ambitious works. Biographies of librarians were less numerous and, on the whole, less successful; but here one might well mention Garrison's *John Shaw Billings*, Kingdon's *John Cotton Dana*, and the half-dozen useful little volumes in the "American Library Pioneers" series.

By the 1930's there had accumulated a sufficient body of these historical data to enable a few individuals to discern the broad general outlines of the emergence and development of the library as a social institution, to relate it to its contemporary social milieu, and to identify, in a general way, the forces that brought the library to its present state of development and shaped its institutional form. Thus Arnold Borden's speculations on the sociological beginnings of the American public library and Lowell Martin's observations on the public library as a social institution were carried forward in the more comprehensive investigations of Ditzion's *Arsenals of a Democratic Culture* and the writer's *Foundations of the Public Library*. At the same time, the antiquarian approach was not entirely abandoned, and factual studies of individual libraries continued to be produced, many of them limited to unpublished theses sponsored by and carried out in the several library schools. Research in library history is, of course, far from exhaustive (it can, in fact, never really attain completion), but the available syntheses show the major lines of development that characterized the growth of the American public library and reveal it as a part of the process of institutionalization that is characteristic of our culture. One may, therefore, appropriately inquire into the value of these investigations and their true bearing on the practice of librarianship.

What is the real value of library history? Perhaps such a question can best be answered by describing certain situations in which a disregard of library history has resulted in confused thinking and much misdirected effort, consequences which eventually are professionally disastrous and socially regrettable.

THE ADULT EDUCATION MOVEMENT OF THE 1930'S

A quarter of a century ago librarians, inspired by the plans of the American Library Association for an "expanded program" of activities and eagerly seeking a promising cause with which they might ally themselves, seized with missionary ardor upon the newly invented term, "adult education." Though the phrase was new, the idea was at least as old as Benjamin Franklin's *Junto*. The social libraries of the eighteenth and nineteenth centuries were voluntary associations of adults eagerly seeking "self-improvement." But the mortality rate of these organizations was high, in spite of the initial enthusiasm of their founders. The nineteenth century brought with it the lyceum movement, the mechanics' institutes, the literary societies, the associations for the education of the merchants' clerks, and the Chautauqua movement.

In 1925 William Jennings Bryan died in Chattanooga, Tennesse, within the very shadow of the unhappy Scopes affair, and with him went the Chautauqua movement, to which he had contributed so much of his vitality. By this time, too, the old Chautauqua Literary and Scientific Circle was, for many people, little more than a childhood memory; *Acres of Diamonds* had become almost legendary; and even the parent-institution, "simmering in the tepid lakeside sun," would hardly have been recognized by its founders, Vincent and Miller. Already the motion picture, the automobile, and even the radio were making the village get-together less and less important in American community life.

The death of the traveling Chautauquas in the last magnificent gesture of the Jubilee Year may have accentuated the rapidly changing pattern of American culture, but it did not mean that the popular urge for "self-education" had disappeared. If the brown tents of the Chautauqua had been stored away for good, their place was soon to be taken by the American Association for Adult Education and its forums, discussion groups, adult education councils, and directed reading programs.

All the aberrant manifestations of the urge for the intellectual growth of the adult directly or indirectly stimulated a temporary interest in the growth of library book collections. Many of the movements actively included libraries and library promotion as important segments of their operating programs. But even at a time when the public library was itself expanding rapidly in both number and size of collections, every attempt to associate the library movement with that of adult education met with conspicuous lack of success. Virtually every library that owed its existence to the initiative of the lyceums, the Chautauquas, or the literary circles died with the demise of the movement itself.

Yet this eagerness of librarians to ally themselves with a social movement so obviously less stable than their own reappeared with renewed vigor in the 1930's. In this recrudescence of the cultural urge the librarians were, as they had been in an earlier day, the willing, eager, and often misguided disciples. Everywhere librarians began the establishment of readers' advisory services, the formation of forums and discussion groups, the promotion or encouragement of adult education councils, the preparation of selected reading lists for "adult beginners." The American Library Association sponsored "Reading with a Purpose," and all turned to the "A Cube E" for hope, guidance, and inspiration. In scarcely more than a decade, the tumult reached its highest pitch when Alvin Johnson published his *The Public Library— a People's University.* Extremists even went so far as to argue that, if libraries were to play their proper part in adult education, they themselves would have to publish books especially suited to its needs.[8]

No one reflected that the very arguments advanced by Johnson, which then seemed so convincing, were almost identical with those employed a century earlier by Henry Barnard, Horace Mann, and others seeking to promote an incipient public library movement. No one turned back the pages of history to discover that for decades such arguments had fallen on ears that were almost totally deaf to such appeals. No one recalled that every attempt to associate the library with universal "self-improvement" had been conspicuously unsuccessful. No one reflected that attempts to associate libraries with Franklin's *Junto*, the lyceum movement, the self-help associations of mechanics' apprentices and mercantile clerks, the Sunday-school movement, and the literary and scientific reading circles had all failed to achieve permanence. The fact that the library has none of the attributes of "a people's university" bothered no one. In short, there was a universal unawareness of the fact that this entire program was a serious distortion of the historic role of the library in society.

Today the adult education movement, if not dead, is certainly suffering a lamentable malaise; but the popular faith in the self-education of the adult still persists, and, if there has been disillusionment concerning the efficacy of "reading with a purpose" and the generosity of Andrew Carnegie, faith has found restoration in the "American heritage" and the benevolence of Henry Ford.

THE PUBLIC LIBRARY INQUIRY

When Robert D. Leigh and his associated experts in the social science disciplines began their "appraisal in sociological, cultural, and human terms of the extent to which the [public] librarians are achieving their objectives" and set out to assess "the public library's actual and potential contribution to American society,"[9] they unquestioningly accepted the time-honored assumption that "the major objectives of the American public library are . . . education, information, aesthetic appreciation, research, and recreation,"[10] and it was within this frame of reference that the Inquiry staff conducted its investigation. This was in itself a wholly unscientific procedure, but the Inquiry did not stop here. It made further assumptions which Mr. Leigh has stated as follows:

> From their official statements of purpose, it is evident that public librarians conceive of themselves as performing an educational task. The library, however, may also be thought of as a constituent part of public (or mass) communication: the machinery by which words, sounds, and images flow from points of origin through an impersonal medium to hosts of unseen readers and audiences. . . . And the public library's services to its patrons are in direct, though often unacknowledged, competition with the commercial media. One clue, then, to the discovery of the public library's most appropriate role in contemporary society is to see it against the background of the whole enterprise of public communication.[11]

Following this line of reasoning, Campbell and Metzner surveyed, for the Inquiry, the use made of the public library by the adult population in eighty selected communities. Their conclusion was that the public library is "failing to a considerable extent as an agency of mass communication and enlightenment."[12] It is their opinion that "the library suffers from being a quiet voice in an increasingly clamorous world" and "there is reason to believe that through broader services and a more active information program this fraction of the population (which it now serves) could be considerably increased."[13]

Mr. Leigh and his staff of social scientists must have taken some passing notice of the history of the American public library. In fact, Oliver Garceau devotes the opening chapter of his *The Public Library in the Political Process* to a historical consideration of "The Foundations of Library Government." But they could not have read this history with much care or thoughtfulness. Even a cursory examination of the history of the American public library would have made unmistakably clear that the public library never has been, and probably never was really intended to be, an instrument of mass communication. The public library, as we know it today, came about through the effort of small and highly literate groups of professional men—scholars, lawyers, ministers, and educators—who sorely needed books for the performance of their daily tasks and who, through their efforts, convinced their respective communities of the social utility of supporting a public library. Even George Ticknor, who, more emphatically than most, argued for the public library as an agency of popular culture, helped fill the shelves of the new Boston Public Library with titles that more properly belonged in the study of the man of letters.

If one learns anything at all from library history, it is certainly that the public library has never evinced any of the attributes of a mass-communication agency. It has never had a "captive audience"—not even an "elite" captive audience. Similarly, the librarian has never been a "manipulator" who seeks to win the agreement of as large a part of his captive audience as possible to his particular aims. Furthermore, in the library the initiative has always come from the library patron, never from the librarian. The librarian has never been able to bend his patron to his purpose as has the radio commentator or the newspaper columnist. Thus any attempt to study the public library as a segment of the existing system of mass communication ignores history, and the Public Library Inquiry, in so doing, may have committed a costly and disastrous blunder.

THE PROBLEM OF DEFINITION

The misconceptions that underlie both the adult education movement and the Public Library Inquiry derive from the same fallacious definition of the "educational" function of the library. The concept of the library as an educational agency is a direct transfer to librarianship of nineteenth-century faith in the education of the masses, a faith that had its roots in the eighteenth-century Enlightenment and the belief in the idea of progress and the perfectibility of man. Through the influence of nineteenth-century educational leaders, this dogma of human perfectibility was transformed into a general conviction that the intellectual improvement, i.e., the education of the young, was a universal social responsibility—and thus began the ever expanding movement for free, tax-supported public schools.

But this new urge for universal education was met by two opposing forces. The first came with the realization that men are not created intellectually equal and that there are great masses of the population incapable of assimilating the traditional classical scholarship, which in previous centuries had been restricted to the few who could profit from such rigid mental discipline. Hence popular education was expanded, through such instruments as the Morrill Act, to include training in the agricultural and industrial technologies, partly because the basic acceptance of popular education was thereby extended and partly because there was in our increasingly technological culture a growing need for people trained in these skills.

The second counteracting force came with the discovery that our cultural pattern was not singular but dual, that, in addition to the Greco-Roman culture which had up to this time dominated popular education, there was an independent folk culture which was not derivative but had its roots in the hearts, minds, and experiences of the masses of the people.

These opposing forces, then, brought schism to the educational world, but the librarians continued to cling tenaciously to the traditional nineteenth-century concept of education as an attempt to impose upon the public the traditions of classical scholarship and to translate popular culture into "elite" terms. Thus many librarians view their institutions as bulwark against an encroaching flood of cultural mediocrity and seek to explain away their failure to "educate" the masses. This unrealistic infatuation of the librarian with his educational responsibilities arises in part from a desire to share in the prestige that the professional educator has long enjoyed in American culture, but it is in large measure the result of the deterioration of the definition of education itself. During the last few decades the term "education" has been so broadly and loosely applied that it has now very nearly lost all meaning. Today almost every human experience has been described at one time or another as "educational," and even the advertiser who discourses at length on the deleterious effects of certain tobaccos upon the membranes of the "T-Zone" has come to think of himself as a missionary of popular enlightenment.

Such absurdities force a return to the original definition of "education," as derived from the Latin *educere*, "to lead forth." The educator, then, is a leader, one who conducts the student from a world that is familiar to a land that, at least for the student, is unexplored. The librarian, by the very nature of the responsibilities which he has assumed, cannot function effectively as such a leader. Only in a few isolated instances has personal contact between patron and librarian made possible the student-teacher relationship; yet from just such exceptions has grown a whole myth concerning the "educational" role of the librarian in society. So long as the social responsibility of the librarian remains the collecting, organizing, servicing, and administering of the graphic records of civilization and the encouragement of their most effective utilization, he cannot be an educator in the proper sense. To superimpose upon his established functions these irrelevant tasks will certainly confuse his objectives, if it does not actually destroy the true purpose for which the library was created.

This does not imply that the librarian must resign himself to a passive role in society, that he must continue to be "a quiet voice in an increasingly clamorous world." To be sure, the world would doubtless profit from an increase of vocal restraint. The librarian is at complete liberty to promote his services with all the intensity and drive that he deems desirable; but his vigor, if misdirected, can result only in frustration and eventual failure. Nor does this argument suggest that a social agency cannot attempt to change, even drastically, its function in society; but the proponents of such alteration must be aware that the course which they are proposing is counter to the historical trend and may well involve grave risks. To reason that, because educators and librarians both make use of books and ideas, librarians are therefore educators is equivalent to saying that Old Dutch Cleanser is a food merely because it is usually kept in the kitchen and used by the cook.

REASONS FOR THE NEGLECT OF HISTORY

Though one may grant that an understanding of the past is of major importance to those engaged in the social sciences, either as practical workers or as scholars, it still remains true that the uses and limitations of historical study have long been debated. As Crane Brinton points out, "there have always been individuals to whom the study of history seems unprofitable, even vicious, a limitation on the possibilities of soaring that the human spirit not dragged down by history might have."[14] There are a number of reasons for this growing lack of interest in history that is so strikingly characteristic of the historian's colleagues in the other social sciences, even though the popular appeal of history still remains relatively strong.

With the maturation of the social sciences as a recognized field of scholarship has come the development of a whole new constellation of techniques for the isolation, analysis, and investigation of social phenomena. In past centuries man turned to history alone, as today he turns to the entirety of the social sciences, for an understanding of man's social behavior. Then history was the only key to an understanding of man as man. But today history no longer provides the sole textbook for the study of human social, psychological, economic, and political behavior; and, with the evolution of specialized techniques in each of these branches of social science, there has arisen not only a diminution of the prestige of the historian but a concurrent distrust of his methods. Thus social scientists generally have come to consider history, if not actually a sterile and fruitless field of investigation, at least an academic adornment, to be pursued only for its own sake, with little or no thought to practical utility. In short, they would challenge Collingwood's defense of history that "the only clue to what man can do is what man has done" and that the "value of history, then, is that it teaches us what man has done and thus what man is." That the social scientists, in following this line of argument, are pursuing a dangerous path has been suggested in the illustrations above.

The second argument that has been so successfully used against the historian arises from the belief that an increasingly complex pattern of social behavior denies the predictive value of history. If there have been those who have clung to the belief that history does not repeat itself, it is only because they subscribe to the popular adage that even a donkey will not stumble over the same stone twice. In this the social scientists have been strongly supported by the historians themselves, who have been eternally timid in defending the predictive value of their craft even when they must have known that a donkey will stumble over the same stone not only twice but many times. The Bourbons never learn. The great powers of the world relentlessly precipitate wars, fight them, win and lose them, and then go about the business of fomenting future conflicts with policies and practices almost identical with those that brought on earlier international strife. The cynical aphorism that "man learns nothing from history except that he learns nothing from history" is too often true. But man does sometimes learn something from history—though not so much as he should—and the real question is: Does his wisdom increase with sufficient rapidity to avoid catastrophe?

But the third and basic reason for the decline of history may be charged directly to the historians themselves. When Leopold von Ranke first enunciated his conviction that the task of the historian was to recreate the past "wie es eigentlich gewesen ist," he inaugurated a new era of scholarly accuracy in historical writing. At the same time he shackled historians for generations to come to a blind devotion to the fact per se, and from this bondage the historians have even yet been unable to free themselves. The result has been that synthesis and interpretation have been forsaken in the mad scramble to reexamine all history in the light of the new Rankean methodology. Thus has arisen a widespread belief that the true historian busies himself with the minutiae of historical detail, having little or no regard for the significance of the factual remains that he is able to uncover.

Such a criticism does not imply that the Germanic influence in historical scholarship is to be disparaged. The historical documents which Von Ranke found stood in need of just such searching criticism and analysis as his methods could give, and the school of historical writing which he founded merits all the credit given to it. No history can rise above the level of the accuracy in factual detail upon which it rests. But historians have often forgotten that syntheses and interpretations are also *facts* and that their truth to reality is often more important than the lesser values of their constituent elements. Truth itself is absolute, not relative, but the *importance* of truth can display an infinite degree of variation. Robert Maynard Hutchins has said:

> Philistines will ask, what is truth? And all truths cannot be equally important. It is true that a finite whole is greater than any of its parts. It is also true, in the common-sense use of the word, that the New Haven telephone book is smaller than that of Chicago. The first truth is infinitely more fertile and significant than the second. . . . Real unity can be achieved only by a hierarchy of truths which shows us which are fundamental and which are subsidiary, which significant and which not.[15]

Similarly, the question of whether or not General Custer disobeyed the orders of General Terry and of which man was more responsible for the disastrous massacre of the Seventh Cavalry at the battle of the Little Big Horn is less important than the whole fact of governmental stupidity in dealing with the problems of the American Indians. Yet an excessive amount of historical scholarship has been channeled into establishing the truth or falsity of the insignificant trifles, and, for all its good intentions and lofty motives, it has in many ways rendered history a real disservice.

THE REORIENTATION OF RESEARCH IN LIBRARY HISTORY

If the writing of library history is to realize its fullest possibilities, it must be subjected to a drastic reorientation that will bring it into conformity to an underlying philosophy respecting the social function of the library itself. During the last two decades the earlier writing of library history has been severely criticized because of an excessive preoccupation with antiquarian detail and a provincial point of view. This charge that the authors of library history saw the library as an isolated and independent agency existing in a social vacuum was a thoroughly justified and wholesome criticism, and it promoted some useful exploratory thinking about the relation of the library to its coeval social milieu. But it did not go far enough. Even those writers who tried to present the library in sociological terms confined themselves to its institutional structure and form. They described, with a reasonable degree of success, *how* the public library assumed its present institutional pattern, but they did not question the current underlying assumptions about the function of the library in society, and hence they failed to explain *why* it came to be the kind of public agency it now is.

This failure of library history completely to come to grips with the problems of interpreting the social context from which the library arose may be explained in another way. "Man," says Pierce Butler, "is 'a thinker . . . a tool-user, and a social being,' and therefore his culture is trichotomous—'an organic integration of a scholarship, a physical equipment, and a social organization.' "[16]

Valid library history, then, can be written only when the library is regarded in relation to this tripartite division of culture, a phenomenon which not only has physical being, is formed in response to social determinants, but finds its justification as a segment of the totality of the intellectual processes of society. The library is an agency of the entirety of the culture; more specifically, it is one portion of the system of graphic communication through which that culture operates, and its historic origins are to be sought in an understanding of the production, flow, and consumption of graphic communication through all parts of the social pattern.

One may properly conclude, therefore, that the historical emergence and development of the library as an agency of this process of graphic communication must be viewed in a framework of effective investigation into the whole complex problem of the trichotomous culture, a study of those processes by which society *as a whole* seeks to achieve a perceptive or understanding relation to the *total* environment—the physical, the social, and the intellectual.

So long as the process of communication was personal, direct, and immediate, the problem of transmission was a simple and local matter. But as it became possible to extend the communication process to ever greater dimensions through space and time, as the pattern of culture became increasingly complex, and as the informational needs of society became more divergent and even conflicting, an understanding of the historical development of the several aspects of culture becomes mandatory. Although the ultimate aim of such a study is effectively to order our communication processes to the end of greater benefit to society, it cannot proceed toward any valid conclusions without first answering such questions as: What have been the respective roles of the "personal carrier" and of the graphic record in the communication process? How did the main stream of graphic communication grow to its present flood proportions? What tributaries fed its turbulent waters, and how and to what extent did it irrigate the surrounding wastelands of human ignorance? What is the real contribution of libraries to this enrichment of the culture? What can be known of the past that will promote the exploitation of truth and the avoidance of error? What hope is there for the future ordering of graphic communication for the benefit of mankind? Even the mere listing of such questions reveals the depth to which their answers must be rooted in an understanding of the past.

The limitations of the present discussion preclude the possibility of describing in detail a research program in the history of librarianship and bibliographic organization that would contribute to the answering of such questions. But a few topics for investigation may be suggested that should exemplify the kind of historical inquiry which the writer has in mind.

It would seem to be a truism that the history of the library is related to the history of book production itself and that the two should be investigated in relation to each other. Yet we do not know what state of complexity a literature must achieve before society demands libraries of varying degrees of structural intricacy or subject specialization. The profession already possesses a series of histories of individual "special" libraries in medicine, business, industry, commerce, and the like; but all these, placed end to end, do not present a useful history of the special-library movement in this country. No history of special libraries has yet been written that will answer such questions as the following:

1. What kinds of special libraries appeared first?
2. What was the structure of the business or industry at the time the special libraries for that particular enterprise developed?
3. What was the "structure" of the literature of that particular field, i.e., was it largely contained in books, in periodicals, or in special reports?
4. What were the basic informational needs of the enterprise, and what kinds of publications were essential to the meeting of these needs?
5. What was the maturity of the bibliographic organization for the particular field to be investigated; were its materials well organized bibliographically, or were there few bibliographies, guides, and indexing or abstracting services?
6. In all these respects, how does one field compare with another or one period with another in the demands that it makes for library and bibliographic resources?

Such an intensive analysis, not only for the special library but for the public library, the large research library, and the other bibliographic services that have been stimulated by our increasingly complex system of graphic communication, would contribute substantially to our understanding of the place of the library in our society.

Without such a "clear historical consciousness," is the librarian likely "at times to serve his community badly"? Indeed, without such an understanding, he is in constant danger of not serving his community at all. The degree of his success will be largely determined by the extent to which practical considerations are founded upon historic truth. To paraphrase the words of a German writer on archeology, library history is the concern of every librarian, for history is not an esoteric or special branch of knowledge but a synthesis of life itself. When we busy ourselves with library history, librarianship as a whole becomes our subject. History is not an occasional or partial affair, "but a constant balancing on the point of intersection where past and future meet."[17]

FOOTNOTES

[1] Pierce Butler, *An Introduction to Library Science* (Chicago: University of Chicago Press, 1933), pp. 81, 89-90, 101.

[2] John Dewey, *Essays in Experimental Logic* (Chicago: University of Chicago Press, 1916), p. 176.

[3] Crane Brinton, *Ideas and Men* (New York: Prentice-Hall, 1950), p. 19.

[4] R. G. Collingwood, *The Idea of History* (Oxford: Clarendon Press, 1946), p. 10.

[5] *Ibid.,* pp. 10-11.

[6] Louis Gottschalk, *Understanding History* (New York: Alfred A. Knopf, 1950), p. 252.

[7] *Ibid.,* p. 253.

[8] James Truslow Adams, *Frontiers of American Culture* (New York: Charles Scribner's Sons, 1944), p. 230.

[9] Robert D. Leigh, *The Public Library in the United States* (New York: Columbia University Press, 1950), p. 3.

[10] American Library Association, Committee on Post-war Planning, *A National Plan for Public Library Service* (Chicago: American Library Association, 1948), p. 107, summarizing from the committee's *Post-war Standards for Public Libraries* (Chicago: American Library Association, 1943), pp. 19-24.

[11] Leigh, *op. cit.,* pp. 25-26.

[12] So interpreted by William S. Gray, "Summary of Reading Investigations, July 1, 1949 to June 30, 1950," *Journal of Educational Research,* XLIV (February, 1951), 403.

[13] Angus Campbell and Charles A. Metzner, *Public Use of the Library and Other Sources of Information* (Ann Arbor: Institute for Social Research, University of Michigan, 1950), p. 45.

[14] Brinton, *op cit.,* p. 19.

[15] Robert Maynard Hutchins, *The Higher Learning in America* (New Haven: Yale University Press, 1936), p. 95.

[16] Pierce Butler, "Librarianship as a Profession, " *Library Quarterly,* XXI (October, 1951), 240.

[17] C. W. Ceram [pseud.] , *Gods, Graves, and Scholars* (New York: Alfred A. Knopf, 1952), p. 20.

ADDITIONAL READINGS

Colson, John C., "Speculations on the Uses of Library History," *Journal of Library History* 4 (January, 1969), pp. 65-71.

Cutliffe, M. R., "The Value of Library History," *Library Review* 21 (Winter, 1967), pp. 193-196.

Harris, Michael H., *Guide to Research in American Library History* (Metuchen, New Jersey: Scarecrow Press, 1968).

Holley, Edward, "Neglect of the Greats: Some Observations on the Problems of Writing Biographies of American Librarians," *Library Journal* 88 (October, 1963), pp. 3547-3551.

McMullen, Haynes "Research Backgrounds in Librarianship," *Library Trends* 6 (October, 1957), pp. 110-119.

Reichmann, Felix, "Historical Research and Library Science," *Library Trends* 13 (July, 1964), pp. 31-41.

Shera, Jesse H., "The Literature of American Library History," *Library Quarterly* 15 (January, 1945), pp. 1-24.

Vleeschauwer, H. J., "Library History in Library Science," *Mousaion* Nos. 29 and 30, 1958.

II

BOOKS AND READING IN COLONIAL AMERICA

For a good many years American historians were heavily committed to research and writing on the economic and political development of the United States, and tended to overlook the history of ideas. In recent years we have witnessed a steady increase in historical interest in "the life of the mind"; numerous studies have appeared which treat American ideas in relation to the environment or to the prevailing climate of opinion. Along with their growing interest in the "American mind," historians have become increasingly concerned with the impact of ideas, and, more significantly for library history, with the dissemination of ideas.

Merle Curti, in his Pulitzer prize-winning *Growth of American Thought*, outlined this new emphasis by arguing that "the history of knowledge, of speculation and ideas, and of values cannot easily be traced without reference to the institutions especially concerned with making accretions to knowledge and thought and disseminating these. Thus the growth of schools, colleges, libraries, the press, laboratories, foundations and research centers becomes an important condition for the growth of American thought."

This new emphasis on the dissemination of ideas in America encouraged scholars interested in the first three centuries of American history to pay serious attention to one of the primary means of disseminating information during that period: the printed word—whether transmitted by means of books, newspapers, or magazines—and in the repository of the printed word, that is, the library.

As a result, the signficance of library and book history as an integral part of American cultural history seems to be generally accepted among intellectual historians. However, the most painstaking and productive work along these lines has been the result of research undertaken by scholars investigating the colonial period of American history. Louis B. Wright, the author of the first essay in this section, suggested the importance of library history in relation to the pursuit of American intellectual history when he wrote:

> The choice of books brought by the first settlers, or imported as soon as they had established themselves in the wilderness, provides a significant clue to their conception of intellectual and social values. Since these values lie at the foundation of American intellectual and literary history, an understanding of the early colonial attitudes toward the purpose of books is necessary to any study of literary culture in America.

Book, Libraries, and Learning

Louis B. Wright

*Louis B. Wright, prominent American historian and former director of both the Hunt-
ington and Folger libraries, has written widely on early American history. In this essay, he presents a brilliant synthesis of the library, book, and educational history of
the period, and in doing so revises a number of earlier theories on colonial intellectual
life. He proves that books were widely available in the colonies, analyzes the most
popular ones, and shows that the reading tastes of the first colonists, whether they
were Cavaliers or Yankees, did not vary nearly as much as was once believed.*

When prospective colonists, preparing to embark
for North America in the seventeenth century,
came to pack their belongings for the long voyage
in crowded little ships, the decision as to what to
take and what to eliminate was a matter of such vital importance that it might mean success or failure, life or death.[1] Since freight was high and even
the most elementary essentials of life had to be
transported, the wonder is that the emigrants
found room for such luxuries as books. But the
fact is that they did. We can imagine the bewil-
dered worry of many a pioneer, pondering the relative importance of an extra pair of boots or a
stout folio as he chose his indispensables for the
Great Venture. The choice of books brought by
the first settlers, or imported as soon as they had
established themselves in the wilderness, provides a
significant clue to their conception of intellectual
and social values. Since these values lie at the
foundation of American intellectual and literary
history, an understanding of the early colonial attitude toward the purpose of books is necessary to
any study of literary culture in America. Inciden-
tally, the reading habits of seventeenth-century
Americans indicate the continuing influence of
Tudor and Stuart writers, and for that reason even
those students who yawn over what they describe
as the literary desert of America will do well to
contemplate the vitality of English authors in the
New World.

Generalizations about the reading habits of the
seventeenth-century colonists are subject to many
qualifications. Our evidence is often limited. We
cannot be certain that a man read a book because
he possessed it, but it is reasonable to suppose that
pioneers did not go to the expense and trouble of
gathering books merely for show. A large proportion of the inventories do not quote titles but instead make such tantalizing references as "one par-
cel of old books," or "five great books in folio."
Hence it is impossible to say that any author then
available was not known in the colonies. For all
we know, the unspecified parcels of old books
may have contained quartos and folios of Shakespeare. What we can do is to reason from the habits of typical colonists whose records are fairly
complete: letters, diaries, wills, and inventories
provide the clues that enable us to reconstruct the
literary interests of the early settlers. Proof is ample of the presence of books among the posses-
sions of the colonists in the first century of settlement. The ruling classes and even many humbler
folk possessed works which they prized as important to their lives and prosperity. The significance
of their selection of these books is a problem deserving our attention.

Sectional patriotism and prejudice have produced many facile generalizations about the differences in the literary taste of "Puritan" New England and "Cavalier" Virginia. The facts are that
although some significant differences gradually
manifest themselves, the similarities between the
literary tastes of early Virginians and New Englanders are as striking as their differences. Although one is not surprised to find more theological works in the library of a Puritan preacher of
Boston than among the books of a tobacco planter
on the Chesapeake, one may be surprised at the
large number of titles throughout the seventeenth
century common to both sections. This is true

SOURCE: Reprinted from Louis B. Wright, *Cultural Life of the American Colonies*, (New York: Harper and Row, Publishers, Inc., 1957), Chapter 6, "Books, Libraries, and Learning," pp. 126-153, by permission of the publisher. Copyright © 1957 by Harper & Row, Publishers, Inc.

even of books of divinity. The intellectual differences between early New Englanders and Virginians were not so great as some of their descendants would have us believe.

Some literary students of the American seventeenth century have been perturbed over the scarcity of belles-lettres in the luggage of the first settlers. They wring their hands because Shakespeare's plays were neglected and other great poets passed over for dull works of divinity. But such critics have rarely taken the trouble to look at the books the colonists actually read, and they forget that these pioneers were more concerned about self-improvement than poetry. Shakespeare had not yet been made "improving" by legions of schoolteachers.

When the colonist began to select books for his five-foot shelf of essential works, he chose items that he proposed to consult. He may have borne in mind the advice of Henry Peacham in *The Compleat Gentleman* (1622), a handbook that some of our ancestors thought necessary to their life in America: "Affect not as some do that bookish ambition," Peacham had warned, "to be stored with books and have well furnished libraries, yet keep their heads empty of knowledge: to desire to have many books and never to use them is like a child that will have a candle burning by him all the while he is sleeping."[2] Prospective Americans could not yet afford libraries for ostentation, nor had they the inclination to burden themselves with useless books. Books that provided guidance in the way of life that the colonists were marking out for themselves predominated therefore in their literary preferences.

A considerable proportion of the books collected by Americans in the seventeenth century were sheer utilitarian works. Since every man was his own doctor, a few books on chirurgery and medicine were essential, and thousands lived—and died—according to the recipes of Philip Barrough's *The Method of Physic* (1583) or William Vaughan's *Directions for Health, Both Natural and Artificial* (1600), the latter work having been written specifically for the benefit of Newfoundland settlers.[3] Likewise, every man had to be his own lawyer and many citizens came equipped with Michael Dalton's *The Country Justice,* Sir Edward Coke's *Reports,* or Sir Thomas Littleton's *Tenures,* works which not only gave them the information and language to represent the sound and fury of the law but also made it possible for laymen to sit as judges in the local courts, to draw up deeds and wills, and to conduct complicated lawsuits in their litigations over land and property. Books of surveying and engineering were of course considered

necessary. Miles Standish felt that he needed William Barriffe's *Military Discipline*; or, *The Young Artilleryman* to aid him in warding off the Indian and Dutch enemies of Plymouth Colony. Planters of Virginia and New England alike brought along Gervase Markham's various books on farming, horsemanship, and sundry country pursuits. The foundation of Yankee horsetrading was laid by that popular work of one L. W. C., *A Very Perfect Discourse and Order How to Know the Age of a Horse.* But useful as were these technical works, they can scarcely be called literary assets.

Since the greatest amount of information in the most convenient form is usually to be found in an encyclopedia, the colonists brought along such encyclopedic works as Pierre de La Primaudaye's *The French Academy*, a title found in many inventories in the tobacco colonies and in New England. It was one of the books that Miles Standish read when he was not fighting Indians or quarreling with the saints and sinners who crossed his path. The importance of this work in the informal education of seventeenth-century readers on both sides of the Atlantic has never been fully recognized because few students have bothered to look at it. Indeed, one writer on American colonial culture explains this title, mentioned in a will, as the "publications of the French Academy." La Primaudaye's work in reality is an outline of knowledge with a strong emphasis on the natural sciences, heavily moralized to take away any taint of damnation which meddling with God's mysteries might have suggested.[4] Preachers and laymen, tobacco planters and Boston traders, all found *The French Academy* a useful book in their search for information, cultural, scientific, and godly. Other encyclopedias are found in the lists of colonial libraries, even that wondrous collection of medieval lore, *De Proprietatibus Rerum,* but none so frequently occurs as La Primaudaye's compilation. Home study, or "adult education," in America should regard this book as one of its foundation stones. An important reason for the popularity on both sides of the Atlantic of Du Bartas' versified description of the creation in his *Divine Weeks and Works* was the encyclopedic information it contained. While Anne Bradstreet was absorbing enough poetic inspiration from Du Bartas to make her the Tenth Muse, many a less exalted reader was acquiring from the same source information which he accepted as scientific truth about God's creatures, the stars in the heavens, and even the qualities of the angels themselves. Our ancestors loved "books of knowledge" even as we do, even as had their medieval sires before them.

The zeal to perpetuate learning, to keep alive the desire for knowledge, and to provide the instruments of self-instruction accounts for many volumes of a textbook character. Works whose value had been first learned in the English grammar schools were brought along to be used by the children of the settlers or to keep the wisdom of the ancients fresh in the minds of adults. Books of rhetoric and logic, collections of aphorisms and the flowers of eloquence, compilations of similes, dictionaries, and other handbooks of learning were common. Many of these books were reliable works that the fathers of the first settlers might have known. Erasmus, for example, remained popular in America throughout the seventeenth century. Schoolboys in Massachusetts and wealthy planters in Virginia had collections of the adages and colloquies of the great humanist. Harvard College students quoted the wisdom of Erasmus in their exercises;[5] and if men like Ralph Wormeley and Richard Lee of Virginia did not quote him in their speeches, they at least owned his works.[6] Books used in the grammar schools were not completely neglected in later life. John Hull, mintmaster and treasurer of the Colony of Massachusetts Bay, must have remembered the concise wisdom of Erasmus or perhaps that in the *Colloquies* of Corderius when he sat down to write out some aphorisms as his own rules of life.[7] Throughout the century, works of aphoristic wisdom were prized. This quality in Bacon's *Essays* no doubt accounts for their popularity.

The humanistic tradition of the Renaissance, with its insistence upon the cultural discipline of Greek and Latin writers, exerted a strong influence upon the choice of books for American libraries throughout the seventeenth century, despite occasional qualms of a Puritan disturbed in his conscience over too much attention to heathen authors. Some of the early settlers in Virginia and New England had a respectable number of classical works, and as libraries became larger and more numerous during the later years of the century, an increasing emphasis was placed upon Greek and Latin writers, both in the originals and in translation. George Sandys, busily translating Ovid's *Metamorphoses* on the banks of the James in 1622, was not alone in his interest in Latin poetry; and Miles Standish in chilly and pious Plymouth in the 1630's must have derived considerable consolation from his copies of Homer's *Iliad* and Caesar's *Commentaries*. An indication of the classical authors considered necessary to the library of an educated man is found in the inventory of books selected by the Reverend John Goodborne, a minister of the Church of England, who sailed for a plantation in Virginia in 1635.[8] Goodborne, unhappily, died on the voyage, but his library arrived safely to become the subject of a lawsuit which preserved a record of its contents. Destined for a plantation called Merchant's Hope, Goodborne planned to have the benefit there of the works of Homer, Aristotle, Thucydides, Isocrates, Pindar, Seneca, Plautus, Terence, Ovid, Juvenal, Persius, Horace, Cicero, Quintilian, Plutarch, Virgil, Suetonius, Justin, Julius Caesar, Claudius Aelianus, and others. If these were not sufficient to provide ample classical lore, Goodborne made doubly sure by adding Natalis Comes' *Mythologiae,* an anthology much used in the sixteenth and seventeenth centuries. Not all of his classic authors were in their original tongues. Plutarch was represented by a Latin version and North's English translation; Terence was in English; and in addition to a Latin text of Virgil, illustrated with notes and pictures, he had the Elizabethan translation by Thomas Phaer and Thomas Twyne. If this Anglican minister's library seems particularly well supplied with the classics, it is by no means extraordinary in that respect, even for the first half of the century. In New England John Harvard, in the library bequeathed in 1638 to the college that was to bear his name, duplicated many of his Anglican contemporary's classic authors, and added a few others, including Pliny, Sallust, and Lucan.[9] He also had Natalis Comes' *Mythologiae,* a book frequently owned when other works of classic literature were lacking. Like Goodborne he had North's version of Plutarch's *Lives*; in place of Homer in Greek, he had Chapman's translation.

Men of education and culture, brought up in the classical tradition of the English schools and universities, felt that Greek and Latin authors were essential if they were to preserve and transmit the amenities of a cultivated life in New England or Virginia. Literary style was still modeled on Cicero and Quintilian; history was learned from the Greek and Latin historians; much information that passed for science still came from Aristotle, Aelianus, Pliny, and others; the conduct of life was taught by Plutarch, Seneca, Homer, and Virgil; good morality, in some fashion, was extracted from them all, even from Suetonius' *History of the Twelve Caesars*. Since few, even among the sternest Puritans, were willing to deny that the basis of erudition lay in the classics, every colonist who wanted to be learned—or to appear learned—tried to give the impression of an acquaintance with Greek and Latin authors until, at the end of the century, Cotton Mather, himself an inveterate pedant, warned young preachers to stick to the simple style and avoid too much parade of Latin learning.

The tradition that Greek and Latin works were essential to a well-rounded library, as to a sound education, persisted; and when the Century of Enlightenment dawned, it found the bookshelves of Boston scholars and Chesapeake planters graced with the classic works that had come to be regarded as the essentials of a gentleman's library.

As the prevalence of Latin historians in the book lists of seventeenth-century America suggests, historical reading was greatly favored, for it was believed to be highly instructive and useful in providing lessons of benefit to both the individual and the commonwealth. History, Richard Brathwaite had assured the readers of *The English Gentleman* (1630), is "the sweetest recreation of the mind,"[10] a belief that met with general acceptance. Indeed, the value placed upon historical reading was second only to that accorded works of divinity.[11] When near the end of his life Cotton Mather summed up his advice to young preachers, he urged an acquaintance with history as one of the "most needful and useful accomplishments for a man that would serve God as you propose to do."[12] Whether one proposed to be a preacher in New England or a landed gentleman in Virginia or Maryland, histories were necessary to one's reading.

Some of the historical works of the Elizabethan period maintained their popularity throughout the century. William Camden's *Remains of a Greater Work Concerning Britain,* full of miscellaneous lore and apt moralizations, is listed in many wills and inventories, and even his imposing *Britannia,* with its maps and county-by-county descriptions of the British Isles, was frequently owned in the colonies. But the most popular of all histories by an Englishman during the seventeenth century was Sir Walter Raleigh's *History of the World.* Favored by the Puritans because it demonstrated the divine purpose in human events, the book was also well liked by Anglicans. Men like the second Richard Lee, for example, looked upon it as a work of wisdom. Most readers would have agreed with Raleigh's prefatory statement that "we may gather out of history a policy no less wise than eternal by the comparison and application of other men's forepassed miseries with our own like errors and ill deservings." Although it is impossible to measure the influence of Raleigh's *History of the World* upon the political thinking of early American leaders, it is interesting to speculate upon the effect of his digressions on kingship and his skeptical attitude toward the divinity of monarchs. The colonists, like their kindred in England, read Raleigh's

History not merely as a compendium of facts about the ancient world but also as a source of political and moral truths.

In the later years of the seventeenth century, Bishop Gilbert Burnet's *History of the Reformation* was possessed by many readers, but it never encroached on the popularity of that other source of edification about the era of reform, John Foxe's *Acts and Monuments,* more generally called *The Book of Martyrs.* Many a humble man, whose "library" consisted of the Bible and two or three other books, numbered among them Foxe's great folio volume, which supplied the place of any other works of history or biography. No one can calculate the enormous influence of Foxe's descriptions of persecutions by Catholics in keeping alive hatred of Romanism in the breasts of American Protestants. Even yet traditional stories traceable to Foxe can be heard in the hinterland of American prejudice. The consuming interest of the seventeenth century in religious and Biblical matters gave Thomas Lodge's translation of Josephus' history of the Jews a long life in the colonies.

Current history also made its appeal to colonists, who took an eager interest in events in England and on the Continent. Booksellers in the middle of the century found ready buyers for copies of *The Swedish Intelligencer* with its running narrative of the actions of that doughty champion of Protestantism, Gustavus Adolphus. In the later years of the century, colonial readers who wanted to be informed about recent events in England equipped themselves with John Rushworth's *Historical Collections,* giving an account of parliamentary matters in the stormy years of Puritan dissension, and Bulstrode Whitelocke's *Memorials of the English Affairs . . . from the Beginning of the Reign of King Charles I to King Charles II* (1682). The parlimentary bias of these two works did not keep royalists in the South from reading them.

If historical reading was essential for any Englishman, it was doubly useful to the settlers on the fringe of the vast American wilderness. Through their historical reading they maintained a contact with the past and preserved a sense of their own continuity with the great deeds that had gone before. Out of the Americans' meditation upon their own relation to human events came a notion that later matured in the idea of manifest destiny.

That some of the early colonists were greatly concerned with books on politics and statecraft is what one might expect, for the leaders of the colonial enterprise were convinced that they were going out to found a nation. Though these men were not mere armchair theorizers, they did not neglect books that might contain useful suggestions and lessons. Among the books collected by Elder William Brewster of Plymouth was a copy of Sir Thomas Smith's *The Commonwealth of England and Manner of Government,* the standard Elizabethan work on the subject, which was continually reprinted for nearly a century and is frequently listed in colonial inventories. More remarkable was Brewster's possession of Machiavelli's *Prince* and Richard Knolles' translation from Bodin, *The Six Books of a Commonweal* (1606). Both of these books, however, were fairly common in colonial libraries. Whether Machiavelli influenced the good elder of Plymouth and his fellow settlers in their dealings with the Indians and their neighbors, one cannot say; but it is worth noting that such books were read, as references in sermons, pamphlets, and diaries indicate.

Sir Thomas More's *Utopia,* listed in numerous inventories of seventeenth-century libraries, was a book calculated to excite the interest of theoretical statesmen with a new world before them. If prejudice was still too strong for the tolerance and equality decreed by King Utopus, some at least among More's colonial readers undoubtedly yearned for a peace and prosperity like that of the Utopians. And in a few particulars, Utopia was imitated in the colonies. The banishment of idlers from the commonwealth, the insistence that every man have a calling and labor in it, the distrust of extravagant finery, and similar social attitudes were common to New England and Utopia. Colonists could find in this book passages that confirmed their social views or perhaps suggested ideas that remained dormant but alive in the subconsciousness of Americans.

If More's description of an ideal commonwealth was popular with seventeenth-century Americans, one might naturally suppose that Francis Bacon's *New Atlantis* would also attract attention. It was included at the end of the 1627 edition of Bacon's *Sylva Sylvarum,* a work on natural history recorded in a number of libraries. Bacon, throughout the seventeenth century, was a name to conjure with in America, but his reputation was based primarily on *The Advancement of Learning* and the *Essays.* His influence upon American thought is a theme for a book. In North and South, from the first quarter of the seventeenth century onward, he was regarded as an apostle of the new learning, and his *Advancement of Learning* was read and quoted as an authority by preachers,

schoolmasters, and politicians. It was to Bacon that educational theorists looked for wisdom, and it was as a pedagogical expert rather than as a scientific thinker that he was most influential.

The beginning of a scientific spirit, naïve though it may seem, is discernible in the detailed observations of natural phenomena made by a few of the colonists and in their desire for scientific literature. The emphasis upon natural philosophy in *The Advancement of Learning* served to place the stamp of approval of "the great Lord Bacon" upon the normal interest of many educated colonists in things scientific. Although encyclopedic works supplied the ordinary reader with a certain amount of information concerning the world about him, some men wanted more than this, and in the inventories of the period are listed many works dealing with the rarities of the New World, geography, botany, medicine, astronomy, chemistry, and other scientific subjects.

The most influential and, at least until near the end of the century, the largest scientific library in America was that accumulated by John Winthrop, Jr., governor of Connecticut, whose books were freely drawn upon by his neighbors and friends from the time of his arrival in Boston in 1631 until his death in 1676. Jonathan Brewster, for example, was constantly borrowing alchemical books, which served only to confuse a mind already muddled with too much contemplation of esoteric matters. Winthrop's home became a scientific center, stimulating some of his contemporaries to gather books on the subject. Gershom Bulkeley was one of these. His tombstone describes him as being "exquisite in his skill in divinity, physic, and law, and of a most exemplary and Christian life."[13] The last-named virtues did not prevent his probing into God's mysteries and collecting scientific books which he and his Connecticut neighbors read. Scientific interest was undoubtedly stimulated in New England by the dispersal of the library of the Reverend Samuel Lee, who came over in 1686. His library, containing an extraordinary number of scientific books, including works of Newton, was sold in 1693 by Duncan Campbell, the Boston bookseller.[14] Virginians were also curious about natural philosophy, as their libraries indicate. William Fitzhugh, near the end of the century, became greatly interested in mineralogy in the hope of discovering precious metals on his plantation; but his interest did not stop there, for in October, 1690, he was writing to his London factor for a copy of "Cornelius Agrippa's Occult Philosophy in English if it be procured, if not then one in Latin."[15]   Science was one of the many interests of William Byrd II of Westover in Virginia, and his library reflects that curiosity.

The theory of conduct and of man's relation with man was a problem of consuming interest to our soul-searching ancestors, whether they were Puritans or adherents of less rigid sects. In this field they were abundantly supplied with books that provided the essentials of instruction in everything from table manners to the means of attaining a heavenly crown. A Renaissance Italian author, who would have felt singularly ill at ease in Plymouth, was the instructor in manners chosen by Elder Brewster to be the Emily Post of the Pilgrims. He was Stefano Guazzo, whose *Civil Conversations* in an Elizabethan translation was prized by Brewster and other colonial Americans. Native English authors on problems of conduct, however, were not overlooked, and, to balance any pagan advice that the Italian might have offered, Brewster had Robert Cleaver's *A Godly Form of Household Government,* a guide in domestic affairs long used in English households. Brewster's neighbor, Governor Bradford, got along without an Italian manners book by sticking to the Reverend William Gouge's treatise, *Of Domestical Duties,* a recent work that united much practical and pious advice. This book and treatises like it commonly found in colonial libraries joined religious authority and bourgeois expediency in emphasizing a standard of conduct as useful to a pioneer society as it was to Gouge's London parishioners.

A determination of colonial leaders to duplicate the best features of the life they had left in England was responsible for a general interest in books concerned with the traditional rationale of conduct. Although the choice of particular books within this type was determined by individual attitudes and points of view, there was widespread agreement on the utility of books with the moral slant of Cleaver and Gouge, but not all the favorite treatises on conduct were necessarily of Puritan origin. John Harvard bequeathed his college a copy of King James's *Basilikon Doron,* doubtless with a hope that future Harvard students would overlook the royal intolerance of Puritans and remember only the excellent advice on the conduct of young men. Nor did the Anglican and royalistic flavor of *The Whole Duty of Man* in the later seventeenth century prevent its acceptance in New England as well as Virginia, though Cotton Mather sneered at the inclusiveness of the title.

While it is true that the older and more pagan Renaissance culture, described by Castiglione in *The Book of the Courtier* and Henry Peacham in *The Compleat Gentleman,* was less at home in the Bay Colony than in Virginia, where men still read these old books, both regions displayed considerable interest in the accomplishments of the gentleman, and bought books of instruction. Elder Brewster had a copy of *A Help to Memory and Discourse,* one of the better-known conversation manuals, and the records of Boston booksellers show frequent importations of a similar book called *The Academy of Compliments.* Colonial Americans were determined that their conversation should not display a provincial rusticity if handbooks could prevent it. The great concern of the colonists, however, was less with the externals of behavior than with deeper problems of conduct that determined reputation and character. When they sought books of guidance in this field, they usually chose highly moralistic works. In the later years of the century they were likely to turn to two of the most edifying books in this genre, *The Whole Duty of Man* and *The Gentleman's Calling.* How far their conduct was patterned on the admonitions of their books we can only guess.

The appetite of the seventeenth century for works of divinity has provoked the scorn of later and more sophisticated generations. Theology, we have been told, was meat and drink to a Puritan, and books of piety were his daily recreation. Of religious controversy, he made a sad-faced sport, and hurled thunderbolts from Calvin, or the Church Fathers, and buried his opponents under deep-piled quotations. We have come to think of the Puritans as a race created in the image of William Prynne, with the literary habits of their prototype. This picture is true only in part, for we are inclined to view it out of perspective and to scoff without understanding. We forget that Puritans had no monopoly of pious reading; that works of divinity and books describing the means of attaining the good life were regarded as essential to every man who pretended to civilized culture. Sectarian beliefs may have influenced the selection of certain books, but readers generally agreed that pious books were essential. For example, Ralph Wormeley, secretary of the colony of Virginia and a most unpuritan gentleman, given to horse racing and lavish hospitality, collected during the last half of the seventeenth century a library of approximately 375 titles, of which more than 120 were books devoted to religion and morals.[16] No one ever accused any of the Carters of excessive piety, yet of the books listed in the inventory made in 1690 of the personal property left by John Carter of Lancaster County, Virginia, nearly a third were religious works, including several titles by Richard Baxter, the sermons of that favorite Jacobean preacher Nicholas Byfield, and the most ubiquitous of all devotional books, Lewis Bayly's *The Practice of Piety.*[17]   Few inventories fail to show a considerable proportion of religious books, and if Virginians had more interest in the sermons of Lancelot Andrewes, Jeremy Taylor, and other Anglicans than was displayed by their brethren of the Bay Colony, nevertheless a remarkable number of the same sermons and books of devotion are common to both regions.

Many of the preachers who stirred England in the reigns of Elizabeth, James I, and Charles I, and published sermons to guide their countrymen, exerted an influence on the American colonists for a century or more. The most widely read of these preachers were perhaps Richard Greenham, William Perkins, Henry Scudder, John Preston, Nicholas Byfield, and Richard Sibbes, all men of Puritan leanings. The works that made them influential, however, were not polemical fulminations but sane and sensible suggestions for leading a Christian life. Much of their advice was eminently practical. We are prone to forget that religion in the seventeenth century was vitally related to man's daily existence, that a pattern of life that ignored religion was unthinkable; even reprobates whose personal behavior belied this belief were not likely to deny the theory. Indeed, the notion that God prospered his servants and sent afflictions upon sinners was so universal that many a seventeenth-century settler must have regarded the reading of *The Practice of Piety* or the sermons of a worthy preacher as a sort of insurance policy.

Seventeenth-century citizens were likely to set themselves up as connoisseurs of sermons heard from the pulpit or received from the press. Hence, even among laymen, there was a semiprofessional interest in works of divinity of a type read today only by the more scholarly of our clergymen. A desire to ponder the raw materials of sermon making helps to account for the innumerable commentaries on the Scriptures which circulated in the colonies. Even Anglicans owned and read Calvin's explanations of the Bible, one of the favorites being his observations on the Book of Job. The struggling colonists were peculiarly fascinated with the contemplation of Job's sufferings. A work that had a great vogue in this country in the last three decades of the seventeenth century was Joseph Caryl's *Commentary on the Book of Job,* first published, 1651-66, in twelve quarto volumes, but brought within the compass of two great folios in the second edition. This was one of Samuel

Sewall's favorite works, though he usually turned to Calvin in an emergency. When, for instance, at the turn of the century, Josiah Willard was risking damnation by wearing a periwig, Sewall prayed with him and recommended a course of reading in Calvin's *Institutes.*[18] Sewall's *Diary* provides much useful information about the reading of works of divinity by laymen of New England in the later years of the seventeenth century.

Pious books, good for English readers, were also good for Indians, New Englanders believed. A passage in Mather's *Magnalia,* commenting on John Eliot's translations into Indian of the Bible, the *Practice of Piety,* and Richard Baxter's *Call to the Unconverted,* describes the effect of the last-named work upon a godly young chief who "lay dying of a tedious distemper, and would keep reading of Mr. Baxter's *Call to the Unconverted,* with floods of tears in his eyes, while he had any strength to do it."[19] The works of Richard Baxter were not exclusively reserved to Puritans. In the second half of the seventeenth century, Baxter's various works were common to the libraries of both New England and the southern colonies. Of all the sermons read in the seventeenth century, however, those of William Perkins, the great Elizabethan teacher and preacher of Christ's College, Cambridge, were received with greatest favor by both nonconformists and churchmen.

The main reason for the interest in sermon reading was not theological but devotional and practical: men looked to these divines for wisdom and guidance in both spiritual and temporal affairs, for help in establishing and following a pattern of life fulfilling their ideas of dignity and honor. When readers turned to their favorite sermon writers, they found exhortations and admonitions mingled with common-sense advice on everyday problems. Perkins' writings furnish many examples, but his sermon-essay entitled, *A Treatise of the Vocations,* which first appeared in the 1603 edition of the collected works,[20] is perhaps the most significant. This little treatise epitomizes the gospel of work which became the cornerstone of American economic progress. Long before Poor Richard, Perkins emphasized the prudential qualities of diligence and thrift; he demonstrated that the proper way to live acceptably before God was to fulfill one's worldly duties; and he clearly pointed out that idleness is sin, efficiency a duty, and persistence in one's daily vocation a heavenly virtue, perennial elements in our creed of success. If heaven was the destination of the seventeenth-century citizen, this world was an important way station in which he could not spend his time in idle whittling. Preachers like Perkins constantly reminded their readers of a mundane as well as a spiritual duty.

A good deal of solemn nonsense about the taste of the American colonists for religious literature has been written by facile critics who have never read more than the titles of the books in colonial libraries. It is sometimes implied that the colonists were devoid of literary taste or aesthetic judgment because they seem to have preferred piety instead of plays, poetry, and romances. If such critics would read the books owned by our ancestors, they would discover that many despised sermons and treatises were written in sinewy, straightforward prose and are full of ideas and good sense. Such books were not the handiwork of half-literate fanatics, as we are sometimes led to believe, but of shrewd and intelligent university men, whose piety did not keep them from being practical social thinkers. From them our ancestors learned to follow closely reasoned and logical argument, to discipline their minds to analytical exposition, to appraise questions raised by their authors. It is not unreasonable to assume that such reading provided as much intellectual nourishment as our forebears would have derived, let us say, from meditating upon the devious plots of contemporary romances and plays. If no pretty poetry, clever drama, and urbane essays graced American literature in the seventeenth century, it is not a sign that our ancestors' minds were stultified with theological reading. We should remember that they were busy establishing a mode of existence and setting patterns that America was to follow in succeeding generations.

Not all seventeenth-century readers confined their interests to solemn treatises, but one should always remember that the prevailing attitude toward literature was so distinctly purposeful that many of our ancestors made themselves believe that they could gain instruction even when reading romances. This fact is important when we come to judge of the quality of belles-lettres in early American libraries. In the seventeenth century few readers admitted even to themselves that they read merely for idle diversion. Idleness was sin, and books—if they were good books—did not encourage this vice. Even at the end of the century, when settled prosperity had relaxed the more rigid life of the earlier period for many Americans, the proportion of trivial books that one finds recorded in inventories and booksellers' lists is small. Though in the later years of the century, especially in Virginia, there is evidence of an increasing inter-

est in polite literature written by modern or contemporary authors, relatively few trifling or flippant works were sufficiently prized to get themselves preserved in the records. Some ballads and sorry pamphlets, it is true, were imported. It was verily a proof of witchcraft, Cotton Mather thought, that a Boston child in 1688 went into convulsions at the sight of a catechism, but read glibly from jestbooks and made "cunning descants upon them."[21] But jestbooks, ballads, and idle tales were not characteristic of any colonial libraries that we know about. If numerous copies of the *History of Dr. Faustus* were imported by Boston booksellers in the 1680's and nineties, the reason must be found in the abnormal concern over magic and witchcraft in those years, not in a sudden shift to light reading. When colonials bought books, they wanted something substantial, something worthy and respectable, something to do them good.

George Lyman Kittredge[22] and Samuel Eliot Morison[23] have called attention to the wide reading, particularly in the English poets, revealed by the commonplace books of three Harvard youths: John Leverett, later president of Harvard College; Elnathan Chauncy, son of a Harvard president; and Seaborn Cotton, later a minister. If some of the passages written down by these boys show a normal interest in the theme of love and fair ladies, others indicate the age-old tendency to cull flowers of wisdom for future use. Though some of their contemporaries doubtless disapproved a familiarity with Shakespeare's *Venus and Adonis,* or the worldly poetry of Herrick and Cleveland, few would have questioned the virtue of reading Spenser, whose works provided Elnathan Chauncy with twenty pages of excerpts. And definitely improving was an acquaintance with *The Mirror for Magistrates,* Warner's *Albion's England,* Fairfax's version of *Jerusalem Delivered,* Barclay's romance *Argenis* (which even Michael Wigglesworth did not eschew), and other modern writers. These commonplace books, which have already been adequately described by others, suggest that Elizabethan and early seventeenth-century poets and prose writers exerted a strong influence upon some seventeenth-century Americans. Men still believed that the function of the poet was to teach and to delight and they did not completely omit recent English authors in their search for delightful instruction.

Probably the most widely read English poet in America in the seventeenth century was George Herbert, though he shared honors with Francis

Quarles and other serious poets of the period. Evidence of their influence has been pointed out by Leon Howard in his introduction to Philip Pain's *Daily Meditations.*[24] Puritans especially approved of Herbert's prophetic lines from *The Temple:*

> Religion stands on tiptoe in our land,
> Ready to pass to the American strand.

Michael Drayton, in epistolary verses written to his friend George Sandys, then in Virginia, refers to the possibility of the flight of poetry also to America. But Sandys' translation of Ovid's *Metamorphoses* was the only really literary evidence of this flight for years to come.

One might suppose that John Milton would have appealed to the serious and purposeful colonists, but we should remember that the growth of Milton's reputation as a poet began late in the seventeenth century. His controversial and prose works naturally reached the colonies before his poetry. Records of six or eight copies of *Paradise Lost* in the colonies before 1700 have been preserved,[25] but Milton's great reputation in America was an eighteenth-century development.

The reading of fiction in early America was not entirely unknown, but our ancestors were too busy with the sharpening of their wits, with mundane affairs, or with a serious concern for their souls to have time for much "escape" into the world of romance. A few bold spirits, both male and female, bought old-fashioned romances of the kind Anthony Munday had translated, or the newer and more sugary stories of Scudéry or La Calprenède; booksellers imported a supply of Deloney's narratives for Boston shopkeepers; an occasional library had a copy of *Don Quixote;* but the stories that were best received were those written in an exalted vein. The reputation of Quarles as a divine poet took the curse off his verse romance, *Argalus and Parthenia,* sufficiently to make it fairly popular. Sidney's great name persisted and the *Arcadia* was not wholly unknown even in frontier settlements. John Allyn of Hartford, writing to Fitz-John Winthrop in 1673, alludes playfully to incidents in the *Arcadia.*[26] An imitation of the *Arcadia* by Sidney's niece, Lady Mary Wroth, a novel entitled *The Countess of Montgomery's Urania,* enjoyed a considerable vogue. Such stories were capable of a moral interpretation, and they were full of good instruction in the manners and conduct of gentlemen. Our ancestors may have enjoyed them as romance, but we can be sure that those who owned copies considered them improving. Bunyan's *Pilgrim's Progress,* published in Boston in 1681, was undoubtedly regarded as a moral treatise and not as a novel.

No one who has assessed the evidence properly will say that seventeenth-century America was without literary culture; nor can anyone who understands the books gathered by the colonists assert, as some have done, that the Puritans of New England confined their literary interest to theology.[27] The traditional literary heritage of England was transmitted to the New World, and if didactic interpretation, which had always been strong, acquired still greater emphasis, it resulted from the serious purposefulness of the colonists, whether in New England or elsewhere. They regarded their reading as one means of attaining the kind of life that they desired. As the patterns of life in New England and the southern colonies became differentiated, variations in their literary taste developed, but that is another story. A significant fact is that in the seventeenth century, colonists of varied sectarian beliefs drew inspiration and instruction from so many of the same literary sources. Writers of the early Renaissance, of Elizabethan and early seventeenth-century England, continued to influence Englishmen in America. If this literary tradition produced no urbane school of letters in the wilderness, it provided nourishment for a developing intellectual life that came to maturity in the later eighteenth and nineteenth centuries.

By the early years of the eighteenth century, increasing prosperity and urbanity led to the multiplication of private libraries in all the colonies, the beginnings of libraries designed to serve a wider public, and a well-developed book trade in such towns as Boston, New York, Philadelphia, and Charleston. Already in the seventeenth century, private libraries provided reading matter for many more readers than the households of the owners. The failure of neighbors and friends to return borrowed books provoked more than one bitter comment in the correspondence of the day.

Two of the most noteworthy book collectors were Cotton Mather in Boston and William Byrd II of Virginia. Both had the instincts of the bibliophile and loved books for their own sakes. Mather accumulated between 3,000 and 4,000 titles before his death in 1728,[28] and Byrd had a library of more than 3,600 titles at his death in 1744.[29] Their books were varied in subject and included everything from religious tracts to recent books on natural science. Works of history and the Greek and Roman classics were numerous. Despite the difference in social points of view of these two men, their libraries were strikingly similar.

A number of other bibliophiles in the eighteenth century gathered libraries of distinction. Thomas Prince, minister of the Old South Church, collected more than 1,500 volumes, many dealing with civil history. At his death in 1758, his books were stored in the tower of the church. Though many were stolen by British soldiers during the occupation of Boston, a considerable number survived the Revolution and eventually found their way into the Boston Public Library. Thomas Hutchinson, the last royal governor of Massachusetts, had a fine library surpassed in excellence only by the Mathers' collection of books.

James Logan, who came over as secretary to William Penn in 1699, and lived in Pennsylvania until his death in 1751, brought together a library of more than 3,000 volumes, notable especially for classical and scientific works. Great as was Logan's interest in science, he remained always a humanist and looked back to the literature of Greece and Rome for inspiration. In the controversy over the ancients and the moderns, he gave his allegiance to the ancients, but was wise enough to take what suited him from the moderns too.[30] Logan had one of the best scientific libraries in North America, for he himself had a deep interest in botany and other aspects of natural science. He kept his books in a small house near his home in Philadelphia and made them available to serious students.

On Logan's death he bequeathed both house and books to the city of Philadelphia for a public library. He stands in the front rank of the founders of practical and useful libraries for the benefit of the public, albeit he was not the first in the colonies to have such an idea. Long before, Robert Keayne, a Boston merchant who died in 1656, left a bequest providing for a library for the town; but though mention is made from time to time of the "public library," it appears to have fallen early into decay and to have disappeared altogether in the fire of 1747.[31] Although New Haven, Concord, and Dorchester had little collections called town libraries in the seventeenth century, they were of no great importance.[32] The establishment of libraries for public use on any considerable scale had to wait until the eighteenth century.

One of the most earnest advocates of libraries as a means of civilizing the colonies was Dr. Thomas Bray, who was responsible for the founding of the Society for Promoting Christian Knowledge (1699), which had as an offshoot the Society for the Propagation of the Gospel in Foreign Parts (1701). Bray himself was a zealous propagandist who labored unceasingly to bring about the official establishment of the Church of England in Maryland, where he personally served for a few months in 1699 as commissary. To improve the status of the clergy, he proposed to provide them with parochial libraries of carefully selected volumes for professional use. Bray sent these parochial libraries to various colonies, but Maryland, as the center of his personal interest, received the largest number. The parochial libraries, composed almost entirely of religious books, were intended for the use of the clergy rather than the public. But Bray also planned provincial libraries for the use of all types of readers. The largest of these was established at Annapolis. In an account dated 1702, Bray listed twenty-nine parochial libraries in Maryland alone, with collections ranging from ten to 314 titles. The provincial library at Annapolis, to which Queen Anne herself had contributed, contained 1,095 volumes.[33]

The care and preservation of the libraries were of concern both to Bray and the colonial governments. Beginning in 1696, the Maryland Assembly passed several laws designed to prevent dispersal of the Maryland libraries through carelessness. In 1704 Bishop White Kennett wrote earnestly to Thomas Hearne, then a young assistant keeper in the Bodleian Library, urging him to go out to Maryland as a missionary and examiner of the libraries established there. Hearne resisted the offer and was thus saved to antiquarian scholarship.

The provincial library established by Bray at Charleston, South Carolina, in 1698, laid the foundation for library development in that colony. The government itself contributed £225 toward the book fund and in 1700 the Assembly passed a law specifying conditions under which the inhabitants might borrow books from the library. This union of private enterprise and government was a long step toward the concept of a public library for the general benefit of the population.

New York appears to have been less receptive to Bray's efforts to establish a library for general use. The books that he sent over, presumably for a provincial library, remained locked up in Trinity Church and were of no use to any except the clergy. Finally, in 1713, the Reverend John Sharpe, who had served in New York as a chaplain of English troops, gave his books to the Society for the Propagation of the Gospel in Foreign Parts to found a public library in New York. What happened to Sharpe's books is not certain, but in 1739 another parson, John Millington, gave books for an institution called the Corporation Library.[34] These little collections preceded the formation of the New York Society Library in 1754. In North Carolina, in 1723, Edward Moseley, in the hope of establishing a provincial library at Edenton, gave a collection of books to supplement those sent over by Dr. Bray.

Bray's efforts to send books to the British colonies in America may not have had far-reaching results, but they helped to focus interest on the need for books and served a very useful purpose in several colonies, particularly Maryland and North and South Carolina. He was concerned primarily with religion. Even the so-called laymen's libraries that he planned to present to colonial Americans were not really libraries, but were small collections of such books as *The Practice of Piety* and *The Whole Duty of Man* for the religious instruction of individuals who received them.[35]

Before the middle of the eighteenth century, the idea that individuals might pool their resources and set up subscription libraries was beginning to take hold. Like so many other things in eighteenth-century America, the impetus for this came from Benjamin Franklin, who in November, 1731, organized the Library Company of Philadelphia. The first members, belonging to Franklin's discussion club called the Junto, paid forty shillings each for their shares. They took in other members to the number of fifty and later increased the membership to one hundred. The earliest shipment of books, which arrived in October, 1732, indicates the changing nature of American libraries. No longer did religious literature predominate. Of forty-five titles not one concerns dogmatic religion. Here are recent historical works along with English translations of Plutarch's *Lives* and Tacitus' *Annals*, geographies, grammars, dictionaries, Boerhaave's *Chemistry*, Parkinson's *Herbal* and other more recent scientific treatises, books, on mathematics, government, politics, agriculture, architecture, and such literary works as *The Spectator, the Tatler,* and *The Guardian.*[36] These were the books that a secular, rationalistic group of ambitious young tradesmen and craftsmen bent upon improving themselves would want to read and study. The Library Company's books are a symbol of a new note in American life, the advance of an independent and forward-looking middle class who saw in self-education the means of raising themselves both economically and socially.

Concerning the Library Company, Franklin wrote with obvious satisfaction in his *Autobiography:* "This was the mother of all the North American subscription libraries, now so numerous. It is become a great thing itself and continually increasing. These libraries have improved the general conversation of Americans, made the common tradesmen and farmers as intelligent as most gentlemen from other countries, and perhaps have contributed in some degree to the stand so generally made throughout the colonies in defence of their privileges."[37]

The Library Company of Philadelphia, first housed in a room in Pewter Platter Alley and later, for more than thirty years after 1740, in the State House, contributed much to the intellectual development of Philadelphia. The librarian was instructed to let any "civil gentleman" read the books during the few hours that the library was open each week, but books could be borrowed only by members, with the single exception of James Logan. In deference to his own interest in books—and his encouragement of the enterprise—he was allowed to take books home.

The proprietary library on the model of the Library Company of Philadelphia, or the "social library" as it is sometimes designated, became an important instrument of popular education, as Franklin implies. Two years after the establishment of the Library Company of Philadelphia, a group of citizens of Durham, Connecticut, in 1733 organized the Book Company of Durham, and similar libraries were soon organized at a half-dozen places in Connecticut. Before the Revolution, it is estimated that at least sixty-four subscription libraries had been organized throughout the American colonies.[38] The probability is that there were many more, all records of which are lost.

The Redwood Library of Newport, Rhode Island, founded in 1747, owed its existence to the approval shown by Abraham Redwood, a merchant, of the purposes of the Literary and Philosophical Society of Newport, which was organized "for the promotion of knowledge and virtue." Redwood proposed to some of the men of the Society that they organize a library, which they did, and received from Redwood £500 sterling as a start.[39] When the first catalogue was published in 1764, the Redwood Library had about 700 volumes, with belles-lettres, science, and history predominating. Only about 13 per cent of the collection could be classified as religion and philosophy.[40]

The Charleston Library Society, organized in 1748 by seventeen of the leading citizens of the town, quickly became an important influence in the cultural life of the South Carolina metropolis. Within two years after its founding, it numbered 130 members and had an endowment for the purchase not only of books but of scientific apparatus. Its members planned an academy in conjunction with the library and proposed to have a professor of natural philosophy and mathematics to lecture at the library. These grandiose plans failed to develop, but the library itself provided a wide assortment of reading in all fields, especially in science, law, history, and philosophy. Despite lip service to the classics, the literature of Greece and Rome appears to have been neglected in Charleston. When Christopher Gadsden in 1764 resigned because the Library Society rejected his proposal to spend 70 per cent of the annual appropriation for Greek and Latin classics, the librarian pointed out that nobody had called for classical works already on the library shelves.[41]

From an early period, New York was more noted for its commerce than its culture, but in 1754, high-minded citizens succeeded in establishing a proprietary library and King's College. The New York Society Library was apparently planned as a sort of adjunct to the college. The articles of subscription drawn up on April 2, 1754, stated that "a public library would be very useful, as well as ornamental to this city and may be also advantageous to our intended college."[42] Like the college, the library was at first dominated by Church of England influences, much to the disgust of the Presbyterians, one of whom published a letter in the *Mercury* for May 12, 1755, pointing out that "no sooner were the subscriptions complete and a day appointed for the election of trustees than a dirty scheme was concerted for excluding as many English Presbyterians as possible from the trusteeship."[43] Despite the displeasure of the Presbyterians, the New York Society Library became a useful cultural institution. Like the Library Company of Philadelphia, the Redwood Library of Newport, and the Charleston Library Society, the New York Society Library continued to grow through the years and to exert a beneficent influence even to the present day.

Circulating libraries, operated chiefly by booksellers and publishers, which came to have considerable importance in the late eighteenth and early nineteenth centuries, had a beginning in our period. In 1762, William Rind, one of the publishers of the second *Maryland Gazette,* advertised a plan to establish a circulating library which he hoped would be useful in "diffusing a spirit of science through the country."[44] About six months later, a stationer in Charleston named George Wood also advertised a proposal for a circulating library, but neither Rind's nor Wood's ventures flourished, and

it was at least a decade before circulating libraries began to have much influence on the reading public.

By the middle of the eighteenth century, the libraries of Harvard and Yale were sufficiently large and varied to play a significant part in the cultural development of their students, faculties, and such others as were fortunate enough to have access to the books. A list of Harvard's books in 1723 showed approximately 3,000 volumes in a wide variety of subjects, and Yale's first catalogue in 1742 listed about 2,600 volumes, including a respectable collection of belles-lettres. At both Harvard and Yale one could find works of the chief English classics. Yale's catalogue listed the works of Chaucer, Spenser, Shakespeare, Milton, Dryden, and contemporary authors such as Pope, Gay, Prior, Addison and others.[45]

Both Harvard and Yale benefited from generous benefactors in the first half of the eighteenth century. Beginning with a gift of Milton's poetical works from Thomas Hollis of London in 1722, Harvard received for many years successive gifts of books and money from Hollis and his son and other members of the Hollis family. In 1724 Hollis wrote to the Harvard Corporation a letter that is still timely: "If there happen to be some books not quite orthodox," he warned, "in search after truth with an honest design, don't be afraid of them. A public library ought to be furnished, if it can, with *con* as well as *pro,* that students may read, try, judge; see for themselves, and believe upon argument and just reasonings of the Scriptures. 'Thus saith Aristotle,' 'Thus saith Calvin,' will not now pass for proof in our London disputations."[46] Hollis also showed unusual clairvoyance in anticipating a central repository for little-used books when he wrote to a member of the Harvard Corporation urging him, if necessary to make room for modern books, "to remove the less useful into a more remote place, but not sell any."[47]

The Yale library's most important gift in the first half of the eighteenth century was a donation in 1733 of nearly 1,000 volumes from George Berkeley, Bishop of Cloyne, who took a deep interest in American affairs. He had hoped to found a college in Bermuda and had lived from 1728 to 1731 in Newport, Rhode Island. When he left Newport, he donated his ninety-six-acre farm to Yale along with his library, a well-selected collection embracing the major branches of learning.[48] To Harvard he also gave a few books. Thanks to gifts from generous benefactors, the libraries of both Harvard and Yale continued to grow. By the time of the great fire which destroyed the library in 1764, Harvard had a collection of nearly 5,000 books.

The libraries of the other colonial colleges were less important. The College of William and Mary received several small gifts of books from time to time, but it too suffered from fire, and its library probably never totaled as many as 3,000 volumes before the Revolution. Princeton received a gift of several hundred books from Governor Jeremy Belcher and by 1760, when it published a catalogue, it had a library of 1,261 volumes.[49] King's College (later Columbia) received gifts of books from several benefactors before the Revolution, but it could not boast a library of any distinction in our period. The College of Philadelphia had no adequate library in the period before the Revolution.

Bookselling in colonial America was centered chiefly in Boston, New York, Philadelphia, and Charleston, but elsewhere printers and stationers frequently had small stocks of books, and general merchants sometimes advertised schoolbooks and other works of interest to their customers. Between 1669 and 1690, Boston had twenty booksellers, and from this time onward Boston was an important book market.[50] It supplied books to most of New England and frequently shipped them to more distant colonies. The booksellers of Boston were sufficiently numerous in 1724 to found a trade association, and their importations of books multiplied in the eighteenth century until they represented a fair cross section of contemporary publication in England. In 1732 Richard Fry imported 1,200 copies of the Wiltshire poet,

Stephen Duck,[51] a fact that may account for the quality of some eighteenth-century American verse. Dr. Alexander Hamiltion of Annapolis on a visit to Boston in 1744 attended a book auction and commented: "The books that sold best at this auction while I was there were *Pamela, Anti-Pamela, The Fortunate Maid,* Ovid's *Art of Love,* and *The Marrow of Modern Divinity.*"[52]

By the early years of the eighteenth century, New York had at least four booksellers. But in the colonial period, New York never rivaled Boston as a book market. Philadelphia printers and shopkeepers frequently advertised books and by the middle of the eighteenth century the town could boast at least a half-dozen booksellers. Best known was Benjamin Franklin, whose printing shop offered a variety of books on many subjects. After 1731, the newspapers of Charleston carried frequent advertisements of books for sale, an indication that Charleston was a good book market for the colonies of the far South.

The advertisements of eighteenth-century colonial papers indicate a steady market for contemporary English publications and do not suggest that the cultural lag was longer than the time for books to reach the colonies after publication in England. Throughout the colonial period, the interest in books was a vital and growing manifestation of the American genius for self-improvement. Franklin's comment that American tradesmen and farmers were as well read as gentlemen elsewhere was something more than the empty boast of a superpatriot. Americans had learned that books would provide not only inner satisfactions but material rewards as well.

FOOTNOTES

[1] The portion of this article dealing with the seventeenth century in part is reprinted by permission from an essay entitled "The Purposeful Reading of Our Colonial Ancestors" in *ELH, A Journal of English Literary History*, IV (1937), 85-111.

[2] Henry Peacham, *The Compleat Gentleman* (London, 1622), p. 52.

[3] Cf. Louis B. Wright, *Middle-Class Culture in Elizabethan England* (Chapel Hill, N.C., 1935), pp. 586 ff.

[4] *Ibid.,* pp. 555 ff.

[5] Samuel Eliot Morison, *Harvard College in the Seventeenth Century* (Cambridge, Mass., 1936), I, 178.

[6] For an inventory of Ralph Wormeley's library, see *The William and Mary College Quarterly*, II (1893-94), 169-174; for Richard Lee's library, *ibid.,* pp. 247-249. Wormeley's inventory is dated 1701; Lee's, 1715; but both represent collections made in the latter part of the seventeenth century. For identification of Lee's books, see Louis B. Wright, "Richard Lee II, A Belated Elizabethan in Virginia," *The Huntington Library Quarterly*, II (1938), 1-35.

[7] *The Diaries of John Hull, Mint-Master and Treasurer of the Colony of Massachusetts Bay* in *Transactions and Collections of the American Antiquarian Society*, III (1857), 117-118.

[8] "A Virginian Minister's Library, 1635," *The American Historical Review*, XI (1905-06), 328-332.

[9] Alfred C. Potter, "Catalogue of John Harvard's Library," *Publications of the Colonial Society of Massachusetts*, XXI (1919), 190-230.

[10] Edition of 1630, p. 220.

[11] Wright, *Middle-Class Culture*, pp. 297-338.

[12]Cotton Mather, *Manuductio* (1726), p. 58.

[13]See C. H. Hoadly's introduction to Gershom Bulkeley's "Will and Doom, Or The Miseries of Connecticut by and under an Usurped and Arbitrary Power," *Connecticut Historical Society Collections,* III (1895), 70-269.

[14]A catalogue of the library was printed by Campbell and distributed prior to the sale. A few photostatic copies of the original catalogue, preserved in the Boston Public Library, have been distributed by the Massachusetts Historical Society. For a comment on Samuel Lee, see Samuel E. Morison, *The Puritan Pronaos* (New York, 1936), pp. 139-141.

[15]*Virginia Magazine of History and Biography,* III (1895-96), 8.

[16]Philip A. Bruce, *Institutional History of Virginia in the Seventeenth Century* (New York, 1910), I, 425-426; *The William and Mary College Quarterly,* II (1893-94), 169-174.

[17]Inventory in *The William and Mary College Quarterly,* VIII (1899-1900), 18-19. See Louis B. Wright, "The 'Gentleman's Library' in Early Virginia: The Literate Interests of the First Carters," *The Huntington Library Quarterly,* I (1937), 3-61.

[18]*Diary of Samuel Sewall* in *Collections of the Massachusetts Historical Society,* 5th Ser., VI (1879), 37.

[19]Cotton Mather, *Magnalia* (Hartford, Conn., 1853), I, 569.

[20]Wright, *Middle-Class Culture,* pp. 170-185.

[21]Mather, *Magnalia,* II, 462.

[22]George Lyman Kittredge, "A Harvard Salutatory Oration of 1662," *Publications of the Colonial Society of Massachusetts,* XXVIII (1935), 1-24.

[23]Morison, *The Puritan Pronaos,* pp. 46-53.

[24]Philip Pain, *Daily Meditations,* 1668, ed. Leon Howard (San Marino, Calif., 1936).

[25]Leon Howard, "Early American Copies of Milton," *The Huntington Library Bulletin,* No. 7 (1935), 169-179.

[26]*Collections of the Massachusetts Historical Society,* 6th Ser., III (1889), 435.

[27]See the protest of C. A. Herrick, "The Early New Englanders: What Did They Read?" *The Library,* 3rd Ser., IX (1918), 1-17.

[28]Thomas Goddard Wright, *Literary Culture in Early New England, 1620-1730* (New Haven, Conn., 1920), p. 178.

[29]Louis B. Wright, *The First Gentlemen of Virginia* (San Marino, Calif., 1940), p. 333.

[30]Frederick B. Tolles, "Quaker Humanist: James Logan as a Classical Scholar," *The Pennsylvania Magazine of History and Biography,* LXXIX (1955), 415-438.

[31]C. Seymour Thompson, *Evolution of the American Public Library, 1653-1876* (Washington, D. C., 1952), pp. 13-14.

[32]*Ibid.,* pp. 15-18.

[33]Joseph Towne Wheeler, "Thomas Bray and the Maryland Parochial Libraries," *Maryland Historical Magazine,* XXXIV (1939), 246-265.

[34]Thompson, *Evolution of the American Public Library,* pp. 31-32.

[35]*Ibid.,* pp. 28-29.

[36]Austin K. Gray, *The First American Library* (Philadelphia, 1936), pp. 11-12.

[37]Max Farrand (ed.), *The Autobiography of Benjamin Franklin* (Berkeley, Calif., 1949), p. 86.

[38]Thompson, *Evolution of the American Public Library,* pp. 54-55.

[39]*Ibid.,* p. 53.

[40]Jesse H. Shera, *Foundations of the Public Library* (Chicago, 1949), p. 39.

[41]Frederick P. Bowes, *The Culture of Early Charleston* (Chapel Hill, N.C., 1942), p. 62.

[42]Austin B. Keep, *History of the New York Society Library* (New York, 1908), p. 136.

[43]*Ibid.,* p. 139.

[44]Shera, *Foundations of the Public Library,* p. 132.

[45]E. P. Morris, "A Library of 1742," *The Yale University Library Gazette,* IX (1934), 1-11. *A Catalogue of the Library of Yale College in New Haven* (1742) has been reproduced in facsimile (New Haven, 1931).

[46]Josiah Quincy, *History of Harvard University* (Cambridge, 1840), I, 433.

[47]*Ibid.,* I, 432.

[48]The collection given Yale is listed in Louis Shores, *Origins of the American College Library, 1638-1800* (Nashville, Tenn., 1934), pp. 244-262.

[49]Thomas J. Wertenbaker, *Princeton, 1746-1896* (Princeton, N.J., 1946), p. 106.

[50]Carl Bridenbaugh, *Cities in the Wilderness: The First Century of Urban Life in America, 1625-1742* (New York, 1938), p. 129. Cf. Thomas G. Wright, *Literary Culture in Early New England, 1620-1730* (New Haven, 1920), *passim.*

[51]Bridenbaugh, *Cities in the Wilderness,* p. 452.

[52]Carl Bridenbaugh (ed.), *Gentleman's Progress: The Itinerarium of Dr. Alexander Hamilton, 1744* (Chapel Hill, N.C., 1948), p. 112.

The Colonial College Library

Kenneth Brough

The nine colleges established in colonial America each had libraries, but in most cases they were little more than conspicuous "treasures," guarded jealously and seldom used. Budgets were small in the early colleges, and the money available for books was extremely limited. Most books were acquired through the generosity of friends of the colleges, though a few were purchased with money raised by means of special student fees, or, in some cases, lotteries. Since books were scarce, costly, and in constant danger of being destroyed in the frequent fires which plagued the early colleges, it is not surprising that the regulations governing their use were considerably more conservative than is currently the case. The brief selection which follows suggests the flavor of the rules governing the use of early college libraries.

The college library dates back to the beginning of the college itself. John Harvard's bequest to the institution which took his name included all his books, a collection of 329 titles totaling over 400 volumes.[1] Tradition has it that books played a more dramatic part in the founding of Yale. According to President Clap's narrative, the eleven founders met at Branford in 1700 and formally presented books, saying either these words or to this intent: "I give these Books for the founding a College in this Colony."[2] Even though it seems improbable that the founding took place in just this way, as Oviatt so ably demonstrates,[3] the legend still clings pleasantly to the Yale Library.

In his study of the libraries of the nine colonial colleges, Louis Shores traces their development from earliest beginnings through 1800. He points out that due to the general scarcity of books in the colonies and also to losses by fire and by pillage during the Revolution, the library attained no great size in those early days. Warning that he bases his figures on sketchy records, Shores estimates that by 1790 Harvard had 12,000 volumes, the largest accumulation. Second in size, William and Mary had only one-fourth of this number. The average annual rate of accession for the entire period ranged from 30 volumes at William and Mary and at Yale to 100 at Brown. Even when one takes into consideration the fact that these figures are but rough approximations, one can conclude that the library of the colonial college was small and grew slowly. Accumulated chiefly as the result of direct gifts, and with theological works predominating, probably a considerable proportion of the collections had little bearing on the educational program of the college, regardless of the intrinsic worth of the books.[4]

Regulations concerning use failed to make up in liberality for any shortcomings of the library in size. The rules ordered in 1667 by the Harvard Overseers stipulated that "No Schollar in the Colledge, under a Senior Sophister shall borrow a book out of the Library," and further, that "No one under master of Art (unless it be a fellow) shall borrow a Book without the allowance of the Praesident."[5] The Yale Trustees voted a rule with closely similar provisions in 1723.[6]

The Harvard library laws of 1765 provide a good example of the accessibility of books in the American college toward the end of the colonial period. Junior sophisters by then had the borrowing privilege. To obtain any book not among those set aside "for the common Use of the College," however, undergraduates had to procure "an order under the Hands of the President, one Professor & One Tutor to the Librarian to deliver what Books they shall judge proper for the Perusal of such a Student." Students could borrow as many as three volumes at a time. They had to exercise some foresight concerning their needs, however, since they could take out books only once every three weeks. On Friday the librarian lent and re-

SOURCE: Reprinted from Kenneth Brough, *The Scholar's Workshop: Evolving Conceptions of Library Service,* (Urbana: University of Illinois Press, 1953), pp. 2-5, by permission of the author and publisher. Copyright © 1953 by the Board of Trustees, University of Illinois.

ceived books from nine until eleven o'clock in the morning and from three until five in the afternoon or longer if necessary. The rules also required that he "wait on any of the Gentlemen in the Instruction or Government of the College, whenever they have Occasion to go into the Library," and on each Wednesday that he "attend . . . on such Gentlemen as shall obtain Leave from the President, Professors & Tutors, to study in the Library."[7]

Restrictive as these rules may seem today, they permitted practices which to the more conservative of that era must have appeared completely reckless. The libraries of Oxford and Cambridge still had books literally in chains. Potter quotes from a revealing letter written to the Harvard authorities in 1725 by Thomas Hollis, a resident of London and a benefactor of the Harvard College Library:

> Your library is reckond here to be ill managed, by the account I have of some that know it, you want seats to sett and read, and chains to your valluable books like our Bodleian library, or Sion College in London, you know their methods, wch are approved, but do not imitate them, you let your books be taken at pleasure home to Mens houses, and many are lost, your (boyish) Students take them to their chambers, and teare out pictures & maps to adorne their Walls, such things are not good; if you want roome for modern books, it is easy to remove the less usefull into a more remote place, but do not sell any, they are devoted. Your goodness will excuse me, if I hint to you what I think faulty.......

Throughout the colonial period college libraries, like the colleges themselves, remained in the stage of small beginnings. Books were few and precious, and in the thoughts of college authorities their safekeeping rose in importance far above any desire to make them immediately useful. The library had no necessary bearing on the studies of the undergraduates. Students brought from home the books they needed, or they purchased them from their predecessors or from booksellers.

FOOTNOTES

[1] S. E. Morison, *The Founding of Harvard College* (Cambridge: Harvard University Press, 1935), p. 264.

[2] Thomas Clap, *The Annals or History of Yale College* . . . (New Haven: Printed for John Hotchkiss and B. Mecom, 1766), p. 3.

[3] Edwin Oviatt, *The Beginnings of Yale (1701-1726)* (New Haven: Yale University Press, 1916), pp. 158-69.

[4] Louis Shores, *Origins of the American College Library, 1638-1800* (Nashville, Tenn.: George Peabody College, 1934).

[5] Colonial Society of Massachusetts, *Publications,* XV (1925), 194-95.

[6] F. B. Dexter (ed.), *Documentary History of Yale University under the Original Charter of the Collegiate School of Connecticut, 1701-1745* (New Haven: Yale University Press, 1916), p. 238.

[7] Quotations from the Harvard library laws of 1765 which appear in this paragraph are taken from the "Holyoke Code of 1767" as reproduced in Colonial Society of Massachusetts, *Publications,* XXXI (1935), 369-75.

Franklin and the Library Company of Philadelphia

Margaret Korty

Perhaps the most significant development in colonial library history was the introduction and spread of the social library in the colonies. Ben Franklin, finding that books were costly and difficult to acquire in Philadelphia, hit on the novel idea of pooling the resources of a number of young men in order to buy books. His idea bore fruit in what he termed the "Mother of all the North American Subscription Libraries," the Philadelphia Library Company, and set a pattern that was to be copied again and again in America and Europe.

For years Franklin's role as the founder of American subscription libraries was overlooked. However, Margaret Korty has recently authored several important studies analyzing his contribution in this area. The following selection describes the events that led to the establishment of America's first subscription library, and suggests how significant a development it was. The widespread growth of subscription (or social) libraries after the Revolution is dealt with in a later chapter.

BEGINNINGS IN THE JUNTO

When Benjamin Franklin arrived in Philadelphia for the first time, he noted that

> there was not a good Bookseller's Shop in any of the Colonies to the Southward of Boston. In New York and Philadelphia the Printers were indeed Stationers, they sold only Paper, &c., Almanacks, Ballads, and a few common School Books. Those who lov'd Reading were oblig'd to send for their Books from England.[1]

It is no wonder then, that this young man sought out friends who enjoyed books and enjoyed talking about them; he began to gather around him young men with similar interests. In the fall of 1727, he tells us,

> I had form'd most of my ingenious Acquaintance into a Club for mutual Improvement, which we call'd the Junto. We met on Friday Evenings. The Rules I drew up requir'd that every Member in his Turn should produce one or more Queries on any Point of Morals, Politics or Natural Philosophy, to be discuss'd by the Company, and once in three Months produce and read an Essay of his own Writing on any Subject he pleased. Our Debates were to be under the Direction of a President, and to be conducted in the sincere Spirit of Enquiry after Truth, without Fondness for Dispute, or Desire of Victory; and to prevent Warmth all Expressions of Positiveness in Opinion, or of direct Contradiction, were after some time made contraband and prohibited under small pecuniary Penalties.[2]

Three of the members of this Junto were fellow workers at Keimer's printing shop: Hugh Meredith, later Franklin's partner; Stephen Potts, later Franklin's bookbinder; and George Webb. Others were Joseph Breintnall, "a Copyer of Deeds for the Scriveners"; Thomas Godfrey, a glazier and "self-taught Mathematician"; Nicholas Scull, a surveyor; William Parsons, a shoemaker; William Maugridge, a joiner; William Coleman, a merchant's clerk; and Robert Grace, the only member with some wealth. For the most part, these were men with more interest than principal. The Junto met at first in a tavern, but later moved to a room in a house owned by Robert Grace,[3] in Pewter-Platter Alley (or Jones's Alley).

On Franklin's first trip to England, he became familiar with the literary discussions that went on in the coffee-houses and taverns, and even became a participant as author of *A Dissertation on Liberty and Necessity, Pleasure and Pain.*

> My Pamphlet by some means falling into the Hands of one Lyons, a Surgeon, Author of a Book intitled *The Infallibility of Human Judgment*, it occasioned an Acquaintance between us; he took great Notice of me, call'd on me often, to converse on those Subjects, carried me to the Horns a pale Ale-House in [blank] Lane, Cheapside, and introduc'd me to Dr. Mandevile, Author of the Fable of the Bees who had a Club there, of which he was the Soul,

SOURCE: Reprinted from Margaret Barton Korty, "Benjamin Franklin and Eighteenth-Century American Libraries," *Transactions of the American Philosophical Society* 55 (December, 1965), pp. 5-11, by permission of the author and publisher. Copyright © 1965 by the American Philosophical Society.

being a most facetious entertaining Companion.
Lyons too introduc'd me, to Dr. Pemberton, at
Batson's Coffee House, who promis'd to give me an
Opportunity sometime or other of seeing Sir Isaac
Newton, of which I was extremely desirous; but
this never happened.[4]

Between this experience and his boyhood memory
of Cotton Mather's neighborhood benefit societies
in Boston, he worked out a plan for the Junto,[5]
borrowing additional ideas from John Locke's
plan for a mutual improvement society.[6]

Franklin was interested in reading, in discussion,
and in self-improvement. These were the three
functions which the Junto fulfilled for all of its
members. Each member had to qualify himself
by promising to love mankind, to respect one
another, to believe in freedom of speech and of
worship, and to love truth for truth's sake. The
"Rules for a Club Established for Mutual Improvement" were drawn up in 1728 as regulations for the Junto. They were refined in later
years, but remained essentially the same in
that there were twenty-four "queries" which
formed the basis of discussions of the group.
Among these queries were:

1. Have you met with anything in the author you
   last read, remarkable, or suitable to be communicated to the Junto? particularly in history,
   morality, poetry, physic, travels, mechanic
   arts, or other parts of knowledge.
2. What new story have you lately heard agreeable for telling in conversation?

Other questions dealt with morality, business,
and hospitality.[7] Among the proposals which
Franklin brought before the Junto in 1732
were these:

> That these queries, copied at the beginning of a book,
> be read distinctly at each meeting; a pause between
> each, while one might fill and drink a glass of wine.
> That, if they cannot be gone through in one night,
> we begin the next where we left off; ...
> When any thing from reading an author is men-
> tioned, if it exceed a line, and the Junto require
> it, the person shall bring the passage or an abstract
> of it the next night, if he has it not with him.
> When the books of the library come, every mem-
> ber shall undertake some author, that he may not
> be without observations to communicate.

In that year the queries were enlarged to include
one on literary criticism: "How shall we judge
of the goodness of a writing?" Franklin's own
proposed answer was, in part: "To be good, it
ought to have a tendency to benefit the reader,
by improving his virtue or his knowledge. . . . it

should be *smooth, clear,* and *short*."[8] Thus, the
Junto was beginning to depend more upon books
to stimulate discussion.

Not long after the club meetings had moved
into a separate room in the house of Robert Grace,
Benjamin Franklin proposed:

> that since our Books were often referr'd to in our
> Disquisitions upon the Queries, it might be con-
> venient to us to have them all together where we
> met, that upon Occasion they might be consulted;
> and by thus clubbing our Books to a common
> Library, we should, while we lik'd to keep them
> together, have each of us the Advantage of using
> the Books of all the other Members, which would
> be nearly as beneficial as if each owned the whole.
> It was lik'd and agreed to, and we fill'd one End of the
> Room with such Books as we could best spare.
> The Number was not so great as we expected; and
> tho' they had been of great Use, yet some Incon-
> veniencies occurring for want of due Care of them,
> the Collection after about a Year was separated,
> and each took his Books home again.[9]

Franklin took advantage of this opportunity
while the books still remained in the Junto meeting
room. He set down on paper a few "Observations
on my Reading History in Library, May 9, 1731."
Noting the destructive effect of private and party
interests, he came to the conclusion that:

> There seems to me at present to be great Oc-
> casion for raising an united Party for Virtue, by
> forming the Virtuous and good Men of all Nations
> into a regular Body, to be govern'd by suitable
> good and wise Rules, which good and wise Men may
> probably be more unanimous in their Obedience to,
> than common People are to common Laws.

Franklin never carried out his plan for a dream
world, though he from time to time kept making
notes for starting on the *"great and extensive
Project"* by establishing a "Society of the *Free
and Easy."* a society free from vice and easy from
debt.[10]

Though the books were dispersed, the discussions
continued, and this first abortive attempt at a
library was not in vain. "Finding the Advantage of
this little Collection, I propos'd to render the
Benefit from Books more common by commencing
a Public Subscription Library." Thus was born
the first subscription library in America, the Library Company of Philadelphia. The Junto continued in existence for many years and became
influential not only in furnishing intellectual
and moral stimulation for its members, but also
in "preparing the Minds of People"[11] for other
public improvements to come.

FORMATION AND EARLY YEARS

It was only a matter of a few months between the dispersal of the Junto library and the establishment of the Library Company of Philadelphia. Franklin had recorded using the Junto library on May 9, 1731, and the Instrument of Association of the Library Company was drawn up on July 1, 1731.[12] Franklin's *Autobiography* reveals his genius for organization:

I drew a Sketch of the Plan and Rules that would be necessary, and got a skilful Conveyancer, Mr. Charles Brockden to put the whole in Form of Articles of Agreement to be subscribed; by which each Subscriber engag'd to pay a certain Sum down for the first Purchase of Books and an annual Contribution for encreasing them. So few were the Readers at that time in Philadelphia, and the Majority of us so poor, that I was not able with great Industry to find more than Fifty Persons, mostly young Tradesmen, willing to pay down for this purpose Forty shillings each, and Ten Shillings per Annum. On this little Fund we began. . . . .

The Objections, and Reluctances I met with in Soliciting the Subscriptions, made me soon feel the Impropriety of presenting one's self as the Proposer of any useful Project that might be suppos'd to raise one's Reputation in the smallest degree above that of one's Neighbours, when one has need of their Assistance to accomplish that Project. I therefore put my self as much as I could out of sight, and stated it as a Scheme of a *Number of Friends,* who had requested me to go about and propose it to such as they thought Lovers of Reading. In this way my Affair went on more smoothly, and I ever after practis'd it on such Occasions; and from my frequent Successes, can heartily recommend it. The present little Sacrifice of your Vanity will afterwards be amply repaid.[13]

Franklin's method of recruiting subscribers was a success, but to took several months to accomplish the purpose. The Junto members, too, were busily engaged in recruiting. All of the original members of the Junto became subscribers except Hugh Meredith, who one year before had sold out his printing partnership to Franklin to pay off his drinking debts and departed for North Carolina.[14] At length, the Instrument of Association had been completed by the signature of fifty subscribers. Benjamin Franklin wrote out a summons to the directors of the Library Company, and Joseph Breintnall, the secretary, signed it.

To Benjamin Franklin, William Parsons, Thomas Godfrey, Thomas Cadwalader, Robert Grace and Thomas Hopkinson, Philip Syng Junr., Anthony Nicholas, John Jones Junr., [and] Isaac Penington.

Gentlemen,
The Subscription to the Library being compleated You the Directors appointed in the Instrument are desired to meet this Evening at 5 o'Clock, at the House of Nicholas Scull to take Bond of the Treasurer for the faithfull Performance of his Trust, and to consider of, and appoint a proper Time for the Payment of the Money subscribed, and other Matters relating to the said Library.
Philada. 8 Novr. 1731 Joseph Breintnall, Secy.[15]

The treasurer was William Coleman. In this first official group, the treasurer, the secretary, and four directors (Franklin, Parsons, Godfrey, and Grace) were all members of the original Junto. Thomas Cadwalader was a physician; Thomas Hopkinson, a lawyer; Philip Syng, a silversmith; Anthony Nicholas, a blacksmith; John Jones, a cordwainer or leatherworker; and Isaac Penington, a landowner.

At the meeting of November 8, 1731, Franklin urged that the "monies" be collected from the first twenty-five subscribers. Members who lived in town could pay at Nicholas Scull's on November 10; members who lived out of town paid at Owen Owen's on November 22 and 29. By December 14, the twenty-fifth subscriber had paid his money. After New Year's Day, the subscription was thrown open again, and twenty-five more subscribers purchased their shares. Two directors, William Parsons and Isaac Penington, were tardy with their payments, but responded to a polite mandate from Franklin.[16] Franklin printed and distributed a final notice to the Library Company subscribers, dated March 25, 1732:

Sir, Next Saturday Evening Attendance will be given at N. Scull's, to receive the Money subscribed to the Library, of those who have not yet paid; when you are desired to appear without Fail, either to pay or relinquish; that it may then be known who are, and who are not concerned.[17]

With a capital of one hundred English pounds and an annual income of twenty-five pounds in dues, the Library Company was now ready for its first book order.[18] According to the Minutes of March 29, 1732,

Thomas Godfrey at his meeting informed us that Mr. Logan had let him know he would willingly give his advice of the choice of the books . . . and the Committee esteeming Mr. Logan to be a Gentleman of universal learning, and the best judge of books in these parts, ordered that Mr. Godfrey should wait on him and request him to favour them with a catalogue of suitable books.[19]

James Logan was a man of wealth and position in Pennsylvania. He had a large private library, devoted not only to classics, but also to mathematics,

botany, astronomy, history, and literature.
Franklin accompanied Godfrey out to Stenton,
James Logan's home,[20] and the list was completed
by March 31, for the first book order:

Puffendorf's Introduc'n 8 vo.
Dr. Howell's History of ye World 3 vols. Fo.
Rapin's History of England 12 vols. 8 vo.
Salmon's Modern History
Vertot's Revolutions
Plutarch's Lives in small vol.
Stanley's Lives of ye Philosophers
Annals of Tacitus by Gordon
Collection of Voyages 6 vols.
Atlas Geogra. 5 vols. 4to.
Gordon's Grammar
Brightland's English Grammar
Greenwood's   "   "
Johnson's History of Animals
Architect: by And^w Palladio
Evelyn's Parallels of the ancient and modern
   Architecture
Bradley's Improvmt. of Husbandry and his other
   books of Gardening
Perkinson's Herball
Helvicius's Chronology
Wood's Institutes
Dechall's Euclid
L'Hospital's Conic Sections
Ozanam's Course of Mathem. 5 vols.
Hayes upon Fluxions
Keil's Astronomical Lectures
Drake's Anatomy
Sidney on Government
Cato's Letters
Sieur Du Port Royal moral essays
Crousay's Art of Thinking
Spectator
Guardian
Tatler
Puffendorf's Laws of Nature etc.
Addison's Works in 12 mo.
Memorable Things of Socrates
Turkish Spy
Abrdgmt. of Phil. Trans. 5 vols. 4to.
Gravesend's Nat. Philos. 2 vols. 8vo.
Boerhaave's Chemistry
The Compleat Tradesman
Bailey's Dictionary—the best
Homer's Iliad and Odyssey
Bayle's Critical Dictionary
Dryden's Virgil
Catalogues[21]

Franklin's influence is shown in some of the

books that he wrote about in his *Autobiography*
— the *Spectator,* Socrates, Plutarch, *Moral
Essays* of Port Royal, Addison, etc. This was a
practical library; there was not one work of
theology on order. Filled instead with dictionaries,
grammars, an atlas, histories, and books on science
and agriculture, it was suited to the tastes and
purses of young tradesmen.

Thomas Hopkinson carried the order and the
bill of exchange for forty-five pounds made out to
Peter Collinson, mercer, in London. Collinson
responded not only with aid in supplying the
books, but also with the first donation to the Library— "Sr. Isaac Newton's Philosophy and Philip
Miller's Gardening Dictionary."[22] Later he added
Barclay's *Apology.*[23] Benjamin Franklin dictated
the return letter of thanks on November 7, and
it was "copied fair" and sent under the signature
of the secretary. In it, Franklin pointed out that:

> An Undertaking like ours, was as necessary here, as
> we hope it will be useful; there being no Manner of
> Provision made by the Government for publick
> Education, either in this or the neighbouring Prov-
> inces, nor so much as a good Booksellers Shop nearer
> than Boston.[24]

This was the first of many years of correspondence
between Peter Collinson, agent in England, and the
Library Company, much of it going through the
hands of Benjamin Franklin.

The books arrived in October, 1732, and were
unpacked and placed on shelves in the library
room of the house owned by Robert Grace in
Jones's Alley. A labeling committee was appointed,
and the books were catalogued according to a
system used in Queens' College, Cambridge,
England. This system lists size first (folio, quarto,
octavo, and duodecimo), before any consideration
is given to author or subject.[25] To protect tne
binding, the books were covered with sheathing
paper.[26] Franklin printed the catalogue of the
books; at the meeting of December 11, 1732,

> B. Franklin was asked what his charge was for
> printing a catalogue . . . for each subscriber; and his
> answer was that he designed them for presents, and
> should make no charge for them.[27]

In all the time between July 1, 1731, when the
Library was first formed, to November 14, 1732,
there had been no librarian. The first librarian,
Louis Timothée, was selected on November 14,
1732, and served to December 10, 1733.[28]
Timothée, a language teacher, was a native of
Holland, who had come to Philadelphia in 1731,
and was employed by Benjamin Franklin as

journeyman and editor of the *Philadelphische Zeitung,* first German-American newspaper.[29] He was at this time living in the house of Robert Grace, where the books were kept. The agreement between Timothée and the directors of the Library Company, written in Franklin's hand,[30] provided for a salary and room rental together of three pounds for the first three months, with future salary to be arranged. The librarian was to be in attendance on Wednesdays from two to three o'clock, and on Saturdays from ten to four; he was to lend to any subscriber one book or set of books at a time upon receipt of a promissory note to pay the value of the book set down in the catalogue; he "shall not lend to, or suffer to be taken out of the Library by, any Person who is not a subscribing Member any of the said Books, Mr. James Logan only excepted." Franklin printed the promissory notes according to the following form:

> I promise to pay Lewis Timothee or his Order, the Sum of   for Value received. Nevertheless, if within   from the Date hereof, I return undefaced to the said Lewis Timothee a Book belonging to the Library Company of Philadelphia entituled   which I have now borrowed of him this Bill is to be void. Witness my Hand   Day of   [31]

After Timothée (now Lewis Timothy) left for Charleston, South Carolina, to print the *South Carolina Gazette* in partnership with Franklin, Franklin served as substitute librarian from December 10, 1733, to March 11, 1734, a period of three months and one day. William Parsons was then selected as librarian and served until 1746.[32] On April 26, 1733, Franklin inserted an advertisement in his *Pennsylvania Gazette* to give notice to the subscribers that May 7 would be the time for electing officers and for paying their first annual installment of ten shillings apiece, with a reminder that a penalty was exacted for late payment. Penalties were not only for the subscribers in general, but also for directors. Attendance at monthly meetings was disappointing, so Franklin conceived a novel cure for the situation and presented his proposal to the directors on May 28, 1733. Only five directors were present to sign the agreement that

> upon every Failure of attending at any of the aforemention'd Meetings We will at our next Appearance in a Meeting of the said Directors . . . forfeit and pay for Each of us One pint of Wine . . . . No Reasons shall be pleaded for Absence.

The other directors endorsed the agreement later,

and it became an annual ritual, with variations.[33] The agreement signed by the directors on May 22, 1738, required the payment of one shilling for absence. In that year, Franklin was tardy once and absent once (March 12, 1738/9); absentees ranged from two to six per meeting. The agreement of May 11, 1741, changed the penalty to sending a proxy in the shape of "two bottles of good wine."

The directors now felt it time to court the favor of the proprietors, and on May 14, 1733, a committee composed of Franklin, Thomas Hopkinson, William Coleman, and Joseph Breintnall was appointed to draft an address to Thomas Penn, who had recently arrived in Pennsylvania. The language was rather flowery for a Quaker community, for example: "May your Philadelphia be the future Athens of America." Thomas Penn was pleased with the petition for his "Countenance and Protection," asked questions about the new venture, and gave a short oral reply. On May 31, Franklin and Hopkinson returned to receive the reply in writing because the directors wished to print his response:

> I take this Address very kindly; and assure you, I shall always be ready to promote any Undertaking so useful to the Country, as that of erecting a *common Library* in this City.[35]

The business of the library went on as usual, but two major changes were made during the short term that Franklin served as librarian (December 10, 1733, to March 11, 1734). First, the library was opened to nonsubscribers upon a deposit equal to the value of the book and a rental fee.[36] Second, it was proposed in the Minutes of February 11, 1734, "that the time of the Librarian's attendance should be only one day in the week (it having been found by experience that the borrowers of books did not commonly come to the Library on Wednesday)."[37] The hours were set for Saturday from four to eight o'clock. The care of the library was turned over to William Parsons on March 14; the books were removed to his house, and an inventory was taken. There were 239 volumes plus sixteen "Notes of Hand" for books checked out, plus twenty-five periodicals, and a few other pamphlets and papers. The directors agreed that they would continue the "Printing the Notes to be given by all Borrowers of Books out of the said Library."[38] Book selection was done in various ways, but most of the selection was done by the directors themselves with some help from the subscribers. Suggestions were taken from John Clarke's *An Essay upon Study and* John Locke's *Some Thoughts Concerning Education*, and the library eventually acquired *A General History of Printing*, by Samuel Palmer, the London printer who had hired Franklin back in 1725.[39]

New members were admitted from time to time. An example of the form used was one written by Franklin on August 27, 1734, for the admission of John Mifflin, a Quaker merchant.

> Such of the Directors of the Library Company as approve of John Mifflin's being admitted a Member are desired to shew their Consent by subscribing their Names hereto.[40]

In the fall of 1734, John Penn arived from England, but it was the next May before the Library Company presented an address to him which had been written by Franklin, Coleman, Hopkinson, and Breintnall. The language of this address was also flowery, but it gives some hint that there was already some dissatisfaction with the Penn government, though it showed nothing of the future conflict between Franklin himself and the Proprietors. It, too, speaks of the Library Company as being a "Publick Library" erected to promote "Knowledge and Virtue." The address was printed in the *Pennsylvania Gazette*, June 5, 1735. In his reply to the Library Company, John Penn promised that:

> I shall always be ready with Pleasure to promote so good and necessary an Undertaking, as the erecting a Publick Library in this City.[41]

Both John and Thomas Penn had the welfare of the Library Company at heart. John donated an air pump, and Thomas donated a lot in 1738, located on the south side of Chestnut Street between Eighth and Ninth. The lot was never used for the intended purpose of building, but was used instead as rental property.[42]

The directors of the Library Company did not feel ready to build, but they did feel cramped for space. Franklin at this time was serving as clerk to the Pennsylvania Assembly, and it occurred to him to petition for use of a room in one of the vacant offices of the State House. Permission was granted in the fall of 1739, and the books were actually removed from the house of William Parsons, then librarian, to the "upper room of the westernmost office of the State House" on April 7, 1740.[43] This office was located in the west wing of the building, with an outside stairway,

for the same wing also housed the doorkeeper of the Assembly and his family. The two wings of the State House had been constructed in 1736 to provide a safe place for the keeping of state papers. They were, however, not Indian-proof, and during the early years were subjected to indoor teepee fires when Indian delegations were lodged in the upper story of the eastern wing. Not until a separate building was constructed for the use of Indian guests, were the state papers and the books of the Library Company out of danger.[44]

After the books were moved to the State House, now known as Independence Hall, a committee, which included Franklin, was appointed to make a catalogue, and on April 13, 1741, reported "that they have done so; whereupon it is agreed that two hundred of them shall be printed by B. Franklin."[45] In 1733 and 1735, Franklin had printed broadsheet lists of the works available to members of the Library Company, but no copies of either list have survived. The 1741 *Catalogue* recorded 375 titles listed according to size of book. History (114 titles), literature (69 titles), and science (65 titles) were the most popular subjects. Most of the books were in English. Only thirteen were in foreign languages; ten of them were gifts, and in each case of a foreign title order the Library Company also owned an English translation.[46] So far, the language policy followed Franklin's original scheme for an English library.[47] To fill up a blank page at the end of this 1741 catalogue, Franklin wrote "A short Account of the Library." It was approved by the directors and included in the printed catalogue.[48]

Obviously at this time, Franklin was doing all the printing work of the Library Company; besides forms and catalogues, he inserted advertisements of its meetings in the *Pennsylvania Gazette*, did bookbinding and repair work, furnished account books and paper, and even took care of "ye mending Library stairs."[49] He had been excused from two years of annual payments (April 24, 1732) for his printing services.[50] Although he was in the business of selling books, he did not sell books to the Library Company; rather, he probably waited for the Library Company to order new books from London, and then, judging by how well they were received, ordered his own multiple copies for sale.[51] He also used materials owned by the Library Company in his publications. The 1741 *Catalogue* lists in the manuscript collection three documents of Pennsylvania history—Charles II's Charter to Penn, Penn's Charter of Liberties for Pennsylvania, and Penn's Charter of the City of Philadelphia. The year before, these three were gathered together and published by Franklin. Robert Grace donated Gauger's *Fires Improved* to the Library Company; since Grace was the manufacturer of Franklin's improved stove, it is likely that Franklin consulted that book in the design of it.[52] He printed his description of the stove, *An Account of the New-Invented Pennsylvanian Fire-Places*, in 1744.[53]

As early as 1739, the directors began to discuss the possibility of seeking a charter from the Proprietors. After some difficulty in getting approval on its exact wording and terms, the charter was finally signed by Governor Thomas on March 25 and approved by the subscribers on May 3, 1742; by-laws were also adopted at this time. Benjamin Franklin's name stood first in the charter list of subscribers. Franklin, Hopkinson, and Coleman prepared an address of thanks to the Proprietors, John, Thomas, and Richard Penn. In 1746 Franklin printed the text of the charter, the by-laws, and a list of "Books Added to the Library Since the Year 1741."[54]

Franklin took over the secretaryship of the Library Company after the death of Joseph Breintnall in 1746, and held this position until 1757, when he left for England. He was succeeded by Francis Allison, who served for a period of two years, and then by Francis Hopkinson.[55] Hopkinson decided to collect all the old minutes into one volume, but found that some had been lost because Franklin had written some of his minutes on scraps of paper and on backs of correspondence.[56] No wonder Hopkinson was confused—Franklin wrote the December, 1748, minutes on the bottom of Peter Collinson's bill for books sent to the Library between June 16, 1742, and October 15, 1745.[57] Franklin, himself, admitted "I found myself incorrigible with respect to *Order*."[58]

Franklin played host to the visiting Swedish naturalist, Peter Kalm, sent over by the Swedish Academy of Sciences in 1748, and introduced him to Philadelphia's men of learning, including James Logan. Kalm was interested in every detail of life in the colonies, as is evidenced in the detailed diary he kept of his *Travels in North America*. He was particularly impressed by the size of the Library Company's book collection, kept in the State House, which he mistakenly called the "Town Hall."

> On one side of this building stands the *Library* which was first begun in the year 1742 on a public spirited plan formed and put into execution by the learned Mr. Franklin. ... There is already a fine collection of excellent works, most of them English; many French and Latin, but few in any other language. The subscribers were kind enough to order the librarian, during my stay here, to lend me every book which I should want without any payment. The library is open every Saturday from four to eight o'clock in the afternoon. Besides the books, several mathematical and physical instruments and a large collection of natural curiosities are to be seen in it. Several little libraries were founded in the town on the same principle or nearly so.[59]

In the eyes of a European, the Library Company could hold its own.

FOOTNOTES

[1] *The Autobiography of Benjamin Franklin*, ed. Leonard W. Labaree and others (New Haven: Yale University Press, 1964), p. 141.

[2] *Ibid.*, pp. 116-117.

[3] *Ibid.*, pp. 117-118, 130.

[4] *Ibid.*, p. 97.

[5] Carl Van Doren, *Benjamin Franklin* (New York: Viking Press, 1938), p. 75.

[6] Dorothy F. Grimm, "Franklin's Scientific Institution," *Pennsylvania History*, XXIII (1956), pp. 441-446. See also Franklin's donation to the Library Company of Philadelphia listed in *A Catalogue of Books Belonging to the Library Company of Philadelphia; A Facsimile of the Edition of 1741 Printed by BENJAMIN FRANKLIN, With an Introduction by Edwin Wolf 2nd* (Philadelphia: Printed for the Library Company of Philadelphia to mark the 250th Anniversary of the Birth of Franklin, 1956), pp. 28-29.

[7] Jared Sparks, ed., *The Works of Benjamin Franklin* (10 vols.; Boston: Tappan, Whittemore, and Mason, 1836-1840), II, pp. 9, 12.

[8] *Ibid.*, II, pp. 551-553.

[9] Labaree, *Autobiography*, p. 130.

[10] *Ibid.*, pp. 161-163.

[11] *Ibid.*, pp. 142, 173.

[12] George Maurice Abbot, *A Short History of the Library Company of Philadelphia; Compiled from the Minutes, together with some personal reminiscences* (Philadelphia: Library Company of Philadelphia, 1913), p. 3.

[13] Labaree, *Autobiography*, pp. 142-143.

[14] Van Doren, *op. cit.,* pp. 100-101.

[15] Leonard W. Labaree, ed., *The Papers of Benjamin Franklin* (8 vols. to date; New Haven: Yale University Press, 1959–   ), I, pp. 209-210.

[16] Austin K. Gray, *Benjamin Franklin's Library* (New York: Macmillan, 1937), pp. 7-8.

[17] Labaree, *Papers,* I, pp. 229-230.

[18] Gray, *op. cit.,* p. 8.

[19] Abbot, *op. cit.,* p. 5.

[20] Library Company of Philadelphia, Minutes (Manuscript), I, p. 6 (March 30, 1732). Frederick B. Tolles, *James Logan and the Culture of Provincial America* (Boston: Little, Brown and Co., 1957), p. 213.

[21] Gray, *op. cit.,* pp. 9-10.

[22] *Ibid.,* pp. 10-11.

[23] Library Company of Philadelphia, *A Catalogue of the Books, Belonging to the Library Company of Philadelphia; To Which Is Prefixed, A Short Account Of The Institution, With The Charter, Laws, and Regulations* (Philadelphia: Bartram & Reynolds, 1807), p. 16.

[24] Labaree, *Papers,* I, pp. 248-249.

[25] Gray, *op. cit.,* pp. 10-11.

[26] Library Company of Philadelphia, Minutes, I, p. 19 (Jan. 8, 1732/3).

[27] Abbot, *op. cit.,* p. 7.

[28] Library Company of Philadelphia, *Catalogue* (1807), p. xxxix.

[29] Labaree, *Papers,* I, p. 230, n. 2. Van Doren, *op. cit.,* p. 103.

[30] Edwin Wolf, 2nd, "B. Franklin, Bookman," *American Library Association Bulletin,* L (Jan., 1956), p. 15.

[31] Labaree, *Papers,* I, pp. 251-252.

[32] Library Company of Philadelphia, *Catalogue* (1807), p. xxxix.

[33] Labaree, *Papers,* I, pp. 321-322.

[34] *Ibid.,* II, pp. 205-206.

[35] *Ibid.,* I, pp. 320-321. *Pennsylvania Gazette,* May 31, 1733.

[36] Library Company of Philadelphia, Minutes, I, pp. 37-38 (Jan. 14, 1734, new style).

[37] Abbot, *op. cit.,* p. 8.

[38] Labaree, *Papers,* I, pp. 360-361.

[39] Edwin Wolf, 2nd, "Franklin and His Friends Choose Their Books," *Pennsylvania Magazine of History and Biography,* LXXX (Jan., 1956), pp. 14, 34.

[40] Labaree, *Papers,* I, p. 373.

[42] *Ibid.,* II, pp. 33-35.

[42] *Ibid.,* II, pp. 207-210.

[43] Abbot, *op. cit.,* p. 9.

[44] U. S. National Park Service, *Independence National Historical Park, Philadelphia, Pa.,* by Edward M. Riley ("National Park Service Historical Handbook Series," No. 17; rev. ed., Washington, D. C.: Government Printing Office, 1956), p. 3.

[45] Abbot, *op. cit.,* p. 9.

[46] Wolf, "Franklin and His Friends Choose Their Books," pp. 13-15.

[47] Albert Henry Smyth, ed., *The Writings of Benjamin Franklin* (10 vols.; New York: Macmillan, 1905-1907), X, p.9.

[48] Library Company of Philadelphia, *Catalogue* (1741; 1956 facsimile edition).

[49] George Simpson Eddy, *Account Books Kept by Benjamin Franklin, Ledger "D", 1739-1747* (New York: Columbia University Press, 1929), p. 79.

[50] Library Company of Philadelphia, Minutes, I, p. 10 (April 24, 1732).

[51] Wolf, "B. Franklin, Bookman," p. 16.

[52] Wolf, "Franklin and His Friends Choose Their Books," pp. 33-34.

[53] Van Doren, *op. cit.,* p. 117.

[54] Labaree, *Papers,* II, pp. 345-349, 359.

[55] Abbot, *op. cit.,* p. 29.

[56] Wolf, "B. Franklin, Bookman," p. 15.

[57] Labaree, *Papers,* III, p. 351.

[58] Labaree, *Autobiography,* p. 156.

[59] The 1742 date refers to the date of charter. Peter Kalm, *The America of 1750; Peter Kalm's Travels in North America,* ed. by Adolph B. Benson (2 vols., New York: Wilson-Erickson, 1937), I, p. 25.

ADDITIONAL READINGS

Boorstin, Daniel, *The Americans: The Colonial Experience* (New York: Random House, 1958), Chapters 45, 46, 47.

Jackson, Sidney, "Seldom Snug, and gave no scandal: Or The Junto and After," Stechert-Hafner *Book News* 24 (May, 1970), pp. 133-136; 25 (November, 1970), pp. 1-3.

Jennings, John M. *The Library of the College of William and Mary in Virginia, 1693-1793* (Charlottesville: University Press of Virginia, 1968).

Korty, Margaret, "Franklin's World of Books," *Journal of Library History* II (October, 1967), pp. 271-328.

Shores, Louis, *Origins of the American College Library, 1638-1800* (New York: Barnes and Noble, 1963).

Wright, Louis B., *The First Gentlemen of Virginia: Intellectual Qualities of the Early Colonial Ruling Class* (San Mareno, California: Huntington Library, 1940).

Wright, Thomas Goddard, *Literary Culture in Early New England 1620-1730* (New Haven: Yale University Press, 1920).

III

LIBRARIES IN THE NEW NATION

From small beginnings before the Revolution, American libraries grew and diversified in the years prior to the Civil War. Indeed, if any one phrase could characterize the library scene in the new nation it would be "growth and diversity". For in addition to the few college and subscription libraries surviving from the colonial period, a number of new types were added to America's inventory of libraries—the mechanic and mercantile libraries, school district libraries, and Sunday school libraries, the latter numbering in the thousands. Furthermore, the growth of college and subscription libraries was phenomenal, a growth that is amply documented in the following pages.

This period in American library history might well be termed the "experimental age." As is the case with most experimental models, whether they be libraries or cars, many of the experiments carried on before the Civil War were later modified or completely replaced. Thus, many of the types of libraries described in the following pages either are no longer in existence, or are relatively insignificant. What is important is an understanding of the societal needs which created these new libraries, yet later caused them to fall from favor and decline. The essays that follow attempt to provide this understanding.

The Expansion of the Social Library

Jesse H. Shera

Prior to 1850, public tax-supported libraries as we know them today were nearly non-existent. The nearest approximation were the subscription or social libraries which were voluntary associations of individuals for the purpose of buying books to be owned jointly by all those who belonged. This method for the provision of library services worked fairly well, and in time nearly every sizable town in the country had tried a social library system at least once. In New England alone over a thousand were established prior to 1850.

In a very real sense these libraries were the direct ancestors of the American public library. On one hand they illustrated the value of library services to the people of America's towns and cities, but on the other, they proved that the principle of voluntary support was a shaky foundation upon which to build effective public library service. In the following essay, from his now classic treatment of the predecessors of the American public library, Jesse Shera analyzes the reasons for the extensive growth of the social libraries in New England and pinpoints the reasons they proved inadequate to meet that area's needs for good library service.

The Revolutionary War and its aftermath of political uncertainty and economic depression were only pauses in the advance of the social library. No new libraries were established in any New England state during the years 1776 and 1777, and only three or four such institutions appeared during the remainder of the decade, [1] but the 1780's produced more new social libraries than the entire previous half century. [2] The new nation, having successfully survived its initial vicissitudes, was again prepared to focus attention upon cultural undertakings and to resume the establishment of social libraries at the level attained before the interruption by the war.

The year 1790 may be considered a mid-point in the history of the social library in New England. During the preceding half century the institution passed through an age of experimentation, adaptation, incipient growth, and final recognition as a wholly satisfactory library form. The fifty years that followed brought to the social library a period of expansion that might be characterized as its "golden age." During the twenty-five years between 1790 and 1815 the social library experienced unprecedented growth; literally scores of New England towns, especially in Connecticut, Massachusetts, and New Hampshire, organized

such book clubs. The editors of the *Massachusetts Register* for 1802 estimated that "though it would ... require much time and pains to obtain a complete enumeration" of these libraries, "at a random conjecture they now probably amount to one hundred in Massachusetts."[3] Many, as later tabulation will show, were small and short lived, but at this time there were also laid the foundations of some of the most important future collections. The Boston Athenaeum, the American Antiquarian Society, the Massachusetts Historical Society, and the Social Law Library all were begun during these years.

Evidence of the vitality of the social library movement at the turn of the nineteenth century is to be found not only in the enactment of general permissive legislation providing for the establishment of such libraries but also in the eagerness with which local booksellers competed for social library patronage. Such merchants openly boasted that the titles they stocked were particularly appropriate for the shelves of library societies and vied with each other in offering substantial discounts for quantity purchase.[4] "Purchasers for Public, Social, and Private Libraries are respectfully solicited for their favors; and all orders for Books to be had in Boston will be promptly an-

SOURCE: Reprinted from Jesse H. Shera, *Foundations of the Public Library,* (Chicago: University of Chicago Press, 1949), Chapter 3 "The Social Library. I: Origins, Form, and Economic Backgrounds," pp. 68-85, by permission of the author and publisher. Copyright © 1949 by the University of Chicago.

TABLE 1

Distribution of Libraries, Six New England States by Date of Establishment, 1776–1850*

	1776–80	1781–85	1786–90	1791–95	1796–1800	1801–5	1806–10	1811–15
Conn.	3	9	24	61	29	21	19	14
Mass.	5	6	15	35	34	20	33	24
R.I.	–	–	–	3	6	2	6	1
Me.	–	–	2	4	8	6	4	5
N.H.	–	–	1	18	54	51	23	24
Vt.	–	–	2	4	10	5	5	3
New England	8	15	44	125	141	105	90	71

	1816–20	1821–25	1826–30	1831–35	1836–40	1841–45	1846–50	TOTAL
Conn.	14	18	15	9	11	2	4	253
Mass.	31	30	35	24	23	15	25	355
R.I.	4	8	6	4	2	2	21	65
Me.	17	4	5	8	2	8	6	79
N.H.	9	23	27	15	5	8	8	266
Vt.	2	3	5	3	3	1	–	46
New England	77	86	93	63	46	36	64	1,064

*The term "library" as here applied may be interpreted to mean social library in all its forms. A very few truly public libraries, such as those of Peterborough, N.H., Wayland, Mass., and Boston, Mass., have been included, but their number is so small as to make no real difference. Academic, circulating, private, and school libraries have been excluded.

The data for this and the following tables of this chapter have been taken wherever possible from the surviving records of the individual libraries. In many cases, however, these records have not been preserved, and it has been necessary to rely upon such secondary sources as are available.

swered at the most liberal discount."[5] Henry Knox, proprietor of the London Book Store in Boston, added a not too subtle flattery to his offer of special discounts to "Those Gentlemen in the Country who are actuated with the most genuine Principles of Benevolence in their Exertions to Exterminate Ignorance and Darkness, by the noble medium of SOCIAL LIBRARIES."[6] But Charles Pierce, bookseller of Portsmouth, New Hampshire, wasted no idle words of flattery when he offered a discount policy that would seem to have presented almost unlimited possibilities to ingenious patrons:

G. Pierce is determined to sell all his articles at such prices as that purchasers cannot better themselves elsewhere. The regular discount to Libraries is 10 percent, but if any other person in Boston, Newburyport, or Portsmouth, will make 12, he will make 15. And if they make 15 he will make 20 percent, even should he lose by the articles he is determined not to be undersold.

His Books and other articles are nearly all marked by a Boston catalogue, but if higher in any instance than can be purchased elsewhere, he will deduct from said prices. Every favor gratefully acknowledged. PORTSMOUTH, Aug. 5, 1806.[7]

Quite evidently the increasing popularity of the social library offered to the book-dealers a promising field for exploitation, and the more enterprising were by no means reluctant to encourage the movement by emphatic price reduction.

During the years immediately following 1815 the social library entered another phase. Whereas the twenty-five years between 1790 and 1815 were for the most part a period of vigorous and general expansion, those between 1815 and 1850 were characterized by less striking growth, a pronounced tendency toward experimental adaptation of the social library form to special purposes, and during the closing decade a marked decline. During the early years of the nineteenth century the social library was overwhelmingly a "general" collection, evincing no dominant single interest or purpose on the part of its membership. Indeed, it has largely remained thus throughout its history. But with the appearance of the short-lived lyceum movement, and the growing concern of the workers with vocational subjects, there emerged a strong tendency to develop social libraries, the collections of which were pointed toward some specific reading end. The extent of this diversity is apparent from Table 2.

In a sense these were "special" libraries in the restriction of their collections to some precise area of print or in the limitation of membership to a homogeneous group based on sex, age, or occupational interest. The importance of these

TABLE 2

Distribution of Social Libraries by Type of Interest, 1733–1850

TYPE	NO.
General	906
Mechanics and mechanics' apprentices . . .	30*
Juvenile and youth	21*
Ladies libraries	20†
Lyceum libraries	20‡
Young men's libraries	16
Theological	16
Historical	14*
Agricultural	12*
Manufacturers and factory workers	6
Science (including natural history)	4
Law	3
Masonic lodges	3†
Medical	3
Military	3
Periodical clubs	3
Mercantile	2
Antislavery	1
Fire company	1
Music	1
Total	1,085

*One example before 1800.
†Two examples before 1800; includes sewing-circle libraries.
‡No examples before 1820.

special associations is much greater than their numbers would indicate. They were of consequence by virtue of their novelty and the degree to which they revealed a desire to adapt the social library form to differences in reader interest. But, most important of all, these specialized types reveal the great diversity of interests that contributed to the development of the concept of the public library. Each was within itself the crystallization of a desire, or cluster of desires, that when added to its fellows composed a totality of forces that converged to bring tax support for a truly public library service.

In addition to being a period of experimentation, the twenty years before 1850 were an era of consolidation and replacement. The average expectation of life of the social library was not great. Relatively few survived their founders.[8] Many lapsed into inactivity long before their lives were actually terminated by official decree. As Table 3 shows, a number were absorbed by later institutions, but most slipped quietly into oblivion, leaving only a meager record to tell of their ephemeral existence. Specific data on the duration of life are available for only four hundred and thirteen of almost eleven hundred, but from Table 4 it is apparent that about half of these existed less than thirty-five years. Further, it is safe to assume that those libraries for which there is no record proba-

TABLE 3

Distribution of Social Libraries According to Their Ultimate Disposition

DISPOSITION	NO. OF LIBRARIES
Libraries still extant	32
Absorbed by other libraries still extant . . .	76
Taken over by town as free public library .	53
Subtotal	161
Absorbed by libraries later themselves defunct	73
Sold at auction	65
Dissolved and books divided among the membership	75
Destroyed by fire but not revived	12
No surviving record of disposition	699
Total	1,085

bly existed for only a very brief period. In consequence, many towns that could boast of a social library during the decade of the 1790's found themselves in 1830 either without any or with one that was but a ghost. Under the influence of the cultural ferment that swept through New England after the termination of the War of 1812 many new libraries were established, old ones reorganized, or existing institutions merged and the life-cycle begun anew. By 1850 two hundred and fifty-nine New England towns had established more than one library, and though every case did not represent the substitution of a new library for one that was defunct, the proportion is sufficiently great to indicate that such replacement was common. Distribution by states of towns having more than one library is as follows: Massachusetts, eighty-six; Connecticut, seventy-eight; New Hampshire, fifty-six; Maine, eighteen; Rhode Island, sixteen; and Vermont, five; totaling two hundred and fifty-nine.

Above all, the period of 1825-50 was significant for the beginning of a movement that eventually

TABLE 4

Distribution of Social Libraries According to Length of Life

DURATION OF LIFE	NO. OF LIBRARIES
Still extant or lasted over 100 years	60
75–99 years	11
50–74 years	53
40–49 years	53
30–39 years	70
(35 years and up . . . . approximately 212)	
20–29 years	62
10–19 years	63
5– 9 years	28
2– 4 years	13
Total	413

replaced most of the social libraries with municipally owned institutions that were actually public both in support and in patronage. During the years immediately preceding the middle of the century the social library had reached a stationary though not decadent stage. Numerically the number of libraries was great. In 1840 Horace Mann, surveying the library resources of Massachusetts, reported that the returns of his census indicated no less than two hundred and ninety-nine such institutions, with an aggregate of 180,028 volumes having an estimated value of $191,538 and available to 25,705 proprietors or other persons having access to the books "in their own right." [9]

Considered collectively, such numbers are impressive. It may be said that the agglomeration of social libraries that covered New England was in itself a great public library system. Every town then had its social library, as it was later to have its public library. As organizations they were not essentially democratic in control or patronage, but practice strongly modified their theoretical limitations so that their collections were in reality rather widely available to the community at large. Fees were generally low, and it is quite doubtful whether any serious reader was denied access to the books because of poverty. The variety of types of the social library likewise represented a genuine attempt on the part of incorporators to meet diverse wants. Though many classes of society were not adequately represented, neither were they entirely ignored. It is, then, not an exaggeration to say that this network of social libraries was more than a forerunner of the public library pattern—it *was* a public library system based on the ability of the patron to pay for the services he received. The failure of the social libraries to attain the later results of a public library system arose not from any inadequacy of the whole to achieve a sufficiently comprehensive distribution but from the weakness inherent in voluntary societies. Viewed collectively, the large numbers of social libraries do constitute an impressive picture; examined independently, the component libraries are revealed as being far from strong.

Factors in the Decline of the Social Library

Expressed in terms of absolute numbers of titles and contrasted with libraries of the present day, the size of the book collections of the social libraries was small. Even when considered in relation to contemporary university libraries or the

private libraries of scholars and wealthy patrons, except in a few instances, they were not impressive in size. From Table 5 it appears that data are available for only three hundred and eighty-six institutions, of which over half had no more than one hundred volumes. Though there is a tendency for the data to cluster about the round numbers of one hundred or one thousand, such inaccuracies scarcely invalidate the major conclusion that the book stocks were small, an inference that is further substantiated by the absence of information concerning the size of book collections in the remainder of the libraries.

TABLE 5

Distribution of Social Libraries by Size of Book Collections, Prior to 1800

NO. OF VOLS. IN LIBRARY	NO. OF LIBRARIES
10,000 or more	6
5,000–9,999	13
3,000–4,999	12
1,000–2,999	50
800– 999	16
500– 799	34
300– 499	46
100– 299*	141
Less than 100	68
Total	386

*A total of 137 libraries estimated their collections at 100 volumes, the other 4 gave more precise figures.

Data relative to the size of the original membership are even less abundant, being available for but sixty-six associations (Table 6) of which over half fall within the group of from twenty-five to forty-nine members. Obviously, such information does not indicate the eventual size of the membership, but statistics on that point are so meager as to be practically worthless. The surviving record reveals that in many instances the membership of the societies grew very little beyond the numerical limit of the founding group. Local historians may boast in vague terms about the "prosperity" and thriftiness of these little groups, but much too frequently enthusiasm for sporadic manifestations of indigenous culture has obscured strict historical accuracy.

There is no precise gauge by which one may measure the financial stability of these social libraries, though some insight may be gained from the scattered statements revealing the limitations imposed upon their financial structures. The general permissive legislation of the several states usu-

TABLE 6

**Distribution of Social Libraries Established
1790-1850 By Size of Membership
at Time of Organization**

NO. OF MEMBERS	NO. OF LIBRARIES
100 or more	1
75–99	4
50–74	21
25–49	39
Fewer than 25	1
Total	66

ally placed a limit on the amount of property, exclusive of book stocks, these libraries might hold —$500.00 in Massachusetts; $5,000.00 in Maine; $1,000.00 in New Hampshire; $2,000.00 in Rhode Island. In general it may be said that the proprietary libraries represented the larger capital outlay, but even the stock of these sold at prices that, with only a few exceptions, were quite low. In two-thirds of the institutions for which data are available, shares ranged from $1.00 to $4.00 per unit, and in only a few instances was the cost in excess of $25.00. Entrance fees were even less, the majority being but a dollar or two. In more than half of the examples annual dues were only $1.00.

Though this information is available for a limited number of all the social libraries known to have existed, yet when the composite results of the sample are examined—revealing limited book stock, small numerical membership, and circumscribed financial structure—the conclusion cannot be other than that most of the libraries were very weak indeed. Even the Boston Athenaeum, despite its relative financial strength, more than once hung precariously between survival and extinction. To those who, in the middle decades of the nineteenth century, became interested in the encouragement of public libraries, especially the proponents of the school-district libraries, it was clear that the shifting sands of voluntary support were not a sufficiently solid foundation upon which to build a universal library service.[10] As Rev. John B. Wight told the Massachusetts General Court in 1854:

> While they have contributed much to a more general diffusion of knowledge and mental culture among their associated proprietors, experience has fully shown that their *permanence* is not to be depended on. With the exception of a few in the large towns which have been well maintained, their fate has been very much as follows. For a few years

after the formation of the library everything goes on well. Its books are read with avidity. New books are occasionally added. Those who have shares find it pleasant and improving to participate in its advantages. But before many years its prosperity begins to decline. Some of the proprietors have deceased. Others have removed from the town. Others have been unfortunate in business. The annual assessments cease to be paid. New publications are no longer purchased. The library gradually falls into disuse. For a long time there are no books in circulation and then perhaps when the attention of some influential-person happens to be drawn to the subject the old library is reorganized or a new one formed, to pass through a similar course of growth, decline and neglect.[11]

TABLE 7

**Distribution of Social Libraries Established
between 1790 and 1850 by Sources
and Extent of Income**

PRICES OF SHARES (PROPRIETARY LIBRARIES)*	NO. OF LIBRARIES
$300.00	1
100.00	2
50.00	2
25.00	2
15.00–$24.00	2
10.00–$14.00	4
5.00– 9.00	18
1.00– 4.00	54
0.50	1
Total	86

ENTRANCE FEES	
$25.00	1
5.00–$9.00	6
1.00– 4.00	16
0.50	2
Total	25

ANNUAL DUES†	
$10.00	5
5.00	4
2.00–$4.00	10
1.00– 1.99	22
Less than $1.00	49
Total	90

*Omitted are certain early institutions that recorded their stock prices in English currency: 20s. for the Book-Company of Durham, Conn.; £50, Philogrammatican Society, Lebanon, Conn.; £10, United English Library, Pomfret, Conn.; £50, Redwood Library, Newport, R.I.; £50, bond required of subscribers to library at Milford, Conn.; and £10, bond required of subscribers to library at Warren, Conn. It is a curious fact that the prices of shares were uniformly higher for those institutions known as Athenaeums.

†Certain institutions scaled their dues: The Young Men's Library Association of New London, Conn. (established 1840), charged men over twenty-one years of age $3.00; boys under twenty-one were required to pay but $2.00. Library Association, North Woburn, Mass. (established 1840), charged men $1.00 per year but women only $0.50 for the same period. The Social Library of Royalston, Mass. (established 1778), accepted grain, butter, flax, or flax seed in lieu of money for membership assessments.

Economic Influences and the Social Library

A discussion of the economic influences upon social library development between the years 1790 and 1850 should be prefaced with a review of the chronology of the social library movement. As was pointed out earlier in this chapter, the history of the social library resolves itself into a series of distinct and clearly defined periods which are summarized in Table 8. Such an outline illuminates social library development during the years between 1790 and the middle of the nineteenth century and provides a frame of reference within which may be surveyed the cyclical character of social library progress. This pattern of library growth reveals certain definite relationships of the social library to the economic and social forces that contributed to its expansion and decline.

TABLE 8

The Chronological Periods of Social Library Development

I. 1733–90
    The first half-century of the social library
    From the foundation of the Book-Company of Durham, Conn., to the general acceptance of the social library as a satisfactory form
    A period of beginnings and early growth
II. 1790–1840
    The second half-century of the social library
    The social library's "golden age"
    A period characterized by two subordinate phases:
    1790–1815: A period of lush growth and great numerical increase during the first decade but with a marked decline in the rate of increase just prior to and during the War of 1812
    1815–40: Revival of interest during the cultural ferment that followed the Peace of Ghent
    A period of experimentation and replacement
    Vanguard of a free public library system
III. 1840–90
    The decline of the social library
    The birth of the public library movement as a real force in American library development
    Increasingly important competition from the public library brought declining influence to the social library
    Relatively few social libraries established in New England after 1890

Perhaps the most striking of all is the similarity among the several New England states. In all but Maine, which did not become a state until 1820, the ten years between 1795 and 1805 were the most prolific period of library establishment. A second crest was reached between 1825 and 1835, this time with Maine more nearly conforming to the trend in the other states. The intervening years evince alternating crests and troughs of lesser magnitude, but all, save Maine, exhibiting a relatively high degree of coincidence. The obvious inference that may be made is that, in all the states, essentially similar forces were operating to encourage the formation of libraries. Furthermore, Maine is an exception only in the extent to which it represents a time lag; its profile is approximately the same as that of its sister-states.

A second fact is that library establishment was not a continuously increasing process but was cyclical. Periods of rapid expansion were followed by years of less vigorous activity in the creation of new institutions. The growth that characterized the decades before 1790 may be described as rising sharply. But after the peak at the turn of the century fluctuations became pronounced and well defined. Three major factors are responsible for this cyclical quality. As has been previously stated, the replacement of neglected institutions by new and, at least temporarily, more vigorous successors accounts in large measure for the crests.

Recurrent periods of saturation prevented the establishment of new institutions. Finally, there was a tendency for the formation of libraries to follow in general the trend of the business cycle. If one were to superimpose upon the graph of library growth in New England a chart of wholesale price fluctuations in that region during the same period, the coincidence would not be perfect but the configurations would be strikingly similar. Over the second half of the eighteenth century, when the social library movement was gaining momentum in Massachusetts and other New England States, Boston was steadily improving its economic relations with the outside world. The trend of prices for its major export commodities—rum and codfish—moved upward in contrast to its imported goods—tea, cotton, and flour.

Likewise the period of prosperity that followed the sharp depression of the Revolutionary War and postwar reconstruction years is coincident with the peak in library establishment at the end of the century. Thereafter the parallel is somewhat less accentuated, but crests in business activity as indicated by wholesale price fluctuations are evident just prior to the 1820's and during the 1830's, and in both instances the prosperity they produced must have helped to cement the economic foundations of the library development that followed. It is not wise to press too far a strictly economic interpretation of the library movement, particularly if such a point of view excludes the social and cultural factors which so profoundly influenced library growth. But neither should this expansion of library agencies be dis-sociated from general economic conditions. Library formation during the Colonial period necessarily waited upon adequate economic ability for its fullest expression, and library history following the establishment of the Republic displays the same economic dependence.

The cyclical character of social library formation emphasizes anew the uncertainty of voluntary support as a motivating force in library promotion. Clearly, the trend of library establishment, far from being the ever upward progress of an urge that pressed constantly forward in its demand for expanding library resources, reveals an inconstant and shifting desire—an uncertain groping toward cultural values that waxed and waned as the social and economic forces about it surged forward or ebbed. Libraries were promoted because a few people felt the need for books and had adequate, or at least partially adequate, resources for a beginning. But with the removal of the founders or a faltering of the initial enthusiasm the real instability of the institution was revealed, decadence being an almost inevitable result. Constant vigilance was indeed the price of culture, and there were but few in most communities who were both willing and able to give to the social libraries the care and attention that they demanded of their members.

The urge toward library formation that followed the creation of the new nation was, in its social mileu, much like that which came after the Peace of Utrecht and the resultant rise of a prosperous Colonial economy. A sharp period of depression succeeded the Revolutionary War. The problem of bringing the Colonies under one unified government was no easy task. But even more disturbing was the serious dislocation of the Colonial economic balance. In spite of American dissatisfaction with England's colonial policy, the confederation found itself, after the close of the Revolution, without any direction. Public debt, instability of the currency, unpaid soldiers, and, above all, disrupted trade seriously undermined the earlier Colonial economic structure. Prosperity had not immediately followed the signing of the peace; and by the impact of subsequent economic maladjustments the whole institution of property, the foundation stone upon which the social order rested, was assailed.

The adoption of the Constitution and the formation of the Union marked the beginning of a new commercial era for all New England. Compelled by adverse circumstances, the Yankee mer-chants had, in the Far East, tapped a new source of wealth. From this thriving trade with China developed fortunes that brought renewed prosperity to New England ports. From this revival of commercial activity there arose a new wealthy class. Elias Haskett Derby, Israel Thorndike, Simon Forrester, and William Gray left estates that were appraised in the millions. Few represented old families, some began as laborers or sailors, and many were but one generation removed from a "shirt-sleeve" origin.

As in the days when a thriving foreign trade brought wealth to New England ports and gave impetus to the social library, so a half-century later the revival of commerce helped materially to finance a widely spreading social library movement. The fortunes of the library had gone full circle and once again a period of striking development was coincident with a prosperous maritime trade.

The prosperity that was characteristic of the 1790's came to an abrupt termination during the first two decades of the nineteenth century. The grievances that brought the United States into a second major conflict with Great Britain are not the concern of the present study. It is important, however, that, in an attempt to avoid the ruinous consequences of another war with England, Thomas Jefferson signed an act forbidding American vessels destined for foreign countries to sail from any American port. By this legislation it was hoped that, through economic pressure, England could be brought to terms without resort to arms. But this embargo brought New England's economy to the very brink of catastrophe. Farmers and mechanics as well as those directly concerned with foreign commerce felt keenly the loss of oversea trade. A Rhode Island citizen complained: "There is but little market for the productions of our labor . . . . Our crop of hay will but little more than pay for the making. What last year brought twenty will this year bring but ten dollars. Pork at the last market of it was worth ten cents, now it will command but little more than five."[12] On the other hand, the cost of imported necessities and luxuries advanced sharply. George Cabot prophesied aright when he wrote from Boston soon after the embargo was proclaimed that unemployment would be an immediate consequence.[13]

Concerning the economic maladjustment that preceded the War of 1812 it is important to point out that once again the trend of social library formation is seen to follow closely that of general economic conditions. The depression in the early years of the nineteenth century was reflected in a decline in the rate of library growth. Many smaller social libraries, later replaced by a second generation, died of an economic starvation that was a direct consequence of the ruin confronting New England enterprise.

The Peace of Ghent that terminated the second war with England came with a suddenness that astonished the entire nation. In spite of Clay's condemnation of it as a "damned bad treaty," his skill had been much more successful in dictating its terms than one would have expected from the blundering that characterized the prosecution of the struggle. Though the nation had been brought to the verge of ruin and dissolution, the recovery was rapid. For a brief period after the return of peace Massachusetts enjoyed a revival of maritime prosperity. But this foreign trade concentrated to an increasing extent in Boston while such smaller towns as Newburyport, Salem, and Marblehead failed to convalesce from the effects of the war until they began to participate extensively in the new trend toward manufacturing.

If the embargo and the war had brought serious consequences to the shipper, they had acted almost as a protective tariff to industry; and Yankee ingenuity, frustrated by increasing restriction on the seas, turned its attention to the latent power of the New England rivers and streams.

In the wake of industrialization came a complete transformation in New England life. The problems of the industrial worker assumed greater proportions in contemporary social and political thought. Social cleavages appeared that tended to stratify community relationships along entirely new and different lines. For the first time in its history New England began to struggle with the influx of a large group of non-English immigrants, especially the Irish.

Notwithstanding the restlessness and turmoil released by these new forces, southern urban New England in general and Boston in particular was growing wealthy as never before. The city on the banks of the Charles was rapidly becoming a regional capital, and it was with justification that its citizens were assuming an obvious self-esteem. With the statesmen of Virginia it had shared leadership in the formation of the new nation, and it

had played an important part in both the wars in which England had been defeated.

> No one could guess what happy fortunes lay before the valiant young republic, and Boston hoped for a special dispensation [writes Van Wyck Brooks]. The old dream of a Puritan commonwealth, a true city of God, lingered in the New England mind, and it seemed as if the appointed hour had come. Cotton Mather had foretold this hour. Jonathan Edwards, on his lonely rides over the forest hills of leafy Stockbridge, had seen the millennium approaching. Bishop Berkeley, on his farm at Newport, had prophesied the golden age. The hard conditions of life in earlier days had yielded to more propitious circumstances. The time was surely ripe; and what wealth was unable to compass might be left to piety and reason.[14]

Boston was not the only place in New England where a new urge was manifest. Along the coast and through the hinterland, during that period when the social library was enjoying a second growth, the spindles were weaving a new pattern for New England life.

> In every corner of this New England country, where the ways of the eighteenth century lingered on, a fresh and more vigorous spirit was plainly astir. On the granite ledges of New Hampshire, along the Merrimac River, in Essex and Middlesex counties . . .or westward, on the lovely Housatonic, life was filled with a kind of electric excitement. The air resounded with the saw and the hammer, the flows of the forge, the bells in the factory-towers. In all directions the people were building turnpikes, hundreds of miles of straight lines that cut athwart the old winding roads. The Green Mountain boys had erected their State House. Dwellings were going up in clearings and meadows. . . . Villages, towns sprang from the fields. A current of ambition had galvanized New England.[15]

Clearly, the fortunes of the social library movement were reflections of the undulations in economic activity from the middle of the eighteenth century to the middle of the nineteenth. As money became relatively abundant and enterprise prosperous, libraries flourished; when business activity receded, the libraries were much more likely to fail. Save in the very few instances where endowment was sufficient to provide a buffer to depression, these institutions were so directly dependent upon the day-to-day incomes of their members that they reacted as delicate barometers of economic activity.

FOOTNOTES

[1] In January, 1778, was formed the Library Company of Royalston, Mass., and on November 5, 1779, a social library at Farmingbury, Wolcott, Conn., was established. At about this same time there was founded the United Library Association at Templeton, Mass., and a social library at Green Farms, Conn., though the exact dates of these last are

not known (from Trumbull MSS in Yale University Library; also see L. B. Caswell, *History of the Town of Royalston, Massachusetts* [Royalston: Published by the town, 1917], pp. 106-8; D. Hamilton Hurd, *History of Worcester County, Massachusetts* [Philadelphia: Lewis, 1889], I, 146).

[2] Fifty-one libraries between 1731-80; fifty-nine libraries between 1781-90. See Table 4.

[3] *Massachusetts Register and United States Calendar* (Boston, 1802), p. 60. This estimate approximates to a surprising degree the totals for the Massachusetts area given in Table 1.

[4] In 1796 Joseph Nancrede, Boston bookseller, announced: "To country-Booksellers and shop-keepers, purchasers for Social Libraries, and others who buy in quantities a considerable abatement will be made from the usual retail prices" (from title-page of Joseph Nancrede's catalog of books [Boston: Joseph Nancrede, 1796], also carried on the 1798 ed.). E. and S. Larkin, in 1802, and Lincoln and Edmonds, in 1814, pressed similar offers: ". . . purchasers of Social and Private Libraries are respectfully requested to favor the publishers of this Catalogue with their orders, who will engage to furnish them on the most liberal terms; and such scarce books as are not to be had in town, will be immediately procured, if to be had in England" (E. & S. Larkin, *Catalogue of Books for Sale* [Boston: Larkin, 1802], p. 2).

[5] *Catalogue of Books in the Branches of Divinity, History, Biography, Classics, Poetry, Miscellanies, Etc., for Sale at Lincoln and Edmonds' Theological and Miscellaneous Book-Store* (53 Cornhill, Boston: Lincoln & Edmonds, 1814), p. 1.

[6] *Massachusetts Gazette*, March 31, 1774.

[7] *Catalogue of Books for Sale and Circulation by Charles Pierce at His Brick Book Store, in Daniel-Street, Portsmouth, New Hampshire* . . . (Portsmouth: Printed for Charles Pierce, 1806), p. 105.

[8] The social Library Society of Belfast, Me., is an excellent example of an organization built around a single individual, a Mr. Price, who kept the society active as long as he lived in the community. After his departure, however, the library steadily declined and finally became extinct (see Joseph Williamson, *History of Belfast* (Portland: Loring, Short & Harmon, 1877), pp. 319-20. Likewise, the Proprietors' Library Association of Dover, Mass., was largely motivated by the efforts of the Rev. Ralph Sanger, and his departure brought decline and extinction to the organization (see Frank Smith, *A Narrative History of Dover, Massachusetts* [Dover: Published by the town, 1897], pp. 343-45).

[9] Massachusetts Board of Education, "Third Annual Report of the Secretary of the Board," *Common School Journal*, II (1840), 122-28. To obtain this information, Horace Mann sent out a questionnaire to all Massachusetts towns, asking the number, size, value, and patronage of libraries, either social or school district. Information was also obtained on lyceums, mechanics institutes, literary societies, and other mediums of "adult education." Mann's results probably exaggerate the true state of affairs because of the part played by local pride in encouraging the reporting as active of many institutions that were probably quite defunct.

[10] See Sidney Ditzion, "The District-School Library, 1835-1855," *Library Quarterly*, X, No. 4 (October, 1940), 545-77.

[11] John B. Wight, "A Lecture on Public Libraries Delivered in Boston in the Hall of the House of Representatives, 1854, and in Several Other Places" (unpublished MS in the possession of Mrs. John B. Wight of Wayland, Mass.).

[12] An address to the citizens of Rhode Island, November, 1808, quoted by James Truslow Adams, *New England in the Republic* (Boston: Little, Brown, 1927), p. 252.

[13] Henry C. Lodge, *Life and Letters of George Cabot* (Boston: Little, Brown, 1877), chap. xii, "New England Federalism and the Hartford Convention."

[14] Van Wyck Brooks, *The Flowering of New England* (New York: Dutton, 1937), p. 5.

[15] *Ibid.*, p. 46.

For a Broader Culture: Athenaeums

Charles Seymour Thompson

In the first half of the nineteenth century, a variation on the social library theme came in the form of the athenaeum. As did the social libraries, these institutions usually sold shares of stock which were purchased by members. The athenaeums, especially those in the larger cities of Boston and New York, were patronized by the most influential citizens of their communities. Through a varied program of lectures, library, and reading-room services, the athenaeums strengthened appreciation of the library's role in the cultural life of the community.

In the following essay, Charles Seymour Thompson traces the development of athenaeums, and suggests their significance to American library history.

"The science of the learned, the taste of the refined, and the improved and cultivated character of the citizens at large . . . require a fostering care." (Memoir of the Boston Athenaeum.)

"Yesterday I was at the Athenaeum," a friend wrote from Liverpool in 1802 to William Smith Shaw, in Boston; "a handsome room for the reading of newspapers and magazines, with a good library. The genteel part of the inhabitants frequent the library and read, for books are not allowed to be taken away." "I visited the Athenaeum," another friend wrote a year later; "having a public news-room on the lower floor, and a large library and reading room on the second. It has been instituted about ten years. Dr. Currie and Mr. Roscoe were the original advocates of this institution. Roscoe spends much of his time in reading, and probably wrote much of his *Lorenzo* here."

These letters were an inspiration to Shaw, a young graduate of Harvard whose chief interest was advancement of the cause of learning in America. Everyone who saw the Liverpool Athenaeum spoke of it "with delight and admiration." London had its London Institution, with a valuable library and a reading room where "the foreign and domestick journals and other periodical works, and the best pamphlets and new publications" were provided "for the use of the proprietors and subscribers." Boston had nothing of the sort. It had the Boston Library Society, and the American Academy of Arts and Sciences, but these were not enough. "The taste of the refined, and the improved and cultivated character of the

citizens at large" required more than they could give. Intellectual independence was too slowly following political independence. Something was needed, Shaw said, "to stimulate our countrymen to some important mental exertions." Our "literary men" ought to "awake from their stupid lethargy" and "rescue our country from the scorn and derision which now lie so heavily upon her."

For all who would keep abreast of contemporary literature, science, and political and philosophical thought, periodicals were essential. Newspapers had broadened their scope and acquired new importance. Pamphleteers could not be overlooked, but their productions were not easily obtained in America. Desire for access to these sources had led to formation of the Charleston Library Society in 1748, and was now manifested everywhere. In 1798 "Mr. G. Painter" issued a prospectus of a reading room to be opened in New York, which promised "every variety of literary and miscellaneous literature for the inquisitive scholar" and "every paper of note, either in Europe or America." Several reading rooms were opened in New York in the early years of the new century, and in 1809 forty or more citizens united in an endeavor to maintain a reading room by subscription.[1] Few libraries had a reading room, and to meet this need was the most distinctive specific purpose of that form of proprietary library to which the name athenaeum was given.

The Boston Athenaeum, first of the type in America, was an outgrowth from the Anthology Society, which had been formed in 1805 to continue publication of a periodical, the *Monthly*

Anthology and Boston Review, which had been begun as a private venture. Among the first acts of this Society was a vote "that a Library of periodical publications be instituted for the use of the Society." This was a beginning, but Shaw could not forget his vision of a library in Boston similar to the Athenaeum of which his friends had written from Liverpool. At a meeting of the Society in May, 1806, after much discussion "relative to a reading room to be established in this town," a committee was appointed to consider the proposal.

The result of this action was a prospectus, drafted by Shaw, which proposed establishment of a reading room which would provide not only "an agreeable place of resort, but opportunities of literary intercourse, and the pleasure of perusing the principal European and American periodical publications, at an expense not exceeding that of a single *daily* paper." The annual subscription was to be ten dollars. So attractive was the proposal that more than one hundred and sixty subscriptions were soon received, and the Anthology Reading-Room and Library was opened January 1, 1807, with more than a thousand volumes and a large number of French, English, and American periodicals and papers. Encouraged by this success, the Society soon applied for incorporation on a larger basis, and a charter was obtained for the Boston Athenaeum. Issue of one hundred and fifty shares was authorized, at three hundred dollars a share, and the entire number was easily sold. No person was permitted to hold more than three shares. "Subscribers for life" were admitted for one hundred dollars, and in 1808 provision was made for admission of annual subscribers at ten dollars a year.

A "large and commodious" reading room was advertised as "the first department" of the Athenaeum, and the first bylaws provided that "no book, pamphlet, review, magazine, or newspaper shall be taken by any proprietor, subscriber, or visiter, out of the rooms." Not until 1826, when the privilege of borrowing was made available to proprietors for five dollars a year, was circulation permitted. The "next branch" was the library, which was to contain "the great works of learning and science in all languages; particularly such rare and expensive publications, as are not generally to be obtained in this country." "We must, at least for some time, think of popularity," wrote Joseph S. Buckminster, who had been authorized to make purchases while abroad, "and I know of no method so likely to procure it as to keep our

rooms furnished with abundance of magazines, pamphlets, and *new books.*" Shaw accepted only with reluctance the necessity of some concession to popular taste. There must be, he said, some "miscellaneous books, useful to the loungers, such, perhaps, as a complete edition of the English classics, such as the Spectator, Guardian, Etc., with Drake's Essays on these periodical writers, Etc. Etc."

The vision had become a reality. In 1806 Shaw had written to a friend: "I have very little doubt, that in a few years we shall see a library in our beloved Boston inferior to none in America." And in 1807 he wrote: "Depend upon it, that the establishment of the Athenaeum, the rooms of which are to be always accessible at all hours of the day, is one of the greatest strides toward intellectual advancement that this country has ever witnessed." To this institution, for establishment of which he had worked so earnestly, he now gave his devotion so completely that he became known in Boston as "Athenaeum Shaw." Serving sixteen years as librarian, without salary, he had a large part in building the foundation for the Athenaeum's growth as a center of learning and culture, "one of the oldest monuments," said Josiah Quincy, "which patriotism and public spirit, and the love of learning, in this country, ever raised."

Soon after opening of the Athenaeum inquiries concerning its organization and management began to come to Shaw from other cities: in 1808 from Brunswick, Me., where a reading room was being established; in 1809 from John Pintard, a trustee of the New York Society Library, who tried unsuccessfully to arouse interest in formation of an athenaeum in connection with the Society Library and the Historical Society; [2] in 1810 from Salem, where one had been formed by union of a Social Library of 1760 and a Philosophical Library of 1781, and from Providence, where an effort was being made to establish a similar institution; in 1814 from Portland and from the recently organized Athenaeum of Philadelphia. They came also from smaller communities: in 1817 from Frankfort, Ky., where a "public reading-room, or miniature Athenaeum" had been opened, and from Lexington, Ky., where one was being organized. Lexington, Shaw was informed, had "five houses for public worship, a college, not yet in operation, a theatre, court house, jail, and a large number of smart shops," and it was "allowed" that there were one hundred and twenty private coaches in the city. Now it wanted an athenaeum.

In New York the name was first given to a "literary institution," the activities of which were confined to the reading and discussion of literary productions submitted by members. In 1824 a new institution was formed, also called the New-York Athenaeum. The most prominent feature of this, however, was an extensive program of public lectures, and acquisition of a library was to be kept in view as an object after expenses of the lectures had been met. After 1828 the lectures were discontinued, and a small library and reading room was maintained until 1839 when, after long negotiations, a merger was effected with the New York Society Library.[3]

The "first and immediate object" of the founders of the Athenaeum of Philadelphia was "the collection, in some central place, of American and foreign periodical publications of politics, literature and science, maps, dictionaries and other books of reference to which access might be had at all hours of the day." Thus in Philadelphia, as in Boston, a place was found for an athenaeum, to supplement the other libraries of the city, even though among these were the Library Company of Philadelphia and the American Philosophical Society.

In Providence the plan to organize an athenaeum in 1810 was not successful, although it received encouragement from the itinerant orator James Ogilvie. Organization was effected, however, in 1831, and within five years 2,400 volumes were acquired, but the Providence Library of 1753 was still in existence, and it was found that two libraries could not be satisfactorily maintained. In 1836 the two institutions were merged into one, which was incorporated as The Athenaeum.

The Portland Athenaeum was organized in 1819 as a reading room, "without reference to the formation of a library," because the city was still served by the Library Society of 1765. Here, as at Providence, consolidation was soon effected, with the purpose of enlarging the older institution and of "giving it a more elevated and diffusive character, better suited to the wants of the age, and spirit of the times," and in 1826 a new Ath-enaeum was organized, which purchased the property of the Library Society.

At Portsmouth, N. H., an Athenaeum was established in 1817, with a library which was open one hour twice a week and a reading room open every day but Sunday until nine in the evening. Before the middle of the century the name athenaeum was given to libraries or reading rooms opened in Eastport, Rockland, and Saco, Me.; Manchester, N. H.; Windsor, Vt.; Cambridge, Fall River, Nantucket, New Bedford, Newton, and Roxbury, Mass.; Londsdale, R. I.; Rochester, N. Y.; Westchester, Pa.; Petersburg, Va.; and Zanesville, Ohio.

Many of the small athenaeums differed little from other proprietary libraries, apart from maintenance of a reading room, and in them the name lost much of its original connotation. Of the athenaeum in general, however, it may be said that it represented a broadening of interests; an increasing desire to read for general culture and intellectual stimulus. America was held in low esteem abroad, charged with supremacy of commercial interest, with lack of creative ability in literature, in science, in art. This reputation the athenaeum endeavored to cast off. Through the reading room it strengthened appreciation of a library's place in the intellectual life of a community. Through foreign publications it made war on provincialism. Although science and industry, business and commerce, were within its province too, it stressed the aesthetic, rather than the utilitarian. The word *taste* was frequently employed in defining its purposes, implying general culture and refinement, "the embellishment of life by all those arts which give to polished society its chief ornament and grace." It fostered both "those deep investigations of science and exquisite refinements of taste, which are necessarily confined to a few," and "that love of intellectual improvement and pleasure, and that propensity to reading and inquiry, which are capable of being diffused through considerable portions of the community."

Two streams, the cultural and the popular, were drawing closer together.

FOOTNOTES

[1] Austin B. Keep, *History of the New York Society Library* (New York, 1908), pp. 314-16.
[2] *Ibid.,* pp. 275-76, 289-92, 314-15.
[3] *Ibid.,* pp. 325-62.

Libraries in the Ohio Valley Before 1850

Haynes McMullen

For years Haynes McMullen's essays have illuminated the picture of nineteenth century library development. In the following paper McMullen discusses the availability of books, and the types of library services provided to those who settled the Ohio Valley prior to 1850.

As we look back from the present date to the year 1900 we may feel that we are considering a period of rapid change in the United States. But if one of the citizens of Cincinnati or Louisville looked back in 1850 over an equal period of time he would have seen far greater changes. Most of the Ohio valley was in hands of the Indians in 1785, and the whites in the central part of the valley were not to be completely safe from raids for another ten years. It would be many years before steamboats, canal boats, and railroads would come. By 1850, almost exactly a fourth of the population of the United States was in the valley; rich lands were under cultivation, business was booming and even literature and the arts were enjoyed, at least in the larger towns.

For bookish purposes, we do not need to concern ourselves about the exact boundary of the Ohio valley because most of the activity took place within a hundred miles of the river's banks. But we must remind ourselves that a somewhat different culture developed north of the valley, near the Great Lakes, where the New England influence was stronger; nor do we have to consider too carefully the southern limits of the valley somewhere in the hills of Kentucky, Tennessee, and northern Alabama. Our concern is with the population of the central part of the valley which was always a mixed one. Southerners mingled with people from the middle Atlantic states and mixed as best they could with some New England Yankees. In later years, the people of the valley received immigrants coming directly from Europe, particularly from Germany.

Almost from the beginning, the people used books. Of course the earliest backwoodsmen traveled light and knew that books would not help them stay alive in hostile country. But the books came in before the Indians left. In Kentucky, for example, one of the early schools, Transylvania Seminary, seems to have had a library by 1790[1] but Kentuckians were not safe from Indian raids until 1794 when the white Americans, at the Battle of Fallen Timbers, defeated all of the Indians within striking distance of the state. Seven out of the thirteen original trustees of the Transylvania Seminary met death at the hands of Indians.[2]

And the books came before the animals disappeared too. The story of the "Coonskin Library" in Athens County, Ohio has been retold often. The founders paid their subscriptions in furs which were taken to Boston, where they were sold and, in effect, converted into books.[3]

In order to find out how people in the valley used books, it may first be well to get some idea about the extent of use. Of course no one will ever know how many books were there by 1850. The census taken in that year listed books in private and public libraries, but a few years later, officials of the Bureau of the Census admitted that the figure was highly inaccurate.[4]

One indication of the extent of use of books is the number of libraries which were organized. Not including libraries owned by individuals, schools, or Sunday schools, there were more than 500 of these collections before 1850 in the states which may be thought of as constituting the Ohio valley: Kentucky, Tennessee, Ohio, Indiana and Illinois.[5]

To study the use of books by the people of the valley, any of seven different lines of investigation could be followed. 1. The ideal way would be to search for references to books in large numbers of diaries and letters. 2. Printed travel narratives would tell what men and women from the eastern United States or Europe thought the people were reading. 3. The advertisements in newspapers of

SOURCE: Reprinted from Haynes McMullen, "The Use of Books in the Ohio Valley Before 1850," *Journal of Library History* 1 (January, 1966), pp. 43-56+, by permission of the author and publisher. Copyright © 1966 by the School of Library Science, Florida State University.

the region would list what the booksellers hoped the people would buy. 4. The lists of early imprints would indicate what reading matter was produced in the region. 5. A study of school textbooks would indicate materials which could have influenced the thinking of large numbers of people. 6. Any remaining family libraries would show us what individuals bought and, presumably, read. 7. The printed catalogs of early social libraries would list the books which were gathered for common use.

The present study is based mainly on the last-named of these sources, the catalogs listing the books which the people agreed to read. But first, we should briefly consider the other six kinds of sources.

Diaries and letters come very close to showing us the reasons for the use of books. But references are so scattered that an investigator might read for months without obtaining a sample that would be large enough to represent the various times and places where reading took place.

Some information about the reading habits in the valley has been gathered for us by travelers from Europe and from the eastern part of the United States who often commented frankly on the state of culture in the early west, including the use of books and libraries. Generally they were quite favorably impressed if they visited Lexington before 1830[6] and were less favorably impressed if they visited Louisville or Cincinnati later. The famous Mrs. Trollope, who was a resident of Cincinnati for a while around the year 1830, thought that Americans read too many newspapers. She wrote: "In truth, there are many reasons which render a very general diffusion of literature impossible in America. I can scarcely class the universal reading of newspapers as an exception to this remark; if I could, my statement would be exactly the reverse, and I should say that America beat the world in letters. The fact is . . . they are all too actively employed to read, except at such broken moments as may suffice for a peep at a newspaper." And a little farther on in her report on the domestic manners of the Americans, she says "the only reading men I met with were those who made letters their profession."[7]

These newspapers supply one of the clearest kinds of evidence about the use of books. One student of literary culture in the region has observed that, in the earliest days, the advertisements for books occupied an amount of space second only to that of advertisements for land sales.[8] The earliest papers listed a small number of very practical books, but later ones listed a great variety of works of history, biography, travel, and general literature.[9]

These advertisements may provide a better index of book reading than do the lists of early imprints in the valley. It would seem that most early printing was either a necessary record of governmental activity, or an attempt at persuading other people to adopt the author's viewpoint, or, in fewer instances, an attempt to turn a profit by pirating a popular eastern or British work of literature.

But perhaps this judgment is unduly harsh. Thought of in another way, the output of the early presses can be considered as quite representative of what people read. Byrd and Peckham, in the introduction to their *Bibliography of Indiana Imprints, 1804-1853,* quote Abraham Lincoln's cousin who said of the early days: "We lived the same as Indians 'cepting we took an interest in politics and religion." The bibliographers point out that many of the early books and pamphlets were about one or the other of these two areas of concern.[10]

If the newspapers advertised only the books which the booksellers felt were salable, and if the printers produced mainly what some author wished to have distributed, we may learn more about the use of books by studying the ones which were most widely distributed and most heavily used, the school texts. In the earliest schools in the valley, texts were rarely to be had and students brought from home any book that was available; but soon the texts came in, and the tattered condition of remaining copies is witness to their heavy use. The Ohio valley even became the source of one of the most famous of them after the first McGuffey reader was published in Cincinnati in 1836.

Textbooks made up a large part of the reading of those who read very little, but a small part of the reading of people who read widely. The interests of this latter group are revealed by a few of the old family libraries which still exist. Two of these belonged to a prominent Kentucky family, the Browns of Frankfort. The first and most famous member of the family was John Brown, who had served in the Revolution under Lafayette before he settled in Kentucky in the 1780's and successfully entered politics. His home, *Liberty Hall,* was built in the 1790's and contains several thousand books, many of them used by members of the family before 1850.

The library as it exists now may not represent the entire range of tastes of a cultured family of those days because books could have been removed at any time. But there are enough books to show that the family's literary tastes were not bizarre: Scott predominated, as he should have in any normal home; there is some Dickens, and Melville's *Omoo* is present. Of course there are many authors who have since lost their lustre, ranging from Henry Kirke White, the poet admired by Southey, to the Canadian, Thomas Chandler Haliburton, whose book, *The Clockmaker, or Sayings and Doings of Sam Slick* was considered funny by his contemporaries.

The shelves at *Liberty Hall* contain almost nothing in the field of politics outside of federal documents but there is a little history—for example, a translation into English of Charles Rollin's very popular *Ancient History* and, less well known, William Atherton's *Narrative of the Suffering & Defeat of the North-Western Army under General Winchester,* printed in Frankfort in 1842.

Much of the library is predictable—a little science, some medical books (at least one of the Browns was a physician), a few religious books intended for laymen and a few miscellanies of the gift-book type. There are some uplifting children's books—for example, Maria Edgeworth's *Moral Tales* and her *Parent's Assistant; or Stories for Children.* Some Latin classics are there, but the books in French are more noticeable; instead of a few, there are hundreds—standard Eighteenth Century authors, of course, but also volumes on a variety of subjects. At least one member of the family visited Lafayette and other notables in Paris.

Orlando Brown, a son of the founder of the family, built a home on the same street in Frankfort, in 1835, but the collection there may be considered as part of the family library, as inscriptions in some of its books attest. The subject matter of these books is similar to that of the collection in the older house.

Family libraries, such as the ones in the Brown homes, can tell us only a little about the use of books because there are not many such libraries, and they represent the taste of a few people. To find out what larger numbers of people were reading, we must turn from the private libraries to the ones which were gathered by library associations. These collections were among those which were called "public" libraries, a term which was used to include school and college libraries, libraries gathered by any kinds of societies or government agencies—in fact, almost any kinds except tax-supported libraries freely open to all citizens, a type which was extremely rare.

The exact number of organized libraries which were held by groups of people in the Ohio valley through 1850 may never be known, but enough records remain to give some idea of their extent. Omitting collections in educational institutions of less than college grade, and following the political divisions, the totals are close to these figures: 96 in Kentucky; 300 in Ohio (though many of these were in the Western Reserve, north of the valley); 50 in Indiana; 48 in Illinois (partly outside of the valley); and 40 in Tennessee. By omitting libraries in western Pennsylvania and western Virginia (later to become the state of West Virginia) we may offset the libraries which we have included from outside the valley.

These were all libraries of the type which were then called "public" but they varied greatly as to freedom of access. College libraries were often open to townspeople but most other collections could be used only by members of some kind of association or by people who paid some kind of a fee. Of all of these collections, the ones which most directly expressed the general reading interests of the users were the "social" libraries. By the strictest definition, a social library was a collection owned by the members of a society which had been formed for the express purpose of establishing a general library, that is, one which was not specialized in subject-matter. Other libraries fit some part of this definition, as when the members of a lyceum listened to lectures and operated a library or when lawyers formed a library association limited to law books.

The social libraries which fit the strict definition of the term were the most common type in the Ohio valley in the earliest days; most of the other kinds appeared only after 1820. Ohio had its first social library, the Belpre library, also called the Putnam Family Library, in 1796, and at least 187 others were founded there through the year 1850. Kentucky's first, the Lexington Library, was also established in 1796 and there are records of 51 more in that state through 1850. The first social library in Tennessee for which a definite date can be set is the Nashville Library Company of 1813, but there is evidence that a library existed in Knoxville in 1801.[11] Only four more were established in Tennessee. Indiana's first was the Vincennes Public Library of 1806; eleven more were established before 1850. Illinois had a total of 13, starting with the Albion Library in 1818 or 1819. The size of Ohio's share, 188 out of the total of 271, was partly attributable to the large number of people from New England who came to that state. One study has shown that social libraries, in the Midwest, were most frequently founded in areas where New Englanders settled.[12] This kind of association well suited the temperament of the Yankee settlers. Their neighbors of southern origin observed that they were inordinately concerned with the life of the mind and that they also were inclined to obtain what they wanted at the lowest possible price. However, Ohio's predominance may be attributable partly to her larger share of the people from outside of New England. During much of the time she had from about a third to a half of the white population in the region, no matter what its origin.

Concerning most of the social libraries in the Ohio valley, almost nothing is known; but about a few of them, much can be learned. Each of at least seven of them issued one or more printed catalogs. The earliest of these catalogs was the one printed for the Lexington Library in 1796, at a time when it was not only a social library but also the library for Transylvania Seminary and was still called the Transylvania Library.[13]

This collection of about 400 volumes included the standard histories of the day—Gibbon's *Rome*, Rollin for the ancient world, Russel on modern Europe, Hume's *England* and Robertson's *Scotland*. Of more interest are a few on American history that came closer up to date—for example, David Ramsay's *History of the American Revolution*, presumably the American edition of 1789. The authors of the small group of travel books had visited all five continents. There was much good advice for the young—Chesterfield's *Letters to His Son* and several volumes from other authors, addressed to young ladies. The small literature section was well balanced between poetry, drama, and fiction; it contained far more plays than did most collections of equal size. Another even smaller section, "Natural History, Philosophy, Surgery, Medicine, Farriery, Arts, and Agriculture" exhibits no preponderance of any of these subjects unless it be veterinary medicine; there are more books relating to the ills of horses than to the ills of men, a situation understandable in a little city which had possessed a racetrack for the past seven years.

For several years after this catalog was issued, Lexington was the second largest town in the West, second only to New Orleans. But such river towns as Cincinnati and Louisville were to outstrip it soon after steamboats came. Citizens of each of these last-named villages organized libraries long before their towns grew to dominate the heart of the region.

At Cincinnati a social library was established in 1802 but it soon died, and it was not until 1814 that another one opened, the Circulating Library Society of Cincinnati, which issued a printed cata-

log in 1816.[14] Almost half of the thirty-six page pamphlet is taken up with preliminary matter pointing out that the society will be delighted to welcome new members and that the circulation rules will insure the equitable use of the collection by everyone. Fines began at six and a fourth cents and country borrowers were permitted to keep books longer than were city borrowers.

The circulation rules were typical for this kind of library and the list of books includes many titles which appear in library after library. By this time, readers were beginning to have Scott's novels available, but they did not realize it yet because he was still writing them anonymously. There are more from the pen of Maria Edgeworth than any other, but it is pleasant to note recognition of native American literature; not only *Knickerbocker's New York,* but also *Modern Chivalry* by the Pittsburgh writer, H. H. Brackenridge. There is as much poetry as fiction, but little drama. Again, we find standard histories, travel to far places, and biographies of great men. By now, books about American events, places, and people are evident, but they are in a minority. It is not surprising to find a copy of the *Natural and Statistical View, or Picture of Cincinnati and the Miami Country* by that peppery young promoter of the West, Dr. Daniel Drake—especially since he was president of the library association.

At Edwardsville, Illinois (not very far from the area which drains into the Ohio), the collection owned by a social library was so small in 1819 that a single sheet was all that was necessary to list its 216 volumes.[15] At Harrodsburg, Kentucky, in 1824, a library association used only six small pages of its catalog to list 186 titles but nine of its seventeen pages were needed to give the rules for the use of the books.[16] The small Harrodsburg collection was properly diversified. It included works of history, biography, philosophy, ethics, religion, general literature, and a few dictionaries. Some of the items were to be found in all libraries: Thompson's *Seasons,* Plutarch, Milton, and *The Spectator.*

North of the river, at Vincennes, the library association of 1806 seems to have issued a printed catalog in 1813[17] but there is no recent record of the existence of a copy. Another catalog was published in 1838, listing about six hundred titles in at least three times that many volumes.[18]

The Vincennes collection was remarkably similar to that of other libraries, except that the section "Tales, Novels, and Romances" was beginning to forge ahead of other sections, showing a trend which was to continue for at least a hundred years in all American libraries where the users were to have a voice in selection. In the Vincennes catalog, this fiction section included 115 titles; "Voyages and Travels" had 82; "History," 70; "Lives and Memoirs," 65 and so on. The figures would be larger if the collected writings under "Miscellaneous" were to be distributed to their proper places. New writers appeared and new subject interests manifested themselves; for example, there were a few volumes on phrenology.

The early county libraries of Indiana seem to have been organized as social libraries with some governmental help, so their collections should have been similar to those of the purely social organization and, indeed, this was the case. A manuscript catalog for one of them, the Monroe County Library at Bloomington, is still in existence.[19] It is undated, but seems to have been compiled about 1846, and lists 833 titles, acquired in the years since the library had opened in 1821.

The people of Monroe County had at their disposal many books which had regularly appeared in collections elsewhere in the valley and the general balance of subject matter was the same, too. As in other libraries, the books on agriculture, commerce, and science made up a very small fraction of this collection, even though these were areas of human activity which had changed rapidly in the years of the library's life and were surely of concern to its users.

As the towns in the Ohio valley grew in size in the years before 1850, a division of the people into social classes began to appear. However, the lines between classes were not sharp and movement from one class to another was possible. As the classes developed, two kinds of libraries came from the East, each of them intended for young men of what we might now consider the lower middle class. The earliest type consisted of apprentices' or mechanics' libraries, two of which appeared in 1821, one at Cincinnati and one at Columbus. Another type which came in the 1830's was the mercantile library, intended for young clerks. At least twenty apprentices' or mechanics' libraries existed in the Ohio valley before 1850, but possibly not more than two mercantile libraries, one founded at Cincinnati in 1835 and another at Louisville in 1842.

Throughout the country the mechanics' libraries were founded and partly controlled by older businessmen as a benevolent activity, so presumably their collections reflected the opinions of the elders about what the young men should read. The mercantile libraries, on the other hand, were usually formed by the young men themselves so their catalogs reveal the tastes of the users. The preamble to the constitution of the Young Men's Mercantile Library Association of Cincinnati starts with these words: "We, the Subscribers, young men of the City of Cincinnati, being desirous of adopting efficient means to extend our information upon mercantile and other subjects of general utility, have associated ourselves for the purpose of establishing a Library and Reading Room."[20]

The printed catalog which these young men issued in 1838 shows that the means they adopted was to assemble a collection which was as much like that of a social library as they could make it. Out of almost 1200 volumes, only 16 were placed in the section headed "commerce." Looking at the list of books, one would assume that the collection had been assembled for the pleasure and instruction of any group of gentlemen with catholic tastes.

In Louisville, the Mercantile Library Association issued three catalogs before 1850. Its catalog of 1843, like the one from the Cincinnati association, exhibits a very general and typical collection. There are more books about commerce (38 volumes) and about the same number under the heading "Mechanics and Useful Arts." For their lighter moments, the young clerks of Louisville had 286 volumes of fiction.[21]

There were other kinds of libraries in the valley which disclosed the tastes of their owners. More than a score of the lyceums had libraries and there were at least four atheneum libraries before 1850. It is difficult to decide whether some of these were really literary and debating societies which gathered collections of books or whether they were basically library associations whose members occasionally listened to lectures. The Zanesville Atheneum issued a catalog in 1843 which looks like one from a social library except for its greater emphasis on newspapers and periodicals,[22] an emphasis commonly found in atheneum collections.

Another kind of collection which represented the reading interests of the users was the library of the college literary association. There were more than thirty-five of these in the valley before 1850.

The libraries of the colleges themselves are examples of collections which were broad in subject matter but were selected by one group partly for its own use and partly for the edification of another group. By comparing them with the libraries which were chosen for the pleasure of their users, perhaps we can learn something more about the freely chosen collections.

These college libraries had little relation to the college curriculum for two reasons: First, the classwork seldom required use of the library and second, the collections contained many gifts because presidents of western colleges regularly went on begging tours to the East and brought back books as well as dollars and promises of dollars.

At least eighty colleges in the region had libraries but fewer than a dozen seem to have issued printed catalogs. One of those which published its catalog was Indiana University, then known as Indiana State University, located in the same town as the Monroe County Library.[23] Its catalog of 1842 lists more than 1400 volumes and bears a general resemblance to the catalogs of social libraries. In history, biography, and travel, the collection could have served a library association well; in literature, Scott was still there, and other favorites as well, but there were more books in foreign languages than a social library would be likely to have. This state university did not neglect religion; if anything, its library had more than the ordinary number of sermons and included several books calling attention to the errors of the Catholics.

Another college, Georgetown, in Kentucky, issued a catalog in 1848 which shows a wider range of subject matter and more foreign language material than did the one from the Indiana college. At Georgetown the differences from the social library were even more pronounced; the largest class is theology and the library seems to contain more scholarly material than a social library would: for example, there are Bibles in Bengali and Burmese. But this college collection also includes more scurrilous material: the section on polemic theology includes Maria Monk's *Awful Disclosures,* reporting about murders and worse which took place in a convent in Canada. The presence of this little book in a Baptist school may indicate that good men believed the lady's story; let us hope they did not enjoy it.

Many other kinds of libraries in the Ohio valley could show us how its people used books in the years before 1850, but most of the others were specialized in content and were used by small groups. Some of these more specialized collections should be mentioned, because they indicate the reading interests of some of the people in the valley. At least half a dozen historical societies had collections in the 1830's and 40's; there were twice that many law libraries, beginning around 1800, about equally divided between those owned by associations of lawyers and those owned by governmental units. The only kinds of specialized collections which were outstanding, when compared with eastern libraries, were a few that be-

longed to medical schools. The ones belonging to the Medical Department of Transylvania University and the Louisville Medical Institute contained many books on medicine, biology and chemistry which had been bought in Europe. A recent writer on American medical history has called the Transylvania collection one of the finest medical libraries in the United States around the 1820's and 30's.[24] There were some theological libraries and even agriculture had a few special collections: at least half a dozen agricultural societies had tiny libraries.

IN CONCLUSION

It seems likely that many people in the Ohio valley brought with them or purchased from booksellers a few reference books for intensive use at home. But many people turned to one of several hundred "public" libraries in order to obtain general reading matter at a reasonable cost. The printed catalogs of these libraries reveal collections which were remarkably similar. They all show these characteristics:

1. The collections were well balanced. History, biography, and travel were well represented; fiction was always present, but it never predominated; poetry was always to be found, but there were few books of plays. There were books in the fields of religion and ethics but these never overshadowed the others. Scientific and technical books were present, but always in small numbers.

2. The smaller collections put heavy emphasis on standard works; the larger ones contained lighter or more current material as well.

3. Works by European authors predominated at all times, but the number of books by Americans increased gradually through the years. A very small number of the books in these libraries were on the subject of the Ohio valley or some part of it. Of course, only a few such books existed, but even fewer are listed in the catalogs.

4. There were almost no books in foreign languages, though translations from Latin were common, there were some from French and Greek, and a few from German and Spanish.

Finally, it seems clear that when people in the early Ohio valley banded themselves together to buy books and to read them, they selected the ones that would help them to maintain contact with their cultural heritage from the old world. For them, books were links with the finest part of the life they had left behind them.

FOOTNOTES

[1] The Seminary had been given a collection of books before this. The minutes of its trustees imply that it was in use by 1790.

[2] Charles R. Staples, *The History of Pioneer Lexington, Kentucky, 1779-1806* (Lexington, Ky.: Transylvania Press, 1939), p. 303.

[3] Charles M. Walker, *History of Athens County, Ohio* (Cincinnati: R. Clarke, 1869), p. 368.

[4] U. S. Census Office, *Ninth Census, Volume I, The Statistics of the Population of the United States . . .* (Washington: Government Printing Office, 1872), pp. 472-73.

[5] This figure and the figures about the numbers of libraries of various kinds, appearing later in this paper, are based on several early lists and recent studies. The principal national surveys are these: Charles C. Jewett, *Appendix to the Report of the Board of Regents of the Smithsonian Institution, Containing a Report on the Public Libraries of the United States of America, January 1, 1850,* (Sen. Misc. Doc., 31st Cong., 1st Sess., No. 120 Washington: Printed for the Senate, 1850); William J. Rhees, *Manual of Public Libraries, Institutions, and Societies, in the United States, and British Provinces of North America* (Philadelphia: J. B. Lippincott, 1859) and U. S. Bureau of Education, *Public Libraries in the United States of America, their History, Condition, and Management: Special Report, Part I* (Washington: Government Printing Office, 1876).

[6] Several commentators are named and quoted by J. Winston Coleman, Jr. in "Lexington as Seen by Travelers, 1810-1835," *Filson Club Historical Quarterly* XXIX (July 1955), 267-81.

[7] *Domestic Manners of the Americans* (London: Whittaker, Treacher & Co.; New York: reprinted for the Booksellers, 1832), pp. 88, 89.

[8] James M. Miller, *The Genesis of Western Culture; the Upper Ohio Valley, 1800-1825* (Columbus: The Ohio State Archaeological and Historical Society, 1938), p. 147.

[9] Ibid., pp. 147-49.

[10] Cecil K. Byrd and Howard H. Peckham, *A Bibliography of Indiana Imprints, 1804-1853* (Indianapolis: Indiana Historical Bureau, 1955), p. viii.

[11] Mary U. Rothrock, ed., *The French Broad-Holston Country, a History of Knox County, Tennessee* (Knoxville, East Tennessee Historical Society, 1946), p. 115, citing Knox County Court Records, Estate Book I, p. 157.

[12] Haynes McMullen, *The Founding of Social and Public Libraries in Ohio, Indiana and Illinois through 1850,* University of Illinois Library School Occasional Papers, No. 51, March, 1958, p. 9-10.

[13] The only known copy, now in the Transylvania University Library at Lexington, has lost part of its title-page. However, enough remains to indicate that an advertisement in the *Kentucky Gazette* for April 16, 1796 probably contained its exact wording. The advertisement called it "A Catalogue of Books in Transylvania Library, Lexington, Containing Upwards of Four Hundred Volumes—For the Year 1796."

[14] Cincinnati Circulating Library, *Systematic Catalogue of Books Belonging to the Circulating Library Society of Cincinnati. To which are Prefixed an Historical Preface, the Act of Incorporation, and By-Laws, of the Society* (Cincinnati: Looker, Palmer and Reynolds, 1816).

[15] Edwardsville Library, *A Complete Catalogue of All the Books now in, or belonging to, the Edwardsville Library . . . Drawn for the Use of the Shareholders, at the Library Room, Edwardsville, Nov. 30, 1819* (Edwardsville, Ill.: H. Warren, 1819).

[16] Harrodsburg Library Company, *A Catalogue of the Books belonging to the Harrodsburg Library Company. To which is prefixed the By-Laws and Regulations. Incorporated December 1823* (Harrodsburg, Ky.: H. Miller, 1824).

[17] A catalog of that date is mentioned in the volumes by Jewett, Rhees, and the U. S. Bureau of Education, mentioned above.

[18] Vincennes Library Company, *A Catalogue of the Vincennes Library, with the Charter and Constitution Prefixed* (Vincennes, Ind.: R. Y. Caddington, 1838).

[19] Monroe County Library, Bloomington, Ind., "Catalogue of Books in the Monroe County Library," ms., n.d.

[20] Young Men's Mercantile Library Association of Cincinnati, *Catalogue of Books belonging to the Young Men's Mercantile Library Association* (Cincinnati: Daily Express Office, 1838), p. 5.

[21] Louisville. Mercantile Library, *Catalogue of the Louisville Mercantile Library . . .* (Louisville, Ky.: Prentice and Weissinger, 1843).

[22] Zanesville Atheneum, *A Catalogue of Books in the Zanesville Atheneum . . .* (Zanesville, Ohio: Edwin C. Church, 1843).

[23] Indiana State University, Bloomington, *Catalogue of the Library of Indiana State University* (Bloomington, Ind.: M. L. Deal, 1842).

[24] William Frederick Norwood, *Medical Education in the United States Before the Civil War* (Philadelphia: University of Pennsylvania Press; London: Oxford University Press, 1944), p. 294.

The Sunday School Library

F. Allen Briggs

Today the Sunday school library, where it still exists, is usually an insignificant adjunct to the church. In the nineteenth century however, Sunday school libraries were an important and influential part of American life. Seen by their founders as supplements to the educational system, they were intended to serve children and adults alike. In the following paper, F. Allen Briggs traces the development of Sunday school libraries—which at one time numbered over 30,000—and outlines their historical importance.

The Sunday-school library, once an important source of reading matter for most of the population of nineteenth-century America, was an institution far different from the modern library, but in its history may be seen the development of many of the ideas which characterize library service. Historians of the American library either have taken a condescending attitude toward the Sunday-school library, calling it a "professional poor relation,"[1] or have judged the library by its most narrow and conservative examples. A detailed examination of the Sunday-school library as it existed in the first sixty years of the nineteenth century brings to light many interesting facts about the institution. Fascinating are the advantages set forth, how the libraries were administered, the size of the collections, the books held, and the methods of selection used.

The first Sunday-school libraries were designed to replace the premium books given in the early Sunday school when a scholar had been faithful in attendance and conduct. Superintendents felt that once a book had been awarded as a premium, it was lost to the school; but, if the award were the opportunity to read the book, the stock of the school would not be depleted. Where once a scholar received a volume of his own at the end of the school term, with the advent of the Sunday-school library his reward for attendance and good conduct was the privilege of withdrawing a book from the school collection.

The first Sunday-school libraries were simple, but, as they grew in number and size, the organization became increasingly complex. As first formed in schools of one teacher or, at most, a few teachers, the problems of collecting, filing, and distributing the books were easy to solve; the volumes could be a part of the lesson for the day, and the teacher, or the superintendent, could check them out to the students. When the library grew to four or five hundred volumes and the students to more than a hundred, a special device had to be invented to meet the situation. As the system became more complex, those in charge of the school had to remind themselves frequently of the advantages to be expected from this adjunct of the Sunday school.

There never had been much doubt in the minds of the authorities about the value of *good* reading. A Sunday school for which a rather complete record remains was the South Parish Sabbath School of Portsmouth, New Hampshire; the fortieth annual report of the superintendent, published in 1858, shows a development and attitude that was typical of others throughout the country.[2] When the school was formed in 1818, the custom was begun of giving, at the end of each term of twenty-six Sundays, a book to each scholar who had attended twenty times; in addition, two books, of larger size, were given to "each class of scholars who had excelled either in recitation or behavior." The final service of the term, however, was not all sweetness and light, for at the time of rewarding the superintendent also publicly rebuked those who had not attended faithfully or behaved properly.

The gift system was abolished in 1827, but, the report says, "those books, small though they were, carried joy and pleasure into many a family of children."[3] Upon the abolishment of the premium books, the school instituted a library.

In his *Sabbath School Teacher*, published in

SOURCE: Reprinted from F. Allen Briggs, "The Sunday School Library in the Nineteenth Century," *Library Quarterly* 31 (April, 1961), pp. 166-177, by permission of the author and publisher. Copyright © 1961 by the University of Chicago.

1837, the Reverend John Todd set forth eight reasons for the existence of a library:

a. It will create a taste for good reading.
b. It will interest those with books who otherwise would never have them.
c. A Library occupies the vacant hours of the children.
d. A Library will create taste and draw out genius.
e. A Library will refine and elevate intercourse between parents and children and between the children themselves.
f. A Library will attach Scholars to the School.
g. A Library will do good where nothing else can reach [the parents].
h. The Library is a powerful means of convicting the soul, and building it in holiness.[4]

J. W. Harper, in 1827, recommended "small libraries of judiciously selected works, to which, under proper restrictions, the meritorious scholars have access." As an afterthought he added: "Teachers are also allowed to read the books."[5] Sixteen years later, the annual report of the Sunday School Union of the Methodist Episcopal Church declared that "no more powerful auxiliary to our enterprise exists than a good library,"[6] and its value was made plain by a letter which appeared in the *Christian Advocate and Journal*. Here a superintendent reports that all except one family in the community attended Sunday school and drew books from the library. The children thus excluded became so eager for the privilege that they persuaded their parents to join the school.[7]

Advocates of the Sunday-school library claimed for it three chief advantages: it could inform, indoctrinate, and convert; it could improve and cultivate not only the morals but also the tastes of its users; and it was a valuable device to promote both interest and attendance at Sunday school. With these advantages in mind, it is not difficult to understand why the plan grew greatly during the period.

The problems confronting the Sunday-school librarian were those facing any person who works in a similar capacity; he had to provide for the storage of the books, for the selection of books by the students entitled to them, for the charging of such books to students, and for the eventual return of the volumes to the shelves. An investigation of some of the regulations of midcentury Sunday-school libraries and of some of the manuals for establishing such collections gives definite ideas of the methods by which the enterprise was conducted.

The usual storage place for the books was a bookcase; sets of books were often sold with a bookcase in which they might be stored.[8] Authorities usually recommended that the library be kept in a separate room, but the fact that the schools often were not a part of a church or, if they were, that the churches had not yet begun to make elaborate provision for Sunday-school rooms in their building plans, made the site most frequently a rather dark corner of the auditorium or the vestibule.

The East Liberty Presbyterian Church of Pittsburgh had an ingenious system of storage which also provided limited access to the books by the students. The volumes were kept in a room, the walls of which were of glass cases open to the inside. The students could walk around the room, observe the names of the books they wanted, and give the numbers of these books to the librarian, who then picked up the volumes and issued them.[9] The system was an improvement over the usual plan when the student had no contact with the book as he selected it, but, since many of the books were so small that the name could not be put on the spine, the advantage was not great. J. A. Lyons suggested that the most valuable piece of library equipment was a "Good Lock that everybody's key will not fit."[10]

Books were usually kept in a central locked case or cabinet which was opened only on Sunday and usually only in the presence of the officials of the school. The books themselves were arranged on shelves according to the numbers assigned to them, alphabetically or in the order in which they had been purchased. There was little attempt to divide the collections according to subject matter. Since the spines were usually dark, the numbers were put on little squares of paper and glued to the books; the use of white ink was not recommended until late in the century. For the Sunday-school library the librarian was thought of chiefly as a book caretaker.

Since the library was often in a distant corner of the building, the problem of allowing students to come to it was a considerable one. The First Parish Church, Needham, Massachusetts, provided: "No Scholar must leave his seat for the purpose of obtaining books from the Library."[11] Fourth Universalist, Boston, regulated that "scholars *must not* leave their seats for the purpose of procuring any [books],"[12] and the Church Street M. E. Sunday School of Boston had a similar prohibition.[13] Because such regulations existed in most libraries, students were not allowed the privilege of seeing in advance the books they were to read.

The catalog was the device by which choice of books was usually made. Sometimes they were handwritten and were posted at various places throughout the school; when the school was sufficiently prosperous, however, there was a printed list, the titles usually in alphabetical order with no indication of content. Sometimes the length of the book was suggested by listing the number of pages, and some libraries marked children's books with a star. Students were often given one copy of the catalog; second copies had to be paid for. Before coming to school on Sunday, each student was expected to study his catalog and decide which books he wanted. He then wrote the numbers of the books on a slip of paper, or on a card provided for the purpose, and handed it to the librarian. It was suggested that he pick ten books so that he might get one if the other nine were out. The librarian tried to issue to each child one of the books selected. Such a plan tended to make the children choose books on the recommendations of their fellows, because books selected at random from the catalog too frequently proved uninteresting. Once a book was back on the shelf without a recent reader to recommend it, it was almost certain to remain there. The system itself helped to promote the disfavor into which old books fell—one of the faults of the Sunday-school library.

At the beginning of the era of the Sunday-school library, as noted above, privilege of drawing books from the collection was a reward for good behavior at school. Later, however, this provision was relaxed, since the children who needed good reading got it least frequently. One book at a time was all that most schools would permit a student to withdraw, and, at least in the Parish Library of the Trinity Church, Geneva, New York, he had to pay a dollar for a library card, good for one year.[14] This idea of charging money for the use of the library, in effect in 1837, is similar to the custom of the social library and suggests a possible connection between the two types. Books usually had to be returned before new selections could be obtained, and lost books had to be paid for. First Parish, Brighton, Massachusetts, had a special rule: "No pupil is entitled to receive a book from the Library until the last borrowed has been returned."[15] Library privilege was usually granted to any regularly enrolled member of the Sunday school but the number of books he could use was limited.

The libraries were usually open only on Sunday; some seem to have been open during part of the week, but the author of *Sunday School Libraries: Their Uses and Abuses* objected to the practice.[16] The library was generally open during the hours of the Sunday school; such was the practice of the Church Street M. E. Library, South Boston,[17] the Brighton Evangelical Sabbath School Library,[18] and the Sabbath School Library of the Presbyterian Church of University Place, New York.[19] The Trinity Church Library, Geneva, New York, was open immediately after divine services.

After the child had made his choice, the librarian charged the books according to the selections. The method of keeping a record of the persons to whom the books went varied; during the early period a charge book in which each student had a page for his record was kept. By 1850 the use of a card for each child had generally supplanted the charge-book system, but it was not until the last quarter of the nineteenth century that a separate card for each book came into general practice.

The period of withdrawal varied. First Parish, Needham, Church Street M. E., South Boston, and the University Place Presbyterian, New York, all provided that the student could keep his selection for two weeks. Fourth Universalist, Boston, Trinity Church, Geneva, New York, the Little Falls Friends Library,[20] the Brighton (Massachusetts) Evangelical Library, and the West Parish Association of Boston[21] all permitted a four-week borrowing period. The author of *Sunday School Libraries: Uses and Abuses* and other writers of manuals for the library indicate that the shorter period was more usual.

Fines were collected for lost or overdue books; only the Little Falls Library "Regulations" (of the handbooks studied) gives the amount of the overdue fine, which, in this case, was six and one-quarter cents,[22] probably per day. All the regulations provided that a lost book must have been paid for before a student was again entitled to borrowing privileges. Practically, however, manuals and discussions suggested that the librarian not insist on collection; too strict regulation sometimes made the child absent himself from Sunday school and thus defeated the purpose of the enterprise.

One of the strictest provisions of the schools was that books were not to be exchanged after they had been charged. This interdict provided against one student's lending a book to another or the immediate exchange of a book at the library if the borrower did not like the one he received. Even if he had already read it, the next Sunday was the earliest he could made an exchange.

Edward Eggleston, in his Sunday-school *Manual*

gives a rather elaborate system for conducting a Sunday-school library;[23] his discussion of "out-of-date" plans throws some light on previous practices. He mentions as unsatisfactory the teacher-check plan, the librarian-check plan, and the brass-check plan (in which each child had a brass plate with a hole in it; the check was hung on a nail over the place of the book he had borrowed). Eggleston advocated the "pigeon-hole and card" plan, in which a separate space was walled off for each book; each child had a card on which he wrote the name of the book he wanted and gave it to the librarian, who replaced the book by the card. A box of some sort for returned books was also suggested.

From the pains with which Eggleston details his scheme it may be inferred that such orderly procedure was the exception. Behind the various criticisms of the Sunday-school library may be seen a librarian whose intentions were good but who was careless, or who had a will of iron and made an autocracy of the endeavor. Books stored helter-skelter with no one really sure of who had what, a scheme that assigned the unlikeliest book to each reader, or the pandemonium that resulted as every student clamored for his choice—such probably was the pattern in many churches. The purpose of the plan was often good, but the voluntary nature of the administration led to inefficiency.

Specific information about the size of collections in the Sunday-school libraries is difficult to locate, but some information is contained in the United States census figures for 1850.[24] Although these figures are probably not accurate, inferences about library size, for 1850 and thereafter, may be made. Based on the census figures, the average size of a Sunday-school library in 1850 was 120 volumes; in 1860, 335; and in 1870, 249. It is probable that many collections were larger than the averages that the census figures indicate.

A second clue to the size of Sunday-school libraries is the number of books listed in available catalogs. Catalogs noted above represent libraries ranging in size from 220 to 550 books; the size of other libraries, based on their catalogs, was as follows: First Congregational Church of Stonington, Connecticut, owned 800 books in 1836;[25] the library at Old South Church, Boston, contained 420 books in 1861;[26] the first Reformed Dutch Church of Brooklyn, New York, published a catalog of about 450 volumes in 1860;[27] the Union Park Street Sunday School Library catalog, Boston, listed about 1,200 volumes in 1878.[28] The New Haven Sabbath School Union, organized in

1822, had a library of 250 volumes in 1825,[29] and the First Parish Sabbath School, Cambridge, Massachusetts, established in 1816, had 300 volumes in 1826 and 550 the next year.[30] Bullard reports that the library of the First Congregational Society, Methuen, Massachusetts, consisted of 300 volumes in 1836 and of 647 volumes in 1844; the circulation from 1842 to 1844 was 2,750.[31] The same authority cites a library in East Medway, Massachusetts, as containing 800 volumes in 1844; and the First Church, Farmingham, New York, had more than 100 volumes as early as 1821.[32] Often the number of books became so large that the collection was not useful; one of the chief defects mentioned in *Sunday School Libraries: Their Uses and Abuses* is their unwieldy size. Particular attention is called to a collection of 1,100 books which served a school of sixty-six pupils. The author of this pamphlet advocated a library of about 300 volumes because, with that limited number, the teacher could know all the books and could select desirable reading for his students—reading which would amplify the lesson of the day and which would meet individual differences.[33]

A third method of estimate, though less accurate, may be suggested. Many publishers issued uniformly bound libraries for purchase by Sunday schools. These sets numbered from 40 to 300 volumes and were so variously priced that any school could find one set that it could afford; however, the sets were designed to be nuclei, and the libraries certainly increased their holdings through subsequent purchases from the same publisher or in the general market.

The collections probably did not grow indefinitely; aside from the wear and tear inherent in the use of the books, many librarians made it a practice to dispose of old stock. Often the old books were donated to the mission churches, particularly in the West; in *Design, Character, and Uses of Sunday School Books* the author suggests: "When a library has been some years in use, let it be presented to some destitute school or neighborhood, and let a new library be bought to replace it."[34] Although internal evidence indicates that this publication was probably circulated by a publisher of Sunday-school books (the American Sunday School Union) who would profit from the new purchase, the advice was followed. The First Congregational Church of Stonington, Connecticut, occasionally sent old books to "destitute Sunday-schools in the southern and western parts of our country."[35] The library of the Palestine Church, near Genoa, Nebraska, was made up of books from Massachusetts, Connecticut, and Chicago Sunday schools; some, as the bookplates bear witness, had been sent from one of the eastern states to Chicago, where they were used and again passed on to Nebraska.[36]

Although there was great variation in the size and character of libraries, it may be assumed from the evidence that the average library of a small Sunday school contained between 200 and 300 books and that, in larger schools, though the totals became greater, they never reached anything like the size of the usual public library in a twentieth-century small town. In progressive communities the books were new, being replaced frequently, while in other centers one set of books, with only minor additions each season, gathered dust for many years.

Of course, the whole purpose of the Sunday-school library was to give its readers the advantages of the information to be found in the books. To appreciate the value of such a library, then, it is necessary to form some idea of its contents. Three possible methods of arriving at this knowledge suggest themselves: catalogs of various collections may be observed and analyzed; the publications of one of the firms supplying the libraries may be examined; and, finally, if such a library can be found, the material in it may be read and critically considered. Although none of these methods reproduces the experience of a person with access to the Sunday-school library itself, perhaps a combination of the three will give some appreciation of the fare offered.

Most of the available catalogs are simple alphabetical lists of the books held. Catalogs previously mentioned were analyzed and the books, based upon the author's knowledge, divided into seven classes: doctrines, histories, travel books, sermons, juvenilia, narratives, and memoirs. The study of the titles reveals wide variations of types, but space does not permit such detailed analysis.

Several conclusions may be drawn from the study of the catalogs. In the first place, the Sunday-school library changed in the type of book offered as the enterprise became older. In the early collections the chief interest was in books of doctrine and biblical exposition; in later examples the interest was in stories—to a growing extent in fiction. Whether this change resulted from an altered taste on the part of the users of the libraries, or whether the later lists represent what people read and the former what someone thought they should read, is uncertain. In any event, it is obvious that the later Sunday-school library consisted chiefly of a collection of stories rather than of tracts.

A second general tendency noted is an increasing liberalism; titles in the last library studied (South Congregation Sunday-school library, Boston, Massachusetts) did not differ greatly from those to be found in the typical public library of the time,[37] whereas those in the first collections were severely restricted in type. It is, of course, probable that the libraries in communities prosperous enough to have printed catalogs would contain a greater variety of books than would libraries for which no lists are available.

A third trend was in the growth of series books. In the earliest listings the only items which might be considered as "series" were numerous volumes of the same person's works, usually sets of sermons. In later catalogs, however, the books in sequence were frequently noted, the volumes coming from the religious as well as the secular press.

The content of the libraries may also be suggested by an analysis of the publications of one of the firms which frequently supplied books to the Sunday-school libraries. The American Tract Society published widely in the nineteenth century and maintains a fairly complete file of its publications. The following estimate is based upon reading 270 works from its 1845 list. These items are typical of those offered to the purchaser of didactic books, but, since the organization was conservative, it is safe to say that the books read represent the tradition before 1840 rather than later. Sermons took first place with 188 volumes. Most of them were complex both in idea and in structure; certainly, if difficulty of the task performed produced a feeling of virtue, reading one of these sermons on Sunday must have occasioned considerable holy glow. Next most numerous were narratives, sixty-three of the books falling in this category. A great many—fully a third—had an English setting, perhaps explained by the fact that much of the published material of the day was pirated from England. More than half of these books contained, as a part of the title or in the preface, a statement that the tale was true. Most of them concerned young persons but not children; 90 per cent contained at least one deathbed scene. In all the stories emphasis was upon the goodness exemplified and not on the events retold—the didactic theme.

There were fourteen question-and-answer books, or dialogs, most of them catechismal or designed to help in conversion; for example, No. 63— *Twenty-two Reasons for Not Being a Roman Catholic*. In the seventeen memoirs the chief interest was not in the life or death of the subject (which usually occupied many pages) but in the ideas or literary remains of the person. Two publications dealt with the work of the Society, and there was one long poem, theological in subject and crude in verse.

Expositions of moral or ecclesiastical doctrine accounted for the remaining fifty-eight volumes. Most were didactic; the chief difference between them and the sermons is that the sermons were usually more unified and with a single theme, while the doctrinal expositions were often discursive and dwelt on several points.

In addition to the narrative material already cited, many of the other books used stories as illustrations. In fact, almost every book contains some thread of narrative. These tales were uniformly lugubrious in character; many of them dealt with the untimely death of the young or with the picturesque death of the old.

The third method of appraising a Sunday-school library of the nineteenth century is to read its books. Most such libraries have disappeared into wastepaper drives and garbage heaps, but in a little country Baptist church near Genoa, Nebraska, there is a dark corner containing a disused cabinet and several shelves of books from an old library. The collection itself came to the Nebraska hills sometime after 1880, when the church was organized, but the library represents an earlier period; though one book has a copyright as late as 1863, all the rest are older. The books had been sent to mission churches by organizations farther east.

With duplicate copies omitted, there are eighty-two titles in the collection. Of these, thirty-two are non-narratives and fifty are stories. The non-narratives include biblical quotation and criticism (4), Baptist doctrine (3), general doctrine (7), children's doctrine (6), biographies (11), and one book of advice to adults.

The fifty books in the narrative group are more difficult to classify. There is one book of poetry, one historical narrative (although one of the novels has a pseudohistorical background), three books which might be called simple novels, three missionary stories, and seven which are definitely deathbed descriptions. Ten of the volumes are collections of short tales, some of which might be called short stories; and twenty-two can only be classified loosely as stories of varying degrees of interest and purpose.

Most of the narratives are short, from thirty-two to thirty-six pages in length, while the average is about seventy pages. Most frequently the author is not given; all are "written down" to children. The plot is not a strong element in any of the

stories; simple chronology is almost the only basis of organization. One group, less than 10 per cent of the total, seems representative of the worst opinion generally held about Sunday-school books; in the others, the deathbed and the precociously pious do not dominate.

Finally, how were books selected for the Sunday-school library? In this matter there was a sharp division of opinion between two groups. One believed that there were certain doctrinal and scriptural books which the students should read and that these books should be put into the library whether or not anyone wanted to read them. The other group regarded the Sunday-school library as equally responsible for the cultural and religious development of the children, and such critics insisted on literary excellence as well as doctrinal soundness. Most of the libraries seem to have subscribed to the first precept and practiced the second, preferring collections which would be read rather than those which merely ought to be read.

The two leading non-denominational publishers, the American Tract Society and the American Sunday School Union, subscribed to both ideas, edification and interest.[38] The Massachusetts Sabbath School Society agreed but suggested that books be segregated or marked for "Week-day reading" and "Sabbath reading."[39] Some attention was paid to style; Jacob Abbot, prolific writer of children's books in the period, spoke about the necessity of naturalness and not "writing down" to children,[40] and his books often show that he followed his own prescription; but most of the publications are either simperingly simplified or ponderously adult in style.

The chief difficulty in the selection of books was inherent in the method of purchase. Frequently, the librarian was not the purchasing officer, or, if he was, his interest was not deep. The yearly appropriation would be made, and some person who was going to the town where the nearest Sunday-school bookstore was located would be charged with buying the year's supply of new reading material. Since the books bought cost an average of less than fifty cents each, and since the purchaser rarely took more than an hour or two from the duties which had carried him to the city, he gave very little attention to the items bought; usually he took whatever the seller recommended. An even worse situation was apparent when a check was sent to the bookseller and a blanket order for books was given. Sometimes a catalog of volumes on hand was included, but more frequently the only information given was the date of the last purchase, so that only books published after that date would be sent.

Still other libraries bought on a bid basis; the bookseller who could furnish the most books—titles unselected—for the money got the contract.[41] As a result of haphazard buying, there was not much chance that the library would receive the best books; books printed from worn-out plates and on poor paper, as well as of ancient and worthless content, were the frequent lot of the Sunday school.

There were some brighter elements in book selection for Sunday-school libraries. Various manuals for the instruction of the librarian propose relatively sound selection policies,[42] and some libraries must have tried to follow the instructions. Perhaps the most constructive movement of the time was the organization of a committee of Unitarian ladies who recommended books for inclusion in Sunday-school libraries.[43] Their selections were sound and varied, but many denominations shied from the Unitarian label.

Despite the good precept of those who wrote about Sunday-school libraries, the choice of books was usually the weakest element in the system, and the disfavor into which the libraries fell resulted from poor selection. Most libraries were selected from one of two sources: from a Sunday-school library bookstore of from a publisher's catalog. Books selected from a catalog were usually bought without the privilege of return; the catalog gave only the title, with no description of the contents of the book and sometimes without even the name of the author.[44] Denominational schools could be fairly sure that the doctrine would not offend if they purchased from the publishing house of their sect, but the quality of the books depended on the fluctuating policy of the organization.

At the bookstore books might be handled or read by the person responsible for selection, but frequently he was in a hurry or ignorant of the type of literature desired. Booksellers tended to push items on which they made the largest profit, and, since items from reputable publishers, especially if they had philanthropic support, were so closely priced that a large profit was impossible, mediocre books were often purchased. In spite of the high aims of the Sunday-school library, it is not surprising that it lost much of its potential influence through its inefficient selection of books.

The Sunday-school library, which had its beginning about 1825 as an economical means of circulating information and awarding prizes to worthy pupils, by 1850 became the leading medium for distributing didactic literature in America; it continued to grow into the third quarter of the century but fell into disrepute and disuse by the end of the century. The aims of the library—to teach morals and religion while cultivating taste—were broad, and efficient persons worked out satisfactory plans for administering the collections. However, two major factors contributed to the failure of the enterprise: faulty administration and the generally haphazard schemes of book purchase. A struggle between the dual purposes of informing and entertaining dominated; unfortunately, those who tried to inform through books were often so unskilled in their art that their productions left the impression that all religious, didactic books were dull and boring.

FOOTNOTES

[1] Frank Keller Walter, "A Poor but Respectable Relation: The Sunday-School Library," *Library Quarterly,* XII (July, 1942), 731-39.

[2] *Fortieth Annual Report of the Superintendent of the Portsmouth South Parish Sabbath School, Presented June 13, 1858* (Portsmouth, N. H.: Portsmouth *Journal,* 1858).

[3] *Ibid.*

[4] Rev. John Todd, *The Sabbath School Teacher* (Northampton, Mass.: J. H. Butler, 1837), p. 163.

[5] J. W. Harper, "Methodist Episcopal Sunday School Association," *Christian Advocate,* I, No. 24 (February 17, 1827), 1.

[6] *Christian Advocate and Journal,* XVII, Nos. 35 and 867 (April 12, 1843), 137.

[7] *Christian Advocate and Journal,* II, Nos. 44 and 96 (July 4, 1828), 2.

[8] The "Christian Library" of the American Tract Society and the "Family Evangelical Library" of the American Sunday School Union are priced in the catalogs to include a bookcase.

[9] E. E. Hale, *Sunday School Libraries,* quoted in a review by Martha H. Brooks, *Library Journal,* IV (September-October, 1879), 338-43.

[10] J. A. Lyons, *The Sunday School and Its Methods: A Practical Treatise for Earnest Workers in This Department of the Church of Christ* (Nashville, Tenn.: Southern Methodist Publishing House, 1883), p. 68.

[11] *Catalogue of Books Belonging to the Library of the Sabbath School, Connected with the First Parish Church, Needham, May, 1857* (Boston: Alfred Mudge & Son, 1857).

[12] *Catalogue of Books in the Sabbath School Library of the Fourth Universalist Society* (Boston: Eugene Bettes, 1860).

[13] *Catalogue of the Church Street M. E. Sunday School Library* (South Boston: Mattapan Register Press, 1859).

[14] *Catalogue of the Parish Library of Trinity Church, Geneva, New York: Published for the Use of the Congregation, December, 1837* (Geneva, N. Y.: J. T. Brandt, Printer, 1837).

[15] *Catalogue of the Sunday School Library of the First Parish, Brighton, 1878* (Brighton, Mass.: John Adams, 1878).

[16] *Sunday School Libraries: Their Uses and Abuses Considered by a Superintendent* (Philadelphia: American Sunday School Union, n.d.).

[17] Information from catalogs and other sources already cited will not again be noted unless the text leaves some question as to the source. Generalizations, such as those in the preceding and following paragraphs, are made from all the catalogs cited in this article.

[18] *Catalogue of the Evangelical Sabbath School Library, Brighton* (Boston: Davis & Farmer, Printers, 1859).

[19] *Catalogue of the Sabbath School Library of the Presbyterian Church of University Place, New York* (New York: R. Craighead, Printer, 1858).

[20] William C. Dunlap, *Quaker Education in Baltimore and Virginia Yearly Meetings with an Account of Certain Meetings of Delaware and the Eastern Shore Affiliated with Philadelphia, Based on Manuscript Sources* (Philadelphia: Science Press, 1936), p. 168.

[21] *Catalogue of Books Which It Is Proposed To Obtain for the Formation of the Library of the West Parish Association* (Boston: William Bellamy, 1825).

[22] Dunlap, *Quaker Education*, p. 169.

[23] Edward Eggleston, *The Manual: A Practical Guide for the Sunday School Work* (Chicago: Adams, Blacker & Lyon, 1869), pp. 42-48.

[24] *A Compendium of the 7th Census, June 1, 1850* (Washington, D. C.: Government Printing Office, 1853), p. lxiii; *A Compendium of the 9th Census, June 1, 1870* (Washington, D. C.: Government Printing Office, 1873), p. 505.

[25] Richard A. Wheeler, *History of the First Congregational Church, Stonington, Connecticut (1678-1874)* (Norwich, Conn.: Davis, 1875), p. 133.

[26] *Catalogue of Books in the Old South Sabbath School Library* (title-page missing; publication date established by librarian, Boston Public Library, as 1861).

[27] *Descriptive Catalogue of the Library of the Sunday School Attached to the First Reformed Dutch Church, Brooklyn, Edited under the Pastoral Care of Rev. Elbert S. Porter, D. D., by a Superintendent* (New York: John Gray, 1860).

[28] *Catalogue of the South Congregation Sunday School Library, Union Park Street, Boston* (Boston: John Wilson & Son, 1878).

[29] *First Annual Report of the ASSU, 1825* (Philadelphia: American Sunday School Union, 1825), p. 43.

[30] Asa Bullard, *Fifty Years with the Sabbath Schools* (Boston: Lockwood, Brooks & Co., 1876), p. 162.

[31] *Ibid.*, pp. 161-70.

[32] *Ibid.*

[33] *Ibid.*, pp. 12-22.

[34] *Design, Character, and Uses of the Books of the American Sunday School Union* (pamphlet reprinted from *The Biblical Reportory*, no date or publisher given; probably American Sunday School Union, about 1840).

[35] Wheeler, *History*, p. 133.

[36] From observation of the collection.

[37] I also consulted *Catalogue of books in the Sabbath School Library of the Trinitarian Congregational Church, Taunton, Mass.* (Taunton, Mass.: American Republican Office, 1859); and *Catalogue of Books in the St. Stephen's Sunday School Library, Boston* (title-page missing; date estimated by librarian, Boston Public Library, as 1859-60).

[38] *Third Annual Report of the ASSU, 1827* (Philadelphia: American Sunday School Union, 1827), p. 41; *Ninth Annual Report of the American Tract Society, 1834* (New York: Daniel Fanshaw, 1834), pp. 15-17.

[39] *Third Annual Report of the MSS, 1835* (Boston: Massachusetts Sabbath School Society, 1835), p. 9; see also *Sunday School Libraries: Their Uses and Abuses . . .*, pp. 3-4; and Bullard, *Fifty Years*, pp. 170-71.

[40] Quoted in *Design, Character and Uses*, pp. 15-16.

[41] See Hale (n. 9 above); and *Uses and Abuses*, pp. 3-10.

[42] Lyons, *The Sunday School . . .*, pp. 358-84; John S. Hart, *How To Select a Library* (Philadelphia: J. C. Carrigues & Co., 1870), pp. 12-17; *Dodd and Mead's Sunday School Annual for 1871* (New York: Dodd & Mead, Inc., 1871).

[43] Preface to *A Catalogue of Books for Unitarian Sunday Schools, Recommended by the Ladies Commission* (Boston: John Wilson & Sons, 1867), pp. 3-5 ff.

[44] This may be noted by examining catalogs of the day.

Mechanics' and Mercantile Libraries

Sidney Ditzion

Mechanics' and mercantile libraries represent the first form of cooperation between business and American libraries. These libraries were an integral part of the social library movement and provided services mostly to young men interested in mercantile careers. Sidney Ditzion, a professor of history at New York University and the author of a number of important works on American library history, has written the definitive study of these libraries, which for many years offered significant services to America's business community.

MECHANICS' AND APPRENTICES' LIBRARIES

It was at the end of the second decade (1820), about the time when the subscription libraries were beginning to show signs of weakening, that interest in mechanics' and mercantile libraries began to appear. (The mercantile libraries will be treated separately; the writer feels that their history presents problems which require independent treatment.)

Although the cause both of the failing strength of the subscription library and of the rise of mechanics' libraries may be traced to the expanding economic limits of the American middle class—so that its lower branches embraced larger and larger portions of the urban population of the period— the conception of the mechanic-apprentices' library was neither new nor indigenous. It grew out of the workingmen's lecture idea started at Glasgow in 1760 and continued by Birkbeck in 1799. The first Artisans' Library seems to have been established at Birmingham in 1795 to distribute useful reading to the working people at the subscription price of a penny a week. By 1823 Glasgow and Liverpool both had mechanics' institutes and the libraries that went with them.[1]

In 1823, when Timothy Claxton of the London Mechanical Institute came to Methuen, Massachusetts, he found that there had been established in this town in about 1819 the Methuen Social Society for Reading and General Inquiry. Although Claxton seems to have classified this as a mechanics' institution,[2] it may merely have been one of the social library clubs which were quite popular in New England. The first institute libraries of im-portance were those established in Boston, Portland, Philadelphia, and New York in 1820. Of these only the ones in Boston and Philadelphia were newly organized institutions. The General Society of Mechanics and Tradesmen had been organized in 1785 (incorporated 1792) as a mutual benevolence society for the assistance of mechanics in financial distress and for aid to their widows and children. The Mechanics' Library of Portland, Maine, was established by the Maine Charitable Mechanics' Organization whose purpose at the time of incorporation (1815) was to relieve "the distresses of unfortunate mechanics and their families, to promote inventions and improvements in the mechanic arts, by granting premiums for said inventions and improvements, and to assist young mechanics with loans of money."[3]

The movement for libraries seems to have been accelerated—if not initiated—by such popularizers of science and education as John Griscom and William Wood. Griscom's activities consisted largely in traveling about, gathering before him groups of mechanics and merchants, apprentices and clerks, for lectures on science.[4] Wood, a liberal merchant who had been instrumental in stirring up feeling in the United States in favor of the Greek cause and in behalf of the Polish exiles, had his hand in the establishment of at least a half-dozen libraries. His first triumph was the Apprentices' Library of Boston, the success of which seems to have stimulated him to further operation in the field of library establishment. New York, Albany, Philadelphia, New Orleans, and other cities received his personal attention in library building.[5]

SOURCE: Reprinted from Sidney Ditzion, "Mechanics and Mercantile Libraries," *Library Quarterly* 10 (April, 1940), pp. 197-219, by permission of the author and publisher. Copyright © 1942 by the University of Chicago.

Interest in establishing an apprentices' library and school in New York dates back to 1819, when the Library Committee of the General Society reported the benefits to be derived by educating the apprentices whose parents had not been able to afford to send them to school:

> every means that can be devised to further the improvement of such . . . in order to remedy, as far as practicable, the privation suffered in their early years, and which . . . . cannot be more effectually promoted than by affording to all who are desirous of improving themselves, the means by which to attain that object, to wit: the gratuitous reading of elementary, moral, religious and miscellaneous books, and such others as may have a tendency to promote them in their several avocations.[6]

On November 1, 1820, this same committee announced that it had rented rooms in the Free School Society building on Chatham Street. On November 25 a library of 4,000 volumes was publicly opened, blessed by the presence of the mayor and several members of the common council and state legislature at the inaugural ceremonies. In the evening of the same day the library was crowded with apprentices who borrowed nearly 300 books. The number of applicants who took advantage of the privilege dissipated all fears that the library would not be used.[7] In 1829 the library possessed 10,000 volumes and was used by sixteen hundred apprentices in that year.[8] By 1857 the institution was serving a city population of nearly three-quarters of a million people, "of which the working classes form a large majority."[9] And so the society kept expanding its services, soon adding to its clientele the female operatives of the city, offering elementary-school facilities (until public education was free in New York), expanding its physical plant and book collection (60,000 volumes in 1880).[10]

At Philadelphia (1820) "it was agreed to form a Society for the purpose of establishing a Library for the free use of apprentices"[11] "believing that many benefits would arise from the establishment of a library of suitable books for the use of apprentices; that it would promote orderly and virtuous habits, diffuse knowledge and the desire for knowledge, improve the scientific skill of mechanics and manufacturers."[12] It is interesting to note at this point that, although the mechanics' libraries were started with the same general purposes as the subscription libraries of the previous century, they were sustained entirely at first by the associative effort of employer groups in manufacturing towns. A study of the backgrounds of some of the moving spirits of the Apprentices' Free Library of Philadelphia reveals a configuration of surprising scope and breadth of interest. There

were Thomas Kimber, a Quaker bookseller and stationer, who at one time held the position of controller of the public schools; Samuel L. Shober, a boot and shoe manufacturer; Daniel B. Smith, a pharmacist and member of the Academy of Natural Sciences, American Philosophical Society, Franklin Institute, and Historical Society of Pennsylvania; Robert Evans, a flour merchant who "employed his leisure time in literary and scientific studies, with talents and acquirements remarkably devoted to the good of his fellow creatures"; and Roberts Vaux, early abolitionist, writer, educator, humanitarian, and politician.[13]

Before attempting an analysis of the social ideas which motivated these mechanics' institutes with their libraries, schools, museum collections, and exhibits of models of mechanical invention, something needs to be said of the variations from type which were established in the 1840's and 1850's. There is much evidence to show that institutions incorporated toward midcentury attempted to embrace the whole of a community population and required membership dues from all users. Fees were generally lower for those below thirty-five years of age.[14]

As has been remarked, the original idea behind the mechanics' institute was the protection and support of the widows and children of members. When industries began to multiply libraries and other educational instruments were instituted to cover a larger incidence of indigence among the urban industrial population.[15] The boast of the Library of the General Society continued for many years to be that it was the only library in the city "especially designed for the use of that portion of the community the most in need of information, and the least able to pay for it, viz., the working boys and girls of New York."[16]

With the development of city life and its attendant evils middle-class humanitarianism began to accommodate its content to new conditions. Those who agitated for support of apprentices' libraries pointed to the moral and social effects of occupying the leisure hours of youth in the wholesome pastime of reading. These institutions were signally adapted to keeping young men—later, young women—out of bad company.[17]

Employers were impressed with the importance of encouraging virtue and discouraging vice[18] and were reminded of what might result from "the hard labor, the fatigues, the crosses, the vexations of the day" if reading were not provided for evening hours.[19] Toward the end of the nineteenth century when sweatshop conditions were beginning to make a widespread impression on the people the General Society of New York offered its facilities as an evening's refuge from the arduous, "oft times pernicious and hurtful" conditions of the factory.[20] In short, books were to provide a new attraction to insure the security and blessedness of the home against the "temptations of idleness and vice," and to draw the younger generation of mechanics away "from the haunts where they annoy others and seriously injure themselves."[21]

> When the labor of the day is over, instead of the apprentice scouring the streets, visiting bar-rooms or theatres, mingling with idle, vicious companions, he takes his seat in this library with a rich intellectual repast before him, or, being privileged to take a book home with him, he trims his lamp and reads aloud to his little brothers and sisters, scattering good seeds among them to take root hereafter . . . . .[22]

Realizing that apprentices were not disposed to solid reading after a laborious day, library managements introduced into their collections novels and light magazines. If this practice did not meet the level of serious learning, it did prevent exposure to the moral uncertainties of the streets.[23] Of course, it was hoped that novel reading would build up the habit of reading and, since many of the novels were historical, it would lead to the study of history.[24]

The crime-prevention argument, which was used in later years to promote all types of educational institutions, appeared to a small extent in connection with the mechanics' institutes. Whereas fear of punishment could only "restrain from the commission of grosser crimes," intelligence was looked to for the habituation of men in honesty and morality, and education was depended upon to warn men against questionable conduct.[25] The Rochester Young Men's Association presents an instance of direct cause and effect; it was after the first crime punished by execution in the history of Monroe County that ways and means were sought to provide "means of rational amusement" for young men in order to keep them out of trouble.[26]

If one takes an overview of the social changes of the first half of the nineteenth century, humanitarianism recedes to a secondary position as a force which motivated the establishment of mechanics' and apprentices' libraries. A primary force consisted in the changing character of apprenticeship. The educational advantages of indentureship were no longer as valuable as they had been formerly. The master having more than one apprentice—the number growing larger as the mode of manufacture increased in size and complexity of unit—

could no longer give the same time and attention to such general education as the terms of indentureship required. The actual manufacturing process was rapidly changing and improving, a condition which made it difficult for any one master to give appropriate technical education to his apprentices. These and other considerations (to be discussed later) militated toward the establishment of "schools and libraries for the use of apprentices and the improvement of the arts."[27] The school functions of these institutions were performed by public lectures and formal evening schools.

Symptomatic of the underlying purposes of the mechanics' and apprentices' libraries were the museums, the fairs and exhibits of mechanical prowess, and such slogans as "the promotion of the Mechanic Arts and the dissemination of useful knowledge."[28] The prosperity of large industrial cities was by axiom a result of the skill, ingenuity, and enterprise of mechanics. Was it not, then, sensible for the wealthy citizens of a community to insure future prosperity "by doing something for Apprentices."[29]

The employers who supported these institutions were divided as to motive. It was a difference between those who still thought that there was "room for all" and those who did not relish the idea of competition from young blood.[30] The purely trade societies, dominated by exployers—employee domination was rare—did not aim at increasing the number of competitors. They did not grant loans. Their benefits to the employed consisted only in the enhancement of skill and the possibility of an increased wage.[31]

The employers in the other camp, however, recognizing the needless struggle which they had suffered for lack of education in their youth and realizing the value of such education in attaining a place of respectability in the business world, went about setting up their mechanics' societies for the purpose of

> elevating the character of those concerned in them to their just standard, and advancing their general interest and welfare. To attain these ends it behooves us, while we labor to meet competition on fair grounds and to encourage each other in our several avocations, to provide the means of instruction and improvement to our apprentices.[32]

The spirit of free competition expressed here passed out of existence with the Civil War.

Beneath many an argument which spoke of community and national progress, of increased physical security and comfort (which would follow from the spread of scientific and mechanical knowledge), lay the more direct and convincing appeal to the individual.[33] "The object of our institution is," said George Emerson, "to give persons, whose time is chiefly occupied with the business of labor, knowledge of a kind to be directly useful to them in their daily pursuits."[34] Lest the mechanics persist in their suspicion of theoretical knowledge to be derived from books, Emerson proceeded to demonstrate how a knowledge both of the principles of mechanics and of the nature of the materials used in manufactures would save time and prevent the failures which were so frequent when the trial-error method was used. "A few principles of philosophy [enter the mind, then] it ceases to be a dark mechanical process . . . . . He [the mechanic] begins to penetrate the reasons and acquires a new mastery over his own instruments."[35]

Books assisted not only in the mastery of the processes of production but also in the revelation of vast power in the broad expanse of knowledge which had hitherto been the property of the privileged few. The multitudes from workshop and field could now march triumphantly through the "gates of the temple of science" and share in the complete culture of the times.[36] Here we had the basis of true equality, i.e., the equal opportunity to rise in proportion to one's talent and effort. Herein lay the incentive to the good life. Ambition begets knowledge; knowledge begets wealth and power. These "certainly do create differences among men . . . . [but] they are prizes equally open to all: and this is real equality."[37]

Just as the Old World class structure united with ignorance to keep economic power in the hands of the ruling class, so did the exclusive possession of knowledge keep political power in these same hands. But in the United States no one had any reason to withhold knowledge from another since there were no classes. One person's gain was not another's loss. Political slavery was indeed made possible by ignorance; but whatever of freedom was allowed by tyranny to remain would be adequate to work out a complete restoration through revolution. "The aim of the philanthropist and the patriot should be . . . . to guard against the occurrence of the necessity which sooner or later will inevitably drive men to the ultimate resort of the oppressed."[38]

There is evidence which shows that this bright light of exuberant democracy was, at an early date, beginning to fear the shadow of class antagonisms. Paternalism was slightly polluted by self-interest. The benefits of a mechanics' institute were immediate to the apprentice but ultimate to the community in the form of "their [apprentices]

faithfulness, and in the greater security of property, and even of life." How immeasurably better it was to see the apprentice reading patriotic biographies than to have him waste his time in vicious pursuits "either in the company of his contemporaries in outdoor meetings, striving for notoriety, even by extravagance in speech, bordering on blasphemy; or, in the more retired rendezvous . . . . whilst he is stealing his own destruction, is ruining his employer."[39]

These ideas, ill defined in the early history of apprentices' libraries, took on clarity in the 1870's and 1890's when industry began to be harassed by organized labor. In speaking of the Apprentices' Library, the *New York Observer* of September 6, 1877, said: "Too much encouragement cannot be given to institutions of this description. They are the antidotes of strikes and communism, the only educators of many of our voters."[40] In 1894 and 1895 the annual reports of the General Society of Mechanics and Tradesmen used the subject of technical education as the springboard of an attack on the trade-unions. The patriotic sentiments of the employers who comprised the General Society were appealed to in an effort to have the society's school used as an instrument for combating the foreign leadership and un-American practices of the unions.[41] Former Mayor Abram S. Hewitt, in a stirring speech which was incorporated in the 1894 report, spoke of time-honored American freedom of contract. The "antidote" front this time had to be broadened to include "anarchism" and "populism," diseases which would destroy society itself if they were not checked. "The small fraction which has made itself so conspicuous and so noxious during the last ten years must be checked and relegated to their proper position in the social scale. If they will not work, let them starve." In any case the wealthy must be left in peace to perform their invaluable services to society.[42]

The idea of "indefinite perfectibility" with regard to man and his institutions appears in connection with the educational activities of mechanics' institutions, although the phrase itself—and its variants—has been abandoned. Faith in progress was indeed justified by the undeniable spread of intelligence in the period.[43] By dint of its republican institutions in which no class had political power which it feared to lose, the United States had the possibilities of rising to unknown heights. Each citizen had the opportunity of rising to the full measure of his abilities, and the totality of intelligence knew no bounds. So then, since "a comparative estimate of nations and cities depends upon the state of knowledge in a body of people," what indeed could be the limit of our progress?[44]

And more, there was a very compelling political reason for supporting institutions of this kind. The republican form of government depended for its very life upon the education and elevation of the mechanic and laborer.[45] Whether or not this country was to pass back into the hands of despots and oligarchs hinged on the maintenance of workers' education.[46] The world was awaiting the results of this experiment in self-government! Upon its success hung the fate of universal freedom! Knowledge was the one and only safeguard against failure!

What we see in the social backgrounds of the mechanics' and apprentices' libraries are the same solid virtues of the middle class which first organized subscription libraries nearly a hundred years before. We see the same outlook on scientific knowledge as the key to progress in economic as well as political realms. Three new elements enter the situation:

1. Extreme individualism has been modified to allow an increasing number of less fortunate young men to partake of the springs of knowledge
2. In some quarters the confidence in, and the desirability of, everyone's rising to a position of economic independence was put to question
3. National economic and political ends were added to the small group aims of the century before

These new ideas were manifestly functional to the growth of a distinct wage-earning class, the emergence of contradictions which were inherent in free-competition economics, the rising feeling of national self-consciousness with an accompanying desire for cultural independence.

MERCANTILE LIBRARIES

In giving the mercantile libraries separate treatment the writer does not wish to indicate that they were at all points distinct from the mechanics' institutions. There is some reason to believe that many general subscription libraries were called mercantile because they were established in trading towns where the mercantile proportion of the community population predominated.[47] Many communities had institutions of this kind which catered to both a mechanical and a commercial clientele but which were called by one or the other name. In at least one place a mechan-ics' library seems to have opened as a result of a misunderstanding of the nature of the local mercantile library.[48]

However, where in the larger cities two institutions existed side by side, the mercantile libraries were organized and run with a social philosophy quite different from that of the apprentices' libraries. They were established in the early 1820's, not by the employer merchants, but by groups of young clerks and merchants who were just starting in the profession. Another difference was that the libraries were at first the sole educational feature. Discussion groups and mutual-improvement circles and museum features were added only after the mercantile library was well under way.[49] The introduction of lectures (New York Mercantile) is first intimated in 1829, when one finds mention of a proposed building "with a hall devoted to the purposes of teachers connected with our institution."[50] Lecturers were invited to address the membership, wealthy men were exhorted to endow annual lecture series, and by 1839 the lecture feature was firmly intrenched as an auxiliary service.[51]

The New York Mercantile Library Association[52] was the outcome of a meeting of merchants's clerks at the Tontine Coffee House on November 9, 1820.[53] Its organizers found cause to boast not only of the excellence and grandeur of the literary institution they had conceived but also of the youthfulness of the group which was responsible for it.[54] Setting the association in motion, however, was not enough. The officers soon began to complain that, whether for lack of inclination or money or because of the poor location of the library, the number of young clerks and merchants who were joining was not enough to support the library.[55] Confident that the clerks were remaining outside the association because of disinclination rather than "opposing circumstances," a circular was sent to the City's merchants asking them for their blessing.[56]

Shortly afterward it was announced with keen satisfaction that the chamber of commerce had voted not only to donate two hundred and fifty dollars to the association—the more gratifying because funds were not solicited—but also to become patron saint to the clerks' venture.[57] The jubilance with which this action was received was due mostly to the fact that the approval of the merchants and their influence with clerks would cause an increased membership. But this still did not make a going concern. The next step was to map a campaign to get merchants to donate books and to pay subscription fees for their clerks. The "honorary" members—merchant donors—were appealed to for assistance in the campaign.[58]

A year later the opening wedge was begrudgingly conceded:

> We must have a still greater increase of subscribers. These constitute our strength, our chief dependence. We desire the approbation of our employers; we are truly thankful for their aid; we are anxious that they should continue their donations, yet our members should feel that the effective force comes from them.[59]

From this it was but a step to amend the constitution to include life-subscriptions at twenty-five dollars and annual subscriptions (for merchants) at five dollars.[60] By 1835 the older merchants probably had the controlling voice in the New York Mercantile Library Association—at least the annual report of that year would make it seem so.[61]

On the whole, the membership in mercantile library associations must have lived on a higher social plane than the readers in mechanics' libraries. The need for uplift, which the writer has treated under the general term "humanitarianism," does not figure as frequently or as seriously with the protagonists of mercantile libraries. Ornate but mild figures of speech set forth the moral value of a mercantile library or describe the exemplary conduct of its young members.[62] The importance of excluding immoral and irreligious books is mentioned;[63] the necessity of counteracting the penny press, with its general tone of ribaldry and mendacity, its details of "horrible murders," "infamous seductions," and "astounding defalcation," is stressed.[64] In general, those who sought recreation from the library shelves would not "have a taste for idle pursuits and dissolute pleasures."[65]

Employers were urged to see the benefits for themselves. Among the members of the mercantile library association they would see "none who are frequenters of the dram-shop, none who seek the society of the vicious and profane, and few, if any, who are devoted to the theatre."[66] The employer who prized honesty in those to whom he intrusted his property would see in this institution a teacher of correct principles.[67] Finally, before hiring a clerk, it would be well to find out if he is a member of the mercantile library and "what is the character of his reading."[68]

Perhaps the best humanitarian plea made in behalf of a mercantile library was that delivered by John Gourlie in 1839. This address spoke of the temptations to which many of the clerks, away from home and without parental influence, were exposed.

> The ardent spirit of youth, its tender susceptibilities, and that love of independent and unrestrained action which it exhibits, are the weak points which are first assailed by the temptation to error. From the counting-house, after the labours and occupations of the day are over, the thoughtless footstep ofttimes leads its victim to the brothel or the gambling table.[69]

In the days of universal gloom in the depression of 1837 the New York Mercantile Library claimed that in a crisis like this the importance of its facilities was "more palpably felt than at any other time." The unemployed, with little in the business world to occupy their attention, could spend their idle hours in profitable reading. Peculiarly enough, thought the officers, in these times of suffering and distress, the association has been in a favored position. Its social utility had increased![70]

Because of the exalted position which the clerks held in their libraries as compared with the lowly place of the apprentices in theirs there is little in the mercantile library literature which refers to utilitarian benefits from the employers' point of view. Citations which speak of a clerk or apprentice as too busy to read[71] or of professional reference material of direct utility in the transacting of business[72] are rare.

The highest function of a mercantile library association was to afford adequate educational facilities for those who were destined to become the future merchants of Boston,[73] San Francisco,[74] New York,[75] or any other trading city. Some assurance must be had that when the unassuming clerk takes on the merchant's cloak and enters into competition with the older men of the community the respectability of the merchant class would be sustained.[76]

The practical advantages of the mercantile library were soon evident to the merchant community—even to that sector which had thought at one time that it would "divert the attention of the young men from their professional duties."[77] On the contrary, successful practice of the merchant's calling required that he set aside a given time during the working day for reading. It was a grievous error to believe that the merchant could get along merely on what he learned in the conduct of enterprise. He had to know the latest laws and regulations which governed his trade; he had to be aware of production and consumption trends, of monetary expansion and contraction. The market was becoming so intricate that experience had to be supplemented by study if property were to remain secure. Another fallacy was the idea that educated men succeeded less frequently than their uneducated competitors. While this may have been true in the early settlement of the country when the population urgently needed foreign goods and when competition was almost nonexistent, it no longer was the case. The country had grown, competition had stiffened, and education had become the *sine qua non* of a respectable successful life.[78]

The merchant was under obligation to himself and to his profession, not only to learn what was useful, but also to inform himself as widely as possible so that he could command the utmost respect and make his greatest contribution to community life.[79] One had to have a care that the favored position which the merchant had in society was maintained.[80] No knowledge was foreign to the merchant: geography, history, economics, the humanities—all were within his sphere. "The merchant should possess an intimate practical acquaintance with human nature—a knowledge of the human heart—its affections and passions; he should be, indeed, a moral philosopher, although not wrapt up in the abstract speculations which both begin in the closet and end there."[81]

Whatever temptation one may have to define the merchants' conception of culture—with all its breadth—as utilitarian, is dispelled if one takes at face value the overwhelming stress in the annual addresses on the purely literary and humanistic studies. Wealth was despised (!) as an end in itself. Cultural elevation was sought as solace and substance of preoccupation in times of commercial adversity,[82] in old age,[83] and in retirement.[84] Foremost in the minds of some of the merchants was a desire to achieve real class distinction—to rank with the most cultivated classes in society.[85]

Standard and classical works had a preferred place in the library collection. Works of the imagination (fiction) and magazine literature were tolerated only in so far as it was hoped that such reading would start the clerks on the road to more serious studies.[86] In line with the general high cultural level at which the mercantile library associations were aiming many of the poems and papers read at annual meetings represented the last work in scholarship.[87] A favorite theme was the history of the world told in terms of the mercantile profession. It was regularly demonstrated how the superiority of some nations was traceable to the activities of its merchants;[88] how New York

and Boston had grown great on the foundations laid by commerce; and how the charitable, scientific, and literary institutions in these cities had been founded by the merchant class.[89] In place of specific history the clerks sometimes heard long hymns to commerce, to ships, to the sea, to the merchant and his love of literature and the arts, to his knowledge of science and its applications.[90]

In addition to the practical and cultural values of literary and scientific knowledge the merchant could think of another, perhaps oblique, advantage to the acquisition of learning. As the nation and its cities grew in size and complexity, new political responsibilities would devolve upon the citizens. In order to protect their own special interest the merchants had to send to the councils of the city and nation men who could "do proud" by the profession. "But, unfortunately, such has been the want of cultivation among our business men, so little way have they traveled out of the daily routine of the counting house, that it might be difficult to find any considerable number, who united to practical experience sufficient acquired knowledge to qualify them for filling those honorable stations."[91]

Another indirect benefit of the library association to the merchants was its contribution toward producing mutual good feeling, as well as discouraging the discordant spirit of partisanship whether political, religious, or other.[92] More positively, it was asserted that no member who took his reading seriously ever "defrauded his employer, or abused his confidence." "This it is [literary pursuits] which will render them good citizens—elevate them into patriots, and insure to society a race of men, whose intelligence and love of order will preserve it from the storms of civil revolution."[93] Moreover, an educational corrective had to be supplied for the benefit of those who had recently come to our shores and hadn't as yet been adequately informed as to the meaning of our institutions. Some measures had to be taken to modify their misinformed opinions which were beginning to produce disorder in certain circles.[94]

Whatever "correct" information the clerks failed to get from their reading they sometimes got from a lecturer. During the hard times of the late 1830's Edward Everett held forth on the erroneousness of instituting a comparison between the producing and the accumulating classes. While accumulation was the basis of commerce, he explained, it did not create commerce. In order to satisfy needs and desires, the enterprise of exchange was necessary; it was in this process of mutually beneficial exchange that accumulation was possible. It was a system of mutual accommodation. The difference between barbarism and civilization was inherent in the security gained by accumulation of capital. When one considered, too, that production could not go on without capital, that labor could not be employed without capital, it was incomprehensible that anyone should draw contrasts between capital and labor or should dislike the capitalists as a class. Just look at the comforts which have been produced for man by capitalist enterprise. It is unthinkable that government should invest in the branches of industry necessary to supply the wants of men. Capital must be given a free hand to expand.

When one came to analyze the causes of prejudice against capital he would see that it was a carry-over from the Old World where, in a semifeudal stratified society, the poor had reason to hate the rich. In the United States laws and unprecedented opportunity left the path open to all.

Large accumulations were necessary in order to keep smaller ones in action. Joint stock companies were justifiable as an instrument which allowed large capital investment on the part of those who possessed comparatively small accumulations. No money was hoarded; everything was invested in further business operation.

As desirable as equality of condition was, it was wrong to achieve it by an equal division of fortunes among the people. This would result only in general impoverishment. The right inheritance laws, philanthropic practices, "an effective system of popular education, would unquestionably restore harmony and concord to society and bring the great mass of the physical strength of the community into alliance with its moral and intellectual elements."[95]

DECLINE OF THE MECHANICS' AND MERCANTILE LIBRARIES

Although the mechanics' libraries continued to serve their purpose well beyond the middle of the century,[96] they gradually fell prey to the oncoming public libraries and to the weakening of their own economic base. Some interest was still being shown in mechanics' libraries in the last quarter of the nineteenth century;[97] but it is safe to say that by that time those in the smaller communities had died or had been absorbed by the public library. The apprentices' libraries in the largest communities seem to have persisted for several reasons: viz., the wealth of the organizations behind them, their

large, well-developed book collections, and even the sheer impetus acquired in the days of their popularity. An early example of the merger of one of these libraries to form a public library occured in Cincinnati—in 1856 the library of the Ohio Mechanics' Institute was combined with the Common School Library.[98] A somewhat later instance is noted at St. Joseph, Missouri, where the Mechanical Library was annexed to the public library of that city.[99]

Mercantile libraries suffered the same fate as the mechanics' and apprentices' libraries. Whereas they managed to keep alive in a few large cities, they virtually disappeared under the name "mercantile" in the hundreds of cities where they had existed. Even in Boston the Mercantile Library had to relinquish its identity.[100]

As in the case of the decline of mechanics' libraries, the sources yield very little which would explain their disappearance. One must infer that the mere existence of the public library with its superior book stocks caused the obsolescence of the older form. However, there is adequate evidence that hard times were felt keenly by the mercantile libraries;[101] that the number of subscribers fell off and income decreased correspondingly.[102] After the depression period, 1873-78, the removal of the Mercantile Library in New York brought the suggestion that the new building be constructed with a view to its ultimate transformation into a free public library.[103] There began to grow a consciousness that even the smallest fee would tend to keep readers out of libraries. It was noted that when the Mercantile Library of Peoria, Illinois, was turned over to the city and made free the borrowers register increased from 275 to 4,500.[104] In 1900 there was a proposed merger of the Philadelphia Mercantile with the Free Library of Philadelphia. The directors voted down the proposal.[105]

If one seeks the meaning of the rise and decline of the "occupational" libraries which flourished in the first half of the nineteenth century, he finds something like this: With the disappearance of equal position and wealth in all sectors of the American middle class some agency had to be instituted to carry on its cultural and utilitarian aims. In the first years of the mechanics' library institutions there was a great deal of stress on educating the apprentice upward to the solid position of the enterprising middle class, As there was an increase in the wage-earning portion of the lower middle class, and as it became less usual for the working mechanic to rise, paternalistic zeal transferred its attention to obtaining tax-supported free libraries.

The merchant group, at first secure and confident, seems to have lost its cohesiveness after the Civil War. The activities of finance and industrial capital doubtless made it difficult for merchants to continue maintaining a separate group interest. The greatest single factor to make inroads on the "territory" of these institutions was the free public library, whose position became stronger as the wage-earning group moved to numerical dominance in the American population.

FOOTNOTES

[1] C. R. Aurner, "Mechanics' institutions," *Iowa journal of history and politics*, XIX (1921),389-413.

[2] *Ibid.*

[3] William J. Rhees, *Manual of public libraries, institutions, and societies in the United States and British provinces of North America* (Philadelphia: J. B. Lippincott, 1859), p. 73. Benjamin Franklin, by the terms of his will, dedicated a large portion of his wealth to similar purposes. See Francis Newton Thorpe (ed.), *Benjamin Franklin and the University of Pennsylvania* ("U. S. Bureau of Education circular of information," No. 2 [Washington: U. S. Government Printing Office, 1892]), pp. 119-21.

[4] John H. Griscom, *Memoir of John Griscom* (New York: R. Carter & Bros., 1859), pp. 320-44.

[5] General Society of Mechanics and Tradesmen of the City of New York, *Some memorials of the late William Wood, Esq., the eminent philanthropist . . . presented in a report of the Apprentices' Library Committee to the General Society of Mechanics and Tradesmen of the City of New York, December 2, 1857* (New York: John Amerman, 1858), pp. 18–26. A letter written by De Witt Clinton to Wood illustrates both Clinton's interest in libraries and the role played by Wood in their establishment. See E. A. Fitzpatrick, *The educational views and influence of De Witt Clinton* (New York: Teachers College, Columbia University, 1911), p. 88.

[6] General Society . . . , *ibid.*, p. 17.

[7] General Society . . . , *Annals of the General Society of Mechanics and Tradesmen of the City of New York from 1785 to 1880; edited by Thomas Earle and Charles T. Congdon* (New York: The Society, 1882), pp. 60-61.

[8] General Society . . . , *Reports of the Library and School Committee* (New York: Mercein, 1829), p. 4.

[9] General Society . . . , *Inaugural address . . . February 4, 1857, by Thomas Earle* (New York: The Society, 1857), p. 3.

[10] General Society . . . , *Report, February 5, 1868*, p. 19.

[11] John F. Lewis, *History of the Apprentices' Library of Philadelphia, 1820-1920* (Philadelphia, 1924), p. 4. The "free" aspect of mechanics' and mercantile libraries had to be eliminated and a small subscription charge for apprentices introduced. The pressure of subscription libraries forced these institutions to charge for borrowing privileges.

[12] *Ibid.*, pp. 24-25 (quoted from the preamble to the charter).

[13] Most of this material was obtained from biographical sketches in the *Dictionary of American biography*.

[14] Rochester Athenaeum and Mechanics' Institute, *The charter and the constitution* (Rochester, 1840), p. 5; Bessie L. Pierce, *A history of Chicago* (New York: Knopf, 1937), I, 286.

[15] General Society . . . , *Annals*, p. 59; General Society . . . , *Charter and by-laws* (New York: Amerman, 1866), pp. 5, 20-22, 43-44; Rhees, *op. cit.*, pp. 73, 378-79.

[16] General Society . . . , *Annual report . . . Feb. 1, 1873*, p. 9; also *New York Daily Tribune*, September 24, 1850, p. 1, col. 3: "If a poor little ragged apprentice boy feels disposed to drink deep at the Pirenean Spring, where is he to go to slake his thirst? He can have access to no private library . . . . If he wanders into the valuable Library, established through the munificence of the late Mr. Astor, he will b told that there is no provision in the bequest which can embrace his case; he looks around with a sigh and . . . he sees the rich and well-educated enjoying the rich banquet, but, alas, he who is in search of knowledge is not an invited guest. He has only the inheritance of rags; his mind is clear, his intellect bright, his desire to learn and improve is intense, but his hands are black from labor, and his dress coarse from poverty . . . . He can enter here, as proudly as those who enter other libraries, there is no rude janitor who will thrust him forth to live and die in ignorance . . . ."

[17] General Society . . . , *Reports of the Library and School Committee*, pp. 4, 11.

[18] From preamble of 1829 quoted in David C. Haverstick, "History of the Mechanics' Library," *Lancaster County Historical Society*, IX (1905), 338.

[19] General Society . . . , *Reports of the Library and School Committee*, pp. 11-12.

[20] General Society . . . , *Annual report, 1894*, p. 13.

[21] John Sergeant, *An address delivered at the request of the managers of the Apprentices' Library Company of Philadelphia, November 23, 1832* (Philadelphia: James Kay, 1832), p. 34; see also *New York Daily Tribune*, September 4, 1850, p. 4, col. 6.

[22] *New York Daily Tribune*, September 24, 1850, p. 1, col. 4.

[23] Young Men's Association, Rochester, *Proceedings of the Young Men's Association at the first annual meeting, Nov. 26, 1838* (Rochester, N. Y.: Printed at the office of the *Daily advertiser*, by Luther Tucker, 1839), pp. 6-7; General Society . . . , *Reports of the Library and School Committee*, p. 9.

[24] General Society . . . , *ibid.*

[25] *American journal of education*, IV (1829), 538-39.

[26] Young Men's Association; Rochester, *op. cit.*, pp. 5-6.

[27] *American journal of education*, IV (1829), 66; Lewis, *op. cit.*, pp. 24-25.

[28] Pierce, *op. cit.*, p. 289; General Society . . . , *Annals*, pp. 319, 329.

[29] Sergeant, *op, cit.*, p. 33.

[30] John R. Commons *et al.*, *History of labour in the United States* (New York: Macmillan, 1935), I, 79.

[31] *Ibid.*, pp. 78-79.

[32] Haverstick, *op, cit.*, pp. 337-38; also General Society . . . , *Annual report, 1857*, p. 17 (from minutes of the meeting, March 17, 1819); General Society . . . , *Annals*, p. 321.

[33] George B. Emerson, "Mechanics' institutions," *American journal of education*, II (1827), 273-78.

[34] *Ibid.*, p. 273.

[35] *Ibid.*, p. 276; also Jesse Torrey, *The intellectual torch* (1815); reprinted Woodstock, Vermont: Elm Tree Press, 1912), p. 3.

[36] Emerson, *op. cit.*, p. 278; John Sayward, "The means and ends," *American laborer*, I (1843), 325; Sergeant, *op. cit.*, pp. 5, 8; also General Society . . . , *Reports of the Library and School Committee*, pp. 6-7.

[37] Sergeant, *op, cit.*, p. 10. A good statement of this and some of the ideas to follow is contained in Torrey, *op, cit.*, passim.

[38] Sergeant, *op, cit.*, p. 19; also *American journal of education*, IV (1829), 541.

[39] General Society . . . , *Reports of the Library and School Committee*, pp. 4-5.

[40] Quoted in *Library journal*, II (1877), 78.

[41] General Society . . . , *Annual report, 1894*, p.21.

[42] *Ibid.*, pp. 36-39; *ibid.*, *1895*, p.42.

[43] Sergeant, *op, cit.*, p. 23; *American journal of education*, IV (1829), 540.

[44] Sergeant, *op. cit.*, pp. 28-31; *American journal of education*, IV (1829), 538.

[45] General Society . . . , *Reports of the Library and School Committee*, pp. 3, 7-8.

[46] General Society . . . , *Annals*, pp. 324-34 (address of President Hutchinson, February 3, 1858).

[47] James L. Goodknight, *Evolution of the American library* (Lincoln, Ill., 1903), p. 4.

[48] San Francisco Mercantile Library, *First annual report of the president, 1853-54*, p.7.

[49] New York Mercantile Library Association, *Annual reports of the Board of Direction of the Mercantile Library Association of the City of New York, from 1821 to 1838* (New York: Reprinted for the Association, 1868), p. 91.

[50] *Ibid.*, p. 46.

[51] *Ibid.*, pp. 91, 99-100; John H. Gourlie, *An address delivered before the Mercantile Library Association at its eighteenth annual meeting, January 8, 1838* (New York: James Van Norden, 1839), pp. 10-12.

[52] The New York association is the basis of this treatment because of the availability and fulness of its reports. Although in the broad details of its history this association seems to typify the setup of others, the writer offers it as a good example rather than as a type.

[53] Gourlie, *op. cit.*, p. 6.

[54] New York Mercantile Library Association, *op, cit.*, p. 3.

[55] *Ibid.*, pp. 10, 16, 32, 37, 39.

[56] *Ibid.*, pp. 10-12.

[57] *Ibid.*, pp. 15-16, 19.

[58] *Ibid.*, pp. 23-24, 29-30.

[59] *Ibid.*, p. 34.

[60] *Ibid.*, p. 39.

[61] *Ibid.*, p. 101.

[62] *Ibid.*, pp. 6, 18, 83, 101.

[63] *Ibid.*, p. 62.

[64] Phillip Hone, *An address delivered before the Mercantile Library Association . . . October 3, 1843* (Boston: W. D. Ticknor, 1843), p. 23.

[65] *Ibid.*, p. 20; San Francisco Mercantile Library, *op. cit.*, p. 8.

[66] New York Mercantile Library Assocaition, *op. cit.*, p. 35.

[67] *Ibid.*, p. 41.

[68] *Ibid.*, p. 54.

[69] Gourlie, *op. cit.*, p. 16

[70] New York Mercantile Library Association, *Seventeenth annual report, 1837*, pp. 9-10.

[71] *Ibid.*, pp. 7-8

[72] New York Mercantile Library Association, *Annual reports of the Board . . . 1821 to 1838*, p. 24.

[73] George W. Tyler, *Address delivered before the Mercantile Library Association of Boston on the Evening of their sixteenth anniversary, March 11, 1836* (Boston: Hitchcock, 1836), pp. 1 ff.; Robert C. Winthrop, *An address delivered before the Boston Mercantile Library Association on the occasion of their twenty-fifth anniversary, October, 15, 1845* (Boston: Marvin & Co., 1845), pp. 7-9.

[74] San Francisco Mercantile Library, *op, cit.*, pp. 12-13; cf. Mercantile Library Association of New Orleans, *First annual report, November, 1858* (New Orleans: William Bloomfield, 1858), p. 4.

[75] New York Mercantile Library Association, *Annual reports of the Board . . .* , p. 25.

[76] *Ibid.*, pp. 32, 40-41, 49-50, 53-54, 57, 62, 67.

[77] Gourlie, *op. cit.*, p. 8.

[78] Tyler, *op. cit.*, pp. 7-8, 26-30.

[79] New York Mercantile Library Association, *Annual reports of the Board* . . . , pp. 42, 50.

[80] Tyler, *op. cit.,* p. 32; Edward Everett, *An address before the Mercantile Library Association* (Boston: W. D. Ticknor, 1838), pp. 35-36.

[81] New York Mercantile Library Association, *Annual reports of the Board* . . . , p. 117; Tyler, *op. cit.,* p. 8.

[82] Gourlie, *op, cit.,* p. 18.

[83] Hone, *op. cit.,* pp. 20-21.

[84] Tyler, *op. cit.,* p. 6; George Lunt, *Anniversary poem delivered before the Mercantile Library Association of Boston, October 3, 1843* (Boston: W. D. Ticknor, 1843).

[85] New York Mercantile Library Association, *Seventeenth annual report,* p. 7.

[86] New York Mercantile Library Association, *Annual reports of the Board* . . . , pp. 4, 11, 77; Hone, *op.* cit., pp. 21, 24-25.

[87] E.g., Robert C. Winthrop, *Algernon Sidney: a lecture delivered before the Boston Mercantile Library Association, December, 21, 1853* (Boston: Whipple, 1854).

[88] Tyler, op. *cit.*

[89] Hone, *op. cit.;* pp. 26-44 of this address consist in a treatise on the study of history and oratory; see also New York Mercantile Library Association, *Annual reports of the Board* . . . , pp. 76, 88, 110.

[90] James T. Fields, *Anniversary poem, delivered before the Mercantile Library Association of Boston, September 13, 1838* (Boston: W. D. Ticknor, 1838).

[91] New York Mercantile Library Association, *Seventeenth annual report,* 1837, pp. 8-9; Gourlie, op. *cit.,* pp. 17-19.

[92] New York Mercantile Library Association, *Annual reports of the Board* . . . , pp. 80-84.

[93] Gourlie, *op. cit.,* p. 16.

[94] Tyler, *op. cit.,* p. 31.

[95] Everett, *op. cit.,* p. 40.

[96] *Report from the Select Committee on Public Libraries; together with the proceedings of the committee, minutes of evidence, and appendix,* pp. 97-104, quoted by James Howard Wellard in *Book selection: its principles and practice* (London: Grafton, 1937), p. 22.

[97] Cf. "Mansfield, Ohio, Library of the Order of American Mechanics (1872)" in C. B. Galbreath, *Sketches of Ohio libraries* (Columbus, Ohio: Heer, 1902), p. 218; also "Altoona, Pennsylvania, Mechanics' Library," *Library journal,* XIV (1889), 483.

[98] U. S. Bureau of Education, *Report on art and industry* (Washington: U. S. Government Printing Office, 1897), III, 614.

[99] *Library journal,* XVI (1891), 284.

[100] William I. Fletcher, "The proprietary library in relation to the public library movement," in Gertrude G. Dury (ed.), *The library and its organization* (New York: H. W. Wilson, 1924), pp. 25-26.

[101] Mercantile Library Association of New Orleans, *op. cit.,* p. 6.

[102] Mercantile Library Association of Baltimore, *Annual report, 1874,* p. 4.

[103] *Library journal,* IV (1879), 443-44.

[104] Henry H. Barber, "The free public library," in A. E. Bostwick (ed.), *The library and society* (New York: H. W. Wilson, 1920), p. 179. Other examples are Tacoma, Washington (1894), and Denver, Colorado (1898). See *American library annual* (1916-17), pp. 277-366.

[105] *Library journal,* XXV (1900), 139.

Read a Book and Sin No More: The Early YMCA Libraries

Doris M. Fletcher

Many of those who supported libraries saw them as forces which could effectively combat evil. The early YMCA founders were especially strong in their belief that YMCA libraries were vital as a place "for young men and others to spend their evenings in, without resorting to the haunts of vice and dissipation."

In the following short paper, Doris Fletcher discusses the reasons these libraries came into existence, how they pioneered in a number of areas (YMCA librarians considered the book expendable!), and the way in which their numbers decreased as the number of public libraries began to increase.

The theme of public relations, which has taken hold of the modern libraries with such vigor, is not so new as our Librarians in the Grey Flannel Suits may think. Several years before the large urban public libraries opened their doors, the YMCA libraries were devising ways of luring the public into their reading rooms, *not* away from anything so simple as our present problem of TV, but from the old problem of *Sin* itself. This, in case anyone has forgotten, takes some doing.

At that time thousands of young men were being spilled into the cities on one of those waves set in motion by the Industrial Revolution, and the nineteenth century was only beginning to concern itself with their welfare. According to the introduction to the 1851 constitution of this country's first YMCA:

> Christians in Boston have long seen with sorrow the allurements to evil that surround the young men of the city, and desired to do something that should counteract them . . . . Many a heart has mourned, many a prayer ascended, on this account

As the New York Association said a year later:

> Our objects are no less than the prevention of the ruin, physical and spiritual, which overtakes so large a portion of the multitude of young men constantly arriving in our city, destitute of Christian associates and connections.

With this as its stated purpose it is gratifying to note that the first act of founding of every YMCA as it spread across the country, was to open a read-ing room and library. Library service, semi-private at best, left much to be desired. William J. Rhees, first librarian of the YMCA in Washington, D. C., describes the situation in his *Manual of Public Libraries:*

> At the time of the formation of the Association [1852] there was no popular or general library or reading-room in the city, open in the evening. It had long been felt that an establishment of this kind was much needed; and in carrying out the plans of the Association it was important to provide a suitable place for young men and others to spend their evenings in, without resorting to the haunts of vice and dissipation.

Offering competition to the "haunts of vice and dissipation" may not be considered the proper province of a library, but it must be admitted the challenge was as great as any library could have. In meeting it, the YMCA libraries were forced into a policy of some quite modern public relations.

In the first place they had to show a hardheaded concern for appearance and accessibility. They wanted no part of the marble stairs in which public libraries eventually delighted. Street level entrances, lights, rugs, white paint, warmth, were considered effective means of battling their enemy, the saloon. Excerpts from paragraphs on "The Choice of Rooms" in the YMCA's *Quarterly Reporter* of April 1858 set forth the ideal library:

> Where rents are not too exorbitant, we invariably prefer that they should be located on the principal street of the city or village . . . . We would have large and distinct, though not ostentatious signs . . . . If

SOURCE: Reprinted from Doris M. Fletcher, "Read a Book and Sin No More: The Early YMCA Libraries," *Wilson Library Bulletin* 31 (March, 1957), pp. 521-522+, by permission of the author and publisher. Copyright © 1957 by the H. W. Wilson Company.

possible, the rooms should be accessible through the entire day.

The rooms should, wherever possible, be upon the first floor . . . . Better have the rooms small, on the first or second floor, than spacious on the fourth or fifth.

The reading room should be carpeted, whenever it can be afforded. There is an air about a bare floor extremely repulsive to many young men . . . . Wall decorations, paintings, engravings, etc., add materially to the attractions of the rooms . . . . The manner of filing the papers, etc., must be left to the taste of the committees, who should, however, lose no opportunity to display the literature to the best advantage. Many a young man has neglected to read a good book or paper because it was not just at his hand.

Library rooms should, where possible, be separate and apart from the reading rooms, that the readers may not be disturbed by those coming simply to draw books.

To man these public-relations-conscious libraries it was natural that the YMCA should require librarians with some rather unique public relations abilities. If we grumble today at the growing demand that we be glamorous and outgoing as well as able and efficient, we should consider without envy the lot of those early YMCA librarians. They were expected to save souls, lend money, rescue the starving, find good boardinghouses for strange young men, suggest places of employment, visit the sick and dying, reform the intoxicated, and always turn a sympathetic ear to those in trouble. Their reports list the good deeds done along with the number of books acquired and circulated.

One would think that with all these social welfare activities the YMCA librarians would be excused from being bookmen, too. But this was not entirely the case. The December 1859 *Young Men's Christian Journal* is unrelenting in its expectations of what a good YMCA librarian should be:

It will become him to ever have an eye single to the important duties of his position. As in the case of one entrusted with the library of a purely literary or scientific institution, he should have a thorough knowledge of books and authors; but he must not rest with this. It will be expected, and justly so, that he will display a readiness to converse with those who frequent the rooms, to aid them in their researches, and, above all to have a deep personal interest in their spiritual well-being.

In many little things the Librarian will need to exercise a constant and scrupulous care; such, for instance, as promptly opening the rooms, properly regulating the same, registering the number of visitors, recording the drawing of books, etc., etc. He should prepare a monthly report of his labors, to be read to the Association. It will generally be his own fault if the document is destitute of interest. His daily intercourse

with the members, and even casual observation, will supply abundant material for valuable suggestion, and render him competent to judge intelligently of the Association's progress and prospects.

In spite of these demands, the job of "librarian" often attracted men who really cared for books. Reuben B. Poole became librarian of the New York YMCA library in 1865 and remained there for thirty years. At the time of his death in 1895 he was president of the New York State Library Association. The Washington YMCA library from the beginning had the services of William J. Rhees, chief clerk of the Smithsonian Institution, author of the work on the origin and history of the Smithsonian, and compiler of *The Manual of Public Libraries, Institutions and Societies,* 1859.

With or without book-wise librarians, the most fortunate influence of the public relations policy possibly came in the book collections. It tended to save them from the fate of becoming exclusively and narrowly theological. Such books proved to be too low a drawing card even in the 1850's. Many of the early annual reports of the individual librarians showed an awareness of public demand which should have helped to broaden their collections. "Travel is most popular," or "Irving is most called for," they noted and no doubt struggled to supply the need as best they could.

They also had good advice to follow in articles in *The Watchman* by Reuben Poole and in the speech by Cephas Brainerd at the Cleveland Convention in 1881:

When young men are clamoring for McCarthy's *History of Our Own Times,* don't run off and buy the costly edition of Dr. Johnson, for the reason that no library is complete without it. When they want *Endymion,* don't buy Dr. South's *Sermons,* valuable in their place as they are. If there is a crowd of medical students in the rooms—as at Louisville—get books in their specialty, that are not in the library of their school. In short, coax the young men, by giving them according to their several appetites, the best literary food they crave, or that they can be made to crave.

And, as might be expected in these libraries, there was now and then evidence of censorship trouble, as much political as moral. In 1853 the Library Committee of the New York YMCA successfully excluded from the library "a book called *Uncle Tom's Cabin.*" But in 1857, when the Library Committee of that same Association withdrew the New York *Express* from the reading rooms, a violent and bitter storm of protest followed. The pamphlet, *Report of the Investigating*

Committee, although published a hundred years ago, has a contemporary ring. *The Express,* as a result of this investigation, was eventually restored.

Since only a small portion (one quarter) of the books in these YMCA libraries were acquired by purchase, it is quite possible that, with a few exceptions, their early collections were handicapped by the gifts they had to accept in the way of discards from personal libraries or heavy, unreadable books given for the improvement and advancement of morals.

But these early librarians, aware of the attractions on the other side of the street, or tracks, counteracted their ponderous volumes with a very astute policy of providing home town newspapers to their homesick public. Boston reports in 1854 some forty or more papers including almost all the available local county papers in New England. New York, Chicago, Washington provided foreign newspapers as well. Usually the YMCA library was the only place in the city where such newspaper collections could be found. Public libraries, when they did arrive, were slow to offer this particular form of reading. The Boston Public had its first newspaper room in 1893.

We are glad to say that so far as clientele went many of these libraries were open freely to the public. In St. Paul any citizen or stranger might use the library, or any young man so long as he had "fair" moral character. In Macon, the YMCA had taken over the Mechanic's Library and any citizen could use the YMCA library by paying $1 a year. In Manchester, New Hampshire, young men were charged $1 and ladies 50 cents. In Montreal, if you were poor or in jail or in the hospital, you might have your books free.

Books in the YMCA were always expendable. Their workers took them wherever they went— into foreign cities, into the railroad towns, into Civil War camps where their "bound volumes" were distributed along with their "loaves of fresh, soft bread."

As a final act of public relations the YMCA libraries can be credited with the unusual act of not outliving their usefulness. When public libraries were established and the American Library Association came into being, the YMCA libraries withdrew from the field. They could not compete and, besides, they had found other ways of keeping their young men from ruin. Their readers and often their book collections were turned over to the public libraries; and, if their original mission of combatting sin was not accepted, at least some of the methods of dealing with it have found favor.

The Rise and Development of School Library Service in Its Relation to Significant Movements in Education

Henry L. Cecil and Willard A. Heaps

From the beginnings of American history, we find a definite conception of the need for books and libraries to supplement the local school system. In the following paper Henry Cecil and Willard Heaps trace the development of an important nineteenth century predecessor of modern school libraries. The tax-supported school district library was in many ways intended to serve adults, but as the authors point out, it also contributed to the future growth of school libraries.

During the early quarter of the nineteenth century a number of prominent Americans having diverse interests embarked on trips to Europe with the avowed purpose of securing new ideas to put into practice when they returned home. Included in one group were Governor De Witt Clinton of New York, William L. Marcy of New York, and Horace Mann of Massachusetts, who were interested in education, especially in methods of educating the young. Horace Mann devoted most of his time abroad to studying various school systems, especially those of Prussia, where the influence of Pestalozzi had been finding its way into the Prussian schools. The inspiration received by these men and brought back to our own shores had a great influence on the origin and growth of school libraries in the United States.

These educational leaders and others of the day realized that the development of intelligent citizens depended not only upon teaching reading but also on providing reading opportunities. It was for the purpose of providing such opportunities that the school district libraries came into being.

A brief résumé of the rise, initial popularity, and decline of these libraries in the first three states providing legislation for them will serve to illustrate the difficulties encountered in the struggle for their establishment and maintenance.

NEW YORK THE PIONEER STATE

Governor De Witt Clinton, in his message to the New York state legislature in 1827 recommending the formation of a better common school system, first proposed that a small library of books should be placed in every school house; but it was not until 1835 that the friends of the free schools saw their hopes realized in the passage of a law which permitted the voters in any school district to levy a tax to begin a library, and a tax of $10 each succeeding year to provide for its increase. Much apathy was shown, and a few districts voted the necessary tax.

In 1838, Governor Marcy decided that something must be done to get the people in a receptive state of mind toward the idea of the district school library. In his inaugural address he recommended that the legislature appropriate a share of the United States Deposit Fund for this purpose. The New York state legislature passed an act respecting school district libraries on April 15, 1839.

After the New York legislature adopted Marcy's recommendation it was provided that $55,000 of the fund should be set aside for three years to be applied to the district school libraries, with a further provision that the towns were also required to raise a like sum for the same purpose. General John A. Dix, then Secretary of State, and ex-officio Superintendent of Schools, from the first a zealous and powerful friend of the movement, was charged with the execution of the law. The law met with favor everywhere except among those who opposed the common schools themselves, so that General Dix's successor was able in 1841 to report 422,459 volumes in school libraries.

In 1842, the number of volumes in the district school libraries had increased to 620,125, a growth in one year of more than 200,000 volumes. In 1843, authority was granted the school districts to use the library fund for the purchase of school apparatus, and after that had been sufficiently obtained, for the payment of teachers' wages, providing that each district containing more than fifty children between five and sixteen years of age should have a library of not less than 125 volumes. Year by year the school libraries grew and multiplied until in 1853 they contained 1,604,210 volumes. Then began a period of decline.

Volumes began disappearing at an alarming rate. Though $55,000 had been appropriated each year for purchase, the number steadily decreased. In the 1875 report the evil was revealed as being worse than ever, as evidenced by the table included in the 1875 report of the Superintendent of Public Instruction.[1]

1860	1,286,536 volumes
1865	1,269,125 volumes
1870	986,697 volumes
1871	928,316 volumes
1872	874,193 volumes
1873	856,555 volumes
1874	831,554 volumes

Since the total amount of appropriations since 1838 had been $2,035,100, the Superintendent recommended that the law be repealed, since it was obvious that library monies had been applied freely to the payment of teachers' wages.

ORIGIN OF SCHOOL-DISTRICT LIBRARIES IN MASSACHUSETTS

School libraries in Massachusetts owe their origin to Horace Mann, who, in 1837, gave up a promising political and legal career to become the first secretary of the first board of education in the United States, the State Board of Education of Massachusetts. Through his influence an enabling school district library law was enacted in 1837, by the same legislature that created the State Board of Education, allowing school districts to raise and expend $30 for one year, and $10 each succeeding year to begin and support a school library, the school committee to select the books. No doubt the legislature was influenced by the Act of the state of New York which had provided somewhat similar legislation in 1835. However, few districts availed themselves of the authority thus granted, and Horace Mann became alarmed, and as a result included in his 1839[2] report a section on district

libraries in which he elaborated on "useful" reading as compared with "amusing" and "fictitious" reading, and indicated that the hope of education in Massachusetts lay with the establishment of a program whereby a school library should be placed in every district in the state. This report is outstanding for its succinct statement of the purposes and values of reading, the more remarkable since it was written a century ago.

Again in his famous 1840 lecture "On District-School Libraries"[3] he outlined the plan, emphasizing that common-school libraries were meant for the poor as well as rich, and that since learning to read was the principle purpose of school attendance, a supply of materials for such reading was a necessity. He went on to elaborate upon good and bad reading, maintaining that it was the function of the school to improve taste as well as to build it.

Four years later, in 1841, there were only 10,000 volumes in all school libraries in the state. It was estimated at this time that 100 towns within the state were without any kind of libraries save private.

The friends of school libraries did not despair, and in 1842, owing to their unwearied efforts, a resolution was passed appropriating to each school district that would raise an equal amount, the sum of $15 for library purposes. Neither this resolution nor that of 1843 extending its provisions to cities and towns not hitherto divided into school districts, gave more than $15 to any one library. In 1842 one-fourth of these districts formed libraries, at an expense to the state of $11,355; they contained by estimate 33,000 to 40,000 volumes.

In 1843 the school library reached its height as shown by the number of applications for their establishment under the law of 1842. The applications for aid gradually decreased from 1843 to 1849 when, according to the report of the State Board of Education for 1849, the value of all the libraries was $42,707 and the number of volumes 91,539. When Mann left the Secretaryship of the State Board of Education in this year, the school library was a definite part of the Massachusetts school system.

But it was not to remain a part of the system for long, for legislation in 1850 repealed the law. In its place an act was passed providing for the establishment and maintenance of public libraries by taxation. This legislation, which became effective in 1851, gave impetus to the growth of town libraries. They became so popular in a short time that they superseded the school libraries.

To Horace Mann must be given credit for educating the people of Massachusetts to the point of becoming library-minded. His lectures and writings on the value of common-school libraries during his whole term of office aroused the interests of citizens in all sections of the state, and made easier the establishment of the town library because it was felt the school library could not fill the two important needs, that of the school and the public.

SCHOOL-DISTRICT LIBRARIES IN MICHIGAN

The Michigan school law of 1837 empowered the voters of each district to raise by tax a sum not exceeding $10 annually for the purchase and increase of district libraries. Each district that levied the library tax became entitled to its proportion of the clear proceeds of all fines collected within the several counties for any breach of the peace laws, and also its proportion of its equivalent for exemption from military service, which fines and equivalents should be paid over by the several officers collecting the same to the county treasurers to be apportioned by the number of children in the townships between the ages of 5 and 17 years.

An amendment, in 1840, directed that the funds arising from fines and exemptions should be used for library purposes only. The Act of 1843 provided for the establishment of township libraries and for the annual income of $25 for each, to be raised by taxation; it permitted the electors, after a library had acquired 200 volumes, to reduce the amount to be raised by taxation to a sum of not less than $10 annually; and it was made the duty of the State Superintendent of Schools to publish a list of books suitable for school libraries. The law also empowered the election of a town to raise by special tax $50 additional for the purchase of books for the library. The act of 1859 authorized the voters of any town to determine what proportion of the amount raised by taxation for school purposes should be used to purchase books for the town library; it also authorized the directors to divide the township libraries into district libraries.

The law of 1869 permitted the electors of any town to unite the several district school libraries and form a township library. The electors of a school district might vote a tax for library purposes.

One of the first acts of the new Michigan State Superintendent of Schools, Mr. Gregory, in 1870, was an attempt to have the law changed, but his attempt failed and he said "If we could have an honest administration of the fine moneys and ten percent of the two mill tax, I am sanguine we should soon be proud of our school libraries."

The Michigan State Superintendent of Schools report for 1873 discusses school libraries and from it the following statement is gleaned:

> While it must be admitted that there are not a few who are decidedly opposed to school libraries as a useless appliance in our school work, and many more quite indifferent to the subject, there are yet a host of earnest citizens and many among them our most active educators, who believe the value of school libraries, properly managed, can hardly be estimated.[4]

While nineteen states, by 1876, had provided legislation of some sort designed to promote the development of public school libraries, the movement in general was considered a failure. Defects in original legislation, lack of state administrative coordination and supervision, and the lack of library techniques and trained personnel for each school were all handicaps to its success.

The school district library, though destined to be superseded in most areas by the town library and the public library of today, nevertheless served an important part in school library development. Although its usefulness in the school was hindered by the fact that it was organized primarily for adults and hence failed to consider children in its selection of books, its administration by school authorities, as provided by law, and its usual location in the school house, guaranteed its future consideration as school equipment.

By 1876 the movement for public libraries was on the ascendancy and with their rise into prominence was to come a new form of school library development.

FOOTNOTES

[1] New York Superintendent of Public Instruction, *Twenty-First Annual Report,* February 10, 1875, p. 26-7.
[2] Horace Mann, *1839 Report* of the Secretary of the Board of Education, p. 10-60.
[3] Horace Mann, *Lectures and Annual Reports on Education,* 1867. Lecture VI, p. 297-330.
[4] Michigan State Superintendent of Schools, *Report for 1873,* p. 70.

The American College Library

Howard Clayton

In the following essay, Howard Clayton traces the development of college libraries in this country from 1800 to 1860. In doing so he pinpoints the social, economic, and intellectual factors which influenced the college libraries' growth, both directly and indirectly. These same factors, to greater or lesser degrees, are affecting library growth today.

When compared to present-day standards, the academic library of 1800 is often thought of as an ineffectual appendage to institutions that were themselves objects of charity. To begin with, no college in 1800 had a collection of more than 13,000 volumes and the smallest of them, Rutgers, probably had a library of no more than one hundred books (28). Moreover, such libraries had to wage a continuous battle against fires, wars, and pillaging, while relying for support on donations from people who lived far from the campus. Then too, the college library of 1800 was hampered by severe physical limitations, for the crude furnishings found in most of these libraries must have seemed austere and uninviting even to people who had grown accustomed to privations.

The academic library of 1800 was weak because higher education was weak. Indeed, the twenty-five colleges existing in the United States when John Adams left the presidency had no more than a foothold in the cultural and economic setting of early nineteenth century America. Moreover, this was as true for the state-supported institutions as it was for the private colleges; in fact, the relative stability of the latter, at least as typified by the nine colonial colleges, contrasted sharply with the marginal existence of the three public universities in Georgia, Vermont, and North Carolina. One reason for this general impoverishment was that the nation had not yet developed a population large enough to supply colleges with students, facilities, and money. For example, only on the coastline between Virginia and Massachusetts did the population of 1800 range as high as from 18 to 45 inhabitants per square mile, and only four of the nation's largest cities could boast of a population which exceeded 10,000 persons. (34:51)

Yet, it should not be presumed these institutions were impotent and without meaning. There is evidence, in fact, that considerable leadership came from among graduates of these colleges. Three of the five men who drafted the Declaration of Independence were graduates of the colonial college; furthermore, four of the five members making up Washington's first cabinet were also products of these schools (33). Such circumstances indicate that even in pre-Revolutionary times, when theology was the cornerstone of its curriculum, the American college was entirely capable of equipping men of action and imagination for service in the demanding field of public affairs.

During the early part of the nineteenth century, then, the American college was playing a useful role even though it was forced to operate on a subsistence basis. This Spartan approach to education meant that while all colleges wanted a library, no institution had the resources to provide for more than a small collection of books. But even if these schools had been able to tap great sources of wealth, they still would have had difficulty in building quality collections, for book publishing was but a tiny enterprise during the early 1800's. Evans (11), for example, lists only 39,162 publications for the entire period 1639-1800, and by their very nature many of these materials could not possibly have been available to all college libraries. The same situation obtained for periodicals, for even had libraries subscribed to every American magazine published in 1800, they would have found that the number scarcely exceeded a dozen.[1] (3), (4), (6), (24).

Such a situation meant that many materials had to be imported from Europe and England. This in itself resulted in a scarcity of books for colleges

SOURCE: Reprinted from Howard Clayton, "The American College Library, 1800-1860," *Journal of Library History* 3 (April 1968), pp. 120-137, by permission of the author and publisher. Copyright © 1968 by the School of Library Science, Florida State University.

prior to 1800; but, as serious as this difficulty was, it still did not have as deleterious effect as did the spirit of illiberality that hampered acquisitions work everywhere during this early time. In 1793, for example, an audit committee of the Trustees found that the purchase of Boyden's *Collection of Prints* by the College of New Jersey—later to become Princeton—was such "a very expensive and totally unnecessary article," that the bill would have to be charged to the president personally (26:304). Because such attitudes were commonplace, it is understandable that the collections at Princeton, Bowdoin, the University of Virginia, and Yale numbered only about 8,000 volumes each in 1829. (3).

Even the meager materials available in the academic libraries of the early nineteenth century were not very well used. Good teaching in that era was necessarily rare; in fact, the faculty had little opportunity to excel. Teachers were usually younger men who aspired to enter the ministry, and as such they were not only poorly paid and motivated, but were often called upon to teach the full range of subjects as well. Furthermore, they had to popularize education, among both students and parents, for if the pupil left school it meant the end of a tuition-paying customer. The president's lot was hardly any better, since he was left with the task of being the sole administrator, of conducting religious services, of raising money, of recruiting students, and of teaching courses to the senior class.

The importance of libraries to education, then, was necessarily limited because men who comprised the faculty could rarely lead a scholarly life. Those who did not enter the ministry, and who could content themselves with a life of self-denial, often stayed with their institution 40 or 50 years. In this process piety supplanted intellectual promise as the prime requisite for an outstanding faculty, and the result was almost always an absence of intellectualism, or spirit of scholarly inquisitiveness. Such a condition not only proved inimical to the academic library, but it also went a long way toward explaining the attitude expressed by Mark Hopkins when he said, "You read books. I don't read books, in fact I never did read any books." (25:504) While modern-day historians would probably credit such an outlook to a naive nineteenth-century faith in experience, rather than to a basic anti-intellectualism, it is nevertheless difficult to believe this concept did not work against the library's development. Therefore, from the standpoint of a librarian, Eliphalet Nott of Union College expressed an equally objectionable attitude when he said, "I care less for Greek than you do, and less for books, generally, as a means of educational discipline." (27:1:155)

If descriptions of early nineteenth-century methods of teaching are valid, it is not surprising that books were unimportant as a means of educational discipline. Classes began early and lasted through the day, being interrupted only by prayers. The customary fare was recitation and textbooks, with little more than singing and the writing of verse to break this cycle. The products of such an education supposedly received a mixture of classical scholarship and theological concepts, the former having come from Renaissance thinking and the latter from Reformation doctrine. Occasionally some far-sighted individual or group could be found who wished to break away from this pattern (2), (17), (19); but such efforts were rare, for the predominant mood concerning genuine liberalization of the curriculum was usually one of intolerance.

Another reason for the relative impotence of the academic library was that many pre-Civil War colleges were sponsored by groups who were neither intellectually minded nor economically affluent. As early as 1776, almost every popular religious sect had either planned or arranged financial backing for a college of its own. But while the training of clergymen supplied the motivation for such exuberance in college founding, not all of these sponsoring denominations actually favored a highly educated ministry. Such a paradox was especially prevalent among Methodists, Baptists, Disciples, Friends, and United Brethren groups, where evangelical fervor took precedence over scholarship and bookish sources of learning. This is understandable when one remembers that the appeal of such sects was to the underprivileged, the rank-and-file, the frontier lay preacher, and the circuit rider. However, the result at many of the colleges founded by such groups was that a situation developed in which it was impossible to determine whether the suffering of the library's quantitative or qualitative standards was more acute.

The religious atmosphere generated at these small denominational schools could also be found at the tax-supported colleges. While many of the new states made constitutional provision for a public university, the schools that ultimately emerged from such foresight took on an atmosphere which in many ways was not very different from that of the denominational college. Twenty-one state universities were founded before 1860 (30:133); yet, because church sponsorship of higher education remained dominant throughout the Middle Period, it was not until after the Civil War that public universities became significant. Tax-supported colleges, then, were caught in the same educational and economic outlook as that which permeated the denominational campus, and because of this it is not surprising that they demonstrated no more zeal for a quality library than did the private schools. Nor is it any wonder that Charles C. Jewett saw fit to characterize American colleges of this time as "mostly eleemosynary institutions. . . . [whose] libraries are frequently the chance aggregations of the gifts of charity: too many of them discarded, as well nigh worthless, from the shelves of the donors." (29:39) From this, it is easy to understand why the library in both types of colleges was typically a collection of gifts, old books, reference works, and standard editions, open only a few hours per week, managed by persons without professional training, and little used by students.

The example of the University of North Carolina is probably typical of the way library programs were developed in public institutions. From the Minutes of the Trustees (38), it would appear that the Board originally had an appreciation for the place of a library in its new university. Indeed, this attitude went beyond mere declarations because from later Minutes, viz., January 3, 1795, it can be seen that the Trustees took direct action in the library's behalf by specifically commissioning a bookcase and a bookplate for its use. Later in the same year, December 7, 1795, the Board went even further, for it then appropriated at least fifty dollars for the purchase of forty-six books whose titles they itemized in the minutes (39). As was the case in other colleges during this period, approval was given for the assessment of student fees so that books could be purchased.

Unfortunately, any good intentions further manifested by the Trustees during the early part of the 19th century proved to be short lived, for the period beginning with 1824 and lasting through Reconstruction was a distressing one for the North Carolina University library. As late as 1869, North Carolina's library was reported to have holdings of no more than seven thousand volumes, and even this figure doesn't give a true picture, because at least 1,897 of these volumes were acquired in 1859, subsequent to the death of Prof. Elisha Mitchell in the preceding year.

The library's plight during the second quarter of the 19th century is seen to be even more dismal when it is noted that from 1824 until 1869 the only other acquisitions were: a gift to the University of sixty volumes; twenty-five volumes from the Smithsonian Institution; 218 state documents; and 1,500 pieces from the federal government (7:5).

Thomas Jefferson was one of the first to be influential in establishing a college that would break this pattern. Jefferson brooded for many years about higher education's lack of concern for modern history, modern languages, and the applied sciences $(16)^2$; moreover, he wanted colleges to espouse frankly the concepts of natural law, reason, and observation. At first, he hoped significant change along these lines could be effected at William and Mary; but, when such efforts came to nothing, he turned his thoughts toward the establishment of an entirely new university that would be structured around some of his most cherished notions.[3] This too, however, proved to be difficult and it was only after many years of frustration and disappointment that Jefferson finally saw his dream become a reality in the establishment of the University of Virginia at Charlottesville.

Among the extraordinary educational achievements of Jefferson was the incorporation of a library into his plan of study. This was no token effort on the part of the nation's third president, for Mr. Jefferson personally planned the library building, chose the initial collection, arranged for its purchase, classified the materials, and played a large part in selecting the first two librarians (9). Great emphasis was placed on the acquisition of a good collection, and because of this Francis Walker Gilmer was sent to Europe to choose materials and arrange for their purchase. In addition, the book company of Cummings, Hilliard and Co., of Boston, was retained to procure other materials over an extended period of time. As a consequence the University of Virginia library in 1826 probably contained all the material common to college libraries of the early nineteenth century, plus good holdings in English, French, German, ancient, and modern literature.

Jefferson was also concerned about how the university library would be serviced. With this in mind, he personally formulated rules for its governance and supervised the cataloging of books. The library began with an appropriation of $10,000, and soon thereafter Jefferson ordered another $15,000 worth of materials from Hilliard. In addition, the library subscribed to all the principal American and English reviews, and owned the standard sets in law and medicine. Other innovations brought about by Jefferson included a library committee, a central location on the campus for the building, and the concept of a collection with authoritative coverage in all fields.

Unfortunately, much of the enthusiasm for such an approach to education ended with the death of Jefferson. After 1826, the library at the University of Virginia went into decline because of lack of income, attention, and interest. With such elements missing, the program was soon curtailed; and, because the initial outlay for library materials and facilities was substantial, a low priority was given to further acquisitions. Even the personal library of Jefferson did not find its way to the college, for the majority of it went to creditors. Ultimately, the university did receive 6,800 volumes of this collection, but this was the last contribution of any size until 1836 when James Madison left part of his library and $1,500 in money to the library as endowment (1:186-7).

Inattention accorded the academic library during this era was the result of circumstances far more complicated than mere official unconcern. Money has already been mentioned as a problem, but it should be emphasized that virtually none of the American colleges before 1860 were ever far from bankruptcy. This was particularly true of the western colleges, for every one of them was reduced to begging from Easterners just so they could keep their doors open. And while it is true that John Lowell, John Jacob Astor, and Peter Cooper all made some contribution to libraries and education before 1860, the huge gifts of the country's noted benefactors did not begin until after the Civil War. Then too, the decision in the Dartmouth College case brought an end to public funds for private education, while those principles that came to be the hallmark of Jacksonian Democracy resulted in a further decline of popular support for higher education.

This latter point is especially important to anyone examining the sociology of higher education, for it illustrates an ambivalence toward advanced learning that has been a traditional part of American thought. Because hundreds of colleges were founded throughout this era, higher education must have been important to innumerable persons who had but little schooling of their own. Yet, a popular notion, simultaneously held, was

that colleges were for America's privileged classes, and from 1800 to 1860 the climate of opinion increasingly became one in which domination by the common man was idolized and rugged individualism ruled supreme. The chief concerns of the country were not along intellectual lines, for the overwhelming majority of persons were more interested in physical work and in earning a living than in mastering theoretical refinements traditionally derived from bookish sources.

Clearing a wilderness, settling land, and fighting the adversities of nature were typical American preoccupations throughout the Middle Period. This being the case, it is hardly any wonder that the concept of a gentleman-scholar, leading a life of leisure and contemplation, was not in favor. The American culture of this time had little need of a specialized labor force and it felt no regret for the absence of a tradition in art and music. Consequently, a hard-working population that was at least twenty-two percent illiterate (35:206) was in no mood to provide vast amounts of money for a college education that was believed to be largely superfluous.

The colleges for their part proved equally obstinate. Attempts to bring about only partial reform in the curriculum were stoutly resisted and all efforts to modernize a basically classical education proved fruitless. George Ticknor was one of the most notable advocates of change, but even he achieved only negligible results at Harvard. In 1823, this noted scholar gave it as his opinion that Harvard's twenty or more teachers, as well as its three hundred students, were busying themselves with the same things that obtained when the college had only a president and a few tutors (31:I:357). Ticknor was anxious to divide the college into departments, limit the choice of subjects and alter the proficiency examinations. He felt that until such changes were effected, instruction at Harvard would always be limited to making certain that prescribed lessons were learned by dealing out punishment when recitations were less than satisfactory.

While it is easy to scorn such teaching and curricula, it should be remembered that many colleges were founded in places where few if any secondary schools existed. This meant that colleges had to undertake a considerable amount of secondary instruction, and in many cases, even elementary training. With an educational program keyed to such a level, it is only natural that the usefulness of a quality library could be nothing more than limited, and in many cases even peripheral. Just how grim the actual situation was can be seen by reviewing a few of the reports which Horace Mann compiled for the Massachusetts Board of Education beginning in 1838 and continuing throughout the 1840's. This noted educator pointed out not only that the state's public schools operated on an average of no more than seventeen weeks per year, but that while 42,164 Massachusetts children did not attend school in the summer, there were at least 23,216 children who went to no school at all, summer or winter (20:I:38). These reports further stated that because the legislature was operating the state's teacher-training institutions on impossibly low budgets, most public school teachers were less than qualified to face the classroom.

Conservatism and penuriousness, then, were significant factors in American education. Such characteristics might have been excusable had the country not been interested in improvement, or if it had been economically bankrupt. However, such was not the case; on the contrary, public and private funds were generously spent on such social and economic improvements as canals, railroads, and highways. Education, for its part, reciprocated by rejecting most suggestions that it contribute to the country's social needs, a circumstance which is reflected in the fact that during the building of the Erie Canal no college except West Point had an engineering program.

Yet, change was occurring. Rensselaer was developed as a special school to help farmers; normal schools appeared as early as 1839; Cooper Union and Brooklyn Polytechnic were opened in the 1850's for the applied sciences; and a municipal college was started as early as 1837 in Louisville. Obviously, learning was beginning to appeal to more than just the upper classes, a fact that was especially welcome on the frontier. While in the West such a trend seemed imperceptible, by 1815 there were at least twelve Kentucky towns, ten Ohio towns, and two Indiana towns with libraries. Equally important were the libraries in the Ohio Valley at such schools as Transylvania College, Kentucky Academy, Ohio University at Athens, Miami University, Cincinnati College, and Vincennes University, all of which were important enough to attract the attention of local chroniclers (40).

But as has always been the case, those schools which placed the greatest confidence in a classical curriculum showered contempt on those that addressed themselves to the needs of society. The most comprehensive assault on practical educa-

tion and curriculum change was promulgated in the Yale Report of 1828 (42). This treatise not only denounced the work of reformers, but it stoutly championed the psychology of learning which emphasizes discipline of thought and furniture of the mind. It unabashedly proclaimed the value of the classics by claiming that only they could give a person what he ought to know. And, implicit in the report was the remarkable reasoning that a single text with recitations is superior to use of the library.

The Yale Report was written by two men who were the personification of stability, conservatism, and caution—Jeremiah Day and James L. Kingsley. Day taught at Yale for sixty-nine years, Kingsley for fifty. Drawing on such lifetimes of service and confidence in the status quo, their Report specifically castigated education intended for mercantile, mechanical, and agricultural pursuits, labeling such teaching as outside the realm of college responsibilities. And of particular chagrin to present day librarians is the fact that it neither said anything for the value of a library in the educational process, nor for its importance to the curriculum. But whatever may be said against it now, in 1828 the Report served its purpose well, for it helped to suppress change until at least the 1850's and to make a permanent fixture of the rigid curriculum until late in the nineteenth century.

But while its impact was shattering, the minority toward which the wrath of the Yale Report was aimed did not give up. A number of scholars had already traveled to Europe and while there they had discovered that libraries and library-centered methods of study could bring about decisive results. Among such travelers were John Motley, Edward Everett, George Ticknor, and Henry Longfellow. During their sojourns they not only discovered how inferior American academic libraries actually were, but they also came to feel that quality libraries in the United States would be necessary if there was ever to be receptiveness to intellectual endeavor among the public at large. A favorite place of study for these American students was Göttingen, and while there they must have been particularly aware of the contrast between European libraries and those at home, for the library at Göttingen contained over 200,000 volumes while the one at Harvard had only 30,000. The impact of a liberally administered academic library was also demonstrated to these men, and especially to Ticknor, for he mentions in his notes (31:I:72) how impressed he was by the fact that the Göttingen library loaned materials to students for as long as necessary.

Ticknor's opinion was that American college libraries were 50 to 100 years behind those of Europe. He also came to feel that a library was the first necessity in education, a point on which he elaborated by stating that Harvard professors did not complain about inferior holdings because they were blind as to what a quality library really was (15:I:257). If Ticknor's indictment was valid, the statement left other colleges in an especially poor light because at this time Harvard easily had the best college library in the United States. Furthermore, the superiority enjoyed at Cambridge was not just a quantitative one, since there is evidence that Harvard had made conscious efforts to raise the quality of its collection. For example, the Ebeling collection of 3,200 volumes, plus 10,000 maps and charts, was acquired from Col. Israel Thorndike in 1818, and with this acquistion Harvard made its first gesture toward becoming a research library (12:I:xi). Even earlier, in 1815, an undergraduate library had been recommended, indicating that the college was enough interested in the collection to be willing to spend some time considering a different theory for its use (14). These combined factors point to the conclusion that Harvard did have a library program of some dimensions, and may at least partially explain why literary societies did not flourish there as they did at most other colleges.

The effect of such forward-looking policies, however, should not be overestimated. For example, the undergraduate library did not become a reality until 1845 (13:1), and despite the fact that in 1821 the college boasted of a well-organized collection, the emphasis apparently remained on preservation rather than on use. This attitude can be seen from the sentiment expressed in a letter from Joseph Cogswell to George Ticknor of January 18, 1854, in which the former said, "At nine A. M. I take my stand inside the railing and there I remain as a fixture until half-past four. They all look wishfully at the books and ask, 'Can't we go into the alcoves and up to the second story,' and when I answer 'No,' they break out into a railing accusation. But it's no use, I tell them, 'You can't do it.' I know not what I should have done if I had not hit upon this plan of a close corporation. It would have crazed me to have seen a crowd ranging lawlessly among the books, and throwing everything into confusion." (10:264)

It is true that this quotation is from a letter written by Cogswell when he was librarian at the Astor Library in New York, and not when he was at Harvard. Nevertheless, he had been one of Harvard's most noted librarians and there is no evidence that in the years before 1854 he was more amenable to unsupervised use of the collection. Nor is there any reason to think that any of his earlier ideas concerning the compositon of a quality collection was different from the one he expressed in another letter to Ticknor at about the same date, "The readers average from 100-200 daily, and they read excellent books, except the young fry who employ all the hours they are out of school in reading the trash, as Scott, Cooper, Dickens, *Punch*, and *The Illustrated News*. Even this is better than spinning street yarns, and as long as they continue perfectly orderly and quiet, as they now are, I shall not object to their amusing themselves with poor books." (10:264-5)

Evidence that Cogswell's convictions, as expressed above, were representative of opinion generally can be found among the rules established by the trustees at the University of North Carolina. In Section VIII, Article 1, of the *Laws of the University* can be found the following, ". . . No person but a trustee or member of the faculty shall be admitted into the room of the library, without the presence of the librarian." But worse, Article 3 of the same Section states, "The encyclopedia shall not be taken out of the library by any student not belonging to the senior or junior classes; and no other shall ever consult them, except in the presence of some member of the faculty." (37) It can only be hoped that such rules were necessary because books were difficult to procure, and not because those in authority wanted to limit free inquiry. Whatever the reasons, however, such an attitude was so widespread, and can be so easily documented, that one must conclude preservation of the collection was an over-riding concern of virtually all college libraries between 1800 and 1860.

Despite the conservatism which pervaded American higher education, and notwithstanding the fact that throughout the period 1800-1860 the idea of going to college was beyond the common man's needs or aspirations, the nation was nevertheless beginning to feel the need for more than an elementary education. One way in which this need was met was through the establishment of land-grant colleges. Although the land-grant movement did not come to fruition until after 1860, the idea was actually conceived much earlier. Such a concept was particularly beneficial to libraries because it stimulated the collecting and disseminating of information, publishing of journals, and writing of monographs on discoveries and experiments. Moreover, between 1800-1860 Congress became aware of its duty to education in other ways. West Point and Annapolis were both established in 1802, while interest in scientific research under government auspices could be seen in the creation of the Smithsonian Institution and the Geodetic Survey. Finally, as early as 1867 Congress established a Bureau of Education. These combined circumstances, when taken as a whole, meant that the nation was maturing intellectually, and that men such as Horace Mann, Henry Barnard, and William T. Harris had actually been successful in implanting the notion that popular education was of value to democracy.

One measure of education's impact on daily living can be seen by examining the nature of book publishing in the West. By reviewing the various checklists of imprints which represent publications issuing from printers in Pennsylvania and Kentucky during the period 1786-1815, and from printers throughout Ohio from 1796 until 1820, Peckham (23) found that no less than 481 books were published solely for purchase on the open market. Furthermore, in Indiana sixty-five such books appeared from 1804-1835, and between 1814 and 1840, printers in Illinois published thirty-two. In making this survey, it was reasoned that titles published with unsubsidized funds would reflect genuine interests in reading, since no printer would risk his capital unless he felt reasonably certain of a profitable return. If this conclusion is correct, it would indeed show that literary tastes did exist west of the Alleghenies and that attention to learning went beyond purely practical application.

It is, of course, easy to overestimate popular enthusiasm for such encouraging trends. Nevertheless, the extent to which reading was effecting America's intellectual awakening can be appreciated by noting that in 1825 the number of periodicals appearing in the United States had risen to 100, and by 1850 this figure was as high as 600 (22:34-2). Of this total, perhaps no more than three professional education magazines were appearing in 1826, although several periodicals of a general nature carried articles on the subject.[4] This number, however, increased significantly between 1825-1850, for more than sixty periodicals in the field of education appeared during this quarter century. While a positive correlation is not synonymous with cause and effect, it is never-

theless interesting to note that throughout the period 1825-1860 new public schools and colleges, as well as reading materials of all types, appeared with increasing frequency throughout the United States (36:351; 506-517).

With such a quickening interest in education, it may not be accidental that college libraries saw fit to extend their services to persons beyond the academic community (21). These libraries were probably the only substantial collections of books in large and sparsely settled areas, and their holdings undoubtedly included materials with appeal to the population at large. Such a circumstance is understandable when it is remembered that college libraries were in large part comprised of gifts, a fact which indicated that these books had first been of personal interest to lay donors. This would also account for the fact that religious materials were over-represented in both academic libraries and those general stores which sold books in addition to everyday necessities (23). It is, therefore, not surprising that college libraries had holdings which were broad in subject matter but not entirely pertinent to the curriculum.

This lack of association with the classroom was largely because college libraries reflected education's emphasis on teaching rather than study, its preoccupation with students rather than scholars, and its disposition toward maintaining order and discipline rather than promoting learning. In such a restricted atmosphere as this, it is not surprising that during the ante-bellum period the academic library made little impact on methods of teaching, and even less on faculty involvement in book selection, seminar study, research projects, and interpretation of the collection. The college library reflected the aims and methods of the parent institution between 1800 and 1860 just as it does today, and because of this, it is understandable that in 1835 no academic library in the United States could have supported a study such as Gibbon's *Decline and Fall of the Roman Empire,* or Wheaton's *International Law.* For the same reason, the research for George Ticknor's *History of Spanish Literature,* as well as for the works of Bancroft and Prescott, was necessarily done in Europe.

Colleges during the Middle Period also contrasted sharply with those of today in that many of the era's leading scholars were not connected with higher education. For example, Prescott, Bancroft, Motley, and Parkman were neither teachers in the contemporary sense nor even men who spent much time on campuses in general.

Moreover, Longfellow and Lowell, though affiliated with Harvard for a time, did no writing for scholarly journals. This may or may not have been one of the reasons why the study of literature was restricted to ancient and hallowed authors, but exclusion of contemporary writers was almost universal in higher education and this resulted in a significant lacuna in all library collections. Such conditions led to a general dearth of library holdings in English literature, and at Oberlin this attitude went so far as to result in the exclusion of works by Milton, Dryden, Cowper, Burns, and Southey.

In such a setting, one would expect at least some students and faculty to feel frustration. Just how many were concerned enough to voice an opinion is not known, but one faculty member at North Carolina University is reported to have said, "Not a volume has been purchased by the trustees during the last quarter of a century. No stranger is ever invited to examine our present collection." (41:12) And a Boston newspaper, the *Atlas*, complained in 1857 about the lack of enthusiasm for acquisitions at Harvard by commenting that the college was spending only $300-$400 per year for the purchase of books while it annually invested at least seven times that amount for the inspection of pickled fish (18:2). The editorial estimates that Harvard had only one book in fifty of those published during the preceding half century.

However, it is easy to be excessively harsh in judging the college library of 1800-1860. The collections were probably as good as the endowments, dormitories, or curricula. And if many libraries remained locked most of the time, while others struggled along with no room which could be locked, it should be remembered this was an era in which higher education looked to the past rather than the future. Reflective thinking and theoretical considerations were rare qualities in any college discipline before 1860. It follows rather naturally, then, that college libraries had only limited significance, especially since librarians of the time considered themselves practitioners and schoolmasters rather than scholars.

Few, if any, of the teaching approaches during this era had any relation to the library. It is difficult to over-emphasize the impact that methods of teaching make on use of a college library; consequently, in assessing the significance of the college library during the Middle Period it is important to remember that with isolated exceptions, even gifted history teachers had pupils memorize and recite words found in a text. After some of the noted educators of America returned from European study, the teaching of history slowly shifted from the memorization of such things as political episodes, military achievements, and intrigue to considerations of Darwinism, social evolution, and the inner-life. Even so, it was probably not until the 1880's that history teaching in the leading colleges of America began to rival that of the European universities.

The studies that were offered also militated against any meaningful library program. Although science had gained a place in the curriculum by 1850, it was not until after the Civil War that the new technology found popularity through application to everyday problems. As late as 1880 much of the science taught in American colleges was still called "natural philosophy," and scientific equipment continued to be known as "philosophical apparatus." And, even though Newtonian science had gained importance as early as the 18th century, it is significant that Aristotelian terminology persisted until almost 1900.

The academic library was equally influenced by the number of disciplines that were not part of the curriculum. University training in anthropology, for example, did not begin until the very last part of the 1800's, and this same subject did not enter the undergraduate curriculum until at least 1920. Moreover, the profession of education, with its scientific orientation, and its emphasis on sociology, psychology, and methods was completely unknown during the first half of the 19th century. Nor were research centers part of university life before 1860, and those branches of knowledge which rely on sophisticated abstracting, indexing, and retrieving were far in the future. Finally, the study of literature was completely different, for mastery of various editions, evaluative tools, concordances, and analytical works played no part in the educational process of that era.

Even today, the academic library is too often challenged only at the graduate level. Yet, it was not until 1852 that one of the earliest attempts at gratuate education was undertaken at Michigan University, and this effort was far from a total success. However, with the advent of the seminar, students were able to come in contact with teaching that discussed sources, authorities, opinions, and established values. As a consequence, the library at last began to be as important as classes, dormitories, and compulsory attendance.

Conditions changed slowly, however, and because of this it is not surprising that reform in librarianship itself was slow. The Dewey Decimal Scheme, for example, did not appear until 1876 and the Cutter System was not invented until 1891. Library science schools did not open until 1887, and Library of Congress catalog cards were not produced until 1901. Academic librarianship in the modern sense, therefore, is largely a creation of the twentieth century.

The contribution of early nineteenth-century college libraries was nevertheless worthy of respect. They were probably of greatest value when they attempted to provide the scholar with transactions of learned societies, for one of the oldest responsibilities in college librarianship is to maintain collections such as these. Moreover, it may be that these early libraries will be remembered not for their failure to develop large research collections and support elaborate teaching functions, but for their ability to work with what they had and to maintain themselves against an overwhelming array of adversities.

If their services and holdings were considered meager, their collections were at least as satisfactory as those that were owned by outstanding teachers, and they did reflect the educational thinking of the day. It may be that this caused the college library to duplicate rather than to supplement the teacher's personal collection which he kept at home, but at least it indicated to the student what kind of books should be owned by an educated man. No college before 1860 was content with itself if it did not have at least some semblance of a library. Perhaps this attitude was the greatest legacy these early institutions could leave, for without such an idea permeating today's colleges and universities, higher education would be quite a different enterprise.

REFERENCES

1. Adams, Herbert Baxter. *Thomas Jefferson and the University of Virginia* . . . U. S. Bureau of Education, Circular of Information No. 1. Washington: Government Printing Office, 1888.

2. Amherst College. *The Substance of Two Reports of the Faculty to the Board of Trustees with the Doings of the Board Thereon.* Amherst, Mass.: Carter and Adams, Printers, 1827.

3. *American Almanac and Repository of Useful Knowledge for the Year 1830.* 2nd Edition. Vol. I. Boston: Charles Bowen, 1833.

4. _____. 1841. Boston: David H. Williams, 1841.

5. _____. 1860. Boston: Crosby, Nichols, and Co., 1860.

6. Beer, William, *Checklist of American Periodicals, 1741-1800.* Reprinted from the *Proceedings of the American Antiquarian Society* for October, 1922, Worcester, Mass.: American Antiquarian Society, 1923.

7. Brewer, Fisk Parsons. *The Library of the University of North Carolina.* Chapel Hill: University of North Carolina, (1870?).

8. Brodman, Estelle. "The Special Library, the Mirror of its Society," *Journal of Library History,* I, No. 2 (April, 1966), 108-124.

9. Clemons, Harry. *The University of Virginia Library, 1825-1950: Story of a Jeffersonian Foundation.* Charlottesville: University of Virginia Library, 1954.

10. Cogswell, Joseph Green. *Life of J. G. Cogswell, as Sketched in His Letters.* Cambridge, Mass.: Privately Printed at Riverside Press, 1874.

11. Evans, Charles. *American Bibliography: a Chronological Dictionary* . . . New York: Peter Smith, 1941.

12. Harvard University. *Catalogue of the Library of Harvard University* . . . 3 vols. Cambridge, Mass.: E. W. Metcalf and Co., 1830.

13. Harvard University. *Eleventh Annual Report of the Librarian of the Public Library of Harvard University, Made to the Examining Committee, July 11, 1842.* Harvard University Archives Library.

14. Harvard University. Memorandum from Andrew Norton, Librarian, to President Kirkland, 1815. Harvard University Archives Library, U A III 50.28.13.

15. Hofstadter, Richard, and Smith, Wilson. *American Higher Education: a Documentary History.* 2 vols. Chicago: University of Chicago Press, 1961.

16. Jefferson, Thomas. *Writings.* Library Edition. 20 vols. Washington: Thomas Jefferson Memorial Association of the U. S., 1903.

17. *Journal of the Proceedings of a Convention of Literary and Scientific Gentlemen, Held in the Common Council Chamber of the City of New York, October, 1830.* New York: Jonathan Leavitt and G. & H. Carvill, 1831.

18. "The Library of Harvard College," *The Boston Daily Atlas,* XXV, No. 2 (Feb. 26, 1857), p. 2.

19. Lindsley, Philip. *The Cause of Education in Tennessee: an Address Delivered to the Young Gentlemen Admitted to the Degree of Bachelor of Arts in Cumberland College at the Anniversary Commencement, October 4, 1826.* Nashville: Banner Press, 1826.

20. Massachusetts. Board of Education. *Report, together with the Report of the Secretary of the Board.* 1st-12th. Boston: Dutton and Wentworth, State Printers, 1838-1849. [Washington, 1947-1952]

21. McMullen, Haynes. "The Use of Books in the Ohio Valley before 1850," *Journal of Library History,* I, No. 1 (January, 1966), 43.55.

22. Mott, Frank Luther. *History of American Magazines, 1741-1850.* Cambridge, Mass.: Harvard University Press, 1939.

23. Peckham, Howard H. "Books and Reading on the Ohio Valley Frontier," *Mississippi Valley Historical Society Review,* XLIV (March, 1958), 649-663.

24. "Periodical Literature of the U. S.," *North American Review,* XXXIX (October, 1834), 277-301.

25. Perry, Arthur Latham. *Williamstown and Williams College.* Printed by the author, 1899.

26. Princeton University. Minutes of the Board of Trustees of the College of New Jersey, April 9, 1793. Princeton University Archives, 300-311.

27. Raymond, Andrew Van Vranken. *Union University, Its History, Influence, Characteristics and Equipment . . .* 3 vols. New York: Lewis Publishing Co., 1907.

28. Shores, Louis. *Origins of the American College Library, 1638-1800.* New York: Barnes & Noble, 1935.

29. Smithsonian Institution. *Fourth Annual Report of the Board of Regents . . . 1849.* Washington: Government Printing Office, 1850.

30. Tewkesbury, Donald G. *The Founding of American Colleges and Universities Before the Civil War.* New York: Archon Books, 1965.

31. Ticknor, George. *Life, Letters and Journals.* 6th ed. 2 vols. Boston: James R. Osgood and Co., 1877.

32. *Union List of Serials in Libraries of the U. S. and Canada.* 3rd ed. New York: H. W. Wilson Co., 1965.

33. U. S. Congress. *Biographical Directory of the American Congress, 1774-1961.* Washington: Government Printing Office, 1961.

34. U. S. Bureau of the Census. *Abstract of the Fourteenth Census of the U. S., 1920.* Washington: Government Printing Office, 1923.

35. _____. *Historical Statistics of the U. S., Colonial Times to 1957.* Washington: Government Printing Office, 1960.

36. U. S. Department of the Interior. *Report . . .* (1869). Vol. II, *Report of the Commissioner of Education.* Washington: Government Printing Office, 1870.

37. University of North Carolina. "Laws of the University of North Carolina Established by the Board of Trustees at their Session in December, 1799," *Faculty Journal,* 1814-1823. University of North Carolina Archives.

38. _____. Minutes of the Board of Trustees . . ., Dec. 3-13, 1792.

39. _____. Minutes of the Board of Trustees . . ., November 15, 1790-December 6, 1797.

40. Venable, William Henry. *Beginnings of Literary Culture in the Ohio Valley.* Cincinnati: R. Clarke & Co., 1891.

41. Wilson, Louis R. *Library of the First State University: a Review of its Past and a Look at Its Future.* Chapel Hill, N. C.: North Carolina University Press, 1960.

42. Yale University. *Reports on the Course of Instruction in Yale College;* by a Committee of the Corporation, and the Academical Faculty. New Haven: Hezekiah Howe, 1828.

FOOTNOTES

[1] Beer lists ten magazines that were started in 1800. Some of these lasted for less than one year and others failed to publish more than a single number. Combining such short-lived journals with those founded in previous years, Beer's *Checklist* indicates that a total of thirteen periodicals were available at one time or another during 1800. The *American Almanac* states that by 1810 this number had risen to twenty-six.

[2] Letter, Thomas Jefferson to T. M. Randolph, July 6, 1787. (*Writings:* VI, pp. 165-169); Letter, Thomas Jefferson to John Adams, July 5, 1814. (*Writings:* XIV, pp. 144-151.)

[3] Letter, Thomas Jefferson to Peter Carr, September 7, 1814 (*Writings:* XIX, pp. 211-221); Letter, Thomas Jefferson to J. Correa De Serra, November 25, 1817. (*Writings:* XV, pp. 153-157).

[4] A review of *Poole's Index to Periodical Literature, 1802-1881,* indicates that entire articles on the subject of education before 1826 were rare. *North American Review, Analectic Magazine,* and *Portfolio (Dennie's)* are representative of magazines that devoted some space to the topic.

The Library of Congress:
The Early Years

David Mearns

For many years Americans suffered at the hands of literate Englishmen, who were quick to point out that the new independence of the young country did not extend into the fields of literary culture. Not only did they see America's literary productions as infantile and inconsequential, but they also ridiculed her libraries for being small, poorly organized, and filled with useless books.

In many ways their criticism of American libraries was just; there were few, if any, that could support serious research. In the early years of the nineteenth century, however, a research library was born, which grew to be the envy of literate nations throughout the world.

From 1800, when the Library of Congress was founded, until 1899 when Ainsworth Rand Spofford resigned as librarian, the fortunes of this great library fluctuated considerably. In 1814 the library was destroyed by the British, only to be replaced by Jefferson's magnificent collection. Again, in 1851, the fine collections were devastated by flames, but were rebuilt to large proportions by 1900. David Mearns, the well known Lincoln scholar and historian of the Library of Congress, describes those difficult years, and provides an exciting insight into the political struggles that have surrounded the "National Library's" growth.

THE PEACE OF GREAT PHANTOMS BE FOR YOU

The Library of Congress was a long time aborning but the quest for origins leads straight to New York's Wall Street where, at the corner of Nassau, the Jacobean City Hall had lately been refurbished, according to the plans of Major Pierre Charles L'Enfant, French artist, engineer, and Revolutionary veteran, for the accommodation of the "general government." There the First Congress of the United States was convened and there on August 6, 1789, Elbridge Gerry, one of eight Representatives from Massachusetts, rose from his place to introduce a motion. A native of Marblehead, graduate at eighteen from Harvard College, formerly a member of the Continental Congress (where he had signed the Declaration of Independence) and a Delegate to the Federal Convention (where he had steadfastly refused to affix his signature to the new Constitution), Mr. Gerry had already established on both sides of the aisle a reputation as a man of parts, who stoutly believed it to be "the duty of every man though he may have but one day to live to devote that day to the good of his country."

Mr. Gerry was to survive for a quarter of a century, and was subsequently to become Minister to France, Governor of Massachusetts, and Vice President of the United States, but his act of patriotism for that eighteenth century Thursday was to move "that a committee be appointed to report a catalogue of books necessary for the use of Congress, with an estimate of the expense, and the best mode of procuring them."

The motion lay comfortably on the table until the following spring, when on April 30, a committee, consisting of Mr. Gerry, Aedanus Burke, of South Carolina, and Alexander White, of Virginia, was appointed for the purpose.

Judge Burke had been born in County Galway, educated at the theological college in St. Omer, France, and following a visit to the West Indies, had emigrated to Charleston where, after service in the militia during the early years of the Revolution, he had been appointed a judge of the state circuit court. His purple obituary, which

SOURCE: Reprinted from David Mearns. *The Story Up to Now: The Library of Congress, 1800-1946* (Washington: Library of Congress, 1947), excerpted.

appeared in the *City Gazette* for April 2, 1802, glistens with such phrases as "In his pure and elevated mind every consideration was deemed subordinate to the freedom and happiness of man"— "His enmities were like those of other men, but his friendships were eternal"—"His acquirements as a scholar, were extensive, classical and erudite. In the walks of history and jurisprudence, and the regions of elegant literature, his attainments were equal and commensurate."—"There was something in him formed for great occasions and splendid exertion."—"Eccentricities at times he had— They were of an agreeable cast, generally harmless, always variable, and appeared but as the coruscations of elevated and uncommon endowments."—"He was an enlightened liberal and genuine republican."

Alexander White was generally regarded as the outstanding leader of western Virginia and one of the ablest lawyers in the United States. Born in Frederick County, son of a former surgeon in the English Navy who had married into a pioneer family, he was educated at the University of Edinburgh, and studied law in London, first at the Inner Temple and later at Gray's Inn. Upon his return to this country, in 1765, he served almost continuously as King's or State's attorney. He took little part in the Revolutionary struggle, but was active in securing the ratification of the Federal Constitution. It is not quite certain that that First Congress and its work meant a fulfillment of his ambitions, for while he was participating in its affairs he confided in a letter (albeit in a letter to a lady) "to associate with the great men of the earth, and to share in the Government of an Empire, to me has no charms."

On Wednesday, June 23, 1790, Mr. Gerry, in behalf of the committee, reported to the House. *The Debates and Proceedings in the Congress of the United States* are silent concerning its contents and only record the fact that it "was ordered to lie on the Table." Fortunately, however, *The Gazette of the United States* supplied the text; the following paragraphs of which seem to have a particular relevance:

> . . . That, as far as the nature of the case will admit, they have in the schedule annexed, complied with the order of the house, having due regard to the state of the treasury.
>
> That, the committee have confined themselves, in a great measure, to books necessary for the use of the legislative and executive departments, and not often to be found in private or circulating libraries.
>
> That, nevertheless, without further provision of books on laws and government, to which reference

is often necessary, members of the legislature and other officers of government may be either deprived of the use of such books when necessary, or be obliged at every session to transport to the seat of the general government a considerable part of their libraries; it seldom happening that they can otherwise command such books when requisite, without trespassing too much on the indulgence of their friends. The committee are therefore of the opinion that a sum not exceeding 1,000 dollars be appropriated in the present session, and that the sum of 500 dollars be hereafter annually appropriated to the purchase of books for a public library, and applied to the purpose by the Vice President, Chief Justice and Secretary of State of the United States, without confining them to the catalogue reported until in the opinion of Congress, the books provided shall be adequate to the purpose.

This, the first official proposal for the establishment of a Library of Congress, is clear on several points: (1) it is clear that the committee contemplated a library for the Government in all its branches, the legislative, the executive and the judicial, and, to the extent that all activities related to the Federal establishment are national activities, it contemplated the formation of a National Library; (2) it is clear also that the committee doubted the present or future adequacy of merely local resources to meet the needs of transacting the people's business; (3) it is, finally, clear that the committee conceived of the possibility of creating a fixed and permanent collection upon the basis of a self-liquidating enterprise. It is less apparent, but it may be implied that the Congress, as onlie begetter, was to have first (though by no means exclusive) call upon the works of these "sundry authors on the laws of nature and nations." One phrase in the report must be read in its eighteenth century meaning; a "public" library was not public at all by modern standards but was actually a subscription or proprietary library in which a relatively small part of the community formed a corporation and made financial investments in exchange for the privilege of borrowing books from a jointly owned stock.

OUR UNION DOES NOT REQUIRE IT

But why was this report tabled? Why was the proposal permitted to languish for a decade? Why was an effort which reflected so much initiative and foresight and conscientious application set aside? There are several possible explanations.

In the first place, there were those who found the idea either frivolous or unrelated to the immediate concerns of a wise and representative democracy. Typical of this attitude was an anonymous contributor to the *Independent Chronicle* of Boston, who over the signature of "An Observer" let go with a terrific blast in the issue for May 13, 1790:

> . . . The late motion respecting the "Library" for Congress, is truly novel—could it be supposed that a measure so distant from any thing which can effect the general purposes of government, could be introduced at this important period? Could any thing be more foreign to the real business of Congress? What connection has a Library with the public? With our Commerce; or with any other national concern?—How absurd to squander away money for a parcel of Books, when every shilling of the Revenue is wanted for supporting our government and paying our debts? How preposterous to originate such a mode to lay out money, more particularly at a time when the utmost stretch of the Treasurer's genius is exerted to provide for the *necessary exigencies* of the government? Provided this motion is adopted, when can we expect to compleat a system of finance? The Treasurer having made no provision, in his report for such an application, additional ways and means therefore must be devised, in order to raise money for this purpose—the question then is, shall our trade be burthened with an additional Impost, to furnish a Library to amuse men who are sent to do the business of the continent.
>
> It is supposed that the Members of Congress are acquainted with history; the laws of nations; and possess such political information as is necessary for the management of the affairs of the government. If they are *not*, we have been unfortunate in our choice—or, should they need the assistance of Books upon any particular subject, they are able to furnish themselves *with little expence* at the circulating Library in the city where they reside. But why the States should be at this expence and the time of Congress taken up in arranging a body of Books for a public Library at this important period, is a piece of policy which no person can reconcile upon any principle of propriety, or expediency.
>
> The motion however seems to claim a *right*, which appears Congress are not empowered to exercise. *"The Powers of Congress"* do not give them this privilege. The design and end of the Constitution are for quite different purposes, than for the amusement, or even instruction of Congress. I would ask wherein is a public Library conducive to the purposes mentioned in the preamble of the Constitution? Our Union does not require it—neither does the establishment of justice—the promotion of the general welfare; the security of liberty to ourselves and posterity. All these are the great objects of the government, but it is supposed that the members are fully competent for these purposes, without being at the expence of furnishing them with Books for their improvement. They may with equal propriety charge the public with all the expence of their cloathing, boarding &c. as to touch the Revenue for Books for their own convenience, entertainment or instruction. The people look for *practical politicks*, as they presume the *Theory* is obtained previous to the members taking their seats in Congress.

Perhaps these considerations of "practical politicks," entertained by subjects worthy of the pen of William Blades, prevailed and forced the abandonment of the proposal. Or again, the collapse may be explained by a loss of interest on the part of the chairman of the committee. Professor Morison, of Harvard, in a penetrating study of Elbridge Gerry has discussed the conflict of the gentleman and the democrat in his nature; a conflict which made him vacillate, carry water on both shoulders, sometimes, change sides. He may have lost interest, for it cannot be without significance that no reference to this episode is found among Gerry's surviving papers. John Adams once complained directly of Gerry's "obstinacy which will risk great things to secure small ones," and another lifelong associate wrote to Jefferson that Gerry was a "Grumbeltonian" who "objected to everything he did not propose." This suggests that he may merely have acted perfunctorily in response to the urging of another, and actually cared very little whether the plan gained acceptance or not.

But the most satisfactory explanation of the moratorium derives from the history of the New York Society Library, a corporation chartered by George III and composed of divers merchants, lawyers, physicians, printers, apothecaries, distillers and "gentlemen," whose collections had been dispersed during the War for Independence, and had been only lately reestablished (in the number of some four thousand volumes) in "the uppermost Room in the South East part of the City Hall" where their continued occupancy was conditioned on the complete convenience of their fellow tenants, "the Gen'l Gov't of the United States." This hazard appears to have been removed by extending the full privileges of the Society to the Members of the National Legislature, and the Society's librarian, the Reverend George Wright, a native of Ireland, rector of the Episcopal Church in Brooklyn, once described as "of rather slender constitution," became in fact, though not in title, the first Librarian of Congress.

OF FURNISHINGS, FOOTWAYS AND FOUNDATIONS

The third session of the First Congress met in Philadelphia and there, on Wednesday, January 19, 1791, there was communicated to the Senate a resolution recently adopted by the directors of the Library Company in that city, providing "that the President and Members of the Senate and House of Representatives of the United States shall have free use of the books in the Library in as full and ample manner as if they were members of the company." To those who had sat in the "Old," or Continental, Congress this generous action was welcomed as a renewal of privileges formerly enjoyed and highly prized. As early as August 31, 1774, when the Company was soon to receive the Congress as its joint tenant of Carpenters' Hall, the Librarian had been instructed to "furnish the Gentlemen who are to meet in Congress in this City, with the use of such Books as they may have occasion for during their sitting, taking a Receipt for them."

And those who had served as Delegates during Constitutional Summer may have remembered a motion of thanks which they had adopted on July 7, 1787, upon receiving word that "the gentlemen who compose the Convention" had been authorized to draw "such books as they may desire during their continuance at Philadelphia."

Now the New Government had again been assured of recourse to the impressive collection (recently installed in its elegant new home on Fifth Street) which the late Dr. Franklin had done so much to found, to foster and to form. It was not surprising that "General" Washington's private secretary, Tobias Lear, should acknowledge so important a courtesy "in obedience to the commands of the President of the United States."

Thus it was that the Members of the American Congress, first as champions of a revolutionary cause, now as the chosen representatives of a free and independent and terribly isolated people, had come, for their endeavors, to depend upon those guides to experience and example which are contained in books. Thus it was also, that for a while they considered themselves relieved of the onerous necessity of fashioning a special library of their own. But gradually the requirements of the legislative process for immediate recourse to authority became so pressing that certain standard works had to be acquired. In the fall of 1794, the Secretary was ordered to purchase copies of Blackstone's *Commentaries* and Vattel's *Law of Nature and Nations* "for the use of the Senate," and from time to time both Houses appear to have added to their routine equipment about fifty titles including such publications as the poems of Robert Burns, Dr. Rush on *Yellow Fever,* Hume's *History of England,* Reeves and Wooddeson on English law, several treatises on elections, Morse's *American Geography,* Varlo's *Husbandry,* Chalmers' *Collection of Treaties,* and two or three periodicals.

It is reasonable to suppose that those who had opposed the Gerry proposal came slowly to discard their skepticism regarding the relationship of literature to law; toward this reversal of viewpoint they were propelled both by the development of their own practice and by the prospect of a radically altered situation.

There were no libraries in the Potomac Marshes, and in the spring of 1800 the Congress was confronted with the eminently practical and inescapable consideration of its imminent removal to the new "Federal City," which was to be the "permanent seat of government."

Something of the sort may have been in the mind of young Harrison Gray Otis, of Massachusetts, then serving his second term in the House of Representatives when on Thursday, March 20, he introduced a resolution calling for the appointment of a committee "to consider what measures are expedient for Congress to adopt, preparatory to the removal of the seat of government, with leave to report by bill or otherwise." On the following day, the question was referred to the Committee on Ways and Means and its chairman, Robert Goodloe Harper, who was also the Federalist leader, reported on March 24 "a bill making further provision for the removal and accommodation of the Government of the United States; which was twice read and committed to the whole House." On April 2, the House "resolved itself into a Committee" to discuss it, and "considerable conversation occurred" with reference to the section which contained an appropriation for furnishing the President's House. After some time, John Rutledge, Jr. sought to put an end to the debate by moving "that the Committee rise, in order that time may be given for learning the amount of money wanting for this object, and because he supposed the Chairman of the Committee, who was absent, might be able to give that information." The proceedings must have been very confusing for the *Annals* report that "the motion was afterwards withdrawn, but renewed by the Speaker, and at length carried."

Mr. Harper was in his seat on Friday, April 4, when the debate was resumed. In the interval which had elapsed since he had originally introduced the legislation he had been gravely disturbed by "some Constitutional doubts," because that controlling instrument prescribed, as he put it, that "the salary of the President should receive no addition nor diminution during his being in office." As a consequence, he proposed, and his colleagues concurred in, language which so amended the act "that the sum to accommodate the household of the President . . . should not operate until after the third of March next." The question then turned to the amount of money which should be allowed for that purpose. Sums of $20,000, $15,000, and $10,000 "were severally named," but a State Rights Democrat, John Randolph, of Roanoke, who considered "the principle itself unconstitutional, moved, in order to defeat the section altogether (it having been amended and being out of order to move its being stricken out) to insert the sum of $500." By a vote of 44 to 42 it was agreed to settle on $15,000. Mr. Harper then proposed an appropriation of $1,000 to cover the expense of removing the public property already "appertaining to the household of the President to the Federal City."

Thereafter Congressman Dwight Foster, of Massachusetts, moved to strike out the fifth section which allotted $10,000 to pave the streets of Washington, but that was "negatived, only 21 rising for it."

The debate continued; James Asheton Bayard, of Delaware presented a successful motion that the secretaries of the executive departments rather than the Secretary of the Senate and the Clerk of the House should be responsible for the suitable accommodation of the Congress. Samuel Smith, of Maryland, moved a new section, which was carried, allowing one quarter additional salary to "the clerks of several offices of the Departments of State, Treasury, War, Navy and General Post Office" to cover the expenses involved in transferring their personal effects to the District of Columbia. Then $9,000 were appropriated "to furnish the two Chambers of Congress, offices, committee rooms &c."

The House, as a Committee of the Whole, "rose when Mr. [Albert] Gallatin [a diehard] moved to strike out the second section, which provided $15,000 to accommodate the President's house with furniture." He took this action, so he declared, "not because it would not be necessary to appropriate something, but he said what that something might be, would be better ascertained by waiting for the proper estimates, and until Congress moved there, when as much as should appear necessary might be appropriated, since it was not to come into use until after the 3d of March." On a rising vote his motion was lost, and "the bill being gone through was ordered to be engrossed for a third reading on Monday."

And so, on Monday, April 7, the bill passed the House and was sent to the Senate, where on the following day it was referred to a committee consisting of James Ross, of Pennsylvania, James Lloyd, of Maryland, and James Hillhouse, of Connecticut. On Saturday, April 12, Senator Ross, for the three Jameses, reported the bill with amendments, on the 15th it received some attention, and on the 17th the Senate resumed its consideration with the result that the second section of the House bill (which related to the expenditures for fitting out the Executive Mansion) was amended and the third and fifth sections were stricken out. In this form the Senate concurred in the bill, and returned it to the House where it was agreed to on Tuesday, April 22. Two days later President John Adams "did approve and sign it." The only point at issue, a point on which there had been a division on strictly party lines, was whether he should have the pleasure of reclining on a new chair, resting on a new bed, or dining at a new table.

As it left the House the bill had contained eight sections, but due to the changes made in the Senate, the interesting seventh section had become the fifth in the new law. Because of its importance to this study it is cited in full—

> . . . That for the purchase of such books as may be necessary for the use of Congress at the said city of Washington, and for fitting up a suitable apartment for containing them, and for placing them therein the sum of five thousand dollars shall be, and hereby is appropriated; and that the said purchase shall be made by the Secretary of the Senate and the Clerk of the House of Representatives, pursuant to such directions as shall be given, and such catalogue as shall be furnished, by a joint committee of both Houses of Congress to be appointed for that purpose; and that the said books shall be placed in one suitable apartment in the capitol in the said city, for the use of both Houses of Congress and the Members thereof, according to such regulations as the Committee aforesaid shall devise and establish.

And so, as part of an appropriation for furniture and footways, the Library of Congress was founded.

• • • •

During these "early years of the Library," wrote Ainsworth Rand Spofford in 1876, "there was little occasion for official work with a view to its wider usefulness; and the care of the few books accumulated (which amounted only to 3,000 volumes up to the year 1814) involved but little time or trouble." When John Beckley died in 1807, Patrick Magruder was appointed to the combined post of Clerk of the House of Representatives and Librarian of Congress.

As work on the construction of the Capitol progressed the Library was shunted to a small committee room, first in favor of the House of Representatives, then the Supreme Court, and then the Senate. In this mean apartment the timbers of the roof and floor were decaying, and as the collections grew in size it became necessary to pile books in disordered heaps. Suitable accommodations were an object of concern and the situation was about to be remedied when the outbreak of the second British war put an end to public works.

The Library's participation in the War of 1812 was both negative and notorious. In the spring of 1813, American forces had captured York (now Toronto), then the capital of Upper Canada, had burned the Parliament Buildings with the library and archives, and had carried off the plate from the church. On August 24, 1814, Washington was captured by the British, and the Capitol of the United States was consumed by fire. The books of Congress were used as kindling. The Library was an ash heap.

The first phase of the Library's history had ended. Influences had combined which had led to its foundation. The collection had been formed in accordance with a narrow notion of the nature of useful books. As for its privileges, they had, in the beginning, been limited to Members of the Congress; the single exception being the President of the United States. Then they had been extended by statute to include the financial agent of the Library, and by Joint Resolution, the Justices of the Supreme Court. But its scope and its constituency alike were limited. There was little reason to fear that the wagon would run too fast. Beyond the Capitol, ruts were deep and its wheels tiny. It was not constructed for the hard wear of the national road. Perhaps the British torch had destroyed it altogether.

SECOND BLOOMING

The Library's second period covered the period from the close of the War of 1812 to the end of the War Between the States. It was a time of subtleties and implications; actions taken were less significant in themselves than they were significant as impulses toward a changing purpose and an enlarging responsibility. These were commitments of the future.

Prior to the late summer of 1814, the Library of Congress had attained an unconscious but remarkably successful anonymity. Aside from mem-

bers in and out of Congress, a handful of officers of government, and a few authors eager to place their works in the center of the national enterprise, the people of the United States were generally unaware of its existence. The bonfire did more than encinder it; it brought it for the first time to public and strangely affectionate notice. Indignation at destruction so wanton and so uncivilized was widespread. Unknowingly, or unmindful of, the precedent of York, the British soldiers were compared unfavorably with the Mohammedans who had destroyed the Alexandrian library. They were vandals, barbarians, goths and all the other names which always are applied to the enemies of culture. Most outraged of all were, quite properly, the Senators and Representatives who were called into extraordinary session on the nineteenth of September. On the twenty-second, Congressman Richard Mentor Johnson, of Kentucky, had just submitted a resolution calling for a committee of inquiry into "the causes of the capture of this city by the enemy; also into the manner in which the public buildings and property were destroyed," when the Speaker laid before the House "a letter from Patrick Magruder, Clerk to this House, detailing the circumstances attending the destruction of his office by the enemy." This communication was referred to a committee for investigation and report. Magruder, a native of Montgomery County, had attended Princeton College for a short time, had studied law, been admitted to the bar, practiced his profession, and served in the Ninth Congress as a Representative from Maryland, where he had served up to his assumption of the clerk-librarianship.

At the time of the British incursion he had been absent from the city, recovering from an illness at a Virginia spa. He had left the Clerk's Office and the Library in the hands of assistants; nevertheless he was made the scapegoat by the investigating committee which, in its subsequent report found that "no preparatory measures" had been "taken to secure the library and papers appertaining to the office of the House of Representatives."

The report went on to point out that:

> . . . As to the absence of the clerk on account of *indisposition,* as alleged, the committee have not examined as to the particular nature and extent of that indisposition. They will only say that it was, or ought to have been, serious and alarming to have justified his absence under the circumstances which then existed. The committee are, therefore, constrained to express the opinion that due precaution

and diligence were not exercised to prevent the destruction and loss which has [sic] been sustained.

As a consequence he was threatened with removal, and on January 28, 1815, he resigned his office, in order "to permit those by whom I am persecuted to attain, with greater ease, an object to which they have been willing to sacrifice not only my family but my reputation." It was accepted two days later.

Meanwhile, as early as September 26, 1814, Senator Robert Henry Goldsborough, of Maryland, had introduced a resolution calling for the appointment of a Joint Committee "to have the direction of the money appropriated to the purchase of books and maps for the use of the two Houses of Congress;" it was passed instantly, and before the day was over the House had given its concurrence. These swift actions had proclaimed the intent of Congress to make the replacement of its library a matter of prompt and proper attention.

THE SUBSTRATUM OF A GREAT NATIONAL LIBRARY

Mr. Jefferson, then living in retirement at Monticello, and inconvenienced by financial stringency and a desire to rid himself of the embarrassment of debt, had made a proposal. On September 21 he had written to his old friend Samuel Harrison Smith, founder of the *National Intelligencer*, at that time Commissioner of Revenue, a long letter, in the course of which he had remarked his presumption that it would "be among the early objects of Congress to recommence their collection." He considered that this would "be difficult while the war continues, and intercourse with Europe is attended with so much risk." On the other hand there was his library. He had "been fifty years making it," and had "spared no pains, opportunity or expense to make it what it is." While Minister to France, he had spent every afternoon, when not engaged, "for a summer or two in examining all the bookstores, turning over every book" with his own hand, "and putting by everything which related to America, and indeed whatever was rare and valuable in every science." In addition, he had had "standing orders during the whole time" he "was in Europe, on its principal book-marts, particularly Amsterdam, Frankfort, Madrid and London, for such works relating to America as could not be found in Paris," with the result that "in that department particularly such a collection was made as probably can never again be effected, because

it is hardly probable that the same opportunities, the same time, industry, perseverance and expense, with the same knowledge of the bibliography of the subject would again happen to be in concurrence." He continued: "During the same period, and after my return to America, I was led to procure, also, whatever related to the duties of those in the high concerns of the nation." He ventured to estimate the size of the collection, supposing it to contain "between nine and ten thousand volumes." It included, so he declared, all that "is chiefly valuable in science and literature generally," although it extended "more particularly to whatever belongs to the American statesman." It was, "in the diplomatic and parliamentary branches . . . particularly full." He had long been sensible that "it ought not to continue private property" and had provided that at his death "Congress should have the first refusal of it at their own price." The loss that Congress had now incurred, made "the present the proper moment for their accommodation, without regard to the small remnant of time" remaining to him and the "barren use" he might make of it. He, therefore, asked of Mr. Smith's friendship, "the tender of it to the Library Committee of Congress, not knowing" himself "of whom the committee" consisted. He enclosed a catalogue, which would enable those gentlemen "to judge of its contents." As for the volumes, "nearly the whole" were "well bound, abundance of them elegantly," and represented "the choicest editions existing." Their value might be determined by appraisers selected by the Committee, and payment for them "made convenient to the public." He would be willing to accept "such annual installments as the law of Congress . . . left at their disposal, or in stock of any of their late loans or of any loan they" might "institute" at the current session, "so as to spare the present calls of our country and await its days of peace and prosperity." Nevertheless the Congress might "enter . . . into immediate use of it, as eighteen or twenty wagons would place it in Washington in a single trip of a fortnight."

He would "be willing, indeed, to retain a few of the books, to amuse the time" he had "yet to pass, which might be valued with the rest, but not included in the sum of valuation until they should be restored at" his "death." On that score he would take pains to avoid mischance, "so that the whole library," as it stood in the catalogue would "be theirs without any garbling." Those books which he would like to retain "would be chiefly classical and mathematical." He would like also to have the use of "one of the five encyclopedias." But he would not press the point.

Then came the famous line: "I do not know that it contains any branch of science which Congress would wish to exclude from their collection; there is, in fact, no subject to which a Member of Congress may not have occasion to refer." This is followed by the statement of his unwillingness to have the collection dismembered—"My desire is either to place it in their hands entire, or to preserve it so here." He was "engaged in making an alphabetical index of the authors' names, to be annexed to the catalogue," which he would forward as soon as it was completed. The letter concluded: "Any agreement you shall be so good as to take the trouble of entering into with the committee, I hereby confirm."

Sometime between October 2 and October 7, Mr. Smith submitted the offer and the catalog to the members of the Joint Committee. Writing to Mr. Jefferson on the latter date, he reported that "the tender was respectfully received . . . with the assurance that no time should be lost in acting upon it." On the ninth, Senator Goldsborough introduced a resolution "That the joint library committee of the two houses of Congress be, and they are hereby, authorized and empowered to contract, on their part, for the purchase of the library of Mr. Jefferson, late President of the United States, for the use of both Houses of Congress." The following day it passed the Senate, without opposition, and was sent to the House, where it was read twice "and referred to a Committee of the Whole Tomorrow."

However, it did not come up until Monday, October 17, when the debate, according to the annalist, was "desultory." Those who opposed the purchase were Thomas Jackson Oakley, of New York a Federalist, Yale graduate, former surrogate of Dutchess County, an outspoken critic of the Madison administration and the conduct of the War, a man of "majestic bearing," a facile speaker who resorted to "but little rhetoric or gesticulation;" John Reed, of Massachusetts, a Federalist, graduate of Brown, former schoolmaster; and Thomas Peabody Grosvenor, of New York, a Federalist, Yale graduate, lately district attorney of Essex County. Their objections were generally the "extent" of the collection, "the cost of the purchase, the nature of the selection, embracing too many works in foreign languages, some of too philosophical a character, and some otherwise objectionable." As an example of those in the first category, mention was made of the works of M. Voltaire; typical of the other was Callender's *Prospect Before Us.*

The outspoken advocates of purchase were Robert Wright, of Maryland, a Democrat, educated at Washington College, successively private, lieutenant and captain in the Continental Army, formerly a senator and governor of his State, always a loyal supporter of Mr. Jefferson; Adam Seybert, of Pennsylvania, a Democrat, graduate of the medical department of the University of Pennsylvania who had continued his studies at Edinburgh, Göttingen, and Paris, member of the American Philosophical Society, chemist, mineralogist, apothecary, and statistician of government revenues and expenditures; Thomas Bolling Robertson, of Louisiana, a Democrat, educated at the College of William and Mary, lately secretary of the Territory of Louisiana by appointment of Mr. Jefferson, first Representative of his State in Congress, a man "capable of using strong denunciatory language" whose comparatively short life was to be crowded "with public activity and office-holding, to which he applied himself with energy and conviction;" Joseph H. Hawkins, of Kentucky, a Federalist, lawyer, former speaker of the State House of Representatives; and John Forsyth, of Georgia, a Democrat, graduate of Princeton, former attorney general of his State.

These gentlemen, according to the official record, "contended that so valuable a library, one so admirably calculated for the substratum of a great national library, was not to be obtained in the United States; and that, although there might be some works to which gentlemen might take exception, there were others of very opposite character; that this, besides, was no reason against the purchase, because in every library of value might be found some books to which exceptions might be taken, according to the feelings or prejudices of those who examined them."

The House adjourned without taking action. Discussion was resumed on the following day. An amendment to set a ceiling price of twenty-five thousand collars was offered, "the debate before its conclusion became rather too animated, and being checked by the Speaker, the question was permitted to be taken" with the result that it was voted down 103 to 37.

At that point the venerable Timothy Pickering of Massachusetts, a Federalist, graduate of Harvard, one-time Revolutionary colonel and quartermaster general, President Washington's Postmaster General, Secretary of War, and Secretary of State, proposed an amendment "the object of which was a selection of part of the library." Mr. Jefferson had gone on record as declining to entertain the suggestion of partition and the Pickering amendment was negatived by a vote of 92 to 56.

Finally Representative Oakley offered an amendment "requiring the sanction of Congress to the agreement for the purchase of the library, before it should become binding." It was adopted and in this form the resolution was ordered to a third reading. It passed the House on October 19, the Senate concurred on the twentieth, and final approval was given on the twenty-first.

The Joint Committee proceeded to secure an appraisal and on November 28, Senator Goldsborough reported a bill to authorize the purchase of the library, said to contain 6,487 volumes, for $23,950, "in Treasury notes of the issue ordered by the law of the fourth of March, one thousand eight hundred and fourteen." It passed the Senate without debate or amendment on December 3.

The discussion in the House took place on January 26, 1815; and the two members of the Joint Committee on the Library who were present were strangely silent.

Joseph Lewis, Jr., a Federalist Representative from Virginia, made a motion for indefinite postponement. It was lost by the narrow margin of 68 votes against 74.

Cyrus King, of Massachusetts, a Federalist, educated at Phillips Academy, Andover, and Columbia College, "moved to recommit the bill with instructions to a select committee to report a new section authorizing the selection of such of the books belonging to said library as might be necessary or useful to Congress in their deliberations, and to dispose of the remainder at public sale." This was "negatived."

Thereupon Mr. King, half-brother of another distinguished bibliophile, Rufus King, "moved to recommit the bill to a select committee [of the three members of the House on the Joint Committee on the Library only one was a Federalist], with instructions to report a new section authorizing the Library Committee, as soon as said Library shall be received at Washington, to select therefrom all books of an atheistical, irreligious, and immoral tendency, if any such there be, and send the same back to Mr. Jefferson without any expense to him"; but "this motion Mr. K. thought proper afterward to withdraw."

It was reported by the patronizing annalist that the "subject, and the various motions rela-

tive thereto, gave rise to a debate which lasted till the hour of adjournment; which, though it afforded much amusement to the auditors, would not interest the feelings or judgment of any reader."

Opposing the bill, in addition to Cyrus King, Thomas Peabody Grosvenor, and Timothy Pickering were Samuel Farrow, a "War Democrat" from South Carolina, whose face bore a scar from a saber wound sustained in the Revolution; Newton Cannon, of Tennessee, a Democrat, lately a Colonel in the Rifles with service in the War of 1812; Alexander Contee Hanson, of Maryland, a Federalist, graduate of St. John's College, journalist and administration critic; and a New Hampshire Federalist, product of Phillips Exeter Academy and Dartmouth College, then serving his first term in Congress, the Honorable Daniel Webster.

They "opposed the bill . . . on account of the scarcity of money, and the necessity of appropriating it to purposes more indispensable than the purchase of a library; the probable insecurity of such a library placed here [there was talk of changing the seat of government]; the high price to be given for this collection; its miscellaneous and almost exclusive literary (instead of legal and historical) character, &c."

The advocates of purchase were Robert Wright, of Maryland, a Revolutionary veteran, James Fisk, of Vermont, a Democrat, Revolutionary veteran, minister of the Universalist denomination and lawyer; John Rhea, of Tennessee, a Democrat, native of Ireland, graduate of Princeton, member of the Patriot Force at the Battle of King's Mountain; and John Whitefield Hulbert, of Massachusetts, a Federalist, lawyer and bank director.

"Enforced with zeal vehemence," these champions of the bill replied to its detractors "with fact, wit, and argument, to show that the purchase, to be made on terms of long credit, could not affect the present resources of the United States; that the price was moderate, the library more valuable from the scarcity of many of its books, and altogether a most admirable substratum for a National Library."

However compelling or unconvincing their arguments may have been, it is a fact of history that the bill was passed by a narrow margin of ten votes, and that on January 30, 1815, it became a law.

The action was momentous for four reasons: (1) the Library of Congress was reestablished, (2) the most distinguished private collection in the United States (it more than doubled the size of the old Library) passed into the possession of the Government, (3) the character of the Library of Congress changed from a "special" library to a "general" library (Mr. Jefferson had said "there is . . . no subject to which a member of Congress may not have occasion to refer"), and (4) Congress consciously secured "a most admirable substratum for a National Library."

• • • •

At the beginning of 1850, when the Smithsonian Institution published *Notices of Public Libraries in the United States of America* it seemed to have been forgotten that in the purchase of the Jefferson collection the country had acquired a "substratum" for a National Library. It had a Library, of course, then grown to "about 50,000 volumes, a few Manuscripts, a series of medals designed by Denon and executed by order of the French government, commemorative of events during the reign of Napoleon; some valuable maps and charts, and busts of several of the Presidents, with a few paintings of interest." The yearly average increase was about 1,800 volumes. The collections were housed in three rooms in the Capitol, "only one of which was originally designed for the purpose." Catalogs had been published as follows: "In 1802 (10 pp. 8vo.;) supplement, 1803 (3 pp.) and 1808 (41 pp.;) in 1812 (101 pp. 8vo.;) in 1815 (170 pp. 4to., containing Jefferson's library;) supplement, 1820 (28 pp.;) and in 1830 and '31 (362 pp. 8vo.)" The last catalog had been printed in 1840 (747 pp. 8vo.) with additions recorded in annual supplements. A new catalog was then in press.

The Library was "open every day during the sessions of Congress," and during a recess, for six hours on Tuesday, Thursday, and Saturday of each week. "Members of Congress, the President and Vice President of the United States, Heads of Departments, Judges of the Supreme Court, Secretary of the Senate, Clerk of the House, agents of the Library Committee, and Foreign Ministers," were "entitled to the use of the library," and were "allowed to take out books." The number of books annually issued on loan was "not known," nor could "the number of persons consulting the library be stated," but both were "very great during the sessions of Congress." Charles C. Jewett, author of the *Notices*, considered the Library of Congress "one of very great value" and "worthy of a minute and accurate catalogue."

Without such an apparatus "it would be comparatively useless . . . were it not for the catalogue of its contents written upon the memory of the librarians." In such a record as he proposed "every book, pamphlet, map, handbill, speech, and important article in a reveiw or magazine, should be entered carefully and accurately under the name of its author, and alphabetical and analytical indexes of subjects should be made." Moreover, this "catalogue should be a model performance." At the same time he recognized the fact that "such an one should not, of course, be required from the present force employed in the library," which was "not sufficient for the regular work of the establishment." Indeed, "the making of a catalogue should be a separate affair."

But at that moment a closer approach to a National Library was forming at the Smithsonian, then rapidly becoming "a centre of bibliographical knowledge," in the hope that one day it might be "worthy of the United States of America," and thereby "release us from a provincial dependence in literary matters upon the libraries of Europe." There the Institution's 6,000 books were accessible to all who wished "to use them in the room."

Toward the close of 1851, Washington was "still one of the best places for study in America." Wrote Charles Hale in the second number of *To-day, A Boston Literary Journal:*

> The Copy-right Library has 10,000 or more late American publications. The Smithson Library has as many books, including Mr. Marsh's valuable collections of Scandinavian literature. The Patent office Library, the Engineer's Library, and the War and [National] Institute Libraries comprise nearly 30,000 scientific books . . . . The House's Library is 12,000 volumes of law books and documents. And among private Libraries we may name Col. Force's invaluable collection on American History and early printing—which in these departments has books no where else in the country.

As for the Library of Congress, it was, Mr. Hale begrudgingly conceded, "a valuable collection of miscellaneous and law books," but "valuable as it was, there were circumstances attending its collection" which diminished his regard. For example,

> It was collected by different committes,—of course without any continued system, and it exhibited quite curiously the whims of Congresses and Congressmen.
> For instance, there was always a demand for Heraldry books. In compliance with this the Committees kept it up to the time, in all the English publications of that sort. Our Members from the West thronged that alcove on their first arrival, and many an "honorable gentleman" could not rest till the

chairman of the Library Committee had translated his Latin family motto for him.

There had to be assortments of showy picture books for the danglers who made the Library room their flirting place in the session . . .

Any private person, with the $250,000 spent for this Library, would have had a collection of four times its value. But "Uncle Sam" never gets his money's worth. And yet this was quite too good to lose.

And yet it had been lost.

FLUES, FURNACES AND FUTILITY

It was four o'clock on the afternoon of Tuesday, December 23, 1851. The Librarian was about to close the Library of Congress for the day. It would soon be dark.

He glanced about, "everything . . . appearing to be perfectly safe as usual." The books were in their places within the twelve arched alcoves, "Ornamented with fluted pilasters, copied from the pillars in the celebrated Octagon Tower at Athens." Over the mantel at the south end of the room was the fine portrait of Columbus, believed to have been painted "by the same hand which painted the celebrated likeness of that great man, now in the palace of the Escurial in Spain." It had been presented by George G. Barrell, while serving as our Consul at Malaga. Perhaps William Elliot was right; perhaps it was "in rather too elevated a position to gratify the spectator." Someday something should be done about it. In other parts of the room, on the walls and between the alcoves hung Gilbert Stuart's portraits of the first three Presidents, together with portraits of Peyton Randolph, John Hancock, John Tyler, Bolivar, Cortes, Americus Vespucius, the two Barons, deKalb and von Steuben, and other famous men, American and foreign. On the right of the door leading onto the balcony was Ceracchi's admirable bust of Mr. Jefferson, "elevated on the frustum of a fluted black marble column, based upon a circular pedestal," which was "ornamented at the top by a continued series of cherubs' heads, under a broad band encircling the pedestal," on which were "sculptured the signs of the zodiac." The pedestal had been presented to Mr. Jefferson in France, and bore a Latin inscription which was translated for the benefit of Capitol sightseers: "To the Supreme Ruler of the Universe, under whose watchful care the liberties of North America were finally achieved, and under whose tutelage the name of Thomas Jefferson will descend forever blessed to posterity." (At Monticello, Mr. Jefferson's modesty had induced him

to turn the inscription toward the wall, but here no such compulsions were felt.) "This bust was regarded by Mr. Jefferson's family as presenting the most perfect likeness of him of any extant."

Opposite it was David's head of "the generous and brave Lafayette." It, too, was in marble, "of colossal and bold proportions," and it had been "designed for an elevated position," which it did not hold. As a likeness it was considered admirable. On one side of the base block was inscribed an extract from his speech in the House of Representatives, December 10, 1824, and on the other his last words in answer to the President's farewell in September 1825.

Over the cornice of the alcoves, upon the blocking of the gallery, were several plaster busts; one of General Jackson, another of General Moultrie. They seemed familiar and eminently correct.

The Brussels carpet was clean; the large engravings were out of sight, carefully arranged in the drawers of the tables which furnished the middle portion of the long room. The furnace provided a pleasant warmth. The Librarian locked the door behind him, and, passing through the portico and down the steps, hurried to his home a block or two away. Christmas would come in two days. He probably looked forward to a little rest.

But the following morning was for him one of strenuous and tragic activity, and at the earliest possible moment he sat down to write a letter to James Alfred Pearce, chairman of the Joint Library Committee of Congress:

> . . . It is my melancholy duty to inform you that a fire originated in the principal room of the Library of Congress, this morning, about half past seven o'clock, and that nearly everything in the room was destroyed before the flames were subdued.
>
> The guard who was on duty at the time, told me that when he discovered the fire, having broken open the door for the purpose, it might have been extinguished by a few buckets of water, which unfortunately were not near at hand; but, that it spread in a few minutes so extensively as to be entirely beyond the control of the few persons then in the building with him. The fire soon extended to the roof, which was entirely destroyed, and left the late, beautiful room, with its invaluable contents, a smouldering mass of ruins.
>
> I believe that all the books and other property, in the Committee room, and in the large room adjoining it, are safe and uninjured.
>
> How the fire originated is quite a mystery, as no fire or lights have been used in any of the rooms of the Library for several years. Some have conjectured that the fire was communicated to the woodwork adjacent to the flue used for warming the room; whilst others believe that it was the work of an incendiary.

The latter is my own opinion. A searching investigation will be ordered by Congress, I presume; and I trust that the true cause of the most melancholy event will then be ascertained.

What had happened was this. At a quarter before eight on the morning of December 24, smoke, or flame, or both, were observed by a passer-by who notified the Capitol police. John W. Jones, of the police force, assisted by a certain Mr. Hollohan forced open the main door of the Library, and discovered a large table at the north end of the room afire, as well as a part of the shelving and books in the alcoves on the right. From the statement of Mr. Jones it appeared that when he first saw the blaze he and Mr. Hollohan hastened downstairs to get water and to summon assistance. The opening of the door produced a draft which "lent such vigor to the flames that by the time they returned the whole room was irrecoverably won to the power of the destroying element."

The alarm was given by shouts of "fire" and the ringing of alarm bells. Firemen hurried to the Capitol with their apparatus; and despite the fact that many of them had been up all night "in trying to extinguish a fire at Mr. Baker's Hotel, they worked their engines with great vigor and commendable perseverance." First to arrive was the Columbia Fire Company, followed shortly by the Anacostia. The *National Intelligencer* reported that "the hose [of the Columbia] being in a frozen condition, . . . had to be taken to the new gas factory on the canal to be thawed;" but *The Washington News*, on the authority of the President of that Company dismissed the canard as "entirely erroneous" insisting that "the hose never left the Capitol and was soon put in working order and rendered unfreezable, by means of whiskey." To the exertions of these public servants the salvation of the Capitol was due, for had the large dome caught fire, the building could hardly have escaped total destruction. By "cutting down with their axes the burning roof and dome, the conflagration was confined to the Congress Library." Assisting these "professionals" were the United States Marines from the Navy Yard and "numerous citizens who rendered prompt and willing" help "on a day of remarkable inclemency." Fire departments in Baltimore and Alexandria were getting ready to dash for Washington when they received a telegraphic announcement that the flames had been brought under control.

Thomas U. Walter, Architect of the Capitol explained the cause. Flues from some of the committe rooms passed under the floor of the Library, and close to the partition wall where they entered, an aperture was found quite large enough to admit particles of such light and combustible materials as are used in kindling fires. The fires in these rooms were made up at half-past six o'clock, and the chimney had taken fire. The alcoves of the Library were formed of timbers filled with "brick-nogging;" and the horizontal pieces were let into the walls for the purpose of strengthening the structure, thus affording the means of communicating the fire to the vertical scantling, one of which was placed against the wall in each partition. Mr. Walter declared that "the timbers were too far above the fire place to be set on fire in any other way than by the burning of the chimney, and such an event could not have occurred at any time without communicating fire to the Library." He concluded with a clear conscience: "No human forethought or vigilance could, under the circumstances, have prevented the catastrophe."

• • • •

THE THIRD THRUST

On December 31, 1864, Grant was still in the trenches before Petersburg, Sherman was preparing to strike northward from Savannah, and Sheridan and Thomas were receiving the Northern plaudits which followed their recent triumphs in the Valley and at Nashville. The fact that a member of the staff of the Library of Congress, who had for some years been supplying the place of the absentee Librarian, was on that day appointed by President Lincoln to the post of Librarian of Congress was in and of itself, hardly a transaction likely to figure largely in the public eye. On January 5, 1865, the *New York Times* carried a small paragraph reporting that the new Librarian had on that day entered upon the duties of his office, and beyond this the public interest—if there was a public interest—went unsatisfied. The appointment, however, was to prove an event of the greatest consequence for the development of the institution and for the idea of a national library. The new incumbent was to serve for thirty-two years, and during that time would witness, inspire, or direct developments determining the nature and future of the Library of Congress, and its position in the intellectual and social life of the Nation.

Mr. Lincoln's appointee was Ainsworth Rand Spofford, now in his fortieth year, who had been a member of the Library's staff since September

1861, and had been in charge most of the time, while John G. Stephenson was following the wars and winning mention in the dispatches. If there could be said to have been such things as professional librarians in the America of 1865, Mr. Spofford was certainly not of their number. He was the son of a New England clergyman, the Reverend Luke Ainsworth Spofford of Gilmanton New Hampshire, of the sixth generation of his family in America. As the son of a clergyman, he was of course prepared for college, attending Williston Seminary for that purpose, but in the end medical opinion pronounced that his eyes and lungs were both too weak to enter upon the severe application of college studies, and he had to abandon his intention of matriculating at Amherst. It is pleasant to record that nearly forty years later, in 1882, Amherst bestowed upon him, now famous for his services at Washington, an honorary Doctorate of Laws. Instead he went west, but not too far west, to Cincinnati, and succeeded in outgrowing and completely overcoming these physical handicaps. Herbert Putnam reported of his later years that he gloried "in the assiduity which his hardy, if attenuated, frame permitted: for the weakness of the lungs survived only in a mechanical cough, and the weakness of the eyes was remedied so completely that in his eighty-second year he resisted a prescription for glasses as premature and derogatory."

• • • •

The idea of the Library of Congress as the National Library, to which Mr. Spofford here gave expression, was one which he would preach in season and out for the next thirty-seven years, to Democrats and to Republicans, to politicians and to ordinary citizens, to learned assemblies and to Capitol sightseers alike. There was of course nothing new about the idea, but no one had hitherto taken hold of it with such firmness and fervor, or developed its consequences with such perfect clarity, or made himself its unresting servant. In the end, after manifold frustrations, hopes deferred, and tedious delays, all that he had foreseen and all for which he had labored were to be accomplished. It is for this reason that if anyone deserves the name of Apostle of the National Library, it is Ainsworth Rand Spofford. What was achieved in 1897 was envisaged in 1861—when the Nation was engulfed in fratricidal horror. In time of war, prepare for peace. Mr. Spofford never, so far as we are aware, made any large-scale or sys-

tematic exposition of all that was present to his mind in the concept of a National library. But nearly everything that he published or did from this time forth was a commentary upon this concept, and as we proceed we shall cite many of his brief and partial presentations of the idea, and touch upon the constituent elements as they became a part of his practical program.

We may pause to look for a moment at the institution whose employ he entered in 1861, and of which he became the director something more than three years later. Reduced to its essentials, the Library of Congress in 1861 consisted of two rooms, seven people, and 63,000 books. It required indeed the eye of faith to equate this shoestring outfit with the British Museum, the Bibliotheque Nationale, and the Imperial Library at St. Petersburg, but such an eye was precisely what Ainsworth Spofford brought to his job. The rooms comprised a separate apartment for the Law Library, after 1860 in the old Supreme Court room on the east side of the basement, and the Main Hall of the Library, on the west front of the central portion of the Capitol, directly off and easily accessible from the Rotunda under the dome. It will be recalled that the principal room was a good one, new, commodious, fireproof, and quite handsome for a construction of its date. The door was locked after the horse had been stolen: after the disastrous fire of December 24, 1851, which destroyed half of the entire collections and two-thirds of Mr. Jefferson's books, the Library room was reconstructed out of iron, copper and stone.

The seven persons on the staff of the Library consisted of the Librarian himself—normally absent at this period—three assistant librarians, one messenger, and two laborers. Since the younger Meehan—C. H. W. Meehan was the only member of the "professional" staff who was not dispossessed by the Republican invasion, and continued to serve until 1872—was on duty in the Law Library downstairs, this left just two librarians regularly on hand in the main room during the War. The Law Library was under the control, not of the Joint Library Committee but of the Supreme Court, and Chief Justice Roger B. Taney would have had no motive to replace a deserving Democratic incumbent by a black Republican. These seven men received in salaries the princely total of $9,000, ranging from the absentee Librarian's $2,160, through the assistants' $1,800 and the messenger's $1440, to $500 for the laborers who "did the chars." The Library's entire budget in 1861 amounted to $17,000, the remaining $8,000 being divided into $2,000 for the purchase of law books, $5,000 for other books, $1,000 for contingent expenses.

As for the collection, while it was the largest of the nine libraries then maintained in Washington by various branches of the Government, it nevertheless required a Spoffordian faith to regard it as the National Library of the United States of America. Of the Jeffersonian basis, but a third remained, and that third largely confined to a certain range of classification. After the disaster of 1851, the shelves had been somewhat hastily and unsystematically replenished, and rather with what the book sellers had to offer than with any planned body of acquisitions. There were some rarities but the presence or absence in the collection of any particular rare or unusual item was quite unpredictable and apparently accidental. In one respect the collection departed very radically from any reasonable concept of a National Library: the holdings in Americana were neither large nor distinguished. The best developed section was naturally the separately housed Law Library; in the *Catalogue of the Library of Congress* printed in this year, 1861, the law chapters occupy some 250 out of 1400 pages, and a much greater proportion of their entries are for large sets. By and large, the verdict of William Dawson Johnston is just: "The Library was a good reference library for the average legislator, though it was little more, and aimed to be little more." The printed catalog just mentioned was a complete repertory ot its contents but, as Spofford pointed out, its arrangement involved 179 distinct alphabets and being otherwise unindexed it was not therefore of great service as a finding instrument.

The war years, with Spofford in limited authority, were necessarily ones of limited progress. Nevertheless, what Spofford succeeded in accomplishing with the means at his disposal was sufficiently remarkable. While the turmoil raged without, attendance at the Library was small, being largely limited to Members of Congress, and this gave some opportunity for concentrated and constructive effort. "Mr. Spofford was primarily a collector of books," says Johnston, and the Library began to grow faster than it had ever grown before. With no increase either of the appropriations or of the Library's privileges, but merely by superior attention and energy the collections were increased by nearly one-third in four years and grew from 63,000 to 82,000 volumes. In fact,

the problem of adequate space began now for the first time to rear its head. With, as we have seen, hardly more than two working librarians, he not only kept up the annual catalogs of new accessions, but put through the press in 1864 a complete catalog of the Library based on an entirely new system of arrangement as compared with those issued between 1815 and 1861. This was an alphabetical catalog by authors, and was the only such printed catalog ever to be completed by the Library of Congress. It was also the first general catalog to be manufactured by the Government Printing Office, which had been producing the annual supplements since 1862.

• • • •

On February 7, 1884, Senator Justin S. Morrill, characterizing the Library as "the property of the nation, open to all the people without any ticket of admission," reminded the Congress that "its custody is intrusted to our honor and our enlightened sense of propriety. Our duty is obvious, and its neglect can not escape reproach." Five days later Senator Thomas F. Bayard spoke to the same effect:

> I trust that the present measure is now about to take the form of law, in order that we shall at least see the beginning of that which we all recognize as a duty, and that is the construction of a safe, suitable and worthy building for the preservation of the books of the American people.

At last, on April 15, 1886, it happened.

> *Be it enacted by the Senate and House of Representatives of the United States of America in Congress assembled,* That a fire-proof building, for the accommodation of the Library of Congress, shall be erected east of the Capitol . . . as the commission hereinafter provided shall determine; and the construction of said building, substantially according to the plan submitted to the Joint Select Committee on Additional Accommodations for the Library of Congress, by John L. Smithmeyer, in the Italian renaissance style of architecture, . . . shall be in charge of a commission composed of the Secretary of the Interior, the Architect of the Capitol Extension and the Librarian of Congress . . . and the sum of five hundred thousand dollars is hereby appropriated to commence the construction of said building.

But the building could not actually begin without an additional appropriation for the purchase of land; and one of the very few private letters of Mr. Spofford's which we have shows his personal share in getting this over the hurdle:

> Aug. 5, 1886. To-day I have had a hard day's work,

and at times a hurried and anxious one. It grew out of this being the last day of Congress, and the great importance to the Library Commission of getting through the $35,000 appropriation to make certain the immediate progress of the building. I was on the floor of the House three hours, and Secretary Lamar was there about two hours, watching its chances, removing objections, taking care of Holman, McMillan, Blount and others—for a single member's objection would have killed it at any stage. Randall had made known his intention not to oppose it, and his belief that it would go through. . . . At last after running the gauntlet for the better part of the session, a favorable moment was seized, and the bill got through by unanimous consent! Speaker Carlisle was favorable or it would not have got a chance. At once I hurried it back to the Senate to be enrolled—got the signatures of Sherman and Carlisle, and was made special messenger to carry the bill to the White House for the President's signature. This goal was reached at 3.10 P. M. and both Houses had resolved to adjourn *sine die* at 4. Mr. Cleveland was at lunch, but I sent the bill down to him by Mr. Pruden, the Secretary, and it came back in fifteen minutes with Grover Cleveland's name "approved." This saved the day—and I am again the happiest man in Washington—the last obstacle in the way of the Library Building being removed.

With the circumstances that made the construction of the new Library of Congress the slow work of more than a decade we are not here concerned. They were for Mr. Spofford simply a period of marking time, as the situation continued to deteriorate. Only one important change took place during this period: the enactment of an international copyright law approved March 3, 1891, and effective July 1, 1891. This extended the protection of the American copyright law to authors and artists of foreign citizenship, so long as their books, photographs, chromos and lithographs were manufactured in the United States. It added to the embarrassment of the Library and the Librarian in three ways: it increased the influx of materials, not so much in books, but in musical compositions and works of art; it entailed a foreign correspondence; and it imposed the duty of transmitting the Treasury Department for publication there, a weekly catalog of all publications entered for copyright. But no new clerical help was given to the Librarian, and a Register of Copyrights to take the burden from his shoulders was not provided.

At length the new Library of Congress was ready for occupation, and a new era of the National Library could begin. Mr. Spofford, in his last Annual Report as Librarian, included a brief note of congratulation:

> The completion, since the last annual report of the undersigned, of the commodious and beautiful new Library building is a proper subject of congratulation to Congress and to the American people. Planned throughout with a view to the accommodation and prompt service of a great library collection in all its departments, its utility may be said to have realized the chief end of library architecture, while the beauty of the edifice, both in its exterior walls and interior decorations (all by American atrists) appeals eminently to the public taste.

ADDITIONAL READINGS

Bach, Harry, "The Snows of Yesteryear," *College and Research Libraries* 30 (July, 1969), pp. 301-306.

Ditzion, Sidney, "The District-School Library, 1835-55," *Library Quarterly* 10 (October, 1940), pp. 545-577.

Everhart, Frances, "The South Carolina College Library, Background and Beginnings," *Journal of Library History* 3 (July, 1968), pp. 221-241.

Harding, Thomas D., "College Literary Societies: Their Contribution to the Development of Academic Libraries, 1815-1876," *Library Quarterly* 29 (April, 1959), pp. 94-112.

Held, Ray, "The Early School-District Library in California," *Library Quarterly* 29 (April, 1959), pp. 79-93.

Held, Ray, *Public Libraries in California, 1849-1878* (Berkeley: University of California Press, 1963).

Johnston, William Dawson, *History of the Library of Congress 1800-1864* (Washington: Government Printing Office, 1904).

McMullen, Haynes, "The Founding of Social Libraries in Pennsylvania, *1731-1876,"* Pennsylvania History* 32 (April, 1965), pp. 130-152.

McMullen, Haynes, "Social Libraries in Ante-Bellum Kentucky," *The Register of the Kentucky Historical Society* 58 (1960), pp. 97-128.

Ranz, Jim, *The Printed Book Catalogue in American Libraries 1723-1900* (Chicago: American Library Association, 1964).

IV
PUBLIC LIBRARIES IN THE UNITED STATES

The opening of the reading room of the Boston Public Library at the Adams School House in 1854 heralded the advent of the American public library. These libraries, as defined by one of their most effective administrators, were established by state laws, supported by local taxation or voluntary gifts, and managed as public trusts. Every citizen of the city or town which supported the public library had an equal share in its privileges.

The rise of the American public library has been the focus of a number of studies, all of which attempt to explain the forces which helped create this new kind of library. The four essays which follow are landmark studies on this subject, and while they do not provide the definitive answers to the questions surrounding American public library development, they do provide important insights into the societal factors which influenced, and are still influencing, public library development in this country.

The People's University—The Educational Objective of the Public Library

Robert Lee

The founders of early public libraries in this country had as one of their primary objectives the provision of equal educational opportunities for the country's citizens. The following essay merits our consideration for two important reasons. First, it presents a concise and enlightened summary of public library development, and second, it offers an explanation for the growth of the public library in terms of that institution's educational objectives.

Early Development

On April 9, 1833, the citizens of Peterborough, New Hampshire, without the sanction of state legislation, voted to set aside for the purchase of library books a portion of the state bank tax, which was distributed among New Hampshire towns for schools or "other purposes of education." Thus, the first American town library, open to the public and continuously supported by tax funds, was begun.[1] This new civic institution, however, did not suddenly appear on the American scene. It was the product of almost a century and a half of experimentation in the development of three major types of semipublic libraries: parish and parochial libraries, social libraries (proprietary, subscription, mechanics' and mercantile libraries), and circulating libraries.[2]

The establishment of the Peterborough Library in 1833 was significant in that it set a precedent in the use of public funds. Other free libraries were established during the next two decades in some of the small towns in Massachusetts, New Hampshire, and New York State.[3] The organization of free libraries was relatively slow, however, until 1854 when the city of Boston—one of the large and culturally important cities of the country—established a public library. This marked the turning point in the history of the public library movement in the United States. The organization of a public library by a major metropolitan community, and the formulation by its founders of a rationale for free public library service, provided the impetus needed to set the public library concept into motion.

FOUNDING OF THE BOSTON PUBLIC LIBRARY

In 1839, M. Nicholas Marie Alexandre Vattemare, a former actor and ventriloquist who was serving as an emissary of the French government, toured this country with the object of establishing a system for the international exchange of books. After presenting his proposal to President Van Buren and to members of the Congress, he was asked to visit Boston on the assurance of John Quincy Adams "that of all the cities of the New World none are better qualified to appreciate and support the system."[4]

In April, 1841, Vattemare went to Boston and there introduced his program for the exchange of books and a corollary of his plan, which involved the establishment of a free public library. His purpose, according to Josiah Quincy, President of Harvard College and a former mayor of Boston was "to give the intellectual treasures of the civilized world the same dissemination and equalization which commerce [had] already given to its material ones."[5] Although an enthusiastic response greeted Vattemare's presentation at two public meetings held in Boston in 1841,[6] no official action was then taken. His efforts had no tangible effect in Boston until six years later.

In October, 1847, Mayor Josiah Quincy, Jr., received on behalf of the City a gift of fifty books from the City of Paris. That same month the city council of Boston appointed a joint committee to prepare an acknowledgment to be sent to Paris and to consider the formation of a public library. The members of this committee prepared a report, submitted on October 18, in which they presented

SOURCE: Reprinted from Robert Ellis Lee, *Continuing Education for Adults through the American Public Library, 1833-1964* (Chicago: American Library Association, 1966), pp. 3-11, 116-119, by permission of the author and publisher. Copyright © 1966 by the American Library Association.

the reasons for the establishment of a free library in Boston. "It will tend," they said,

> to interest the people at large in literature and science. It will provide for those who are desirous of reading a better class of books than the ephemeral literature of the day. It may be the means for developing minds that will make their possessors an honor and blessing to their race. It will give to the young when leaving school an opportunity to make further advances in learning and knowledge. It will, by supplying an innocent and praiseworthy occupation, prevent a resort to those scenes of amusement that are prejudicial to the elevation of the mind. It will in addition to lectures established by Mr. Lowell and the libraries and advantages of the neighboring University, tend to make this City the resort of learned and scientific men from all sections of the Country, increasing the intelligence, the character, and the wealth of the City.
>
> . . . .
> Linked together as we are by political and business relations the character and intelligence of the people in every city between Massachusetts and Oregon is of vast importance to the citizens of Boston. If a free public library is established here our example will be imitated.[7]

Library Legislation

In January, 1848, the city council directed Mayor Quincy to apply to the legislature for power to enable the city to establish and maintain a public library. On May 18, 1848, the Massachusetts Legislature passed an act that enabled the city of Boston "to establish and maintain a Public Library, for the use of its inhabitants."[8] This was the first statute passed by a state governing body authorizing the establishment of a public library as a municipal institution supported by taxation. The following year, the New Hampshire Legislature passed the first general library law permitting "any town in the State to raise and appropriate money for the establishment and maintenance of a public library, and to be open for the free use of every inhabitant of the town, for the general diffusion of intelligence among all classes of the community."[9] On May 24, 1851, a similar act was passed by the Massachusetts Legislature. "The object aimed at in procuring the passage of this Act," wrote the Reverend John B. Wight, a member of the Massachusetts Legislature,

> . . . was not merely to prevent the necessity of special legislation, whenever any city or town might wish to have such a library, but to bring the formation of Free Public Libraries before the public mind, that it might recommend itself to universal adoption as an important supplement to the common schools, academies, and colleges, in the subsequent and life-long education of the whole people.[10]

Securing permissive legislation enabling communities to tax themselves was a necessary first step; the more difficult task, however, was for local authorities and enlightened citizens to implement this legislation by actually establishing libraries and obtaining funds for their maintenance.

Everett and Ticknor

In 1850, Edward Everett, a former President of Harvard College and Senator from Massachusetts, became interested in the plan for a public library, and offered to present his collection of American state papers, public documents, and other works if the city would provide a suitable place for them.[11] In a letter to Mayor Bigelow of Boston, dated June 7, 1851, Everett wrote:

> The first principles of popular government require that the means of education should, as far as possible, be equally within the reach of the whole population . . . . This however is the case only up to the age when School education is at an end. We provide our children with the elements of learning and science, and put it in their power by independent study and research to make further acquisitions of useful knowledge from books–but where are they to find the books in which it is contained? Here the noble principle of equality sadly fails. The sons of the wealthy alone have access to well-stored libraries; while those whose means do not allow them to purchase books are too often debarred from them at the moment when they would be most useful. We give them an elementary education, impart to them a taste and inspire them with an earnest desire for further attainment–which unite in making books a necessity for intellectual life–and then make no provision for supplying them.
>
> . . . .
> For these reasons I cannot but think that a Public Library, well supplied with books in various departments of art and science, and open at all times for consultation and study to the citizens at large, is absolutely needed to make our admirable system of Public Education complete; and to continue in some degree through life that happy equality of intellectual privileges, which now exists in our schools, but terminates with them.[12]

Everett continued by describing the conditions necessary for extending educational opportunities: if the public schools taught students how to read and developed in them a continuing curiosity about the world, public libraries would provide the means for continuing the educational process throughout life. Everett's assumption was that with the establishment of a public library the knowledge of this world would be at the disposal of those who could read and who had the incentive to do so.

Everett, in his attempt to establish a free library, was joined by George Ticknor, a professor of foreign languages at Harvard. In a letter to Everett, dated July 14, 1851, Ticknor suggested that a public library "would be the crowning glory of our public schools."[13] He agreed with Everett on all points concerning a free library except one: the nature of the book collection. Ticknor maintained that a library should be organized to serve all classes of people and, to achieve this end, popular books should be provided.[14] He said that the proposed public library

> ... should be adapted to our peculiar character; that is, that it should come in at the end of our system of free instruction, and be fitted to continue and increase the effects of that system by the self-culture that results from reading.
>
> ....
> Now what seems to me to be wanted in Boston is an apparatus that shall carry this taste for reading as deep as possible into society, assuming, what I believe to be true, that it can be carried deeper in our society than in any other in the world, because we are better fitted for it. To do this I would establish a library which, in its main department and purpose, should differ from all free libraries yet attempted; I mean one in which any popular book ... should be furnished in such numbers of copies that many persons, if they desired it, could be reading the same work at the same time; ... This appetite for general reading, once formed, will take care of itself. It will, in the majority of cases, demand better and better books; and can, I believe, by a little judicious help, rather than by any direct control or restraint, be carried much higher than is generally thought possible.[15]

The crucial moment in the establishment of a public library in Boston came in the early part of 1852. On May 24, Everett, Ticknor, and three other citizens were appointed as members of the first board of trustees. Ticknor at first declined to accept the office "unless the library were to be dedicated, in the first instance, rather to satisfying the wants of the less favored classes of the community, than—like all existing libraries—to satisfying the wants of scholars, men of science, and cultivated men generally."[16] No agreement to these terms was made, but Ticknor nevertheless accepted the office. The newly formed board of trustees held its first meeting May 31 and appointed a committee consisting of Edward Everett, George Ticknor, Sampson Reed, and Nathaniel Shurtleff "to take into consideration the objects to be obtained by the establishment of a public library, and the best mode of effecting them, and to report thereon."[17] This report, largely written by Ticknor,[18] was submitted and unanimously

adopted on July 6, 1852. It laid down the fundamental concept on which the American public library system has since developed and was, according to Jesse H. Shera, the leading authority on this period of public library development,

> ... the first real credo of the public library. Modified by experience only in minor detail, it still stands as the best single statement of the relation of the library to the social order. What was said then has been repeated many times since, but seldom with equal clarity and precision.[19]

The 1852 report, because of the extensive influence it has had on public library development and because of its explicit definition of the educational function of a public library, will be quoted at length.

The 1852 Report

The purpose of the Boston Public Library, according to the report, was to supplement the city's system of education. Boston provided "a first rate school education, at the public expense, to the entire rising generation."[20] However, and this particular point was emphasized,

> ... when this object is attained, and it is certainly one of the highest importance, our system of public instruction stops. Although the school and even the college and the university are, as all thoughtful persons are well aware, but the first stages in education, the public makes no provision for carrying on the great work. It imparts, with a noble equality of privilege, a knowledge of the elements of learning to all its children, but it affords them no aid in going beyond the elements. It awakens a taste for reading, but it furnishes to the public nothing to be read. It conducts our young men and women to that point, where they are qualified to acquire from books the various knowledge in the arts and sciences which books contain; but it does nothing to put those books within their reach. As matters now stand, and speaking with general reference to the mass of the community, the public makes no provision whatever, by which the hundreds of young persons annually educated, as far as the elements of learning are concerned, at the public expense, can carry on their education and bring it to practical results by private study.
>
> ....
> The trustees submit, that all the reasons which exist for furnishing the means of elementary education, at the public expense, apply in an equal degree to a reasonable provision to aid and encourage the acquisition of the knowledge required to complete a preparation for active life or to perform its duties.
>
> ....
> ... a free public library is not only seen to be demanded by the wants of the city at this time, but also seen to be the next natural step to be taken for the intellectual advancement of this whole community and

for which this whole community is peculiarly fitted and prepared.[21]

The trustees were of the opinion that a public library, like a public school, would strengthen the "republic government." They reasoned that (1) the building and maintenance of a free nation rested on the wisdom of the people who controlled it; (2) the nation placed upon its electorate an increasing responsibility but had no comprehensive policy for educating the people beyond common school requirements; and (3) a nation which granted freedom of choice to its people must, therefore, provide a means of continuing education which would ensure that choices would be intelligent.

> For it has been rightly judged that,—under political, social and religious institutions like ours,—it is of paramount importance that the means of general information should be so diffused that the largest possible number of persons should be induced to read and understand questions going down to the very foundations of [the] social order, which are constantly presenting themselves, and which we, as a people, are constantly required to decide, and do decide, either ignorantly or wisely. That this *can* be done,—that is, that such libraries *can* be collected, and that they will be used to a much wider extent than libraries have ever been used before, and with much more important results, there can be no doubt; and if it can be done *anywhere*, it can be done *here* in Boston; for no population of one hundred and fifty thousand souls, lying so compactly together as to be able, with tolerable convenience, to resort to one library, was ever before so well fitted to become a reading, self-cultivating population, as the population of our own city is at this moment.[22]

The proposed library, as stated in the report, was conceived of as an institution

> . . . to which the young people of both sexes, when they leave the schools, can resort for those works which are needful for research into any branch of useful knowledge.[23]

The immediate purpose of a public library was to raise the reading tastes of the majority of citizens through the provision of what Ticknor called "popular books." The long-range purpose, once general reading standards were raised, was to make the institution

> . . . a great and rich library for men of science, statesmen and scholars, as well as for the great body of the people, many of whom are always successfully struggling up to honorable distinctions and all of whom should be encouraged and helped to do it.[24]

In attempting to achieve these purposes, the trustees

> . . . would endeavor to make the Public Library of the City, as far as possible, the crowning glory of our system of City Schools; or in other words, they would make it an institution, fitted to continue and increase the best effects of that system, by opening to all the means of self culture through books for which these schools have been specially qualifying them.[25]

The report was submitted to the city council during the latter part of July, 1852. Benjamin Seaver, the mayor of Boston, sent a copy of the trustees' report to Joshua Bates, a successful London banker and former resident of Boston. In a letter to Mayor Seaver, dated October 1, 1852, Bates offered $50,000 for the purchase of books if the city would provide a building for the library.[26] Suitable facilities were provided, and the Boston Public Library was officially opened May, 2, 1854, to all inhabitants of the city over the age of sixteen.[27]

Educational Rationale

The Boston Public Library came into existence, not because the people demanded a library, but because a small number of learned and influential citizens expressed the need for providing equal educational opportunities for adults. The chief motivating forces were: first, effective leadership and benevolent philanthropy, and, second, a firm belief in the social value of education, with, however, an awareness of the limits of formal education, as a permanent means of individual betterment, moral improvement, and political progress.[28] The existing social, economic, and cultural conditions that enabled the founders of the Boston Public Library to put their ideas into practice were: a growing urban area which was rapidly becoming an industrial center; a cultural heritage expressed in a body of literature important enough to be disseminated; and a system of public education producing an increased number of literate adults.

Public education was considered to be the best means of solving social and political problems and the most certain guaranty of continuing progress. The communication of knowledge, it was hoped, would bring about a number of desirable results: improve the personal and vocational competence of individuals; protect and perpetuate republican institutions; dissolve social differences; check demagogues through intelligent use of the ballot; make citizens virtuous as well as intelligent; maintain the prosperity and well-being of the country; make men more efficient as producers; inculcate respect for property rights; curb radical tendencies; and prevent labor uprisings.[29] These convictions about the ends of education were based on the belief that the well-being of the individual was intimately related to the conditions of society as a whole. The goal was a better society, the barrier was ignorance, and the means—public education.

Most of the ideals, many of the conditions, and some of the assumptions that led to the establishment of the public schools led logically to the establishment of the Boston Public Library. This library was organized for the purpose of providing a means by which the citizens of the community could continue to learn through their own efforts. Its role was to serve as a supplement to the public school system. Its function was to provide adults[30] with equal access to books. And, although never publicly stated, this library was initiated as a municipal experiment. The founders made an assumption about the educational value of books and formulated what was, in fact, a statement of belief concerning what a public library could accomplish. Only the events of the future would indicate whether the ideals of the founders of the Boston Public Library could be achieved.

GROWTH OF PUBLIC LIBRARIES

In the period immediately following the establishment of the Boston Public Library, the ideas of Ticknor and Everett were reiterated in many New England communities as the primary reasons for the establishment of a public library.[31] In the 1850's, thirty-five public libraries were organized: thirty in Massachusetts, four in New Hampshire, and one in Maine. During the next decade relatively little progress was made; the Civil War halted the formation of new libraries and the growth of the old. But library development was revitalized between 1870 and 1875, when more public libraries were established than had been in the previous twenty years.

Between 1850 and 1875, the public library movement in the United States began to assume a definite form in the northeastern and midwestern states. Enabling laws for public libraries were enacted in ten states, and free municipal libraries established in eight cities:

Enabling Laws for Public Libraries[32]		Free Municipal Libraries[33]	
Massachusetts	1851	Boston	1854
Maine	1854	Cincinnati	1856
Vermont	1865	Detroit	1865
Ohio	1868	St. Louis	1865
Wisconsin	1868	Cleveland	1868
Connecticut	1869	Louisville	1871
Iowa	1870	Indianapolis	1872
Indiana	1871	Chicago	1873
Illinois	1872		
Texas	1874		

At the end of the third quarter of the nineteenth century there was a total of 188 public libraries in eleven states:[34]

Massachusetts	127
Illinois	14
New Hampshire	13
Ohio	9
Maine	8
Vermont	4
Connecticut	4
Wisconsin	4
Indiana	3
Iowa	1
Texas	1

Since the organization of public libraries presupposed an educated, or at least literate, adult public, it is not surprising that the development of libraries in the different states followed somewhat the same geographical pattern as that of the public schools established earlier.

• • • •

DEVELOPMENT OF THE PUBLIC LIBRARY AS AN EDUCATIONAL INSTITUTION

Four major phases in the development of the public library as an educational institution may be noted:

First Phase

Almost a century and a half of experimentation in the development of three types of semipublic libraries in this country—parish, social, and circulating libraries—prepared the way for the establishment of the first public library, which was organized in Peterborough, New Hampshire, in 1833. The effective beginning of the American public library movement, however, came in 1854, when a public library was established in Boston by a small group of learned and influential citizens.

The Boston Public Library was organized for the purpose of providing a means by which adults could continue to learn through their own efforts. This purpose was based on three beliefs. First, adults were capable of unlimited self-improvement and intellectual progress. Second, books were the principal instrument of education. Third, most adults could not afford to buy the books they needed to continue their education through reading. These beliefs, which were clearly formulated and concisely recorded by the founders of the Boston Public Library, provided a rationale for the establishment of public libraries in this country from around 1855 to 1875.

During this early period of public library development, librarians had a clear understanding of the library's educational aim and of the way in which it was to be implemented. They believed that it was not their responsibility to teach or to instruct the library patron, but instead to provide him with the type of books from which he could gain for himself the knowledge he wanted. In working with a relatively small and homogeneous audience, librarians provided a specific type of educational service which they rendered with as little intrusion as possible into the lives of the persons they were serving.

Second Phase

During the last quarter of the nineteenth century, the public library gradually expanded its services and acquired two additional objectives: recreation and reference. Librarians believed that the provision of recreational reading (namely, popular novels) would lead to more serious reading, contribute to cultural growth, and thereby serve as a steppingstone to the library's primary objective—education. They reasoned that they must first interest the reader before they could educate him; and, to this end, "must commence at his own standard of intelligence." During the late 1870's and throughout the 1880's, the library's educational objective was basic, however, and the other two objectives were subordinated to it. Then, around 1890, when the provisions of recreational reading and informational reference service began to make more and more demands on the librarian's time, confusion arose about which of the library's three objectives—education, recreation, or reference—was primary. In serving an audience composed of persons with diverse reading interests and abilities, librarians had difficulty in making an absolute division between the educational objective and the recreational objective. Furthermore, they were faced with the problem of determining how much time and how many resources should be devoted to each.

With the rapid growth of the public library movement after 1900, librarians directed major efforts toward serving a larger and more heterogeneous audience, responding to more of the recreational reading wants of the people, and increasing library coverage and circulation. The majority of librarians were no longer seriously concerned about whether novel reading led to serious reading. This attitude was fostered and sanctioned to some extent by the development, during the early 1900's, of the organized recreational movement in the United States, which began with the

recognition of the fact that the urban environment offered no adequate outlet for the wholesome energies of either children or adults. Recreation was "socially useful," and therefore it was "good" public policy for libraries to supply recreational reading which would help people pass time pleasantly. Thus the recreational objective soon exceeded the educational objective in terms of emphasis.

Third Phase

Following the Close of World War I, a small group of librarians attempted to revitalize the library's educational objective and to make education once more the dominant function of the public library. This group sought a return to the educational ideals of the founders, attempting to bring those ideals to fruition through a new interpretation adapted to the needs of the 1920's. During this period more public libraries began to function successfully as adult educational agencies. Many of the advances that came about during the 1920's can be attributed to the work of the American Library Association, which, with funds from the Carnegie Corporation of New York, provided encouragement and assistance to libraries in the development of educational services for adults. Although some positive gains resulted from these efforts, the concept of the library's educational commitment was not clearly understood by the majority of librarians.

With the coming of the depression of the 1930's, library appropriations were reduced. Subsequently, there was a reappraisal of essential library services, and some of the leaders of the profession stated that the educational rather than the recreational services of libraries would be more likely to command public respect, especially during the period of financial crisis. Between 1933 and 1938, two attempts were made to formulate comprehensive statements of public library objectives. Each of these statements, which were officially adopted by the American Library Association, represented a step forward in focusing attention on the Library's educational responsibility.

A series of events which occurred between the close of World War II and 1956 resulted in a gradual improvement in the quality, and an increase in the quantity, of educational services for adults through libraries. Two additional attempts were made to formulate comprehensive statements of public library objectives, and in each of these statements the educational function was given first place among the listing of objectives. During this period, two survey studies of library adult education were undertaken which presented the first detailed account of the extent and diversity of the adult educational services to groups provided by public libraries. Several extensive projects were initiated by the American Library Association, with financial assistance from the Fund for Adult Education, which increased the number and type of the adult educational services of libraries. The results of these efforts were that more librarians were gradually acquiring a better understanding of the library's educational responsibility and more libraries were beginning to allocate staff time and resources to the provision of adult educational services and programs.

Fourth Phase

Between 1957 and 1964, increased emphasis was placed on the provision of reference and informational services, less emphasis was given to the provision of materials for recreational or pastime reading, and the concept of educational service to adults was broadened by building the educational aim into many of the library's services and activities and by focusing services on community needs. Reference and informational service in-

creased because of the greater use of the public library by students. The need for providing recreational reading, especially light fiction, decreased because of more diversified recreational outlets for adults—such as television, spectator sports, group activities—and the availability of inexpensive paperbound books for recreational reading. Educational services for adults through the public library were focused more and more on local community concerns, were often planned and cosponsored by the library and another agency, were presented by means of a variety of techniques, and were often more meaningful to adults than the more traditional type of programs presented by libraries during the late 1940's.

Thus, there have been four phases in the development of the public library as an educational institution. First, the library began as a single-purpose institution in which education for adults was the central aim. Next, it became a multipurpose institution in which education, recreation, and reference were the primary objectives, with recreation and reference eventually taking precedence over education. Third, it entered a period of appraisal in which attempts were made to revitalize its educational objective. Fourth, it is currently placing major emphasis on its informational and educational objectives and less on its recreational objective.

FOOTNOTES

[1] Albert Smith, *History of the Town of Peterborough, Hillsborough County, New Hampshire* (Boston: George H. Ellis, 1876), p. 114-17.

[2] Bernard C. Steiner, "Rev. Thomas Bray and His American Libraries," *American Historical Review*, 2:59-75 (Oct. 1896); William D. Houlette, "Parish Libraries and the Work of Rev. Thomas Bray," *Library Quarterly*, 4:588-609 (Oct. 1934); Charles K. Bolton, *Proprietary and Subscription Libraries* (Chicago: ALA Publishing Board, 1917); William I. Fletcher, "The Proprietary Library in Relation to the Public Library Movement," *Library Journal*, 31:C268-72 (Aug. 1906); Sidney Ditzion, "Mechanics' and Mercantile Libraries," *Library Quarterly*, 10:192-219 (April 1940); Charles K. Bolton, "Circulating Libraries in Boston, 1765-1865," Colonial Society of Massachusetts, *Publications*, 11:196-207 (Feb. 1907).

[3] Jesse H. Shera, *Foundations of the Public Library* (Chicago: Univ. of Chicago Pr., 1949), p. 181-99.

[4] Justin Winsor, "M. Vattemare and the Public Library System," *Literary World*, 10:185 (June 7, 1879).

[5] Josiah P. Quincy, "The Character and Services of Alexandre Vattemare," *Massachusetts Historical Society Proceedings*, 1, 2d ser.: 260-72 (1884).

[6] Winsor, *op cit.*, p. 186.

[7] Horace G. Wadlin, *The Public Library of the City of Boston: A History* (Boston: Printed at the Library and published by the Trustees, 1911), p. 8, 9.

[8] Edward Edwards, *Free Town Libraries: Their Formation, Management, and History, in Britain, France, Germany, and America* (London: Trubner and Co., 1869), p. 281.

[9] The complete text of the New Hampshire Act of 1849 is reprinted in Shera, *op. cit.*, p. 192-93.

[10] (Jared M. Heard), *Origin of the Free Public Library System of Massachusetts* (Clinton, Mass.: Printed at the Office of the *Saturday Courant*, 1860), p. 9.

[11] Paul Revere Frothingham, *Edward Everett, Orator and Statesman* (Boston: Houghton, 1925), p. 323.

[12] "A Public Library," *Massachusetts Teacher*, 4, no. 8:255-56 (Aug. 1851).

[13] George Ticknor, *Life, Letters and Journals of George Ticknor* (Boston: James R. Osgood and Co., 1876), 2:301.

[14] *Ibid.*

[15] *Ibid.*, p. 301-2.

[16] *Ibid.*, p. 304.

[17] Wadlin, *op. cit.,* p. 31.

[18] *Ibid.,* Ticknor, *op. cit.,* p. 305; Shera, *op. cit.,* p. 181.

[19] Shera, *op. cit.,* p. 181.

[20] *Report of the Trustees of the Public Library of the City of Boston*, City Document No. 37, July 1852, p. 6.

[21] *Ibid.,* p. 6-9.

[22] *Ibid.,* p. 15.

[23] *Ibid.,* p. 8.

[24] *Ibid.,* p. 20.

[25] *Ibid.,* p. 21.

[26] Wadlin, *op. cit.,* p. 41-42.

[27] Edward Edwards, *Memoirs of Libraries: Including a Handbook of Library Economy* (London: Trubner and Co., 1859), 2:215.

[28] A different interpretation has been suggested by Jesse H. Shera: "The public library, as we know it today, came about through the effort of small and highly literate groups of professional men—scholars, lawyers, ministers, and educators—who sorely needed books for the performance of their daily tasks and who, through their efforts, convinced their respective communities of the social utility of supporting a public library. Even George Ticknor, who, more emphatically than most, argued for the public library as an agency of popular culture, helped fill the shelves of the new Boston Public Library with titles that more properly belonged in the study of the man of letters" ("On the Value of Library History," *Library Quarterly*, 22:246 [July 1952]). Shera's point of view, in the judgment of the writer, is relevant with regard to the early *practices* of public libraries but not with respect to the *motives* of the founders. Shera's interpretation assumes that the founders of the Boston Public Library established a tax-supported municipal library primarily for the purpose of advancing their own personal interests, and, to achieve this end, set about to convince the people of the social value of a public library. The evidence that Shera gives to support this interpretation is that Ticknor "helped fill the shelves of the new Boston Public Library" with scholarly books. The fact is that Ticknor donated some books (not "filled the shelves") from his personal collection. Since almost all public libraries were, and still are, receptive to donations of significant books, and because it was never stated, implied, or assumed that the book collection of the Boston Public Library would consist entirely of popular books, the example that Shera cites as evidence of the motives of the founders is questionable. Moreover, Everett and Ticknor, the two central figures in the establishment of the Boston Public Library, were not "sorely" in need of "books for the performance of their daily tasks." Both men had their own private collection of books, as well as access to the Boston Athenaeum and the Harvard College library. Furthermore, Everett, who served as Secretary of State from November, 1852, to May, 1854, the period in which the Boston Public Library was being established, also had access to the Library of Congress. Ticknor, according to Arthur E. Bestor, Jr., had a private library consisting of "some thirteen thousand volumes" ("Transformation of American Scholarship, 1875-1917," in Pierce Butler, ed., *Librarians, Scholars and Booksellers at Mid-Century: Papers Presented before the Sixteenth Annual Conference of the Graduate Library School of the University of Chicago* [Chicago: Univ. of Chicago Pr., 1953], p. 10).

[29] Merle Curti, *The Social Ideas of American Educators, with a New Chapter on the Last Twenty-Five Years* (Paterson, N. J.: Littlefield, Adams, 1959), p. 51-100.

[30] During the early years of public library development, library books were to be used only by adults. Library service to children did not begin in most libraries until after 1900. See Arthur E. Bostwick's *The American Public Library* (New York: D. Appleton, 1929), p. 81-99.

[31] Leon Carnovsky, "The Public Library in the U. S.," *Libri*, 2:287 (June 1953); William S. Learned, *The American Public Library and the Diffusion of Knowledge* (New York: Harcourt, 1924), p. 68; Sidney Ditzion, *Arsenals of a Democratic Culture* (Chicago: American Library Association, 1947), p. 174; Ernestine Rose, *The Public Library in American Life* (New York: Columbia Univ. Pr., 1954), p. 217.

[32] U. S. Bureau of Education, *Public Libraries in the United States of America: Their History, Condition, and Management* (Washington, D. C.: Govt. Print. Off., 1876), p. 452-56.

[33] *Ibid.,* p. 762-72.

[34] *Ibid.,* p. 1012-42.

Democratic Strivings

Sidney Ditzion

In the preface to Ditzion's book on the social history of the American public library, from which the following paper is drawn, Merle Curti praised the author for writing one of the first library histories to be conceived and executed in terms of modern scholarship in history and sociology. His in-depth investigation of the sources and ground-breaking approach to the problem make his study extremely important. In the paper reprinted here, Dr. Ditzion analyzes the cultural setting of the early library movement, and discusses the librarians' reaction to the societal forces influencing public library growth.

GENERAL POLITICAL AND SOCIAL BACKGROUNDS

One obvious generalization to which our study leads is that the main currents of nineteenth-century American thought, no matter what their origin or direction, supported the foundations and growth of the free library movement. That such a confluence of diverse ideologies, meeting on the common ground of a system of free schools and libraries, was at all possible is to be attributed to the adjustability of the American mind to shifting forces and changing conditions. It was this flexibility which could start with a common heritage—the democratic premise—and could modify, distort, or even pervert it to suit the requirements of widely varying points of view. The tax-supported public library not only answered the criteria inherent in the democratic premise but also offered an instrument as responsive to varying social requirements as democracy itself.

The ideas brought into service by the spokesmen for free libraries were drawn very naturally from the well of rhetoric best suited to the celebration of American institutions. Many of these ideas were observed in those writings of early promoters of the library movement already discussed. The present treatment will be devoted to a description of the cultural setting for library events of the early movement; to the reappearance of these same ideas in the library literature of later years; and to a presentation of new developments which arose in a changing scene.

Republicanism and the Religious Heritage

The concepts of republicanism, risen from the enlightenment, advertised in the Revolution, strengthened in the philosophy of Jeffersonianism and practiced in the era of Jacksonian democracy, were by mid-century deeply engraved upon the popular mind. The doctrines of human rights, political equality, and residence of authority in the whole people, had become firmly fixed in the professed American credo, though sometimes these ideas were not followed to the letter by leaders in political and economic life. When the suffrage was extended in the 1820's bringing the political reality into closer harmony with the democratic ideal, the education of the masses—which had been a corollary of the concept of rationalism—made a new claim upon the attention of New England Whig leaders in politics and society. New institutions were needed to help make the landless, propertyless following of mass political parties more amenable to the rationale of friendly, paternal conservatism. The new voters needed the tempering influence of education to curb their impetuosity.

Even more deeply embedded in the culture of New England and its demographic colonies was the heritage of individual moral worth translated from the earlier Calvinism into a doctrine more conge-

SOURCE: Reprinted from Sidney Ditzion, *Arsenals of a Democratic Culture: A Social History of the American Public Library Movement in New England and the Middle States from 1850-1900* (Chicago: American Library Association, 1947), Chapter 4 "Democratic Strivings," pp. 51-76, 221-226, by permission of the author and publisher. Copyright © 1947 by the American Library Association.

nial to requirements of nineteenth-century America. The individual was the focus of state activity. The individual, moreover, must in obedience to moral law translate his virtue into social progress. The only true function of government was to nurture the individual in his intellectual and economic growth. Moral order, the restraint of evil, and social responsibility were the mainstays of order and security. Universal education and religious conviction were the guarantors of stability. Moreover, the Unitarianism which had quietly revolutionized conservative New England religious thought was a strange transformation of the old struggle against evil ingrained in man's nature. It emphasized, quite to the contrary, the divine goodness attributed to humankind by the religion of enlightenment. Puritan corrigibility had been assimilated into democratic perfectibility and romantic idealism had been added.

William Ellery Channing, who was among the intellectual leaders of this revolution, was himself a product of antagonistic components. At about the turn of the century his Federalist sympathies had been completely tortured out of their original shape by contact with Jeffersonianism and French romantic philosophy. At the same time he experienced the beginnings of a shift away from the state religion of his home region—a shift which was eventually to become a severance of relations from many life-long associations. The humanitarian, egalitarian, and otherwise democratic synthesis of ideas which moulded Channing's later social outlook implied a swerve too sharp for any of the New England intellectuals to follow. Even Ticknor, who had shared many of Channing's more progressive ideas, was prevented from following Channing too far by the intellectual restraints of Boston Brahminism and by the biases of his conservative mercantile associations.

More conservative minds were nursed along the way by Kantian idealism imported by American scholars either directly from Germany, or through Coleridge and Carlyle who were interpreting the immanence of divine spirit for England and America. For those conservatives and sentimentalists to whom the application of cold analytical reasoning was a menace to established institutions, the doctrine of emergence of divinity within the individual was a great comfort. Individual actions —in this system—were motivated by sources which held divine sanction; they were to be encouraged but not controlled.

The transcendentalists attempted to practice a Unitarian idealism which was unconsciously af-

fected by the socialistic doctrines of Fourier. Emerson predicted a world of transition and evolution in which the sole duty of the state was to produce wise, virtuous, and free individuals. The state was to be humane and productive of human welfare; it was to be deprived of its police function. Having assisted in the production of responsible individuals, the state should disappear. Many of these progressive aspects of Unitarianism influenced New England lawyers, ministers, teachers, physicians and merchants, and prepared them for the many humanitarian and educational movements in which they were to participate so prominently.

In all of these ideological systems—Lockean or Kantian, Calvinistic or Unitarian, realistic or idealistic—education was accorded an elevated rank. All were agreed that a state-supported common school education should lay the foundations for necessary intellectual development. All, however, conformed largely to the national philosophy of individualism, and therefore could never cooperate in developing a unified plan of higher education. Such a plan was rendered impossible also by the great variety of coexisting economic, religious and political sects, movements, parties, and economic interests—all of which were competing for prestige, power and control.

Self-Culture

The one idea which was acceptable to all—because it drew spirit and substance from all points of view—was that of "self-culture." Although Channing, in setting down a formulation of self-culture, declared that it was the rightful property of the great fraternity of workingmen, the philosophy was (as a précis will show) congenial to every interest and view. In the first place, the common people were not to concern themselves with their condition of life since personal worth and greatness were more important than worldly goods. The powers of intellect, conscience, love, and the knowledge of God were well distributed among the whole of the people. Self-culture, aided by the self-searching and self-forming powers, with purposive growth and expansion as a goal, would overcome everything standing in the way of the march to perfection. Self-culture embraced the idea of duty (the moral), the aspiration towards the true idea of God (the religious), the disinterestedness which follows the truth wherever it goes (the intellectual), the unfolding and purifying of the affections (the social), and lastly, the ability to make quick decisions when these were necessary for action (the practical). The means of self-culture—the poor were rich in these—were described in summary form as the ability to see the things around one in their true meaning and to put them in their rightful places. These means were presented in many forms: in nature and human life freely revealed to the human eye; in control of the animal appetites; in intercourse with superior minds; in books (books were the true levelers); in the ability to make one's own decisions independently of human opinion and sanction; in one's own condition or occupation; in the opportunities presented by the political relations and duties implied by our free government; and, superimposed on the foregoing elements, in Christianity.

Here was a practical ethical system satisfying to the great mass of politically enfranchised farmers and workingmen, but also perfectly geared to the political, religious and social ideals of those middle-class entrepreneurs of the Northeast who pulled the reins of the economic order. Themselves habituated to a Calvinistic morality which satisfied the moral and, superficially, the religious requirements of this philosophy; possessed as well of a social and economic framework of life based on trust, law and science—thus complying with the social, practical, and intellectual requirements of the creed—the merchant-industrialists of New England were comfortable and secure in their environment. Law and scientific knowledge had minimized life's uncertainties. The political and economic arrangements of the fatherland had favored the individualistic motif which was so favorable to the enhancement of their fortunes. And yet, with all the power which a comparatively unchallenged social order yields to its controlling group, the businessmen continued in obedience to Puritan morality for several decades and resisted with all their strength the rapacious individualism which industrial and financial capitalism introduced.

In the earlier period, these businessmen examined their thoughts and deeds with just as much rigor as did other social leaders. Could they answer the question they put to themselves as to whether they had done their part in the community uplift? Many were the strains in the collective mind of New England which cooperated in public-spirited ventures. It was this mind which founded numerous benevolent and literary institutions. It was this view of life which brought Channing, Everett, Ticknor, the Quincys, and other substantial Bostonians together on the subject of a free public library. How well-suited this institution was as an ancillary to the process of self-culture! How well-adapted as an agency of popular discipline! This type of education, along with the publication of "correct" textbooks, novels, and periodicals, would promote the already manifest desire of the masses to emulate the qualities of the middle class, to act and think in conformity with accepted proprieties. Then, too, one had to consider that the populace had a high potential of political power and a small income surplus to encourage radical independent action. Should the people be left in ignorance? Should the leaders build educational institutions bearing the forbidding label of charity offerings? It was folly to pursue either of these courses.

There were two available methods of avoiding the pauper stigma on popular education, viz., voting tax support and preaching the doctrine of stewardship. Generally both were employed simultaneously. The stewards of wealth often combined genuine religious conviction, complete with its sense of duty and moral obligation, with the practical necessities of their privileged position in society. The need for a well-educated staff of workers in the new industries was, coincidentally, supplied as a by-product of the projected popular institutions. In this most desirable state of affairs, stewardship was highly acceptable; for, as Mayor Smith declared at the laying of the cornerstone of Boston's public library, "when the results of honest industry become instrumentalities for developing the mind, and multiplying resources for bettering the conditions of humanity, society is permanently advanced." In later years the recipients of donations did not always insist upon the "honest industry" element in this formula.

Forward March of Science and Technology

Concurrent with shifting intellectual assumptions, and foremost among the causes and encouragements of progressive thinking, was the revolution in applied science and technology. Nothing confirmed the Jeffersonian promise of indefinite improvement and expansion more than the achievements of science and its accomplishments in the process of revolutionizing industry. Given a universal diffusion of "useful" knowledge the limits of social improvement were indeterminate. Aided by radical improvements in communication and printing, the scientific spirit filtered down to the lower strata of the population and laid the base for a new and genuine mass culture. The intellectual monopoly of the upper classes had been broken—with the consent and encouragement of the former monopolists. Mental development went arm in arm with industrial development and, with the new methods of manufacture, was prerequisite to it. Men of affairs in industry were more than willing to patronize physics and chemistry when the returns were demonstrated to be immediate and tangible. The success of industrial science, reinforced by the inroads made by the Darwinian hypothesis, stimulated an interest in pure science. The scientific outlook permeated all phases of life and, in time, all propositions came to be tested by their observability in reality.

The disinterest of science in sect or belief naturally fostered secularism and therefore greatly encouraged the growth of Unitarianism—the religion of secularism—within the Congregational Church. The disdain of experimental science for rank, caste, or class, prepared the way for the application of new knowledge toward seeking practical results and spreading their benefits far and wide. Such were the claims of equality in a democracy.

The Smithsonian Institution (established 1846) and the American Association for the Advancement of Science (organized Boston 1847) attested to the influence of science and industry upon intellectual interests and institutional arrangements for distributing knowledge. In the course of the debate on the character of the proposed Smithsonian, the arguments developed were on political as well as intellectual grounds. Rufus Choate urged that the greater part of the fund be used to purchase books for a national library. The social idealist and democrat, Robert Dale Owen, insisted that such an institution would deny the claims of democracy by directing its services mostly to the needs of scholars. His suggestion was to devote the funds to the publication of cheap tracts, popular lectures, and a national normal school to improve teaching in the schools of the masses.[1] Owen's failure in Congress was doubtless attributable to the unwillingness of states—both Northern and Southern—to allow the federal educational institutions direct access to the minds of the nation's population. He was unable, moreover, even as one of the regents of the institution, to get any of his ideas accepted. He was beaten in the Smithsonian by the dominating voice of pure science which held power there.

The effects of industry on science and education went beyond the rationale of cognate fields of interest. If the advances in practical science oc-casioned the urgency of an educated people, they also caused a transfer of much mercantile wealth to industry where profits increased their proportions and provided a larger taxable wealth for institutions of popular education. Moreover, under the new distribution, chieftains of industry were more numerous than the old merchant princes and were at least as willing to patronize the arts, sciences and letters. Individual writers on special subjects aided by the power press and cheap paper production, could also look for the patronage of a huge literate population whose small financial surplus permitted a limited satisfaction of their cultural aspirations. The market was flooded with such a profusion of books that, even though these were comparatively inexpensive, no one could hope to possess as many of these books as he wished. At first it was possible to meet this difficulty by supporting small, scantily capitalized libraries. Later, the implications of democracy joined with the exigencies of cultural demand to produce the publicly supported free library.

Cultural Nationalism

The new culture, exhibiting an exuberance of movement, expansion, progress and participation, celebrating individualism, local independence and initiative, and exalting the humane spirit, molded the democratic faith into a religion of nationalism. American literary output was beginning to dispossess the British from American printing presses; American books were being introduced into the British Museum by the bibliophile, Henry Stevens; the English were buying and collecting our scientific and literary productions; men of science were arriving from abroad and delivering encomia on American men of science and their accomplishments; our libraries and other institutions were exhibiting the American product and thereby assisting in the struggle against a middle-class penchant for things foreign. Educational agencies were supplying the means of that self-culture for the lack of which, Emerson pointed out, American intellect and money were fascinated by foreign travel, literature, and art. The national literature of which Channing had written in the *Christian Examiner* (1830) was already proceeding on its triumphant way. Its scope was large enough to encompass every great product of native endeavor. It included in close union all matters moral and physical, humane and scientific. Said Channing, "The expression of superior mind in writing we regard, then, as a nation's literature. We regard its gifted men, whether devoted to the exact sciences, to mental and ethical philosophy, to history and legislation, or to fiction and poetry, as forming a noble intellectual brotherhood . . ."[2] The section of the country most active in this movement of cultural nationalism was the Northeast where leaders of the grand march to supremacy wished to compete with England in things cultural as well as industrial. Conveniently enough, the buzz of intellectual activity created a demand for new publishing houses and offered a new outlet for invested capital.

This religion which was preached in the name of the nation did not share, nor did it wish to share, its fruits with every section of the country. A cultural imperialism, based on the boasts of Yankee background, energy and investiveness, grew up within the larger movement to advertise the nation. New England scholars, at mid-century, could demonstrate how America had become civilized through the medium of the New England mind. The "solid men of Boston" were destined to radiate their great culture to every section of the country. Industry, commerce, and improved methods of communication were to supplement outright migration in the appointed mission.

The Climate of Democracy

These were the principles and ideals, democratic in politics and liberal in religion, which found their way into library campaign and dedication literature from the very birth of the movement. As far back at 1815 Jesse Torrey drew upon the tradition of George Washington, Benjamin Rush, and Samuel Adams when he spoke for a "cause consecrated by religion and enjoined by patriotism," the "universal dissemination of knowledge and virtue by means of free public libraries."[3] The quasi-public subscription libraries, which were established in the period between Torrey's early campaigns and the establishment of the first vigorous free institutions, were founded in part upon these assumptions. The school-district libraries were eminent testimony to the operation of these ideas.

Their fullest expression appeared in the literature of the first Massachusetts free town libraries. This was the institution which would have more regard for the moral and literary wants of the mass of the people than the existing class libraries which catered exclusively to limited numbers of scholars and proprietors. The people were to have a voice in this new free institution and they would see to

it that they got what they wanted. The Boston library, it was said, was destined to rapid growth because, by force of the feeling of common ownership, local publishers, editors, and writers would deem it a pleasure to deposit their books in the public collection. The librarian, for his part, should follow the dictum of "the greatest use to the greatest number" in building his collection. For this was the glory of democracy—an institution accessible to the whole people, rich and poor alike, regardless of race and creed.[4] The New Bedford interests echoed these sentiments and went on to point out the harmonizing influence this institution would have in communities where so many dividing factors were in operation.[5]

Many were the citations in ensuing years of the favorable effect of the mere climate of democracy on the growth of free libraries. Some emphasized the democratic act symbolized by library philanthropy; others, the political significance of this newly manifested desire on the part of the people to procure increased means of physical and intellectual welfare for themselves.[6] Only rarely could a speaker explain away belated library activity on the grounds that the spirit of pure democracy would not have allowed the local voters to accept a gift with a clear conscience. Even to have left such a matter to the people's representatives would have been a violation of the spirit. A popular vote had placed the decision directly in the hands of the people.[7]

Stressing the equality of educational opportunity afforded by public libraries, frequent reference was made to the biographies of self-improved intellectuals, scientists, inventors and political leaders to whom books had been a sole source of early instruction.[8] Similarly, this fundamental equality had its parallel in the equal economic opportunity offered by American institutions, and it was this free source of knowledge which assisted individuals to climb upward in the economic scale. To complete the cycle, the erstwhile poor boys who had been helped to riches by free schools and libraries were already turning back some of their wealth to provide similar opportunities for a new generation.[9]

Equality was the theme again when Joshua Bates urged that library rooms provided for ordinary folk be as comfortable as those provided for the upper classes. The free library was to be an intellectual and literary common where the humblest and the highest would meet on equal terms just as they did at the polls. The library would promote the mutual acquaintance and friendship of all classes; it might even help prevent the dangerous divergence of interest of the wealthy and the poor.[10] "Just in proportion to the degree of intellectual development to which the mass of people have attained, artificial distinctions have faded away (and) the people have become more and more homogeneous and more democratic . . . " The only aristocracy a free library could possibly help to create was "one open to talent and toil . . . the aristocracy of knowledge."[11]

Notwithstanding the very general form in which libraries were dedicated to freedom of religion and politics, the sectarian and party feuds which called the principles of liberty and equality into use were probably different in varying localities and circumstances. Channing pointed specifically to parties based on class consciousness as his chief concern when he called party spirit the bane of self-culture, the destroyer of "truth, justice, candor, fair dealing, sound judgment, self-control, and kind affections . . ."[12] The donors of public libraries were not always as frank and clear.

George Peabody, the foundations of whose fortune had been laid in the South and who had many close personal associations there, forcefully mandated a northern beneficiary of one of his library gifts to eschew periodicals which encouraged sectional animosities. His gift to Baltimore was accompanied by a letter forbidding the "dissemination or discussion of sectarian theology or party politics . . ."[13] Gifts to Bernardston and West Brookfield in Massachusetts were both accompanied by similar restrictions as to religion and politics.[14]

Gerrit Smith's demand for the exclusion of "books unfriendly to truth and purity" probably arose, as one of his biographers claims, from a dogmatism which placed a fixed line between right and wrong and did not recognize degrees of truth and error. This rigid prescription may have been provoked by conservative opposition to rationalistic religious ideas to which Smith was much attracted, or by the threat of Papal power which grew more menacing as immigrants flooded our eastern shores and started to move inland. It may have been a part of his Jeffersonian insistence upon a "manly independent spirit of the people" in working out their own salvation on the basis of knowledge individually interpreted.[15]

The battle cry of freedom in New England and the promotion of libraries as weapons of the crusade were occasionally prompted by the threat of new religious beliefs and recently formed mass political parties. In New England towns of the period, Yankee Protestantism with its Federalist backgrounds was frequently on the defensive against Irish Catholicism and the Democratic Party which championed its cause. This antagonism was generally kept under cover by the "old" merchants and ministers because of the necessity to deal respectably with the "new" people in trade and politics. Occasionally the nativist defense mechanism—which it is claimed was more active than usual in periods of economic depression— broke loose with all the violence of a pent-up hatred suddenly released. On some levels the struggle was physical; on others it spent itself in bitter vituperation.

The will of Judge C. E. Forbes of Northampton was a classic attack of the latter kind. Forbes' testament declared that the collection of the library he was donating was to be gathered under broad democratic principles and was to contain all literary, scientific, historical and theological works with strict impartiality; further, "that none but laymen shall be competent to any employment, or fill any office or exercise any control in the management of the library." Considering that the ministry had always had its place on boards of trustees, this was a conspicuously radical directive to set down in a will. Nor was Forbes to be accused of rationalism, deism, or atheism; he was a member of the Congregationalist church and orthodox in his beliefs. His irrepressible fear of possible control by "new" elements was written down as a defense of intelligence and democracy:

> It has been my aim to place within reach of the inhabitants of a town, in which I have lived long and pleasantly, the means of learning, if they are disposed to learn, the marvelous development of modern thought, and enable them to judge the destiny of the race on scientific evidence, rather than on metaphysical evidence alone. The importance of the education of the people cannot be overrated. It will be found the most efficient if not the only protection against the inroads of a foreign superstition, whose swarms of priests, Jesuits, monks, ministers and agents are let loose upon us, and engaged in the unholy work of enslaving the minds of the multitude, and moulding them into instruments of priestly power. A power built upon the remains of ancient paganism, and sustained in one particular at least by gross fetichism. A power growing out of a monstrous perversion of the precepts and example of the Founder of Christianity, by which poverty, lowliness and self-abnegation are forced to mean worldly grandeur, enormous wealth, a palace, absolutism and an earthly crown. As the contrast, so the antagonism must remain, between the enlightened freemen, and the progeny of the Purple and the Scarlet clad Mother. Let it be deeply graven on the mind, that no strictly Roman Catholic country ever was, or ever can be a free country.[16]

As was to be expected, Forbes' hostility to the ministry was roundly berated. It was difficult for the *Worcester Spy* to understand why the ministry —traditionally associated with books and learning —should have been peremptorily excluded from any participation in the management of a library. The *Holyoke Herald,* speaking the voice of humanitarian democracy, called public libraries a cold comfort for the anxieties of the poor over basic physical needs and declared that, in the prevention of crime, a housing program was more effective than all the public libraries in Christendom.

SPECIFIC CONDITIONS AND IDEAS

Religious Influences

From many points of view one finds himself in agreement with those of Forbes' critics who attacked his generalized proscription of the ministry. We can—without following one extreme interpretation which stresses the Unitarian adherence of George Ticknor, Enoch Pratt, and others in connection with concrete activity in the library movment[17]—point to much historical material which demonstrates great interest, and inferentially, considerable influence of progressive religionists in the library movement before midcentury. Whether the rationale was religious, moral, intellectual, literary, or anything else matters little when we witness the tremendous emphasis placed on books, reading habits and library needs in Unitarian periodicals particularly during the middle decades of the century.[18] Nor were the important Methodist and Congregationalist organs devoid of materials urging the extension of democratic educational facilities. The *Methodist Quarterly Review,* after devoting some space in 1841 to an enthusiastic endorsement of school-district libraries,[19] seems to have abandoned the subject of libraries altogether. The *Congregational Quarterly* included in its first volume an excellent summary statement on the history of the Congregational Library Association[20] and thereafter confined itself to very brief notes on this project.

In several instances religious periodicals threw their weight behind the library movement in more direct fashion. As early as 1849 we find the *Christian Inquirer* quoting Charles Sumner to the effect that "Every sloop-of-war that floats costs more than the largest public library in our country." A year later this same periodical reprinted the *Boston Evening Transcript's* comments on Livermore's *North American Review* article on public librar-

ies.[21] In the following year it carried quotations from the Reverend Wight's manifesto on town libraries, and, in 1853, the Reverend Samuel Osgood's address on popular libraries delivered at the Librarian's Convention, New York City.[22] Additional items on library catalogs, buildings, and other matters of popular interest must have given some impetus to the movement.[23]

Our estimate of the contribution made by men of religion to the library movement should by no means be based solely upon their writings. Their more significant work is shown in the concrete local activities which both preceded the establishment of libraries and nurtured their early days. A religious group might turn its collection to public use. A pastor's wife might start a collection towards a free library. An influential minister might initiate a movement to establish a town library. And how numerous are the instances in which clergymen played their expected educational role in the community, serving as active members of boards of library trustees, making dedication speeches, and pronouncing benedictions upon newly organized free libraries? Then, too, one must not forget the spiritual auspices of some ancestors of the public library, viz., Y.M.C.A. and Sunday-school libraries. The latter, despite the many criticisms heaped upon them for the mediocre quality of their collections, certainly must be given due credit as purveyors of books to the people.[24]

While it is reasonable to assume that the clergy of several sects must have resented the secular nature of the public library movement and therefore opposed it, we know (within the limits of our research) of only one instance in which a public library program was openly obstructed by the religious groups involved. This was the instance of the move to consolidate all quasi-public libraries in New York City in the last decade of the nineteenth century. In the early discussion on consolidation, the Jewish and Catholic library representatives were reluctant to lose their identities in a grand public library merger. However only the Cathedral (Catholic) Library people persisted in vigorous opposition, presenting their case in the following manner:

First, the Cathedral Library is church property, it would not, therefore be suitable to relinquish title to it. Second, if the New York Public Library is to assume complete control of the library administration of New York, we would have no representation on its board of trustees. From that point of view the consolidation would be unfortunate, as the preponderating—

we may say the entire—interests of the present board of trustees are non-Catholic. Third, the purpose of our library would be destroyed by any such consolidation.

We were established in order to counteract the evil influences of public libraries in general, to supply people with innocuous reading, and to minimize as far as possible the harm that can be done by dangerous books . . . [25]

Among the historical materials which relate organized religion to the library movement we find an occasional reference to challenging sects and parties. Inasmuch as such reference is often oblique, it is difficult to determine in whose interest "national unity and power," freedom, and our republican institutions were being preserved by public schools and public libraries.[26] The mention of a prodigious rate of population increase probably indicated an immigration problem. The words "fanaticism" and "ecclesiastical tyranny" certainly pointed to the challenge of a powerful church. The degree of autonomy of the local library, and the loose relationship between it and some state governments rendered this danger a real one. As late as 1914 the New York administrators of state aid to libraries had to explain that a free library was defined (by the Regents' rules) "as one where all the people of the community, regardless of race, sex, religious belief, institutional or professional connections . . . " were welcome. However, aid to church libraries was not altogether out; for this same communication goes on to say,

We have in the past occasionally extended state aid to libraries in churches, but usually in small communities where there was but one church and the people were all of the same general faith. The tendency is away from the use of State money at the present time.[27]

The Informed Voter

On the political front, the strongest threats to democracy were understood to be from ignorant classes who would vote for the wrong parties either because of their own untutored choice or because of the scheming leadership of city politicians. America would be the victim of its own humane spirit if it did not educate and inform its "illiterate blacks and foreign born." The European habit of thought which placed the lower orders in permanent ignorance and subjugation was ill-adapted to the American scene where the populace had already achieved political power and would misuse it unless given proper direction. Unless the correct books were put into the hands of

the people, they would be easy prey for such false and foreign philosophies as were destructive of the foundations of our republic.[28]

Moreover, democratic forms and their enunciation in speech and writing had a function far more positive than the defense of entrenched custom or privilege. Their most legitimate use was to carry forward and insure maximum operation of the government of the people, by the people, and for the people. Having made a complete break with the oppressions and injustices of the old world, the people, in whom the power now resided, must equip themselves "properly to decide the many social and political questions they frequently are called upon to solve." Where every individual thought and deed affected the social mechanism of the whole, it became the interest of the whole to provide the necessary education for its parts.[29] The primary recognition of this need seems to have resulted in early support of state libraries— and indeed the Library of Congress itself; adequate sources of information would assure the framing of good legislation. Provision for libraries in the constitutions of territorial governments probably stemmed from the same basic need.

The very fact that all vital political decisions rested with the voters either directly or through their representatives made it more urgent that we create a responsible citizenry; for any weaknesses in the bulwark of democracy would permit reactionary ideas to gain inroads into our institutions. Differences of opinion, which of necessity must arise in a complex society such as ours, had to be ironed out with intelligence and knowledge which books could help provide; the diffusion of intelligence would offset the activities of secret foes who sought to weaken the foundations of our system. Many a president of the United States had stated this view with emphasis.[30] As truly as Daniel Webster had called the little red school house the "sentry box of American liberty," so could the public libraries be called the "Arsenals of American Liberty."[31]

The logic which had operated so advantageously for the protagonists of publicly supported and controlled schools was recalled to action for the free library; viz., it was at once the obligation and protection of the state to have an informed body of present voters and future leaders. This principle, which would carry great weight even in the presence of a thoroughly educated electorate, was all the stronger in view of the fact that a huge majority of our people had not benefited from an education beyond the common school. Some had been prevented by economic circumstances; some had spent their youth in rural areas where the facilities of a higher schooling were not available; others had chosen the attractions of a business career at an extremely early age. The public library was a natural supplement to the common school in the realm of popular culture; it was a substitute for the town hall in the realm of political education.[32] In periods of national crises, when either war[33] or political unrest[34] was testing the moral fiber of the people, the public library would constitute a steadying factor; it would supply the knowledge with which to temper emotional and intellectual ferment.

The Urban-Industrial Complex

The salutary influence of intellectual and scientific advances upon political forms does not tell the whole story of the new industrial era. Into the complete accounting must go the troublesome sociological problems which rose out of the transition from small-scale, semi-craft manufacturing to large-scale, machine industry. The masses of people who left their farms and intimate villages to run the big factories, developed needs and created problems which sorely taxed the existing institutions and created a demand for new ones. The concentration of capital in the hands of a few canny industrialists was temporarily favorable to the national economy but gave rise to an ever-swelling industrial proletariat whose poverty and degrading conditions of life manufactured social problems which big industrial philanthropy could not begin to solve. The humanitarians and—partly through their agitations—the state stepped in and applied communal resources to the problems which extreme individualism had created. Education and other public services were created to alleviate the lot of the urban producing classes.

Between 1840 and 1880 the populations of prominent mill towns in New England had either tripled or quadrupled. A few grew in even larger multiples.[35] The number and value of manufacturing establishments had increased in similar proportions. The employment requirements of the new mills were so great that ordinarily a market highly favorable to labor would have resulted; but, happily for the owners, the new mass-production machines were comparatively simple to operate and could be run by women and children. This circumstance, combined with the inability of the municipal social conscience to keep pace with rapid growth and change, added to the causes of poverty, slum-living and delinquency. Humanitarians attempted to mitigate these evils with schools, libraries, parks and other public facilities.

The many groups which reacted to the evils of industrialism, whether their philosophies were rooted in idealism, rationalism, or socialism, all gave some thought to the amelioration of the lot of the working classes. The strong note of cooperative idealism which flavored the social thought of this period must have done much to prepare a climate favorable to public action for the betterment of the common man. The Owens, Robert and Robert Dale, and Albert Brisbane taught America much about the social perfectionism of Saint Simon and Fourier. Fanny Wright preached the rights of women and broadcast the basic tenets of a rational, democratic society. Josiah Warren and Stephen Pearl Andrews advertised anarchist doctrines. The Communist Manifesto was imported and translated into American terms. Transcendentalism, disillusioned by the meager accomplishments of America's limitless potential, withdrew from the "strife, injustice, ignorance, and philistinism," and in its seclusion taught how individual worth and dignity could be preserved in a cooperative society. After 1865 the religion of humanity of Walter Rauschenbusch; the labor philosophies of William H. Sylvis, Ira Steward and Terence Powderly; and the new rationalism of Henry George, Frank Lester Ward, and Edward Bellamy lent their weight to the struggle against rugged individualism.

The emphasis of the literature of these movements on the importance of education and self-culture is clear and unmistakable; but their influence on the public library movement was small and indirect. The explanation is that these philosophies, affected as they were by the extremely individualistic motif of their time, were all, excepting neo-rationalism, opposed to the extension of governmental power over the operations of the individual; and education agencies functioning under government authority were conceived by many to be such an extension of power.

William Maclure, the geologist and philanthropist who is closely associated in American social thought with the New Harmony Community, was extremely distrustful of the motives of the "classes who live by the ignorance of the millions." His blanket bequest of funds for the benefit of libraries and reading rooms of workingmen's institutes was based on the premise that laborers constituted the only class which could and would use knowledge for the benefit of society.[36] Similar feelings and suspicions with regard to state power probably prevented the labor movement of the postwar period from supporting the free library movement in the spirit which fired trade unionists of an earlier period to support the struggle for free schools. Labor in the era of big capital was instructed to stay away from the humanitarian representations of the state as well as those of individuals. The worker learned to depend upon self-advancement by fellowship, mutual aid, and cooperative methods.

The real ideological force which fostered the public libraries must be looked for in those islands of communal spirit which rose out of the political and religious backgrounds of democratic America and persisted amid the powerful currents of rugged individualism. This was the spirit of common humanity which fostered abolition, women's rights, the peace movement, prison reform, the mitigation of severe penalties for crime, and the establishment of institutions for the care of the afflicted.

If one should seek a social group which gave the free library direct support he would probably discover that it was a group whose interests were least directly associated with those of the ordinary folk for whom the libraries were primarily opened. The assumption of individualism made by this group permeated every aspect of its life and sought elaborate justification in current intellectual theory. In religion, it believed the individual to be the fundamental moral agent and used the gospel of wealth formulation as its chief instrument for maintaining the *status quo*. In economics, it taught that individual intelligence and ability would win the material prizes of life; that poverty was a temporary status which would soon be overcome by the capable. At any rate, the government must leave the individual's hands free in the economic sphere. Its scientific rationale was a cunning adaptation of the Darwinian hypothesis. The divine right to acquire and defend property was adequately developed by James McCosh, Noah Porter, and Mark Hopkins and shielded by the intellectual prestige of their positions. Carnegie himself elaborated the "law" of competition and the economic applications of the Darwinian struggle for existence. He also gave secular authority to the gospel of wealth.

The secret of how conservative businessmen readily accepted a doctrine so subversive as Darwinism was to accustomed patterns of thought, is revealed in the slogan "evolution, not revolution." In the process of natural selection, nothing

but a man's own deficiencies would prevent him from winning the struggle. When humanitarian workers attacked the wealthy for the existence of poverty-ridden slums, they could be told that such conditions were the natural result of ignorance and shiftlessness. Were not the rich engaged daily in furnishing free popular libraries so that all latent talents and abilities would realize their highest potential development? Of course these institutions had other services to perform. They helped educate productive hands; they would probably endorse and reinforce the views held by donors; they satisfied the need of businessmen for public recognition and also provided reading materials with which the underdog could sublimate his hunger for prestige, power and security.[37]

Various and sundry were the possible impacts of city life under the new industrialism upon the public library movement. By one interpretation, the mere tempo of the new life—with its easier, swifter communications, and the necessity for a larger fund of information to perform the daily business of living—demanded newer instrumentalities for the diffusion of knowledge.[38] To some the use of public money for library service went hand in hand with the efforts of humane government to improve living conditions. This analysis would place public libraries on the list of public functions which urgent sociological factors forced municipal administrations to perform. Uniformed police, city fire brigades, departments of health and sanitation, public highways and parks, and free libraries are lumped together in this interpretation. However, an examination of the chronological relationship between the assumption of these duties by city governments and the opening of local free libraries shows no intelligible correlation.[39] The fact that very large cities of the middle states assumed the obligations of public health and protection at a very early date, and yet did not support libraries until the closing years of the nineteenth century presumably rules out the usefulness of this analysis.

The existence of more pertinent factors is indicated. General regional attitudes toward public education were probably a crucial factor. The problems raised by large immigrant populations have already been noted. The possession of surplus wealth by a generous dominant group was obviously of great consequence. The fact that in 1850 the total taxable personal estate in New York and Pennsylvania combined was one hundred million dollars less than that of New England, although the population of the latter region was half that of the two middle states names,[40] suggests an extremely interesting comparison between the rates at which libraries were established. Instances of taxpayers' resistance to library appropriations were rare in the Northeast. The growth of cities in population, industry and wealth naturally brought with it "increased demands upon the citizens for additional conveniences and improvements." The more complex urban society became, the more numerous were the intellectual and social institutions which were established.[41]

It was generally understood that a town which failed to educate its population would fall behind in the race for business supremacy.[42] Although isolated instances exist where there was appeal to local pride in the name of history and tradition,[43] in practically every other case there was a frank concern for a prosperity which rival cities were seeking to destroy. Boston's claim to being "the most intelligent and cultivated city in America" rested on the successful activities of its businessmen and the solid reading done by its inhabitants.[44] So, too, the reputation of New Bedford was associated bilaterally with municipal prosperity and cultural activity.[45] For some years, the presence of the Astor Library satisfied the local pride of New Yorkers; but they soon became aware that their institution was a counterfeit of the real popular library. Such public libraries were a good thing for all communities but "more especially," said the historian de Peyster, should they be concentrated "in a city like ours, which is the commercial emporium of the New World!"[46]

In the days when smaller cities were competing to attract investment money to local business and real estate, the public library was a feature on a par with light, water and sewer systems;[47] for capital was attracted where symptoms and evidences of growth stood forth. The science of social economy affirmed the obvious claim, made by the Rev. John B. Wight before the Massachusetts legislature, that increased rentals and property values were concomitant with the focusing of commercial and intellectual activity in well-populated cities.[48] As a research student working at the end of the nineteenth century concluded, among the social causes of urban growth were the advantages offered by cities to prospective migrants. The categories of social advantage listed were educational facilities, amusements, a high standard of living, and intellectual associations. Public libraries made a contribution in each of these categories. The public library was placed under the standard-of-living category in an environment as follows:[49]

"Then there are conveniences to be had in the city which in many cases could not be obtained in the country, on account of the small numbers to bear the heavy expenses . . . The field of municipal activity has been constantly widening, until now the city furnishes its residents not only parks and playgrounds, but museums, *libraries* and art galleries; not only hospitals, but baths and washhouses, municipal lodging houses and model tenements . . ." Once there was a sufficient number of public libraries already established in neighboring or competing towns, this fact would be, in fact was, used to goad a town administration into action.[50]

By a curious contradiction of social forces, the same libraries which were being used to attract people from the villages to the cities were also sought for towns and villages in an effort to keep the population in smaller political units. The same groups which were reaping the economic advantages of concentrated manpower soon began to sense perilous political consequences.

> The tendency of population to aggregate in great centers is by all conceded to be one of the most unwholesome symptoms of modern society. In our country it is a tendency fraught with peculiar perils, for no man can doubt that the permanence of our social and political institutions is largely dependent not only on the wide diffusion of wealth among individuals, but on the territorial diffusion of political power. Whatever transfers political power from the country to the city, from a population that is scattered, stable, conservative to a population densely massed, easily moved, ready to be manipulated by designing leaders is a long step towards a political revolution. Whatever tends to make the heated atmosphere of great cities attractive to the most intelligent and energetic part of our population is silently tending to bring about a change which can hardly fail at length to reconstruct the whole fabric of American society.[51]

REACTIONS OF THE LIBRARY PROFESSION

Librarians of the last quarter of the nineteenth century, busy though they were with building collections and developing bibliographic technics, still had time to do a little missionary work of their own. Even where democratic ideas made none too deep an impression, professional aggrandizement demanded that homage be paid to the people's philosophy. In their attempts to fight, wheedle or otherwise influence reluctant taxpayers, library missionaries sometimes offered the prospect of material prosperity and compensating rises in real-estate values.[52] However, the literature of the profession—and library practice as well—adhered closely to the abstract principles of democracy. Emphasis was placed on the democratic conception of the public library as to purpose, source of authority, and control.[53] The future of democracy, the very political and industrial future of the nation, were said to depend upon a system of popular education. A librarian's axiom read: " . . . popular liberty and intellectual intelligence go hand in hand with manufacturing industry."[54]

It was not enough to show how progressive and political idealism had fostered the public library.[55] The taxpayer had to be aroused to a genuine enthusiasm for that *sine qua non* " . . . public treasure which so reasonably demands to be kept and cared for and distributed for common enjoyment at common cost."[56] Anyone who was willing to contribute toward the common defense, must also be willing to share in the defense of the republic—and of civilization itself—against the perpetual menace of ignorance.[57] There was a certain finality in declarations which placed the library alongside sanitation, street lighting, public parks and hospitals as minimum social services which a democratic society owed itself. The backwardness of the South in establishing libraries was attributed to the aristocratic tradition; it was unmistakably true that that section of our nation was slow in learning the democratic principles of cooperation for education purposes.[58]

The sectless, classless character of free libraries was thoroughly exploited by librarians in the effort to raise their institution to the level of public favor enjoyed by the public schools. Little is known either of the pressures which were probably applied in small communities to exclude upsetting theories from library shelves, or of the reactions of individual librarians to "suggestions" offered by men and women of local importance. The organized profession did however speak boldly in one outstanding instance of political meddling where the professional and economic interests of a highly respected librarian were at stake. The Boston Board of Aldermen had tampered with the salary schedule of librarian Justin Windsor without even consulting the trustees of the Public Library. Although the battle was waged in the name of the right of the people to efficient and unhampered library management, other ideas crept into the picture. The public library stood forth as a barricade against such challenges to civilization as the "demagogism" behind railroad strikes and the ignorance of city politicians; for "Light is always the one cure for darkness, and every book that the public library circulates helps to make Alderman O'Brien and railroad rioters impossible."[59]

In general the profession's reaction to social conflicts indicates that it had not yet discerned where its strongest support lay. On the one hand, wealth had shown itself to be favorably disposed by erecting library buildings and by contributing funds for other purposes; on the other, the voting populace had demonstrated its power to vote libraries into being. The most advantageous position to assume, therefore, was a neutrality which favored liberal principles. Librarians were to make themselves cognizant of all matters affecting public interest without entering into local politics personally.[60] It was perfectly proper, though, to denounce editorially the aggressions of a reactionary French ministry against popular libraries.[61]

On the home front the profession showed a great deal of concern over the sharpening consciousness of class aims which was coming to the surface in American society toward the end of the century. One function of the librarian, as he saw it, was to blunt the edge of these differences and to provide a means whereby the rich and poor could live happily side by side. The public library was a great leveler, supplying a literature by which the ordinary man could experience some of the pleasures of the rich, and providing a common ground where employer and employee could meet on equal terms.[62] That librarians did not remark this fraternization of "boss" and worker outside the shop as frequently as did the trustees in their reports, was probably indicative of the hypothetical nature of this meeting of the classes. A librarian at the Astor labeled "entirely fanciful" the idyllic picture of the capitalist and mechanic sitting next to each other in the reading room.[63]

The latter decades of the nineteenth century, marked as they were by some of the most serious strikes in our national history and by an increasing dissemination of socialistic doctrines, provided an opportunity for the profession to sell its agency as a steadying social force. Whatever threat to democratic government might come out of these struggles could certainly be warded off by the spread of " . . . the knowledge of the learned, the wisdom of the thoughtful, (and) the conscience of the upright."[64] By continuing the educational process where the schools left off[65] and by conducting a people's university, a wholesome, capable citizenry would be fully schooled in the conduct of a democratic life. Melvil Dewey gave solemn warning with regard to a reading public which was doing the wrong kind of reading: "To teach the masses to read and then to turn them out in early youth with this power and no guiding influence, is only to invite catastrophe . . . the world agrees that it is unwise to give sharp tools and powerful weapons to the masses without some assurance of how they are to be used."[66]

Though it was agreed that the public library should be a democratic guide to the political and social problems of the twentieth century, there was no consensus as to how such guidance should be put into practice. For instance, the public library was a preserver of democracy whenever, through mass education, it combated the vicious influence of a mercenary press. For a while—during the early years of the daily press—the newspaper had been looked upon as a wholesome medium of mass education; but, when the Pulitzers and Hearsts began to make capital of public ignorance and vulgarity, librarians thought it time to administer an antidote. They realized that a clean, purposeful press was possible "only under circumstances of disinterestedness which were not likely to exist."[67]

There were times, moreover, when the profession overshot the mark in attempting to impress the civic value of its performance upon taxpaying masters. One librarian observed that the well-to-do, satisfied with the *status quo*, were less in the habit of entering upon "troublesome investigations" than were those who had experienced privation.[68] The idea was also advanced that the public library taught the workingman to distinguish his own real interests from "such sham reforms as are brought before them by so-called labor leaders."[69] One over-zealous patriot felt discouraged because of a strong trend exhibited by readers toward research on subjects like heraldry, genealogy and imperialism.[70]

The slogan "Loyalty to City and Country" epitomized another of the aims and functions of the public library in promoting citizenship. The people should learn well the laws under which they lived so that they might serve their country's interests most effectively.[71] Where could they do so more easily than in their free libraries? Further, by supplying reading matter concerned with the history of American independence and the march of democracy, the public library could inculcate patriotic memories, "each of which is a pledge to the nation of unity, prosperity and peace." This service would certainly win the gratitude of patriotic societies which could later be counted upon to help strengthen local-history collections.[72]

The profession evidently concerned itself seriously with the civic education of foreign-born populations in cosmopolitan centers. There was a patent weakness in giving the new citizen the ballot—which he had not enjoyed in his native country—without giving him also the means of developing an intelligence with which to direct its use. Librarians repeatly attested to the fact that their institutions were widely patronized by avid foreign-born readers who were learning for the first time about our history and ideals.[73] When the problem arose of supplying reading matter in languages which immigrants could read, librarians parted company with the super-patriots. If reading in foreign languages tended to engender tender feelings for countries other than their own, a kindly library reception, graced by familiar materials, would build gratitude and loyalty, thus nullifying any other undesirable effects. The library had an Americanizing function; but you could not Americanize the foreign born without reaching them.[74] This was the spirit in which public librarians approached many of their problems of administration and technic: if you would educate people with books, you must ease the way for them by removing barriers which in the past had made libraries unapproachable.

The major ideological currents of this period were directed toward producing a unified nation based on the free informed choice of individuals rather than on measures of indoctrination in behalf of any particular group. As it happened there was a fairly close identity among the requirements of national prosperity, the needs of the new dominant industrial middle class, and the tenets of flourishing individualistic philosophies. Divisive tendencies, having their origins in prejudices of race, section, nationality, creed and class, were present indeed. It was hoped that these could be eased, or perhaps erased, by establishing agencies of enlightenment for adult and youth alike.

FOOTNOTES

[1] Richard William Leopold, *Robert Dale Owen, a Biography* (Cambridge, Mass., Harvard University Press, 1940), p. 219-35.

[2] W.E. Channing, "Remarks on National Literature," in Thorp, W., Curti, M. E., and Baker, C., eds. *American Issues*

(Philadelphia, Lippincott, 1941), Vol. 1, p. 298-312; also, S. G. Goodrich, *Recollections of a Lifetime; or Men and Things I Have Seen* . . . (N. Y., Miller, Orton, and Mulligan, 1856), Vol. II, p. 380-93.

[3] Jesse Torrey, *The Intellectual Torch* (1815; reprinted Woodstock, Vt., Elm Tree Press, 1912), cited in Sidney Ditzion, "The District-School Library, 1835-55," *Library Quarterly*, X, p. 546-548; New York State University, Home Education Bulletin no. 31 (1900), p. 51-2, 92-3.

[4] Cf., "Audiar," *Boston Daily Evening Transcript*, July 18, 1851; Boston Public Library, *Preliminary Report, 1852*, p. 7-9, 13-22; Boston Public Library, Building Commission, *Proceedings on the Occasion of Laying the Cornerstone of the Public Library of the City of Boston, Sept. 17, 1855* (Boston, Moore and Crosby, 1855), p. 16-18, Boston Public Library, *Ceremonies on the Dedication of the Public Library Building, Boylston Street, Jan. 1, 1858* (Boston: G. C. Rand & Avery, 1858, p. 86; also, Providence Public Library, *First Annual Report, 1878-9*, p. 8-9; *ibid., Fourteenth Report, 1891*, p. 9; *Fifteenth Report, 1892*, p. 10; Frederick de Peyster, *The Moral and Intellectual Influence of Libraries on Social Progress* (N. Y., New York Historical Society, 1866), p. 90; *Library Meeting at the Union League Club in New York City, Jan. 20, 1882*, p. 3 (pamphlet in New York Public Library collection classified HB p. v. 11 no. 7); Enoch Pratt Free Library, *Second Annual Report, 1888*, p. 3; Boston Public Library, Roxbury Branch, *Dedication Services of the Fellowes Athenaeum and Roxbury Branch* . . . *July 9, 1873* (Boston, The Fellowes Athenaeum, 1873), p. 9.

[5] New Bedford, Mass. Free Public Library, *Fifth Annual Report, 1857*, p. 3.

[6] North Brookfield, Mass. Public Library, *Dedication of the Haston Free Public Library Building, Sept. 20, 1894* (Brookfield, H. J. Lawrence, 1894), p. 43-5; Herkimer Free Public Library, Herkimer, N. Y., *Proceedings* (Herkimer, The Library, 1896), p. 26-7; Charles W. Eliot, "Why the Republic May Endure," in A. B. Hart, ed., *American History as Told by Contemporaries* (N. Y., Macmillan, 1929), Vol. 4, p. 659.

[7] Newark, N. J. Free Public Library, *Ceremonies Attending the Cornerstone Laying of the New Building, Jan. 26, 1899* (Newark, John E. Rowe, 1899), p. 17-20 (speech of William T. Hunt, editor of the *Newark Sunday Call*).

[8] *Boston Daily Evening Transcript*, Sept. 7, 1850, p. 2 col. 2; *Boston Daily Evening Advertiser*, March 23, 1853 (clipping in Quincy collection at Boston Public Library); Boston Public Library, Building Commission . . . *Cornerstone, op. cit.*, p. 17-18, 47-49; Boston Public Library, Jamaica Plains Branch, *Proceedings at the Dedication of the* . . . *Dec. 6, 1877* (Boston: Issued by the Boston Public Library, 1878), p. 23. Harvard, Mass. Public Library, *Dedication Exercises June 22, 1887* (Boston, Ellis, 1888), p. 20; *Dedication Exercises of the Charles Sedgwick Library and Reading-Rooms, at Lenox, Mass., Jan. 9, 1874* (Pittsfield, Mass., W. H. Phillips), p. 8.

[9] Chelsea, Mass. Public Library, *Proceedings at the Dedication of the New Library Building, Chelsea, Mass., Dec. 22, 1885; With the Address by James Russell Lowell* (Cambridge, University Press, J. Wilson, 1886), p. 28; Boston Public Library, South Boston Branch, *Proceedings at the Dedication, May 16, 1872* (Boston, Rockwell & Churchill, 1872), p. 21; Brookline, Mass. Public Library, *Annual Report, 1859-60*, p. 35.

[10] Boston Public Library, Building Commission, . . . *Cornerstone*, p. 18-19; Boston Public Library, . . . *Dedication, op. cit.*, p. 60; William W. Greenough, "Some Conclusions Relative to Public Libraries . . . May 22, 1874," *Journal of Social Science*, no. 7 (1874), 328; Haverhill, Mass. Public Library, *Proceedings at the Dedication* . . . *Nov. 11, 1875* . . . (Haverhill, C. C. Morse, 1876), p. 14; Rev. J. W. Wellman, "Free Public Library," *Bibliotheca Sacra*, XXVIII (1871), 231; Rev. Dr. Potter, speech in *Library Meeting at the Union League Club in New York City, Jan. 20, 1882*, p. 6-7. One finds occasional use of the idea that books might compensate for lack of money by supplying vicariously some of the opportunities (e. g., travel) possessed only by the rich. Boston Public Library, South Boston Branch, *Dedication* . . . *op. cit.*, p. 20; Harvard Mass. Public Library, *op. cit.*, p, 17.

[11] Providence Public Library, *Exercises at the Opening of the New Building, March 5, 1900* (Providence, Snow & Farnham, 1901), p. 28; *American Bibliophilist*, VII (1875), 239.

[12] William E. Channing, *Works* . . . (12th complete edition . . . ; Boston, Crosby, Nichols, 1853), Vol. 2, p. 387-92.

[13] Newburyport, Mass. Public Library, *Dedication Exercise of the Simpson Annex to the* . . . *Library Building of the City Newburyport* . . . *April, 1882* (Newburyport, 1882), p. 28.

[14] Cushman Library, Bernardston, Mass., *Address Delivered at the Dedication of the Cushman Library in Bernardston, Mass., Aug. 20, 1863, by George J. Davis* (Greenfield, Mass., S. S. Eastman, 1863), p. 14; *Library Journal*, V (1880), 90-91.

[15] Ralph Volney Harlow, *Gerrit Smith, Philanthropist and Reformer* (N. Y., Holt, 1939), p. 232-5; *Woodhull and Claffins Weekly*, VII (Jan. 10, 1874), 8-9.

[16] *Hampshire Gazette*, Feb. 22, 1881, p. 1, col. 4.

[17] George Willis Cooke, *Unitarianism in America* . . . (Boston, American Unitarian Association, 1902), p. 409-10.

[18] R. B. Patton, "Public Libraries," *American Biblical Repository*, XI (1838), 174; O. D., "On Reading," *Christian Examiner*, XXVII (1839), 1-18; *ibid.*, XXX (1841), 49-56; E. R., "Books for the People," *ibid.*, XXXV (1843), 86-111; "Our Book Movement," *ibid.*, LVII (1854), 267-78; *Christian Inquirer* (N. Y.), I (1847), 121 (The Barker Library); *ibid.*, p. 193 (libraries as an aspect of prison reform); "Library of the American Unitarian Association," *American Unitarian Association Quarterly Journal*, II (1855), 186-9; "The Work of the Unitarian Association in the Circulation of Its Literature," *American Unitarian Association Monthly Journal*, IX (1868), 119-32; "Our Freedmen's Libraries," *ibid.*, X (1869), 447 (acknowledgment of receipt of a non-sectarian library by the African Methodist Episcopal Church in Columbia, S. C. from the Freedmen's Department of the American Unitarian Association); *ibid.*, p. 260 (list of books in a typical Freedmen's Library), *The Christian Union* contained an "Educational Notes" column which consistently praised compulsory education laws, educational improvements, library facilities, etc., e. g., III (1871), 215; V (1872), 379-81 (H. W. Beecher's address at Cooper Union); Laicus, "Our Village Library," *Christian Union*, XIV (1876), 269; Edward Everette Hale, "The Chautauqua Reading Circles," *Unitarian Review*, XXVIII (1887), 233-48.

[19] *Methodist Quarterly Review*, XXIII (1841), 321; for remarks on education see *ibid.*, XXXI (1849), 145; XXXII

(1850), 281; XXXIV (1852), 302; XXXVII (1855), 410; LX (1878), 43-67; LXIII (Oct. 1881), 635-54; LXVI (April 1884), 396; LXVII (Jan. 1885), 56; LXXIV (Jan. 1892), 39; LXXVIII (July 1896), 640; LXXVII (Mar. 1895), 308.

[20] *Congregational Quarterly*, I (1859), 70-3.

[21] *Christian Inquirer*, IV (Aug. 3, 1850), 4; *ibid.*, p. 2, on Harvard College Library.

[22] "Town Libraries: Dr. Wayland," *ibid.*, V (Sept. 27, 1851), 4; *ibid.*, VII (Sept. 24, 1853), 1.

[23] *Christian Examiner*, LXXI (1861), p. 454-7; Rev. J. W. Wellman, "Free Public Libraries," *Bibliotheca Sacra*, XXVIII (1871), 209-34; *Christian Union*, XIV (1876), 132-34 (sermon by Henry Ward Beecher, Plymouth Pulpit, on "Reading"); *ibid.*, p. 285, 409 (remarks on the first American Library Association Conference at Philadelphia); "Free Library for New York," *ibid.*, XXXIII (March 11, 1886), 3.

[24] Frank Kellar Walter, "A Poor but Respectable Relation—the Sunday School Library," *Library Quarterly*, XII (1942), 731-9; "How to Improve Sunday-School Libraries," *Christian Union*, VII (1893), 391; National Education Association, *Proceedings, 1875*, p. 188; "Sunday School Libraries," *Pittsburgh Leader*, Jan. 29, 1897 (from scrapbook at Carnegie Library of Pittsburgh).

[25] H. M. Lydenberg, *History of the New York Public Library, Astor, Lenox, and Tilden Foundations* (New York: New York Public Library, 1923), p. 223, 247-54; for Archbishop Corrigan's remarks on the subject, see *New York Times*, April 18, 1901.

[26] E. g., Rev. J. W. Wellman, "Free Public Libraries," *Bibliotheca Sacra*, XXVIII (1871), p. 222-4.

[27] William R. Watson to C. A. Nelson, Jan, 27 1914 (MS in New York Public Library).

[28] Boston Public Library, South Boston Branch, *op. cit.*, p. 19 (address of Rev. George A. Thayer); Boston Public Library, Jamaica Plain Branch, *op. cit.*, p. 9-10 (address of W. W. Greenough, president Board of Trustees); Haverhill, Mass. Public Library, *Proceedings of the Dedication, Nov. 11, 1875*, p. 20-1 (address by Major Ben Perley Poore); Thomas Russell, *An Address Delivered at Dedication of the Hingham (Mass.) Public Library*, p. 10; South Weymouth, Mass. Public Library, *Dedication of the Fogg Library . . . Sept. 14, 1898* (South Weymouth, H. H. Joy, 1898), p. 30-1; Norton (Mass.) Public Library, *Dedication of the Norton Public Library* (Norton, Lane, 1888), p. 49-50; North Brookfield, Mass. . . . *Haston . . . op. cit.*, p. 25-6, 45; Manchester, Vt., *Proceedings at the Opening of the Mark Skinner Library, Manchester, Vermont, July 7, 1897* (Chicago, 1898), p. 31; Buffalo, N. Y. Public Library, *The Record of Its Organization . . .* p. 82.

[29] Boston Public Library, *Preliminary Report, 1852*, p. 5-16; "Canty Carl," "Social Improvements," *Boston Daily Evening Transcript*, Jan. 9, 1850, p. 2 col. 5; Wight's speech to the Massachusetts legislature, in (Jared M. Heard) *Origin of the Free Public Library System of Massachusetts* (Clinton, Mass: Printed at the office of the *Saturday Courant*, 1860); Proceedings of the Librarians Convention Held in New York City Sept. 15, 16, and 17, 1853 (reprinted for William H. Murray, 1915, Cedar Rapids, Iowa: The Torch Press, 1915) p. 15.

[30] *Dedicatory Exercises of the Baxter Building to the Uses of the Portland Public Library and Maine Historical Society, Thursday, February 21, 1839* (Auburn, Maine, Lakeside Press, 1889), p. 8-13; Newark, N. J. Free Public Library, *Opening Exercises . . .* p. 21-3; *Brooklyn Daily Eagle*, Jan. 15, 1897 (reception for Andrew Carnegie); *Exercises at the Dedication of the Fowler Library Building, Concord, New Hampshire, Oct. 18, 1888* (Concord, Republican Press, 1889), p. 60-2.

[31] Uxbridge, Mass. Free Public Library, *Proceedings at the Dedication of the Thayer Memorial Building, Uxbridge, Mass.* (Uxbridge, Compendium Steam Printing Works, 1896), p. 25-6.

[32] New Bedford, Mass. Free Public Library, *Ninth Annual Report*, 1861, p. 6-7; Boston Public Library, South Boston Branch, *Proceedings at the Dedication . . . May 16, 1872*, p. 18; James Blackstone Memorial Library, Branford, Conn., *Exercises at the Opening of the . . . Library, June 17, 1896* (New Haven, Tuttle, Morehouse & Taylor, 1897), p. 36; *Dedication of the Horatio Lyon Memorial Library Building, Erected by Mrs. Carrie R. Bale, for the Monson Free Library and Reading Room Association, March 28, 1882 . . .* (Worcester, Mass., F. S. Blanchard, 1882), p. 25; Harvard, Mass. Public Library, *Dedication Exercises, 1889*, p. 7; Buffalo Public Library . . . *The Record of Its Organization . . .* p. 82; Princeton, Mass. Public Library, *The Dedication at Goodnow Memorial Building* (Princeton, 1887), p. 11; Rev. Jesse F. Forbes, *Address at the Dedication of the Warren Public Library Building, July 1, 1890* (Warren, Mass., Herald Printing, 1890), p. 4-7; *Literary World*, XVIII (1887), 254; *New England Magazine*, N. S. V (1892), 139; *Lend-A-Hand*, XIII (1894), 35; *Midland Monthly*, IX (1898), 24.

[33] Lowell, Mass. City Library, *Annual Report*, 1864, p. 6.

[34] *New England Magazine, supra; Citizen* (Philadelphia) I (1896), 56.

[35] Statistics and materials concerning urban population, wealth, value of products, public services, etc., have been studied from volume 18 of the 1880 *Census*, "Social Statistics of Cities"; analyses made by Turner, *The United States, 1830-1850 . . .* p. 93-103, were extremely helpful.

[36] George Browning Lockwood, *The New Harmony Movement* (N. Y., Appleton, 1905), p. 322-35. A laborer by Maclure's definition had to work with his hands and live by the sweat of his brow.

[37] Douglas Waples, Bernard Berelson, and Franklyn R. Bradshaw, *What Reading Does to People; A Summary of Evidence on the Social Effects of Reading and a Statement of Problems for Research* (Chicago, University of Chicago Press, 1940), p. 7-8.

[38] Boston Public Library, South Boston Branch, *Proceedings at the Dedication, op. cit.*, p. 6-7.

[39] "Social Statistics of Cities," *Census 1880, op. cit.*

[40] F. J. Turner, *United States, 1830-1850; The Nation and Its Sections . . .* (N. Y., Holt, 1935), p. 112; The increase of population in Massachusetts from 1840 to 1860 was 67 per cent, while the increase of property valuation was 200 per cent in the same period (Massachusetts, Board of Education, *Twenty-fifth Annual Report, 1861*), p. 108.

[41] New Bedford, Mass., City Doc. no.1, 1853 (address of the Hon. Rodney French, Mayor . . . April 4, 1853), p. 519; *New Bedford, Massachusetts, Its History, Industries, Institutions . . . passim;* Constance McLaughlin Green, *Holyoke,*

Massachusetts; a Case History of the Industrial Revolution in America (New Haven, Yale University Press, 1939), p. 52-4, 103-30.

[42] Newburyport, Mass., *Dedication of the Simpson Memorial Library, op. cit.,* p. 27.

[43] Lenox Library Association, *Dedication Exercises . . . 1874,* p. 25.

[44] Boston Public Library, Jamaica Plains Branch, *op. cit.,* p. 5 (address of Frederick O. Prince, Mayor of Boston).

[45] New Bedford, Mass. Free Public Library, *Fifth Annual Report, 1857,* p. 2; *Same, Thirteenth Annual Report, 1865,* p. 10.

[46] De Peyster, *The Moral and Intellectual Influence of Libraries . . .* p. 45, 86.

[47] Herkimer, N. Y. Public Library, *Proceedings at Dedication . . .* p. 6-11.

[48] Manchester, N. H., *First Annual Report of the Library Trustees, 1854,* p. 95 (in *Ninth Annual Report* of the City of Manchester); Warren, Mass., Public Library, *Dedication, op. cit.,* p. 8; Harvard, Mass. Public Library, *Dedication,* p. 18; Henry George, *Progress and Poverty . . .* (N. Y., Robert Shalkenbach Foundation, 1937), p. 240-3.

[49] Adna Ferrin Weber, *The Growth of Cities in the Nineteenth Century: a Study in Statistics* (N. Y., Macmillan, 1899), p. 218-24 (Columbia University Studies in History, Economics and Public Law, Vol. 11, whole no. 29).

[50] Unidentified clippings in a scrapbook at the Worcester Public Library. The problem dates are in December 1859. One contains a message by Mayor Bullock citing Everett's speech at the opening of the Boston Public Library building and refers to library reports from Newburyport and New Bedford. "Have We a Lenox Among Us?" *Providence Daily Journal,* February. 3, 1870, p. 2, col. 2; *ibid.,* Feb. 4, 1878. Salem, Mass. Public Library, *Address of Hon. John M. Raymond, at the Opening of the Salem Public Library, June 26, 1889, with a Brief Historical Sketch of the Movement for the Establishment of Such a Library in Salem and a Notice of Libraries Now in Existence in the City* (Salem: Salem Press, 1889), p. 17-18; Arthur Goldberg, *The Buffalo Public Library, 1836-1936* (Buffalo: Privately printed, 1937), p. 114.

[51] *Providence Daily Journal,* Jan. 4, 1878, p. 2, col. 3-6 (address of Prof. J. Lewis Diman of Brown University at the dedication of the Rogers Free Library, Briston, R. I.).

[52] F. M. Crunden, *The Free Library, Its Uses and Value* (St. Louis, Mo., St. Louis Commercial Club, 1893), p. 3; Arthur Goldberg, *op. cit.,* p. 111 (quotation from a letter by Melvil Dewey published in a Buffalo newspaper of the early 1890's).

[53] J. L. Harrison, "Movement for Public Libraries in the United States," *New England Magazine,* X (1894), 709; Crunden, *supra.,* p. 11; C. A. Cutter, "Development of Public Libraries," in U. S. Commissioner of Education, *Report, 1899-1900,* p. 1352-9.

[54] E. Foster, "Argument for Public Support of Public Libraries," *Library Journal,* XVI (1891), C. p. 47; Worcester Public Library, *Seventh Annual Report, 1866,* p. 19; "Why Should St. Louis Have a Free Public Library?" *Library Journal,* XV (1890), 80.

[55] William I. Fletcher, "The Public Library Movement," *Cosmopolitan,* XVIII (1894), 103-4.

[56] *Library Journal,* XXI (1896), 288.

[57] C. A. Cutter, "Development of Public Libraries," in U. S. Commissioner of Education, *Report, 1900-01.*

[58] American Library Association, *Bulletin,* I (1907), 24-35.

[59] *Library Journal,* I (1877), 395, 401, 409, 410.

[60] *Ibid.,* XXI (1896), 234.

[61] *Ibid.,* I (1877), 390; cf. Chapter XI (St. Beuve on censorship in French village libraries).

[62] Newark, N. J. Free Public Library, *Opening Exercises . . . Oct. 16, 1889* (Newark, W. H. Shurts, 1889) (remarks by Lewis H. Steiner on "Library Branches"); *Library Journal,* XXI (1896), 284, A. E. Bostwick, "Economic Features of Libraries," *Library Journal,* XXXIV (1909) 48-52.

[63] Frank H. Norton, "The Astor Library," *Galaxy,* VII (1869), 536-7.

[64] *Library Journal,* XIX (1894), 345; *ibid.,* XIX (1894), 1-4; *ibid.,* XXI (1896), 447-8.

[65] Proceedings, Fabian House Conference, *Library Journal,* XV (1890), 86; Hannah P. James, "Reading Room and Periodicals," *Library Journal,* XXI (1896), 49.

[66] Melvil Dewey, "Libraries As Related to the Educational Work of the State," in U. S. Commissioner of Education, *Report, 1888,* p. 1033-4.

[67] J. N. Larned, "Presidential Address," *Library Journal,* XIX (1894), 3.

[68] *Library Journal,* XIV (1889), 97.

[69] W. H. Brett, "The Present Problem," *Library Journal,* XIX (1894), 5-9; A. L. Peck, "Workingman's Clubs and the Public Library," *Library Journal,* XXIII (1898), 612.

[70] Frank H. Norton, "Ten Years in a Public Library," *Galaxy,* VII (1869), 535.

[71] Jesse Cohen, "The Value of Libraries," *Library Journal,* XVI (1891), 174-5.

[72] Henry Nourse, "The Free Public Library Commission of Massachusetts," *Library Journal,* XXI (1896), 10-13; Angeline Scott, "The Librarian and the Patriotic Societies," *Library Journal,* XXII (1897), 80-1.

[73] *Library Journal,* XV (1890), 55, 100, 106.

[74] Gratia Countryman, "Shall Public Libraries Buy Foreign Literature for the Benefit of the Foreign Population?" *Library Journal,* XXIII (1898), 229-31.

Causal Factors in Public Library Development

Jesse H. Shera

Perhaps only one other book on American library history can claim respect equal to Ditzion's work. That book, Jesse Shera's Foundations of the Public Library, *is considered by all to be a classic in the field. The final chapter of Shera's work, which is reproduced here, is a carefully documented and forcefully argued presentation of the complex mélange of forces which combined to give birth to this new library form. It is interesting to note that Shera and Ditzion were constructing their models of public library growth at the same time, but independent of one another. A comparison of their explanations for the rise of the American public library is both enlightening and thought-provoking.*

Complex social agencies do not arise in response to a single influence; the dogma of simple causation is an easy and ever threatening fallacy. It cannot be said that the public library began on a specific date, at a certain town, as the result of a particular cause. A multiplicity of forces, accumulating over a long period of time, converged to shape this new library form. Some were obviously more important than others, but to evaluate each in precise quantitative terms is impossible. Nevertheless, some generalizations concerning the elements that contributed to the emergence of the public library are possible, and these, together with an indication of the relative importance of each, will be presented in this concluding chapter.

ECONOMIC ABILITY

Among the many social conditions that made the public library possible the one basic element was economic potential. Without financial resources superior to the demands of mere subsistence, no community could assemble and maintain a library. Tax support for libraries presupposes a source from which revenue may be derived. The American public library was evolved and supported by community action; and, because it was dependent upon democratic processes, its advance was slow and its acceptance forced to wait upon general recognition of libraries as at least desirable, if not essential, adjuncts of a culturally sophisticated society. Yet no library was possible in the absence of an available reservoir of wealth. In the advance of tax support for libraries desire and ability were equally important and interdependent; either without the other was incapable of action.

Economic ability contributed to the advance of the library in two major ways: (*a*) the accumulation of private fortunes by philanthropic individuals and (*b*) a rising level of community wealth; and these produced the two aberrant forms of the evolutionary process by which the modern public library arose. These forms are represented by libraries established and supported by (*a*) wealthy philanthropists and (*b*) groups of individuals of more modest means. The former exhibits three variations depending upon the conditions of gift, inasmuch as libraries were inaugurated by an initial gift of expendable money, by an endowment of which the income only was available, and by a combination of expendable gift and endowment.

Private philanthropy antedated tax support by many years because it was simple, direct, and dependent only upon the accumulation of wealth by a generous individual. Philanthropy is a normal process whereby economic inequalities are voluntarily leveled off by individuals acting on their own initiative or in response to public opinion. Public libraries in America may rightly be said to have begun with the bequest of Captain Keayne, and they have been heavily indebted to the generosity of individuals ever since. The first tax-supported libraries drew much of their strength from the donations of wealthy men. Wayland's public library and even the Massachusetts law itself were direct results of a gift from the president of Brown University. The original success of the Boston Public Library can scarcely be attributed to any

SOURCE: Reprinted from Jesse H. Shera, *Foundations of the Public Library* (Chicago: University of Chicago Press, 1949), Chapter 7, "Causal Factors in Public Library Development," pp. 200-244, by permission of the author and publisher. Copyright © 1949 by the University of Chicago.

single influence, but it is certain that the benevolence of Joshua Bates gave to that institution an early stability.

So meager were the first contributions from the town treasuries that the sponsors of early public libraries anticipated that such slender resources would be amplified by private gifts. Edward Everett wrote into the preliminary report of the Boston Public Library trustees his conviction that a large municipal appropriation "was entirely out of the question" and even that there were "advantages in a more gradual course of measures," adding that with only "moderate and frugal expenditure on the part of the City . . . the Trustees believe that all else may be left to the public spirit and liberality of individuals."[1] John. B. Wight said of the Massachusetts library law that it "precludes any large expenditures for library purposes by any city or town in its corporate capacity. It was thought best to leave room for the exercise of private liberality and public spirit in aid of their establishment and augmentation."[2] Likewise, the directors of the Athenaeum of Portland, Maine, when considering the possibility of initiating a public library in their community, remarked in 1855:

> With reference to a free public library, no example is known to us, of any such institution, in this country, established by any municipal corporation or otherwise, which has not had its origin in some large private benefaction, made for the purpose by one or more individuals . . . .
>
> The private generosity, which may be wished for to make this undertaking practicable, has not yet appeared. It may not be unreasonable to *hope*, that coming time will reveal the benefactor, who shall make an effectual contribution to the general intellectual improvement of our city, after the resplendent examples, that have illustrated the annals of some other places; but that chapter in the history of Portland, which shall record such a bounty, is as yet unwritten.[3]

With the independence of New England upon commerce and industry, there developed an economy in which the general income level was relatively low and wealth tended to concentrate in the hands of the few. The public could not afford the costs of adequate library support. Aid through taxation and its resultant spreading of the financial burden over the entire community was, even in its earlier forms, an advance beyond the voluntary association represented by the social library. But only the wealthy were able to give the movement the aid it required.

The dominant characteristic of that benevolence upon which the public libraries of New England were so heavily dependent was the psychology of the generous native son. The individual histories of New England town libraries tell again and again the story of those who, recalling the hardships of youth, returned to their native communities a portion of the rewards gained during a lifetime of economic venturing. The successful Boston publisher Caleb Bingham gave to Salisbury, Connecticut, the library which later became the first collection to receive financial aid from public funds.[4] From London, George Peabody, merchant, financier, and philanthropist, established in South Danvers the Peabody Institute, "in acknowledgment of the payment of that debt to the generation which preceded me in my native town . . . and to aid in its prompt future discharge."[5] Joshua Bates was not a native of Boston, but he had been born at Weymouth in the Bay region and his business life was so closely associated with the capital of Massachusetts that when he received from Mayor Seaver the report of the trustees on the proposed Public Library for Boston, his response was immediate and generous. On October 1, 1852, he wrote to T. W. Ward:

> My own experience as a poor boy convinced me of the great advantage of such a library. Having no money to spend, and no place to go to, not being able to pay for a fire in my own room I could not pay for books, and the best way I could pass my evenings was to sit in Hastings, Etheridge, & Bliss' Bookstore, and read what they kindly permitted me to.[6]

Said John Wight in urging the promotion of libraries under the provision of the Massachusetts law:

> It may be justly expected that in the future . . . as has already occurred, intelligent and far seeing individuals who have risen to affluence in our large cities, or in foreign countries, will be disposed to remember in this regard the place of their birth . . . in the welfare of which they cannot but feel a peculiar interest, by laying the foundation of an institution which will be a rich and increasing source of useful knowledge and mental cultivation open to all the inhabitants throughout all generations.[7]

Of course, not all the benefactions for New England libraries were the contributions of those who from the security of a profitable career remembered the privations of youth, but the philanthropy that contributed so much to the encouragement of public libraries in that region was strongly centripetal, drawing toward its vortex the wealth produced beyond its immediate boundaries. Abbott Lawrence, William Wood, Kirk Boot, William Maclure, and many others who lived in places remote from the recipients of their generosity contributed to the growth of libraries in New England towns which they themselves may never have seen.[8]

The growth of industrialization and of the factory system, with its resultant concentration of capital in the hands of a small proportion of the population, was the real factor behind the expansion of philanthropy. As industry began to return to ownership the rewards of investment and as money accumulated at an unprecedented rate, the individual sought a proper object for his munificence. It was generally acknowledged that a library was a wholesome community influence, and its encouragement could be regarded with the highest approbation. The endowment of a library did not demand extravagant wealth; by comparison to colleges, universities, or art galleries, its requirements were extremely modest. Hence the library could, and did, attract the generosity of men of moderate means—men who, like Francis Wayland or Josiah Quincy, Jr., were able to contribute in a relatively small way toward the support of collections which they sincerely believed to be essential to the encouragement of an indigenous culture.[9]

The libraries which derived support from numbers of small gifts rather than from a single large donation approached the democratic ideal of general community participation. But the great weakness of philanthropy as a medium of library promotion lay in its independence of public desire. It was not a direct expression of popular need. In a sense it was forced upon society; and while it may have been accepted and even fostered by the recipients, it was in its origins a thing apart. In 1785 the inhabitants of Franklin, Massachusetts, wishing a bell for their meetinghouse, communicated the fact to the American minister to the Court of France in whose honor the town had been named. From Passy, Franklin responded with a gift of a library, "sense being preferable to sound," which, though received by the community with appropriate expressions of gratitude, remained for half a century in the hayloft of a barn.[10] Similarly, John Quincy Adams' handsome gift of three thousand volumes, taken from his own rich collection, to the town of Quincy was but slightly esteemed by the recipient municipality; and though provision was made for its preservation, the residents of the community derived little benefit from it.[11]

In an effort to avoid just such misplaced generosity and to broaden the democratic base of the institutions they hoped to found, it became a general practice among donors to require of a community that by voluntary contributions or other means it match the proffered gift.[12] But even at its best, philanthropy, because it lacked the spontaneity of unified collective action, created an institutional superstructure that existed because it had been built upon rather than grown from the life of the town. As a sustaining force in the expansion of the library the importance of private donation is not to be minimized. Many times it saved institutions which would have perished because of the poverty of the communities they endeavored to serve. Moreover, it bridged the gap between the period of the voluntary association and the emergence of tax support by keeping alive social library collections which later were absorbed into the governments of their towns.

Nevertheless, philanthropy, for all the material benefits it conferred, was a contributory rather than a causal factor in public library development. It was not the expression of group action. As an embodiment of the donor's wish to further the welfare of society it was personal and individual, an instrument rather than a cause of public library promotion. But it was not the only medium by which the economic ability of the region contributed to the enthusiasm for public libraries. When the economic structure of New England became more stable and wealth began to accumulate, other social phenomena appeared which stimulated the desire for greater library resources that would be freely available to all who needed them.

SCHOLARSHIP, HISTORICAL RESEARCH, AND THE URGE FOR CONSERVATION

"What is the nest that hatches scholars but a library?" asked Oliver Wendell Holmes,[13] and this one question epitomizes what was probably the greatest single force in the expansion of the public library. In the decades that preceded the middle of the nineteenth century, scholarship, especially as it found expression in historical inquiry and research, was definitely increasing. With the development of settled conditions and the increase of wealth in New England, there appeared a class of professional and amateur scholars who desperately needed libraries, and the accumulation of private wealth richly served the historian. Prescott, Motley, and Parkman were all men of considerable means. George Ticknor, whose *History of Spanish Literature* cost as much to produce as a public building, owned a great house at the head of Park Street, which dominated the Common from Beacon Hill, and there, in its largest and finest room, he kept the most extensive private library in Boston. It was Ticknor who, as a trustee of the Boston Athenaeum, proposed to unite all the libraries of the city with that institution and make the whole freely available to the entire population. On February 2, 1826, he wrote to Daniel Webster:

> We are making quite a movement about libraries, lecture-rooms, Athenaeum, etc. I have a project, which may or may not succeed; but I hope it will. The project is, to unite into one establishment, viz. the Athenaeum, all the public libraries in town; such as the Arch Library, the Medical Library, the new Scientific Library, and so on, and then let the whole circulate, Athenaeum and all. In this way there will be an end of buying duplicates, paying double rents, double librarians, etc.; the whole money raised will go to books, and all the books will be made useful. To this great establishment I would attach all the lectures wanted, whether fashionable, popular, scientific,— for the merchants or their employees; and have the whole made a Capitol of the knowledge of the town, with its uses, which I would open to the public, according to the admirable direction in the Charter of the University of Göttingen, *quam commodissime, quamque latissime.* Mr. Prescott, Judge Jackson, Dr. Bowditch, and a few young men are much in earnest about it.[14]

Having assumed leadership in the movement for establishing the Boston Public Library, Ticknor collected lists of essential books from every interested scholar he could find, planned with C. C. Jewett the accession policies of the new library, and toured Europe purchasing large quantities of books in London, Paris, and Rome.

The growing consciousness of the inadequacy of American libraries was given dramatic expression by Fisher Ames. At the close of a strenuous political career, plagued by rapidly failing health, and furious over a rising Jeffersonian democracy, Ames, with characteristic eagerness to discredit everything American to the eternal glorification of the British, insisted that in all our universities combined there was not a sufficient supply of books to furnish the essential materials for such a work as Gibbon's.

> Nor will it be charged as a mark of our stupidity . . . that we have produced nothing in history. Our own is not yet worthy of a Livy; and to write that of any foreign nation where could an American author collect his materials and authorities? Few persons reflect, that all our universities would not suffice to supply them for such a work as Gibbon's.[15]

The accusation was doubtless just, and it was eagerly snatched by many a mid-nineteenth-century proponent of public library development and bandied about until it became little more than an empty cliché.[16] Finally John Quincy Adams set about collecting at his own expense the titles necessary for the verification of Gibbon's citations.[17] Throughout New England there arose a great outcry from the academicians for more adequate library resources. The *American Alamanac* spoke with feeling of the embarrassment felt by every American scholar who, confronted by the most meager of library facilities, attempts to pursue "one point of science or literature through all or a considerable portion of what has been written on it."[18] In 1850 George Livermore exceeded the charge of Fisher Ames by asserting that the scholar of his generation did not have access to sufficient material to write the history of the *New England Primer*, and C. C. Jewett, with scarcely less restraint, maintained that not one American library could meet the wants of a student in any department of knowledge. In this general opinion Prescott concurred, holding that the American historian was forced to create a personal library if he wished to write extensively on historical themes; and Bancroft, who was relatively poor, found himself obliged, in the preparation of his earlier works, to spend as much as the salary of the president of the United States.

In spite of general dissatisfaction over the poverty of materials, the historians were active. In this sudden outburst of enthusiasm for historical investigation American writers reflected interests that were awakening in England and on the Continent. The aftermath of the Napoleonic Wars brought an aroused nationalism which revitalized historical research. Under the leadership of Niebuhr new standards of critical scholarship in historical writing, both in the search for materials and their objective examination, were established. Macaulay, Grote, and Carlyle in England, Theirs and Guizot in France, and Niebuhr and Von Ranke in Germany were making history popular as never before. American scholars who had traveled in Europe were stirred by the work of these men, and they began to study not only the history of other peoples but also that of their own nation. In increasing numbers young New Englanders with literary tastes were drawn into historical research, as decades before they had been called into the ministry. To the quiet reading-rooms of the Athenaeum came the stalwarts of the *North American Review*: Ticknor, Palfrey, Sparks, Everett, and even Hannah Adams, the first woman permitted to use the collections—locked in while the librarian was at lunch because he was too polite to put her out.

Events had prepared the New England mind for

concentration on history. Old bitternesses and conflicts engendered by the Revolution were forgotten in the nationalism that was sweeping the country. Old men who as youths had fought together in '76 foregathered to relive the battles of Lexington and Concord. Inspired by Webster's orations, the public thronged to the shrine of Plymouth Rock and read again Mather's *Magnalia Christi* and other half-forgotten chronicles of our national heritage.

To the end of encouraging historical research, scholars throughout the New England area united in voluntary associations to promote mutual understanding and to encourage and facilitate the assembly of basic source materials. In 1791 Jeremy Belknap, John Pintard, and Ebenezer Hazard laid the foundation of the Massachusetts Historical Society and its long line of distinguished publications. In 1812 Isaiah Thomas gave his private library to form the American Antiquarian Society and eight years later built with his own money Antiquarian Hall at Worcester where, being in a small town, it would be safer from the fires of large cities and, being inland, less exposed to the ravages of war. In 1821 there was established at Salem, Massachusetts, the Essex Historical Society, which later became the Essex Institute; and the year following both Rhode Island and Maine founded historical societies, the former issuing, appropriately enough, Roger Williams' treatise on the Indian languages in America. New Hampshire, eager to celebrate in 1823 the two-hundredth anniversary of her first Colonial settlement, incorporated her historical society with thirty-one charter members. In Connecticut a state historical society was initiated in 1825, but it did not become active until 1839, when its charter was revived. In 1838 Vermont established at Montpelier the Historical and Antiquarian Society of that state. All over the country, in the middle states and the South as well as in New England, the reading of history was popular as never before; a veritable flood of local histories rolled from the presses, and Parson Weems's *Life of Washington* went through some seventy editions. A generation later James Parton concluded his three-volume biography of Andrew Jackson with the credo of the age:

And to comprehend the state of things in which we find ourselves, it is necessary, first of all, to show every step of the progress by which the present state of things has been reached. It is necessary that the writings of Washington, Adams, Hamilton, and Jefferson should no longer remain in the public libraries with the leaves uncut. It is necessary, in a word, that the educated intelligence of the United States should be-

gin to understand that there is nothing in recent European history half so worthy of study as the history of the United States since the adoption of the present constitution.[19]

In the wake of this enthusiasm for the past came a natural urge to preserve for future generations the more fragile records of the growing nation. Gales and Seaton began their monumental *American State Papers*, and Congress contracted with Peter Force and Matthew St. Clair Clarke for the publication of the "American Archives Series," originally suggested a half-century earlier by Ebenezer Hazard. At the beginning of the century the national Congress, largely through the efforts of Elbridge Gerry, Samuel Latham Mitchill, and John Randolph of Roanoke,[20] had laid the foundation for a great book collection, and though this Library of Congress was to suffer somewhat more than its share of adverse fortune, by the middle of the century it gave promise of ranking among the best of American book collections.[21]

In 1812 Joseph Stevens Buckminster wrote into a preface intended for the first printed catalog of the Boston Athenaeum a plea for the formation of a "complete Bibliotheca Americana," toward which some progress had then already been made,[22] and fifteen years later a similar ideal was proposed for the state of New Hampshire by the trustees of the Portsmouth Athenaeum.[23] As early as 1836 an anonymous writer in the *American Almanac* was urging the creation of a series of regional libraries "under the patronage and direction of the government" that were to be "judiciously placed at the principal centers of population and intelligence."[24]

By 1811 Massachusetts had enacted legislation providing for the exchange of her official state documents for those of other states, thus laying a cornerstone for the future state library, which was established in 1826. Priority in state library establishment belongs to New Hampshire, where in 1818 an act was passed authorizing the secretary of state "to collect and arrange all books belonging to the State," and in 1823 a resolution was adopted appropriating one hundred dollars annually for the increase of the collection.[25]

Much of the passion for the historic became an empty antiquarianism that soon degenerated into mere collecting for its own sake with little or no regard to the value of the materials thus assembled. Libraries eagerly brought together "cabinets of specimens," and historical societies assembled with reckless abandon museums of curios and memorabilia that would have been better forgotten. But at its best this activity did salvage much of value to the historian, and it did help to build up a solid body of source materials upon which might be erected a substantial scholarship. It was through the efforts of such men as William Smith Shaw that later generations have inherited libraries as important as the Boston Athenaeum. Not without reason was he known by his contemporaries as "Athenaeum Shaw":

> That dog of a Shaw [said Judge William Tudor] goes everywhere. He knows everybody. Everybody knows him. If he sees a book, pamphlet, or *manuscript*—Oh! Sir! the Athenaeum must have this. Well, *have it he will*, and *have it he must*, and *have it he does*, for he seldom goes out of a house without having something under his arm; and his large pockets, made on purpose, are crammed. Now, he never refuses anything whatever. With him a book is a book, a pamphlet a pamphlet, a manuscript a manuscript.[26]

This urge to preservation, when in conjunction with the demand of the historian for collections adequate to his research needs, could not fail to influence the course of the public library and contribute to the movement for library establishment a most powerful impetus. Ticknor, despite his predilection for maximum accessibility, wrote into the first report of the Boston Public Library trustees his conviction that there was a basic core of books which should not be permitted to circulate—books which because of their rarity and costliness it was the first duty of the library to provide but which it was the obligation of the library also to protect.[27] Though Ticknor was not reluctant to acknowledge that one of the important functions of the public library was to preserve for posterity the bibliographical treasures of the present, it was Everett who was the high priest of preservation. Writing in 1850 to Mayor Bigelow to offer his collection of public documents to the city of Boston as a nucleus for the proposed library, he asserted:

> Perceiving that a commencement is likely to be made toward the establishment of a public library, I will thank you to inform the city government that this collection is at their service, whenever it will suit their convenience to receive it. I have for nearly thirty years devoted a good deal of time and labor and considerable expense to its formation. It amounts at present to about one thousand volumes. From the foundation of the government up to the year 1825, when I first went to Congress, it contains nearly everything material. While I was in Congress I took great pains to preserve and bind up everything published by either house; and from that time to the year 1840, when I went abroad, the collection is tolerably complete. It is my intention to add to it, as far as they can be procured, the documents since pub-

lished, and I omit no opportunity of supplying the deficiencies in other parts of the series.[28]

Similarly, John B. Wight, in urging upon the Massachusetts General Court the need for state-wide public library legislation, argued: "Such libraries . . . will furnish suitable and accessible depositories for the preservation of important public documents, and the collection of rare and curious books. They will encourage those who are preeminently capable of teaching and improving others to produce works of great utility and interest."[29]

LOCAL PRIDE

The conservational function of the library appeared very early, and the urge toward book preservation has always been a great driving force, but in New England of the 1840's its appeal was especially strong. Everywhere during these years the young Republic evinced the pride of youth that looked with satisfaction upon the past. Perhaps in no other region was this attitude more intensely expressed than in New England. With the statesmen of Virginia, the hardy Yankees had taken the lead in the Revolution. Twice Britain had been defeated, and on both occasions New England had played a noteworthy part. Confronted by the threat of economic domination from the expanding West and the growing industrialism in the middle states, New England was more than ever forced to reflect upon the glory of a former day. Pride in the cultural heritage, the accomplishments of its authors, the development of education, the number of its libraries—all were natural responses to a latent apprehension that henceforth other sections of the nation would dominate American economic life. Even the champions of New England cultural supremacy were haunted by ominous forebodings. An Astor fortune had given to New York the money necessary for a public library, and Boston was truly alarmed. Already men were beginning to express the fear that unless something of a like character were done in Boston, science and literary culture in that city would follow trade and capital to its metropolitan rival. "That Boston must have a great public library," wrote Everett to Ticknor, "or yield to New York in letters as well as in commerce, will, I think, be made quite apparent in a few years."[30] Six weeks earlier he had written to Mayor Bigelow in similar vein:

> The City of Boston expends annually, I believe, a larger sum for Schools and School Houses, in propor-

tion to its population than any city in Europe. Nothing like the same sum is appropriated by the City of London for these purposes. . . . Is it not then a reproach to our City, that,—as far as the means of carrying on the great work of instruction beyond the limits of School Education are concerned,—no public provision exists in favor of those unable to indulge in what is now the expensive luxury of a large library?[31]

The theme was a familiar one in the argument of those who were most seriously concerned with the establishment of the public library. The editor of the *Boston Daily Courier* wrote in his paper for March 26, 1853:

> It is gratifying to observe that the rapid and unremitting growth of this metropolis in population, wealth, all the activities of outward life, and all the materials of physical greatness and strength, is accompanied by an augmenting and sharpened attention to those matters which concern the intellect and morals of the community. What, indeed, is the value of all this wealth—accumulated by the industry, enterprise, and ingenuity of the people of New England, drawn out from our own bosom, gathered from the four corners of the globe, and concentrated in her ancient capital— if we cannot number among its uses that of aiding the intelligence, developing the intellect, and improving the morals of those within its reach?
>
> The interest which is now manifested by the citizens of Boston in the subject of a public library, is one of the encouraging signs of the times, and evidence that the people of this city will not allow it to be out-stripped by any other in a care for the nobler objects of human pursuit. [32]

Boston was not alone in her eagerness to achieve national distinction as a guardian of the cultural heritage and as a patron of libraries. In 1836 a meeting was called to consider the union of the Providence Library and the Providence Athenaeum into a public library for the community as a whole. In supporting the movement an anonymous writer in the *Journal* expressed his conviction that so pre-eminent a municipality would not neglect so important an agency for public enlightenment:

> I . . . trust my fellow citizens in great numbers will join me. I look, then, to the reputation of our beautiful city. I look to the intelligence of its population. I look to the increasing knowledge, refinement, virtue, and love of virtue, of the rising generation, and of the generations to come. All these are deeply involved in the success of the proposed enterprise. What can more worthily appeal to patronage, to any liberal and enlightened community? In this busy, flourishing, and wealthy city, there is not, to our shame, be it recorded, a single building which belongs to our citizens, aside from our school-houses, yet dedicated to the great interests of learning and science. Many towns in New England, quite behind us in population and wealth, have largely surpassed us in the encouragement of

such undertakings. Such an institution as is contemplated it is high time we had.[33]

An appeal to local pride interwoven with the ever effective plea for the necessity of outdistancing one's neighbors gave to the argument a vitality that on more than one occasion strongly influenced popular sentiment in favor of creating a library which in later years, when initial enthusiasm had waned under the pressure of economic restriction, suffered inadequate support. It is difficult to envisage an agency more characteristic of this period than the emerging public library. America, proud of her economic growth but confronted by the ancient tradition of European culture, sought eagerly to demonstrate her awareness of the necessity for preserving her own national heritage. America might anticipate a time when she would become a great power in the economic world, yet in the development of a cultural tradition there would always be the handicap of those centuries when she was an unbroken forest inhabited by only savages and beasts. America could build factories, railroads, and all the other physical properties of a growing industrialism; so, too, she could erect libraries, within the walls of which to assemble the cultural monuments of the entire world, and thus in a measure find compensation for the shortcomings of her national immaturity. Such reasoning was particularly appealing to New England, where the existence of a relatively long Colonial history and the threat of declining economic leadership forced the people to seek in cultural achievement the satisfaction of desire for regional prestige.

THE SOCIAL IMPORTANCE OF UNIVERSAL PUBLIC EDUCATION

Second only to the desire for conservation and local pride was the growth in New England of an awareness of the need for universal educational opportunity. However influential the conservational motive was, its basic appeal was to the scholar, the man of letters, and the leader in political and civil life. It did not arouse the enthusiasm of a large portion of the people. But the public library, if it was to enlist the support of the voters in its campaign for municipal funds, had of necessity to appeal to the popular mind. In this the public library was favored by a spirit that was developing in New England, as elsewhere in America. There was a widespread conviction that universal literacy was necessary, and there was much enthusiasm for education for its own sake. Many believed in the possibility of self-education and the practical value of vocational and technical studies. Finally, there was a prevalent assumption that reading promotes morality. From these convictions there emerged a popular awareness of the importance of the public library to the people, and as the people began to express themselves more freely in political activity, the public library became a necessity.

Jackson's election to the presidency proved the reality of that boundless optimism that characterized the expanding frontier, a seemingly inexhaustible energy that lashed backward over the Atlantic Coast. Even in conservative New England was felt the sudden impact of this robust enthusiasm in the discovery of romance, culture, altruism, self-reliance, and a sense of one's own individuality. Everywhere the spirit of youth was dominant. With the rise of Jackson, the presidency began to seem attainable to every American boy. Democracy became popular to a degree that had never been achieved before, and in its defense Bancroft wrote "history that voted for Jackson on every page." Humanitarian movements developed with all the enthusiasm that attaches to the untried. Social experiments, such as Brook Farm and New Harmony, evinced this same spirit of youthful buoyance and confidence. In New England the trend was a local manifestation of a world movement that swept over Europe in a great wave of humanitarianism, benevolence, and desire for improvement. There it was terminated by the revolutions of 1848; in America it was halted by the cataclysm of the Civil War. But even under the shadow of that conflict popular faith in man's innate competence of social judgment persisted until from Tennessee, Andrew Johnson flung out his challenging credo:

> I believe man can be elevated; man can become more and more endowed with divinity; and as he does he becomes more god-like in his character and capable of governing himself. Let us go on elevating our people, perfecting our institutions, until democracy shall reach such a point of perfection that we can acclaim with truth that the voice of the people is the voice of God.[34]

This affirmation of faith in the perfectibility of man was the very lifeblood of the incipient public library; for, if every man possessed within himself the power to develop a wisdom adequate to the needs of judicious self-government, any agency directed toward the improvement of that intellectual power must necessarily become the recipient

of public support. Wrote Edward Everett to Mayor Bigelow:

> The first principles of popular government require that the means of education should, as far as possible, be equally within the reach of the whole population ... The sons of the wealthy alone have access to well-stored libraries; while those whose means do not allow them to purchase books are too often deprived of them at the moment when they would be most useful.[35]

The theme of democratic necessity was recurrent in the arguments of those who sought to further public library establishment. Its implication was written by Everett into the trustees' report of 1852. It was advanced by Mayor Seaver when he urged upon the Common Council the need for action in support of a public library in Boston. It was repeated by John B. Wight when he persuaded the Massachusetts General Court to enact the law of 1851.

But the argument carried with it a power which many of its most ardent advocates did not foresee, a force which threatened the supremacy of even the conservational motive and which was to reshape the dominant pattern of the public library that was to come. Only Ticknor envisaged the real significance of the democratization of the public library and what it would mean in terms of function. With Everett he shared the honor of having done most to encourage the founding of the Boston Public Library. They were the most powerful members of its first board of trustees, and together they prepared the first report. Each accepted the axiom that the public library, if it were to be an agent of democracy, must be for all the people, but it was Ticknor rather than Everett who could translate this concept into functional terms. In the mind of Everett conservation was still dominant; and though his objective was a collection that would be open to all classes of the population, such a library would remain primarily a storehouse from which the treasures were not to be removed.

On July 14, 1851, Ticknor wrote to Everett encouraging him in his promotion of the undertaking and suggesting that it be

> a library which, in its *main* department and purpose, should differ from all free libraries yet attempted; ... one in which any popular books, tending to moral and intellectual improvement, should be furnished in such numbers of copies that many persons, if they desired it could be reading the same book at the same time; in short, that not only the best books of all sorts, but the pleasant literature of the day, should be

made accessible to the whole people at the only time when they care for it, i.e. when it is fresh and new. I would, therefore, continue to buy additional copies of any book of this class, almost as long as they should continue to be asked for, and thus, by following the popular taste–unless it should demand something injurious–create a real appetite for healthy general reading.[36]

In his reply Everett confessed that the "extensive circulation of new and popular works" was a feature of a public library which he had "not hitherto much contemplated," and, though he admitted that the suggestion was deserving of consideration, he professed a predisposition toward intramural book use.[37] Though Everett was not in agreement with Ticknor's opinion, he acquiesced in the proposal because he believed that it should have a fair chance to prove its true worth, and accordingly he acceded to the incorporation of the principle in the trustees' report.[38] The plan was adopted, and from the beginning book purchase proceeded on the assumption that certain types of materials for which there was an anticipated demand were to be acquired in duplicate.[39] The circulation of popular literature is not inherent in the definition of the public library, but it came to be an important function upon which public support was predicated, and its positive affirmation at the time that the Boston Public Library was founded represents a significant recognition by municipal authority that the supplying of books for popular consumption is a proper public responsibility.

The most significant influence of this expanding belief in the importance of the common people was expressed in the advance of popular education and the support which educators gave to library promotion. During the decade of the 1830's elementary education underwent momentous change. The advent of this educational renaissance brought legislative reforms that began the transfer of the school from the custody of voluntary and charitable associations to newly established state systems of education. The New England mind had long accepted the dual principle that the community had an obligation to educate its children by tax-supported schools; and such opportunities having been provided, the children must be compelled to take advantage of them.[40] Nowhere was this urge to mass education more powerful than in Boston, and, in 1840, Prescott could write of the city that its population had all become "cultivated up to the eyes."[41] The region was a veritable seedbed for education throughout much of the Middle West, but even in New England as late as

1840 a relatively small proportion of the school population was being educated "at public charge" since the condition of the public schools of that day encouraged all who could to send their children to private institutions.[42]

The first to lay bare the defects of the Massachusetts schools was James G. Carter, whose *Letters on the Free Schools of New England* (1826) resulted in the laws of 1826, 1834, and 1837, establishing, respectively, the town school committees, the state school fund, and the first real state board of education. Carter planted the seeds of reform that Horace Mann reaped with such spectacular success, but it was the latter who gave to the Massachusetts public schools the effective leadership they so sorely needed and who influenced educational development far beyond that state. At the same time, Henry Barnard, at first in Connecticut and later in Rhode Island, was promoting similar, though somewhat less dramatic, reforms and establishing himself, largely through his extensive writings, as the outstanding scholar of the great public school awakening. In the extension of schooling to a great number of people, by material improvement in the physical environment, through the advancement of instruction and preparation of teachers, and by giving to their followers a rational social responsibility, both Mann and Barnard saved public education at a critical time from a disastrous school system.

The relations between this educational renaissance and the movement for tax-supported public libraries were far reaching and numerous. There were at least four factors involved: (*a*) a growing awareness of the ordinary man and his importance to the group, (*b*) the conviction that universal literacy is essential to an enlightened people, (*c*) a belief in the practical value of technical studies, and (*d*) an enthusiasm for education for its own sake. Structurally the school and the public library were akin because each represented a substitution of the principle of public support for dependence upon private resources. Largely through the efforts of Mann the public school emerged victorious from a previously losing struggle against the competition of the private school, just as the public library was to supersede the social library. Though the principle of public responsibility for primary education had long been acknowledged by New Englanders and some measure of progress had been made in that direction, it was Carter, Mann, and Barnard who really translated the concept into effective reality at precisely the same time that the need for public libraries was beginning to find expression. Public library development was of necessity forced to wait upon educational reform for the simple reason that an adequate library patronage presupposes an educated, or at least literate, public. Finally the proponents of public education were themselves champions of the public library as a logical extension of the elementary-school system.

"After the rising generation have acquired habits of intelligent reading in our schools, *what shall they read?*" wrote Horace Mann in his third annual report as secretary of the Massachusetts Board of Education, "for, with no books to read, the power of reading will be useless."[43] To answer the question, he surveyed the several counties of the state, requesting statistics on the number of social libraries and lyceums, with the book holdings of each.[44] The results revealed that the social libraries of the state contained an aggregate of one hundred and eighty thousand volumes, and these were available to but one-seventh of the population.[45] Knowing that the average home of the period was stocked with only "the Scriptures, and a few school books . . . [which were] protected by law, even in the hands of an insolvent," in addition to some "of a most miscellaneous character . . . which had found their way thither rather by chance than by design,"[46] and being quite aware that even the social libraries possessed mainly books "of the historical class" as well as "novels, and all that class of books which is comprehended under the familiar designation of 'fictions,' 'light reading,' 'trashy works,' 'ephemeral' or 'bubble literature,' "[47] Mann urged more extensive support for the ill-conceived and abortive school-district libraries.[48] He clearly perceived the weaknesses inherent in the social library form as a medium of general book distribution, while in the school-district library he recognized the essential elements that might develop into the basis for public library support. "Had I the power, I would scatter libraries over the whole land, as the sower sows his wheat-field."[49] That was his aim, and while these school-district libraries did not yield the full return that he anticipated, he did plant in the minds of many a conviction of the need for some form of public library support.

Like Mann, Henry Barnard conceived the library as essential to the cultural life of the people:

> A library of good books, selected in reference to the intellectual wants of the old and the young should be provided in every village . . . [he wrote in his report on the condition and improvement of the Public Schools of Rhode Island, in 1845]. All that the

school . . . all that the ablest lecture . . . can do towards unfolding the many branches of knowledge and filling the mind with various information, is but little compared with the thoughful perusal of good books, from evening to evening, extending through a series of years.[50]

Bernard thought it was, therefore, the responsibility of the community to provide such libraries, equipped with

> reading rooms, furnished with the periodical publications of the day, with maps and books of reference, and if possible with portfolios of engravings and pictorial embellishments . . . To these rooms . . . all classes should have access, and especially should the more wealthy and intelligent resort there, if for no other reason than to bear testimony of their presence and participation.[51]

Barnard also shared Mann's faith in the ability of the school-district libraries to assume the broader responsibility of public library service.

> The school-house is the appropriate depository of the district library, and a library of well selected books, open to the teacher, children, and adults generally of the district, for reference and reading, gives completeness to the permanent means of school and self-education. . . . Without such books the instruction of the school-room does not become practically useful, and the art of printing is not made available to the poor as well as to the rich. . . . The establishment of a library in every school-house, will bring the mighty instrument of good books to act more directly and more broadly on the entire population of the state, than it has every yet done, for it will open the fountain of knowledge without money, and without price, to the humble and the elevated, the poor and the rich.[52]

But he was quite conscious, too, of the social library as an agent of public book distribution, and to encourage its formation he published in his 1848 report as commissioner of the public schools of Rhode Island a detailed account of the Pawcatuck Library Association, together with its constitution and bylaws, and a complete catalog of its holdings.[53] The problem of book selection crystallized for Barnard and Mann alike the entire concept of the function of these "public" libraries. To each the library was more than an instrument for deepening the cultural stream, it was intensely practical and utilitarian.

> The farmer, mechanic, manufacturer, and in fine, all the inhabitants of a district, of both sexes, and in every condition and employment of life, should have books which will shed light and dignity on their several vocations, help them better to understand the history and condition of the world and the country in

which they live, their own nature, and their relations and duties to society, themselves, and their Creator.[54]

Thus wrote Barnard in 1842, and the catalog of the Pawcatuck library which he so warmly praised displayed a wide variety of subjects, including books for the artisan and craftsman as well as the usual assortment of titles in history, travel, literature, and fiction. Mann's choice was equally catholic and eclectic. He, too, emphasized the utilitarian as essential to the selection of books for the district libraries, and though he was wont to warn against a too great indulgence in the reading of ephemeral books, he freely acknowledged that "reading, merely for amusement, has its fit occasions and legitimate office."[55]

A realization of the essential unity of the public school and the public library was not confined to the mind of the professional educator. Laymen throughout New England saw the agencies as interdependent and supplementary. Even to the politician the two were intimately associated; for whenever library legislation was introduced, it was regarded as the proper province of the committee on education, and the library was considered as a logical and appropriate supplement to the work of the public school. As has been shown, the inhabitants of Peterborough who construed the phrase "other purposes of education" as encompassing the library voted to allocate a portion of their share of the New Hampshire State Literary Fund to the establishment of a town library. "It has seemed to me for many years," wrote Ticknor to Everett in 1851, "that such a free public library, if adapted to the wants of our people, would be the crowning glory of our public schools,"[56] and the phrase, repeated by him in the trustees' report of 1852,[57] soon became the rallying cry of all who were concerned with the welfare of the library. A similar point of view had been advanced by Everett himself, when, in 1850 and again in 1851, he expressed to Mayor Bigelow the opinion which in 1852 Mayor Seaver presented to the Boston Common Council.

> Such a library would put the finishing hand to that system of public education that lies at the basis of the prosperity of Boston. . . . I cannot but think that a Public Library well supplied with books in the various departments of art and science, and open at all times for consultation and study to the citizens at large, is absolutely needed to make our admirable system of Public Education complete; and to continue in some good degree through life that happy quality of intellectual privileges, which now exists in our schools, but terminates with them.[58]

There was never any uncertainty about the division of function between the school and the library, for lines of responsibility were clear and distinct. The school was primary and compulsory, the library supplemental and voluntary. The school was pointed at the education of the child, and, though the library might also serve to expand the reading resources of the young, its major objective was to promote the education of the adolescent and the adult. From its inception the public library was conceived as being primarily an agency of self-education. This attitude has been admirably summarized by Ticknor in his letter to Everett: "But I think it important that it [i. e., the public library in general and the proposed Boston Public Library in particular] should be adapted to our peculiar character; that is, it should come in at the end of our system of free instruction, and be fitted to continue and increase the effects of that system by the self-culture that results from reading."[59]

SELF-EDUCATION AND THE LYCEUM MOVEMENT

Faith in the capacity of the ordinary man for self-education and reliance upon personal initiative in extending the opportunities for "cultural development" were not excessively optimistic. Dependence upon voluntary group action for effecting many community undertakings was characteristic of the period. The college graduate of that day was thoroughly familiar with the literary society as an important and almost universal device for extending academic experience. Beyond the college walls these associations had a counterpart in the lyceums and institutes that suddenly became prominent between 1830 and 1850.

From Milbury, Massachusetts, in 1826 Josiah Holbrook set forth his scheme for a "Society for Mutual Education," which later became known as the American Lyceum. Holbrook conceived this new agency as a great national organization that would foster in every town and village the formation of societies designed to enhance the education of the child and encourage continued learning by the adult. Aided by the enthusiastic support of such men as Henry Barnard, Edward Everett, and Daniel Webster and favored by contemporary zeal for the improvement of the common man, the organization spread rapidly. Crowded audiences listened to Emerson, Dickens, Thackeray, or Garrison; and to rapt listeners Wendell Phillips was said to have delivered his discourse on "The Lost Arts" two thousand times. In 1831 a National

Lyceum was formed by delegates from Massachusetts, Maine, and New York. From this parent-organization, state and county subsidiaries extended through the country from New England to the far reaches of the frontier. The national body died in 1839, but its local branches persisted much longer; and when interest generally declined prior to the Civil War, the agency was reborn in the Chautauqua movement, which reached its height in the first decades of the twentieth century.

The lecture platform soon became the focal point of the lyceum, though the original intention of the founders was to use any device for advancing knowledge that might properly be employed by the participants. Debates were common, and the collection of minerals and fossils was encouraged. Interest in the preservation of materials for the study of local history was aroused, and, because the larger program of the lyceum was based upon continuous study and reading of the members, library establishment was fostered. The lyceum, like the school, was book centered.

In 1830 the Lyceum of Middlesex County, Massachusetts, appointed a committee to prepare a model constitution for the guidance of lyceum groups in the surrounding towns. This committee urged the possession of a library as a "primary object with all lyceums"; suggested the purchase of books in biography, travel, and voyages as aids in the development of a taste in reading; and recommended the acquisition of scientific works and encyclopedias as soon as financial circumstances permitted.[60] The Massachusetts State Lyceum boasted in 1832 that, in consequence of its encouragement of popular reading, new libraries had been established and neglected ones revived;[61] and the Connecticut State Lyceum, meeting in special session in 1839, voted favorably on a resolution to encourage the establishment of library collections, suitable to the needs of the older children and adults, in every school district of the state.[62] At a convention held in Boston to consider the benefits accruing from lyceums, the delegates remarked on the instability of the "public libraries," fully nine-tenths of which had either perished or fallen into complete decay, a fact which implied that some more direct and immediate stimulus was needed to encourage the public generally to read.

> It is believed that at least nine-tenths of the public libraries which have been established in New England since its first settlement, have been sold at public auction, distributed among their proprietors, or fallen into neglect or disuse. Nor have those truly benevolent and patriotic institutions, mechanics' and apprentices' libraries, excited that extensive and lasting thirst for reading and information, which might naturally be hoped.[63]

They expected the lyceum to supply this stimulus, and Josiah Holbrook wrote that the "demands immediately and uniformly created for books by the meetings and exercises of Lyceums" had called "into use neglected Libraries and given occasion for establishing new ones."[64] Such statements, however, were largely groundless, for the lyceum movement seems to have contributed little aid to the library. The delegates to the Boston lyceum convention of 1828 were correct in believing that something more than the mere presence of books was required to induce the general public to read. But, supported mainly by the modest admission fees to its public meetings,[65] the lyceum itself was too lacking in stability to contribute much of its slender resources to library encouragement. Yet the movement has significance as an indication of the culture that encouraged the public library. Through the influence of the lyceum the city and the town were brought into closer contact. Everywhere people were being exposed to similar cultural stimuli. Both the library and the lyceum were parts of the general faith in man's ability for self-improvement.

THE VOCATIONAL INFLUENCE

A belief in the necessity of education was further encouraged by a growing demand for vocational training. The rise of industrialization, the rapid growth of a population congested in cities, the increase of the working classes through immigration of new national stocks, and the decline of the earlier apprentice system, all contributed to the need for new social agencies that would satisfy the human urge for the improvement of the individual's economic status. The factory system, the introduction of power machinery, and the extensive utilization of water-power and later of steam, which must be used close to the place of origin, brought together in highly congested areas men, women, and children who were engaged in similar pursuits, who had common economic and social problems, and who quite naturally turned to the formation of voluntary associations for improvement of their working lives. These impulses on the part of the workers were expressed in four major lines of endeavor: (a) the organization of trade-unions and their amalgamation in a national federation, (b) the encouragement of co-operative activities, (c) the formation of workingmen's political parties, and (d) the establishment of newspapers, journals, institutes, associations, and libraries for the education and advancement of the worker. Such early movements suffered heavily in the panic of 1837 and, after the passage of the Homestead Act, lost much of their appeal when an abundance of free land in the West made it relatively easy for the employee to pass to the position of the employer. Nevertheless, a very definite impression had been made on the course of American institutions, and much social legislation had accumulated as a consequence of this early striving.

Concern with the problems confronting the workers did not leave the library untouched. To some extent labor leadership participated in the movement for library establishment, as it had shared in support of public schools. In the case of the library the vocational interests of the workers made its greatest contribution in the form of mechanics' and mercantile libraries that appeared during the first half of the nineteenth century and in the factory book collections in a few industrial towns. It was a utilitarian urge that prompted the mechanics and apprentices to adapt the social library pattern to their specific needs, just as a century earlier Benjamin Franklin and his small group of artisans and other "citizens in the middle and lower walks of life" had met together and pooled their book resources, knowing that their progress would come more rapidly through the mutual interchange of thought and experience.

Basically the mechanics' and apprentices' libraries were an adaptation of the social library form, and they grew directly from the workers' institutes first established in England at the close of the eighteenth century.[66] These institutes spread over England until by 1850 there were some seven hundred such associations there. The main object of these groups was the intellectual development of the artisan, and science was the principal subject considered; though, as time went on, literature, history, and the arts were included. The programs centered about lectures and discussions; more than half of the institutes had libraries, and many also developed elementary scientific laboratories.

At approximately the same time that this movement was gaining headway in England it was also becoming prevalent in America. In 1823 Timothy Claxton of the Mechanics' Institute of London came to Methuen, Massachusetts, where a cotton-mill and a machine shop were in operation. There he revived the defunct Methuen Social Society for Reading and General Inquiry, which had been founded about 1819, and aided in the establishment of a library for the use of the members. In 1826 Claxton moved to Boston where he promoted the Boston Mechanics' Institute. Though the institute was undoubtedly of English origin, Claxton did not introduce it to America. A Mechanics' Library was in operation in Bristol, Connecticut, in 1818,[67] and in 1820 there was established in Boston the Mechanics' Apprentices' Library, the first such library to be formed through the philanthropy of William Wood. Also founded at an early date were the Mechanics' Library of Portland, Maine; the Mechanics' Social Library Society of Nantucket, Massachusetts; and the library of the Salem Charitable Mechanics' Association, the books of which finally found their way into the Essex Institute.

The general development of the mechanics' and apprentices' associations and their affiliated book collections was encouraged by professional educators, particularly Henry Barnard and Horace Mann. Of the Boston Mechanics' Institution the editors of the *American Journal of Education* wrote in part: "It is with much pleasure that we contemplate the prospect afforded by this and similar institutions in our own country; their benefits are perhaps more direct and substantial, and their sphere of usefulness is necessarily much wider, than those connected with any other department of scientific instruction."[68] Such philanthropists as William Wood frequently contributed substantial sums to establish and support these organizations, of which many were created for the protection and support of widows and orphans of mechanics, and, since the argument for the library as a bulwark against the corruption of youthful morals was always potent, the libraries were encouraged by those actively engaged in the prevailing humanitarianism. Basically, the concept sprang from the growth of the industrial system and consequent breakdown of the master-apprentice relationship. Abbott Lawrence strongly felt the absence of adequate training in the industrial arts when he gave fifty thousand dollars for the establishment of a scientific school at Harvard. He recognized that education in law, medicine, theology, and the humanities had been monopolizing the attention of educators when he wrote to Samuel Eliot:

> But where can we send those who intend to devote themselves to the practical applications of science? How educate our engineers, our miners, machinists,

and mechanics? Our country abounds in men of action. Hard hands are ready to work upon our hard materials; and where shall sagacious heads be taught to direct those hands?[69]

These institutes would, in a measure at least, meet this want in the educational system, for their object, as George B. Emerson remarked at the opening of the Boston Mechanics' Institution, was

> to give to persons, whose time is chiefly occupied with business or labor, knowledge of a kind to be directly useful to them in their daily pursuits . . . . The principles of science have hitherto been accessible to those only who were pursuing a course of study preparatory to what are called the liberal professions. The poor and the occupied, if destined to the active pursuits of life, have been almost necessarily debarred from them. By Mechanics Institutions they are offered to all, to the busy, the poor, and the uninformed.[70]

In this plan the lecture was to supplant the personal teaching of a master, but the lecture alone was insufficient if the apprentice was to derive the greatest possible benefit. A library was essential as a supplement to the lecture platform, for the listener, "to derive the greatest advantage from his lecture . . . , must also read."[71]

In general the social philosophy of the mercantile libraries was quite different from that of the mechanics' institutions, though the line of demarcation was not always sharp and there were occasional blendings of the forms. Fundamentally the mercantile libraries were designed to meet the reading needs of the young merchants' clerks and were established by the youthful merchants who were beginning their professional careers. The movement appears to have had its inception in Boston, where, on March 11, 1820, the Boston Mercantile Library was established by a group of young clerks whose initiation fee was the gift of one book on "biography, history, voyages, travels, or work relative to mercantile subjects."[72] Unlike the apprentices' institutions, the mercantile libraries began as libraries and later assumed additional educational functions—lecture courses, museums, or exhibitions.[73] But the two were similar in the advantage they received from the increasing complexity of the occupations each represented. Because of the expanding horizons of applied science, the mechanics and apprentices felt the need for educational mediums that would increase their familiarity with scientific advance. Likewise, the young merchants were keenly affected by the growing intricacy of the commercial structure, the advent of new governmental regulations, the com-

plications of foreign exchange, and the shifting patterns of production and consumption and their impact on market conditions. In addition to its strict professional utility, the mercantile library reflected certain cultural interests. Literature and history, especially the history of the mercantile profession, were conspicuously represented in the book collection since it was generally conceded that no knowledge was foreign to the merchant.[74]

The artisans and merchants were not alone in their response to the need for books. Amid the whirring spindles and in the lint-filled air of the cotton-mills at Lowell, Lawrence, and Peterborough countless girls, newly imported from the rural areas, eager for the adventure of a strange city life, and earning money for the first time, were enthusiastically subscribing to joint-stock pianos for their boarding-houses, studying German, reading the British reviews, and filling the pages of their own literary journal, the *Lowell Offering,* with romantic stories and poetry. Today much of the sentiment with which Harriet Farley and her associates built up the circulation of the *Offering* sounds like courageous whistling to keep up hopes and aspirations that all too frequently were the prey of monotonous toil and heartbreaking loneliness; but some of the girls, at least those in the Merrimack mills, did evince an interest in literature, support subscription libraries, and make plans for a book collection and reading-room of their own.[75] How many such libraries were established on the initiative of the workers is not known, but it is likely that at least some of them were imposed upon the operatives by a management which was perhaps eager to foster its reputation for benevolence. Such were the libraries established in the 1830's at the Union and Phoenix Cotton Mills of Peterborough, New Hampshire,[76] and the Manufacturers and Village Library of Great Falls, New Hampshire, of which the last was sponsored by the Great Falls Manufacturing Company and for the use of which "females" in the employ of the company were required to pay fifty cents per year, though only the subscribers paying a dollar had any voice in the management of the collection. The library of the Pacific Mills of Lawrence, Massachusetts, was assembled in 1854, largely through the efforts of Abbott Lawrence and with the consultation and advice of Henry Barnard.[77] For its support the workers were taxed $0.01 per week, though their wages for the same period varied from $6.75 for men to $1.82 for children, from which "one third of the average" was deducted for board and room at the residence buildings.[78]   At Northfield, Vermont, the Vermont Central Railroad offered the income from a $1,000 bond to initiate a library for its employees, but this library was a joint-stock association in which shares sold at $3.00 each.[79]   Such factory collections differed sharply from the "vocational" libraries formed by the artisans and merchants.   Recreational reading and self-improvement were the major objectives of the former, but probably, as in the case of the library of the Great Falls Manufacturing Company, "ficton" was "most read."   The sudden desire for "culture" that animated the mill girls of Lowell was but a passing fancy—the hard realities of factory toil remained. Twelve long hours of tending the spindles were not usually climaxed by an evening of intellectual pursuit.

The vocational libraries did not live long except in those cases where they were fortunate enough to receive large gifts or to become general social libraries.   A decline in initial enthusiasm on the part of readers and a general disillusionment when reading failed to produce marked increase in either skills or income were the intangible factors in the deterioration of these libraries.   Today the Young Men's Institute Library of New Haven, Connecticut, typifies complete transformation and rejection of primary function.   No longer dedicated to the principle of "mutual assistance in the attainment of useful knowledge," its efforts are now directed toward supplying promptly the current best-sellers to those willing to pay for the privilege, and in its effort to survive it has diverted a measure of popular support from the public library of its own city.   Similarly, in an attempt to save the Middlesex Mechanics' Association from an untimely death the membership subordinated its original objectives until the institution was so changed that Coburn could write of it in his three-volume history of Lowell:

> It used to be a source of boyish wonder, in the seventies and eighties, just what the Middlesex Mechanics' Association and its excellent library in Dutton Street, had to do with mechanical affairs. In conspicuous positions hung several rather awe-inspiring full-length portraits. These were obviously not portraits of mechanics . . . . The library was of a general sort, and the well-informed librarian was not one to whom one would turn for information about gears, shafting, or high-speed steels . . . . Most of those who used the library seemed not to be of the mechanic sort, but rather to be people who preferred its quiet exclusiveness to the democracy of the public library. The Mechanics' Association of 1885 . . . appeared to be one . . . in which an overalled mechanic would be particularly ill at ease . . . in fact the library was some-thing of a Lowell analogue of the Boston Athenaeum.[80]

But if the working classes of the nineteenth century achieved only a temporary success in founding libraries planned to meet their needs, the importance of the vocational motive in public library encouragement is not thereby discredited; for, as the wage-earning portion of the population steadily increased and it became correspondingly more difficult for the uneducated individual to compete successfully with his highly trained fellows, there developed an increasing pressure for any agency that would raise the apprentice out of the ranks of the day laborer and into the middle class.

> Public Libraries will supply the whole people with ample sources for important practical information . . . Where they are provided every farmer will have access to the best books on agriculture, every mechanic to the best books on the arts, every merchant . . . to the best exposition of the laws of trade and the sources of wealth. Would not this be a great advantage? Is it not important to practical men? Would it not much promote their success, to become acquainted with what is already known on the subjects which occupy their attention? And is it not undeserving of remark, that, even in the most simple and uniform operations of labor, it has been found that . . . more is accomplished, and the work better done, by intelligent and well-informed individuals?[81]

These were the rhetorical questions with which Representative Wight challenged the Massachusetts General Court: and in a day when America was prosperous as it had never been before, when both industry and labor were expanding, and when education was regarded by all as the panacea for every social ill, no one could answer in the negative. The argument was convincing.

OTHER CAUSAL FACTORS

In addition to the influences already considered, there were certain other factors which contributed to the growth of public libraries in New England. Primary among these lesser influences were religion, morality, and the church, for, though the proportion of theological works in New England library book collections generally declined after the establishment of the Republic, the importance of organized religion in public library promotion continued. New England religion was bookish, and its intellectual heritage reveals the extent to which the philosophical content of the discipline drew from many sources.[82]   The belief was widely held that reading was a "good" thing in itself and that the act of reading tended to elevate the reader, and this faith in the printed word as an instrument for the building of character was often expressed by the proprietors of corporation libraries. The "promotion of Virtue, Education, and Learning, and . . . the discouragement of Vice and Immorality" was the dual purpose of the Social Library of Salisbury, Connecticut.[83] The members of the Young Men's Institute of Hartford, Connecticut, found themselves unable to estimate "the amount of good accomplished by [its] 25,000 volumes, which have gone forth to exert their silent unobtrusive influence throughout this community." Nor could they ascertain "in how many have the inclinations of vice been diminished; how many leisure hours, which would otherwise have been wasted in idleness, or a thousand-fold worse than wasted, in the pursuit and enjoyment of pleasures which end only in sorrow, have been delightfully employed in the acquisition of useful knowledge."[84] "To excite a fondness for books, to afford the most rational and profitable amusement, to prevent idleness and immorality, and to promote the diffusion of useful knowledge, piety, and virtue" was the objective of the social library of Castine, Maine.[85] Inevitably, those who were campaigning for the creation of public libraries adopted this argument. In addressing the Boston city council on the need for a public library, Mayor Bigelow spoke of it as having an important bearing on the moral as well as the intellectual character of the city.[86] Similarly, Joshua Bates, in setting forth the motives which prompted his gift to Boston, expressed the opinion that, though at first the library would attract only the "worthy young men," later it would "draw others from vice to tread in the same paths, and . . . moral effect will keep pace with mental improvement."[87] "The promotion of virtue," "the reform of vice," "the increase of morality"—with such phrases Representative Wight liberally sprinkled his address before the General Court in support of the Massachusetts law of 1851; for public libraries would "be favorable to all the moral reforms of the day, by leading to more domestic habits of life, by diminishing the circulation of low and immoral publications, and by producing higher and more worthy views of the capabilities of human nature."[88] Small wonder that Francis Wayland looked with such revulsion upon the practice of the Providence Athenaeum in buying "books of at least doubtful character, frivolous, and not innocent . . . because the young people desired them," and "would as soon give a child arsenic because he liked it."[89]

Finally, one must not forget that the parish and church libraries contributed in some measure to the demand for public libraries. Ubiquitous little Sunday-school libraries dotted the intellectual terrain almost as thickly and conspicuously as the Colonial churches accented the New England landscape.[90] That ministers gave to Peterborough, New Hampshire, our first public library and to Massachusetts the law of 1851 was hardly accidental. The position of pre-eminence attained by Puritan intellectualism in the American cultural heritage is clear, and the early public libraries, as shaped by their coeval culture, could scarcely have escaped the influence of the church.

In a sense all the foregoing causal factors in public library establishment may be reduced to a common denominator—personal benefit. As one might expect, the public library received its strongest support from those groups in the community who were in a position to gain from the benefits it offered. Primarily, it was the professional classes—the teachers, scholars, ministers, lawyers, doctors, and especially the historians—who were in the greatest want of adequate book resources, so it was they who assumed leadership in the new movement. They were the most vocal because their needs were the greatest and their training and experience facilitated public expression. Following the example of the learned professions, the young tradesmen and mechanics supported the public library as a potential aid in the mastery of their crafts. Even the publishers and booksellers, who might have been expected to oppose free libraries as possible competitors, encouraged the movement by offering generous discounts to buyers for libraries. As early as the concluding decades of the eighteenth century the practice of competing for the patronage of social library officials was common. The school-district libraries offered an excellent opportunity for actual exploitation. Publishers openly confessed to having reaped a substantial harvest from the sale of hastily assembled sets of standard authors for school library use. "Harper's School District Library" was one such series issued in response to the school-district library laws of New England and New York, and bookmen throughout the region became actively concerned in the passage of legislation providing for the establishment of libraries in the public schools. Soon publisher participation in local politics became so prevalent and subject to so many abuses that the state of New York found it necessary to pass, in 1856, a law forbidding school commissioners to act as the agents of publishers in the awarding of contracts for book purchase.[91] Fear that similar exploitation would be introduced into the management of town libraries was expressed at the 1853 convention of librarians. Edward Everett Hale, though he approved the enthusiasm of the assembled librarians for the formulation of a plan which would promote the establishment of well-selected public libraries throughout the towns and villages of the country, called attention to the danger that the formulation of recommended lists of books for such libraries would serve only to promote publishers' monopolistic practices.

By the middle of the nineteenth century the activities of professional librarians in encouraging library establishment was not conspicuous, but some halting steps in that direction were taken in 1853 when an assembly of eighty-two librarians met in New York City for the purpose of forming a permanent library association that would bring to a focus the professional problems that confronted the practitioners of the craft. These meetings, which were sponsored by Charles C. Jewett, librarian of the Smithsonian Institution; Charles E. Norton, publisher and bookseller; Seth Hastings Grant, librarian of the New York Mercantile Library; Reuben A. Guild, Librarian of Brown University; and Daniel Coit Gilman, then just graduated from Yale, promised much for the encouragement of professional solidarity. But initial enthusiasm sputtered out in forensic appeals for a great national library for reference and research to be subsidized by the Smithsonian gift, Jewett's own grandiose and impracticable scheme for a union catalog of stereotype plates of all American libraries to be deposited at the Smithsonian Institution, and innumerable resolutions providing for library promotion. The group, confronted by the dispersion of its leaders, the financial crisis of 1857, and, four years later, the Civil War, never reconvened, and it was not until the Centennial Exposition of 1876 brought to public notice the library development throughout the country that the profession achieved a real unity. The convention of 1853 accomplished little that was either positive or constructive, yet it revealed a latent professional consciousness that was indicative of future trends.[92]

The factors which contributed to public library development should not be dismissed without reemphasizing the European influence, for many of the ideas which prepared the way for a public library system were not native to America. From England and perhaps from the Continent the idea

of the book club had been imported by migrants who came to the Atlantic coast early in the eighteenth century. A colonial environment altered somewhat the outward form of the agency, and the new social conditions initiated a process of natural adaptation, but these did not obliterate the transatlantic influence. The social and circulating libraries, lyceums, and museums all resulted from the importation and diffusion of institutional forms.[93] The experiences of New England scholars who sought in European universities of the nineteenth century a training beyond that available at Cambridge or New Haven encouraged library formation in this country. Jared Sparks was inspired by the patronage of the British Museum and hoped that the Athenaeum would achieve equal popularity;[94] and George Warren, member of the first board of trustees of the Boston Public Library, submitted materials relating to the Free Library of Manchester, England, for the guidance of his colleagues.[95] Through the efforts of Vattemare and his plans for the international exchange of official publications, France, too, was contributing in a substantial way to the formation of public libraries in her sister-republic.

These European influences upon the American public library were twofold. Directly they contributed to the promotion of the agency by the actual transfer of organizational patterns. The book clubs, the social libraries, and the circulating collections were all either derived from European models or brought to this country by enterprising merchants who sought to exploit the reading interests of the American public, just as they had capitalized on the desires of readers in their native lands. Indirectly, by the example of its own great collections and their organization, Europe suggested to the American mind the significance of the library in the integration of an emerging culture. At Peterborough, Wayland, and Boston, where the initial steps were taken that resulted in the foundation of a public library system as it is known today, the action was characteristically American, but the antecedents of that movement were largely derived from European sources.

Historical scholarship and the urge to preservation, the power of national and local pride, the growing belief in the importance of universal education, the increasing concern with vocational problems, and the contribution of religion—these, aided by economic ability and encouraged by the example of Europe, were the causal factors in the formation of libraries that would be free to all the people. Underlying these was the influence of the people themselves—countless individuals in innumerable towns who had faith in the public library and believed implicitly in its social value. The library movement did not generate "great" leadership. It attracted the support of men who were distinguished in public life—Everett, Ticknor, the Quincys, Mann, Barnard—and it profited much from their efforts. But these men are remembered less because of what they did for the public library than for their achievements in other fields. Community leadership was necessary to give the library movement the impetus and direction it required, but it was essentially a small-town leadership—a leadership that was largely unknown outside its native environs. Today Caleb Bingham, Abiel Abbot, Josiah Eastman, and John B. Wight are almost forgotten, yet it was the cumulative influence of such men that contributed most to the support the library needed. Librarians will continue to honor the names of Winsor, Jewett, Dana, and Brett, as indeed they properly should, but in doing so they should not forget that "the growing good of the . . . [library] is partly dependent on unhistoric acts; and that things are not so ill . . . as they might have been is half owing to the number who lived faithfully a hidden life, and rest in unvisited tombs."

FOOTNOTES

[1] Boston Public Library, *Report of the Trustees . . . July 1852* (City Document No. 37 [Boston: J. H. Eastburn, 1852]), pp. 221-22.

[2] John B. Wight, "A Lecture on Public Libraries Delivered in Boston in the Hall of Representatives, 1854, and in Several Other Places" (unpublished MS).

[3] Portland Athenaeum, *Report of the Directors Submitted at the Annual Meeting of the Proprietors, November 8, 1855*, p. 5; copy in Maine Historical Society.

[4] Charlotte B. Norton (comp.), *History of the Scoville Memorial Library* (Salisbury: Lakeview Journal Press, 1941), pp. 8-10.

[5] Massachusetts Free Public Library Commission, *Free Public Libraries in Massachusetts: Ninth Annual Report* (Boston: Wright & Potter, 1899), p. 93. This was, of course, not the only benefaction of George Peabody. He gave a Peabody Institute to Danvers and to Baltimore, as well as the museums of archeology and ethnology to Harvard and of natural history to Yale, and there were numerous other gifts of lesser magnitude.

[6] Quoted by Horace G. Wadlin, *The Public Library of the City of Boston: A History* (Boston: Boston Public Library, 1911), p. 42.

[7] Wight MS.

[8] William Maclure, who established the Maclure Library at Pittsford, Vt., was moved to do so through the efforts of Thomas Palmer, but Maclure himself had no connection with the town (records in Maclure Library). See, further, the supplementary list of donors of library buildings in the Massachusetts Free Public Library Commission, *op. cit.,* pp. 457-59.

[9] There is perhaps no finer example of this spirit than that of Quincy's gift to the incipient Boston Public Library. In his journal for Tuesday, October 12, 1847, he wrote: "I have determined to endeavor to found a city Library and Museum, and for that purpose to give Five Thousand Dollars on condition that the City double the donation. I have been very prosperous and feel as though it were my duty to improve this opportunity of starting an institution which may, if it 'takes' with my fellow citizens be of great and lasting benefit and honor to the Public."
On the following day, Wednesday, October 13: "Conversed with my wife concerning the Vattemare donation. She entirely approves of everything that is liberal and noble. She is indeed the virtuous woman whose price is above rubies."
The next day, Thursday, October 14, he journeyed to Quincy, where he dined with the family and "walked over the place with my father. Consulted them about the donation, and they all of course approve." Returning to Boston that evening, ". . . sent in my . . . offer of Five Thousand dollars for a Public Library. I, of course, for the present shall conceal my name as it might be looked upon as an electioneering movement."
On January 17 of the following year he wrote: " . . . no one seems to suspect that I am the donor of the Five Thousand dollars, for its [the public library's] commencement. If I can start this during my administration it will be second only to the introduction of water" (MS journals of Josiah Quincy in the Boston Public Library).

[10] Franklin's original letter is reprinted in Massachusetts Free Public Library Commission, *op. cit.,* p. 131; see also Mortimer Blake, *History of the Town of Franklin* (Franklin: Published by the town, 1879), pp. 69-72.

[11] George Whitney, *Some Account of the Early History and Present State of the Town of Quincy . . .* (Boston: Christian Register Office, 1827), p. 44.

[12] One of the best examples of this was the offer of Amasa Manton of Rhode Island, who proposed to give $150 for the purchase of new books to any new public library society which would double his donation. In this way he encouraged the formation of a number of quasi-public library societies in Rhode Island (see Charles Carroll, *Rhode Island: Three Centuries of Democracy* [New York: Lewis History Pub. Co., 1932], II, 1073).

[13] Quoted in *Athenaeum Items,* February, 1938, p. 1.

[14] George Ticknor, *Life, Letters, and Journals* (Boston: Houghton Mifflin, 1909), I, 371.

[15] Fisher Ames, *Works,* ed. Seth Ames (Boston: Little, Brown, 1854), II, 440.

[16] Quoted by an anonymous author in the *North American Review,* XLV (1837), 137, it was used by Judge Story in an address before the Phi Beta Kappa society at Cambridge. It was again quoted in the *North American Review,* LXXI (1850), 186.

[17] *Ibid.,* LXXI (1850), 186. Also A. R. Spofford, "Public Libraries in the United States," *Journal of Social Science,* II (1870), 113.

[18] *American Almanac and Repository of Useful Knowledge* (Boston: Charles Bowen, 1836), pp. 81-82; also 1834, pp. 148-49.

[19] James Parton, *Life of Andrew Jackson* (New York: Mason, 1860), III, 701. John F. Sly, by counting the entries in Jeremiah Colburn's *Bibliography of the Local History of Massachusetts,* finds that twenty-one local histories were published prior to 1830, a total which excludes fragments, "discourses," "sketches," and the transactions of learned societies. Approximately half of these titles were less than one hundred pages in length. Eighteen towns were represented. For the years between 1830 and 1845 thirty comparable histories, representing forty-three towns and villages, were recorded. Between 1845 and 1855 twenty-one new titles were added, of which fifteen were over two hundred and fifty pages in length (John F. Sly, *Town Government in Massachusetts, 1620-1930* [Cambridge: Harvard University Press, 1930], p. 107 n.).

[20] John Randolph was the author of the phrase, "a good library is a statesman's workshop"; and though he owned a large personal collection, he is supposed to have told Nathan Sargent that he would not have in his possession an American book, not even an American Bible (William D. Johnston, *History of the Library of Congress* [Washington, D. C.: Government Printing Office, 1904], I, 24).

[21] Jewett (*ca.* 1850) credits the Library of Congress with fifty thousand volumes, though it then still ranked below Harvard with eighty-four thousand volumes and the Philadelphia Library Company with sixty thousand. It was approximately equal in size to the collections of the Boston Athenaeum and Yale University.

[22] A circular addressed to American authors asking, on behalf of the Athenaeum, for their works and signed by George Livermore, E. A. Crowninshield, and Charles E. Norton [1849] (in Boston Athenaeum), says in part: "The Class [of books] which demands and has received the most anxious care of the Trustees is that which comprises works which relate to America, and in the completion of which we have made some rapid advances. We beg leave, therefore, to call the attention of the public to this subject, and to solicit the donation of any tracts published here or in England, which throw light on our early annals; of works of any kind printed in America, or written by American authors; and, in fine, of anything, even to a single leaf, relating to our literary, civil, religious, natural, or moral History, and to aid us in forming a complete Bibliotheca Americana.

"If the time should ever come, which we fondly expect, when a suitable structure shall be raised in this town, in which to deposit the crowded treasures of this literary institution, we shall then have approached nearer to the accomplishment of a darling object, the formation of a complete American Library."

[23] "The deficiency in the department of American history and statisticks, ought especially to be supplied; and to this end unwearied and individual efforts ought to be made, both by the Corporation and its members individually, until it be supplied. Every publick American library ought certainly to be complete in American history; and in the state of New Hampshire there ought to be at least one library to which every citizen in the State may be able to go with the certainty of being able to find there any needed information in relation to the history of his own country" (Portsmouth Athenaeum, *Annual Report, January 1827,* p. 5; in Portsmouth Athenaeum).

[24] *American Almanac and Repository of Useful Knowledge* (1836), p. 82.

[25] The Vermont state library was established November 17, 1825; that of Maine in 1836; Connecticut in 1854; and Rhode Island in 1868 (state law library).

[26] Quoted by C. K. Bolton, *The Boston Athenaeum, 1807-1927, a Sketch* (Boston: The Athenaeum, 1927), p. 2.

[27] Boston Public Library, *Report . . . July 1852,* p. 16.

[28] Quoted by Wadlin, *op. cit.,* p. 20.

[29] John B. Wight, "Public Libraries," *Common School Journal,* XIII (1851), 261.

[30] Everett to Ticknor, July 26, 1851, in Ticknor, *op. cit.,* II, 303. It is interesting that Ticknor took up the cry of alarm two years later when, in urging the union of the Athenaeum with the Boston Public Library he wrote, almost in Everett's precise words: "Unless a *real* public library can be instituted in Boston, we may justly expect, in the quarter of a century, to fall as much behind New York, with its Astor Library, in the means of intellectual culture, as we do already in the advantages for commercial success ([George Ticknor], *Union of the Boston Athenaeum and the Boston Public Library* [Boston: Dutton & Wentworth, 1853], p. 7).

[31] Letter from Everett to Bigelow, June 7, 1851, quoted by Wadlin, *op. cit.,* pp. 24-25.

[32] *Boston Daily Courier,* March 26, 1853.

[33] Letter from "F" in the *Providence Journal,* January 25, 1836.

[34] Andrew Johnson, *Speeches,* ed. Frank Moore (Boston: Little, Brown, 1866), p. 56.

[35] Quoted by Mayor Benjamin Seaver in his *Message of the Mayor on the Subject of a Public Library, in Common Council [February 19, 1852]* (City Document No. 10 [Boston: No publisher, 1852]), pp. 4-5.

[36] Ticknor, *Life,* II, 301-2.

[37] *Ibid.,* p. 303.

[38] See Boston Public Library, *Report . . . July 1852,* pp. 9-21. These pages were entirely the work of Ticknor; the remaining portions, at the beginning and the end, were by Everett (annotated copy in Boston Public Library). See also Ticknor, *Life,* II, 305. Ticknor did not hold that *all* library books should circulate freely, in fact he divided the library collections into four major groups: (1) books that should not be circulated because of their cost or rarity; (2) books for

which there was a relatively slight demand which, though free to circulate, were not to be necessarily duplicated; (3) books that were to be duplicated as much as the demand seemed to justify; and (4) periodicals, exclusive of news-papers, which were to be circulated on rare occasions when justified by some special need. It was his contention that these categories be completely fluid.

[39] Boston Public Library, *Report . . . 1854*, p. 5, states: "A considerable number of the new books added to the li-brary the present year are duplicate sets of popular new publications, which have been purchased in pursuance to the principle on which the circulation department is founded . . . . It is expected that for a certain class of books this de-mand will be temporary, and that in due time . . . all but a single copy, or very few copies, may be dispensed with.

[40] The first Massachusetts laws relating to education, passed in 1642 and 1647, asserted that it was the duty of the state to compel the education of every child. By the terms of these acts the power was given to the selectmen to en-force its provisions, and parents neglecting the education of their children were subject to fine. Though the law made education compulsory, there was no provision for schools or teachers, and the children were taught either by their parents or by private tutors *(Records of the Governor and Company of the Massachusetts Bay in New England,* ed. Nathaniel B. Shurtleff [Boston: William White, 1853], II, 6, 9, 203).

[41] "We are all becoming cultivated up to the eyes . . . *tiers état* and all. A daughter of an old servant of ours, whose father is an Irish bogtrotter that works on the roads, told me yesterday, 'she had nearly completed her English educa-tion, and was very well in her French, and should only give one quarter more to her music and drawing' " (William H. Prescott, *Correspondence*, 1840, quoted by Van Wyck Brooks, *The Flowering of New England* [New York: Dutton, 1937]), p. 172 n.

[42] U. S. Census Office, *7th Census, 1850: Statistical View of the United States . . . , Being a Compendium of the Seventh Census . . . , 1850* (Washington, D. C.: A. O. P. Nicholson, 1854), pp. 150-51.

[43] Horace Mann, *Life and Works* (Boston: Lee & Shepherd, 1891), III, 8-9; reprints most of his third annual report, for the year 1839; full report appears in *Common School Journal*, II (1840), 113-53.

[44] *Common School Journal*, II (1840), 123-35, 137-39.

[45] *Ibid.*, pp. 125-26.

[46] *Ibid.*, pp. 120-21.

[47] *Ibid.*, pp. 127-28.

[48] *Ibid.*, pp. 151-53.

[49] Quoted by Paul Bixler, "Horace Mann—Mustard Seed," *American Scholar*, VII (1938-39), 32.

[50] Quoted in John S. Brubacher (ed.), *Henry Barnard on Education* (New York: McGraw-Hill, 1931), p. 53.

[51] *Ibid.*, pp. 55-56.

[52] From the Appendix to his fourth annual report as secretary to the Board of Commissioners of Common Schools in Connecticut, reproduced in Brubacher, *op. cit.*, pp. 248-50.

[53] Henry Barnard, *Report and Documents Relating to the Public Schools of Rhode Island, 1848* (Providence, 1849), pp. 424-548.

[54] Brubacher, *op. cit.*, pp. 249-50.

[55] *Common School Journal*, II (1840), 128 ff.

[56] Ticknor, *Life*, II, 301.

[57] Boston Public Library, *Report . . . July 1852*, p. 21. Much of the report deals with the relation of the public li-brary to the public school.

[58] Two letters from Everett to Mayor Bigelow, dated August 7, 1850, and June 7, 1851; quoted by Wadlin, *op. cit.*, pp. 21 and 25-26; quoted by Mayor Benjamin Seaver, *op. cit.*, p. 4.

[59] Ticknor, *Life*, II, 301.

[60] "Middlesex County Lyceum," *American Journal and Annals of Education and Instruction,* I (new ser., 1830), 454.

[61] "Massachusetts Lyceum," *ibid.*, II (1832), 121.

[62] "Connecticut State Lyceum," *Connecticut Common School Journal*, II (1839), 83-84.

[63] "American Lyceum," *American Journal of Education*, III (1828), 719.

[64] [Josiah Holbrook], *The American Lyceum, or Society for the Improvement of Schools and Diffusion of Useful Knowledge* (Boston: T. R. Marvin, 1829), p. 5.

[65] The average price received by Emerson for an evening lecture was $10.00 and traveling expenses. On one occasion, when he received the maximum of $50.00, he expressed grave doubt as to the morality of accepting such excessive re-muneration. A season ticket for a course of ten to fifteen lectures usually cost about $2.00.

[66] The workers' institutes apparently developed from the lectures in natural philosophy given by Dr. John Anderson in Glasgow in 1760. Similar illustrated talks and scientific demonstrations, designed primarily for the laboring man, were continued in the same city by George Birkbeck in 1799. It was during this period that Birmingham became a cen-ter for organizations established to better the lot of the worker, and there was founded in 1795 the first Artisans' Li-brary, which was followed in 1823 by the Mechanics' and Apprentices' Library of Liverpool (Clarence R. Aurner, "Mechanics' Institutes," *Iowa Journal of History*, XIX [1921], 389 ff.).

[67] Trumbull MSS in Yale University Library; E. Peck, *A History of Bristol, Connecticut* (Hartford: Lewis Street Bookshop, 1932), pp. 245-47.

But where can we send those who intend to devote themselves to the practical applications of science? How educate our engineers, our miners, machinists, and mechanics? Our country abounds in men of action. Hard hands are ready to work upon our hard materials; and where shall sagacious heads be taught to direct those hands?[69]

[68] II (1827), 273.

[69] Letter to Samuel A. Eliot, treasurer of Harvard University, June 7, 1847, in Hamilton A. Hill, *Memoir of Abbott Lawrence* (Boston: Privately printed, 1883), p. 109.

[70] George B. Emerson, "Mechanics' Institutions," *American Journal of Education,* II (1827), 273, 278.

[71] *Ibid.,* p. 275. An excellent example of the extent to which these libraries reflected the utilitarian needs of their supporting members and the degree to which their book collections emphasized science and the practical arts is to be found in *Catalogue of the Library of the Massachusetts Charitable Mechanics' Association, 1853* (Boston: Danvell & Moore, 1853), in Massachusetts Historical Society.

[72] This plan was later abolished because the books thus received were generally worthless. Subscriptions were $2.00 annually. There were some two hundred and twenty members the first year, but the organization had a long and difficult fight for survival. It was helped by frequent gifts from Abbott Lawrence. In 1877 its books were added to the collections of the Boston Public Library.

[73] On June 24, 1846, Elliot C. Cowdin of the Boston Mercantile Library Association wrote to James Fenimore Cooper inviting him to lecture before the association, stating that the usual attendance at such lectures was between twenty-five hundred and three thousand (see Dorothy Waples, "An Unpublished Letter from James Fenimore Cooper to Elliot C. Cowdin," *New England Quarterly,* III [1930], 126).

[74] The Massachusetts Historical Society has many printed addresses delivered before the Mercantile Library Association of Boston. These, when taken together constitute a good general statement of the purposes of the mercantile library as conceived by their early promoters: George W. Tyler, *Address Delivered before the Mercantile Library Association of Boston on the Evening of Their Sixteenth Anniversary, March 11, 1836* (Boston: Hitchcock, 1836), 32 pp.; Robert C. Winthrop, *An Address Delivered before the Boston Mercantile Library Association on the Occasion of Their Twenty-fifth Anniversary, October 15, 1845* (Boston: Marvin & Co., 1845); Edward Everett, *An Address before the Mercantile Library Association* (Boston: W. D. Ticknor, 1838); George Lunt, *Anniversary Poem Delivered before the Mercantile Library Association of Boston, October 3, 1843* (Boston: W. D. Ticknor, 1843); James T. Fields, *Anniversary Poem Delivered before the Mercantile Library Association of Boston, September 13, 1838* (Boston: W. D. Ticknor, 1838); Philip Hone, *An Address Delivered before the Mercantile Library Association, at the Odeon in Boston, October 5, 1843* (Boston: W. D. Ticknor, 1843), 44 pp.; Alfred Norton, *An Address Delivered before the Mercantile Library Association, January 19, 1836* (Boston: N. Southard, 1836), 23 pp.

In general the speakers all emphasize the same basic points: (1) The merchants of the rising generation will be trained through the use of library books. (2) The library will improve the morals of the profession by keeping the young clerks out of places of ill-repute. (3) Culture is attainable by the merchant class, and the industrious use of the library will encourage this cultural growth. The one outstanding characteristic of all these addresses is their quality of unlimited optimism.

Ditzion has drawn some interesting parallels between the apprentices libraries and those of the merchants' clerks and, though he has ridden the proletarian theme too hard, has in general given the best consideration of the subject that has yet appeared (Sidney Ditzion, "Mechanics and Mercantile Libraries," *Library Quarterly,* X, No. 2 [April, 1940], 192-219.

[75] The editorials in the *Lowell Offering* reveal that the magazine was under frequent and heavy attack from those who considered it a colossal hoax perpetrated by the management of the mills to discredit any criticism of their labor policies. This controversy—for the case was neither proved nor disproved—must be borne in mind in relation to any quotation from the *Offering.* Certainly there was a tendency to "play up" the cultural aspects of the mill-girls' lives. In reviewing Dickens' *American Notes* for the *Offering,* Harriet Farley challenged his statement that "nearly all" of the girls subscribe to circulating libraries, but though "*nearly all* do not thus subscribe . . . very many are supporters of other libraries" (*Lowell Offering,* III [1843], 96). See also her editorial "Books and Reading," which gives a good presentation of the reading of the mill girls (*ibid.,* pp. 143-44).

"The Improvement Society will meet on Monday evening, March 11th., [1844] at Mrs. Barnes'; and we wish all . . . who are interested in the establishment of a Reading Room to join us on that evening. Mr. Clark, the Superintendent of the Merrimack Corporation, to which we have always belonged, offers his female operatives the use of an excellent room for the purpose, provided they will, by subscription, furnish fuel and lights" (*ibid.,* Vol. IV [1844], inside back cover). This request that the girls furnish fuel and light was not insignificant since at the time they were earning $1.75 a week "clear of board" (*Lowell Offering,* V [August, 1845], 190).

[76] Albert Smith, *History of the Town of Peterborough* . . . (Boston: George Ellis, 1876), pp. 213-14.

[77] *Catalogue of the Pacific Mills Library, Lawrence, Mass., Opened August 21, 1854* (Boston: Darnell & Moore, 1855); copy in Boston Public Library.

[78] "To secure the permanence and increase of the library, the contribution of one cent per week to its funds is made a condition of employment in the Mills" (*ibid.,* p. 3).

The Pacific Mills began operation at the end of the year 1853, though no cloth was marketed until the spring of 1854. So the library was begun less than a year after the mill was opened. In 1867 the mill employed thirty-six hundred people, thus giving the book collection an annual fund of slightly more than $1,800. The mill management made much of the library as an important part of their employee welfare program. At the Paris Exposition of 1867 they boasted that the "Library is managed by the employees, they choosing their own officers for the control of affairs and the selection of books." But the company was careful to see that this did not get out of hand, for it was required that the president of the library association and chairman of the Library Committee be a resident manager of the mill (*Statement of the Pacific Mills Presented to the Special Jury of the Paris Exposition of 1867* [Lawrence: G. S. Merrill, 1868], in Massachusetts Historical Society). The catalog of 1855 lists an unusually broad range of subjects, though proportions are, in general, comparable to those of contemporary social libraries, except that juvenile literature is strong, theology only slightly represented, while history, biography, travel, and the practical arts are most emphasized. Clearly the base collection shows the influence of Henry Barnard.

[79] Lewis C. Aldrich, *History of Franklin and Grand Isle Counties, Vermont* . . . (Syracuse: D. Mason, 1891), pp. 390-91.

[80] Frederick W. Coburn, *History of Lowell and Its People* (New York: Lewis Historical Publishing Co., 1920), I, 263-64.

[81] John B. Wight, "Public Libraries," *Common School Journal,* XIII (1851), 260.

[82] From the citations of Perry Miller's *New England Mind* (New York: Macmillan, 1939) alone, it would be possible to construct a catalog of books which in both quantity and quality would be impressive.

[83] Constitution of the library, 1771, in the Scoville Memorial Library.

[84] Young Men's Institute, Hartford, *Fourth Annual Report, 1842,* p. 7. Henry Barnard II was the first president of this Institute.

[85] Reproduced in U. S. Bureau of Education, "Public Libraries in the United States," *1876 Report* (Washington, D. C.: Government Printing Office, 1876). p. 446.

[86] Wadlin, *op. cit.,* p. 26.

[87] Letter from Joshua Bates to T. W. Ward, October 1, 1852, quoted by Wadlin, *op. cit.,* p. 42. In November of the same year he also wrote to Ward: "My experience convinces me that there are a large number of young men who make a decent appearance, but living in boarding houses or with poor parents, cannot afford to have fire in their rooms. Such persons in past times having no place of resort have often loitered about the streets in the evenings and got into bad company, which would have been avoided, had such a library as is now proposed been in existence. The moral and intellectual improvement such a library would produce is incalculable" (*ibid.,* pp. 45-46).

[88] Wight, "Public Libraries," *op. cit.,* p. 261. In the hands of the professional librarians at the turn of the twentieth century it became an even more potent argument for improving the condition of public libraries. Also see Sidney Ditzion, "Social Reform, Education, and the Library, 1850 to 1900," *Library Quarterly,* IX (1939), 156-84.

[89] MS letter to Judge Mellen, March 25, 1851, Wayland Public Library.

[90] The significance of these Sunday-school libraries has been too much neglected. Of them Jewett wrote: "The aggregate number of books which they contain is very large. These books, though mostly juvenile readers, are always of a moral or religious tendency, and they have vast influence in forming the intellectual as well as the moral character of the people" (Charles C. Jewett, *Notices of Public Libraries in the United States of America* [Washington, D. C.: Printed for the House of Representatives, 1851], Appendix). In addition to their significance as an indication of religious influence, these Sunday-school libraries represented a humanitarian impulse. It should be remembered that in the beginning the Sunday school was a means for educating the poor.

In structure these libraries were akin to the social libraries generally. Their shares sold usually at very low prices. Though individually they were weak, collectively they did contribute to the movement for school libraries and children's collections in later public libraries (see Frank K. Walter, "A Poor but Respectable Relation—the Sunday School Library," *Library Quarterly,* XII [1942], 731-39).

[91] New York State, *Laws,* 1856, chap. 179, sec. 8.

[92] The Proceedings of the 1853 convention are reported fully in *Norton's Literary Register,* III (1854), 62 ff. Reuben A. Guild discusses the reasons why the organization failed to survive in the *Library Journal,* XXVII (1902), c.120-c.121. The history of the conference has been informally written by George B. Utley, "The Librarians' Conference of 1853" (unpublished MS), 120 pp.

[93] The Boston Athenaeum, for example, was directly influenced by the Athenaeum at Liverpool. When the early success of the *Monthly Anthology* encouraged exchanges with the editors of English reviews, its youthful publishers began to feel the need for a supporting reference library and reading-room. "One of our members," wrote Robert Gardiner, "having received an account of the Athenaeum recently established in Liverpool, read it to the [Anthology] Club. We were all at once impressed with the great advantage there would be in having such an institution in Boston; we determined at once that it should be established with the same name" (Robert Hallowell Gardiner, *Early Recollections of Robert Hallowell Gardiner, 1782-1864* [Hallowell, Me.: R. H. & W. I. Gardiner, 1936], p. 96).

[94] "In the reading-rooms are daily congregated more than a hundred readers and transcribers, of all nations and tongues, plodding scholars, literary ladies, and grave old gentlemen with mysterious looks. When shall we see the like in the Athenaeum?" (quoted by Brooks, *op. cit.,* p. 121).

[95] "Proceedings of the Trustees, February 14, 1853," I, 8 (MS in Boston Public Library).

Impact of Carnegie Philanthropy on American Public Library Development

George S. Bobinski

One of the most significant factors in public library growth in this country was philanthropy, and especially the philanthropy of Andrew Carnegie. And yet, this important aspect of American library history was ignored for years. The recent work of George S. Bobinski, however, has now filled this gap in library history; Bobinski wrote his widely respected book on Carnegie libraries after years of careful research, using the original records of the Carnegie Foundation. In the following essay, Dr. Bobinski presents his personal interpretation of the impact of Carnegie's gifts on American public library development.

Biographers, historians, and commentators have written relatively little on the evaluation of Andrew Carnegie's library gifts and their effect on American public library development. Their comments have been brief, sketchy, and for the most part full of praise. Almost no mention is found of the accusation frequently made by contemporaries that Carnegie libraries were merely expressions of Carnegie's exalted egotism and monuments of himself for posterity.

PUBLISHED VIEWS

Burton J. Hendrick, who might be called Carnegie's official and most exhaustive biographer, was the most laudatory. According to him, Andrew Carnegie believed that public libraries were as essential to the development of citizens as elementary education. This idea, however, was not generally accepted and needed momentum to survive. Carnegie gave the concept impetus when he donated money for buildings in which libraries could be established and operated. Hendrick wrote that Carnegie's library benefactions were a carefully conceived campaign to induce the states to establish free libraries as part of the regular educational system and represented the "Gospel of Wealth" in its highest and best meaning. Writing in the early 1930's, Hendrick declared that the free public library was then as much a part of life in the United States as the public school and the church. The American community could not function without it. Funds for libraries were no longer being given by the Carnegie Corporation because America had learned its lesson. Hendrick felt that the free public library had this permanent standing in American society largely because of the influence of Carnegie.[1]

Samuel Morison and Henry Commager concluded that the most effective impetus to the public library movement did not come from official sources or from public demand but from Carnegie's generosity. This generosity was, in turn, the result of Carnegie's genuine passion for education, his persuasion that the public library was the most democratic of all roads to learning, and a mindfulness of his own debt to and love of books. Morison and Commager termed Carnegie's library philanthropy as "not only munificent but wise, for by requiring a guarantee of adequate support to the libraries which he built, he laid the foundations for healthy growth of library facilities after his own gifts had served their immediate purpose."[2] Harold Underwood Faulkner concurred with Morison and Commager. He credited Andrew Carnegie with being the greatest single incentive to library growth in the United States.[3]

Sidney Ditzion, in his study of public libraries in New England and the Middle West from 1850 to 1900, characterized Carnegie's role in the library movement as not that of an initiator but rather as that of a "stimulant to an organism which might have rested long on a plateau had it not been spurred on to greater heights." Ditzion believed that the free library movement began on a firm foundation in New England and probably

SOURCE: Reprinted from George S. Bobinski, *Carnegie Libraries* (Chicago: American Library Association, 1969), Chapter 10 "Impact of Carnegie Philanthropy on American Public Library Development," pp. 183-202, by permission of the author and publisher. Copyright © 1969 by the American Library Association.

would have grown and gained acceptance throughout the rest of the country without Carnegie's help. However, it would have taken a much longer time, because many local officials and politicians were shirking municipal responsibility while waiting for some local, wealthy patron to establish and support a library. Carnegie's novel scheme of helping only those who helped themselves was a deterrent to such evasion.[4]

In the late thirties; William Munthe, a distinguished European observer of the American library scene, stated that Andrew Carnegie's gifts to public libraries in the United States were the evidence of an individual man's faith in the significance of books to society and as aids to the individual in his struggle with life. Munthe lamented the lack of a library philanthropist such as Carnegie in European countries. He felt that new buildings resulted in the increased understanding of library significance by all classes of society. The old baronial European buildings hindered the attainment of library service on the American level.[5]

In the postwar 1940's, the historian Dwight Dumond wrote that Carnegie and the other capitalists of the new industrial empire believed

> . . . that they had a moral obligation to dispense their wealth for the benefit of humanity, and they did so in generous fashion. Their philosophy, that superior intelligence had given them wealth and the same superior intelligence enabled them to spend it more wisely than their less fortunate brethren, belonged to a passing age, but their benefactions were for the most part wisely chosen and hastened the progress of sweeping reforms.[6]

Stuart Sherman stated that Americans would not have accomplished what Carnegie did, even if he had charged less per ton of steel. Instead, we "would have apportioned our little 'surplus' to our tobacco fund and our soft drink for the tranquilization of our nerves and the alleviation of our thirst."[7]

At the beginning of the 1930 decade, Mark Sullivan wrote that it was still too early to estimate the results of Carnegie munificence. But he did think that these benefactions had the effect of democratizing culture. Sullivan concluded, however, that to a generation of Americans who had enjoyed the fruits of Carnegie's gifts Carnegie, himself, was little more than a name over a library door.[8]

Writing more recently, Ralph Munn, formerly director of the Carnegie Library in Pittsburgh, called Andrew Carnegie a great library patron and a stimulator of library development. He credited the benefactor for emphasizing the library as a responsibility of the local government, spurring education for librarianship, and bringing about improvements in library architecture. Furthermore, he felt that the generous and widely publicized gifts gave prominence to the entire library movement. But he also criticized the philanthropist, declaring that Carnegie's gifts to hundreds of small towns throughout the land were, in one sense, a hindrance to public library development. According to Munn, many millions of Americans have known only these small village and town Carnegie libraries and have formed their entire concept of the public library from them. These libraries, too small to provide even the minimum essentials of good service, have been in part responsible for the attitude of benevolent apathy with which so many people regard public libraries.[9]

James Truslow Adams was almost alone in his disdain for Carnegie, the man "who had fought his workingmen's reasonable demands for better living conditions and had replaced native American labor by foreign immigrants for the sake of more complete control over their destinies, [and] had begun to distribute millions for his libraries, buying cheap notoriety on terms so onerous that more than one city, including the one in which I happened to live, declined to accept the money in accordance with them."[10]

A PERSONAL APPRAISAL OF CARNEGIE'S PHILANTHROPY

It seems unnecessary now to consider the question of how Carnegie made his money and whether it was morally right for communities to accept it as library philanthropy. Andrew Carnegie was no worse, and perhaps even better, than the other capitalists and industrial leaders of his time in respect to wages and working conditions. The effects of his surplus wealth on public library development are the only concern here.

Also, little attention need be given the question of whether or not Carnegie gave money for library buildings so that they would serve as monuments to posterity. This may have been one of his motivations, but a far more important one was his belief in the value of books and libraries as a means for self-improvement. It must be remembered that Carnegie did not require his name to be used on the buildings. Indeed, he preferred otherwise. Furthermore, he did not suggest that pictures or busts of him appear in the libraries. Communities wanting to place such objects in their Carnegie buildings had to buy them from commercial sources.

But if immortality *were* a Carnegie motivation, then it has been achieved. While it is true that fewer of the library buildings now officially bear his name and many are being demolished, nevertheless, the Carnegie name has not been forgotten. It has long been associated with libraries, and still is. In fact, many of Carnegie's other activities, and those of the trusts which he established, have been overshadowed in the public mind by his contributions to public libraries. Even at this date, library buildings are still being requested from the Carnegie Corporation. The author, in his research and writing during the last few years, has been impressed by the awareness and appreciation of Carnegie public library philanthropy voiced by the general public.

Carnegie had no master design in mind when he began giving gifts of libraries. A study of the years in which communities were promised buildings reveals a pattern beginning with a few donated libraries in the early years from 1886 to 1896; then a sharp rise from 1898 to a peak in 1903; with a gradual leveling off thereafter to the end of giving in 1919. Carnegie's early gifts of buildings attracted attention and requests for similar benefactions. With faith in this type of philanthropy, Carnegie acceded to the appeals as they continued to increase. Gradually a plan did evolve. The amount given was based on the population. The 10 percent support clause became mandatory for all communities. Application forms were developed and revised through the years. Eventually, even library architecture was regulated. Improvements were made throughout the life of the program as experience taught its lessons.

With the help of hindsight, it is now easy to look back and suggest what Andrew Carnegie could or should have done. It is probably true that Carnegie's gifts to small communities have made it difficult to break away from this pattern of local municipal control for more efficient and economical regional library service crossing city and county lines. It is now recognized that small localities cannot operate successful public libraries, even if they tax themselves heroically. In order to succeed they must pool their resources and services into a county or regional system. Although there has been great progress in this direction, more than two thirds of all public libraries today serve an area with a population of 10,000 or less. Almost 42 percent of all public libraries

serve localities with less than 3000 people.[11] About 2700 public libraries still have an annual income of less than $2000 or book funds of less than $500 per year.[12]

But Carnegie's emphasis on municipal government seemed the most logical at the time. This was the common way in which public libraries were being founded. After all, the appeals did come to Carnegie from the local community. People were not as mobile then, and communities were not able to provide efficient library service on a wide area basis. When Carnegie began giving, there were no county libraries. The county library movement had its beginnings only during the period of Carnegie library philanthropy. In 1903 small, horse-drawn book wagons were serving some sixty-six stations throughout Washington County out of a headquarters library in Hagerstown, Maryland. Carnegie donated $25,000 in that same year toward the support of this library extension service.[13] Funds were contributed for county library buildings as the systems were formed, particularly in the South and West. The terms were the same as those for municipal libraries.

The autonomous, municipal libraries were not only a logical development but perhaps a necessary one. The large number of local libraries scattered all over the United States helped to bring about a public willing to vote local, state, and federal funds for the improvement of public library service.

It is also easy to assert now that Carnegie should have provided each building with books and librarians. But he and his officials felt, and rightfully so, that this was the responsibility of each community. These problems were not peculiar to Carnegie libraries. All libraries needed librarians and larger, better collections. The time was a period of rapid public library growth. The momentum of the establishment of new public libraries was ahead of the development of library service and training.

It was a wise decision on the part of the Carnegie Corporation to stop giving library buildings when it did. For more than twenty years this philanthropy had helped sell the value of libraries, and there were now other needs, as suggested by Alvin Johnson, which were more important and needed early solution in order to gain further support for public library service everywhere, not just for Carnegie libraries.

The program of Carnegie benefactions had been been generally very successful. Relatively few of the 1679 buildings in 1412 communities were failures as libraries. Even the percentage of those not acceding to the 10 percent support clause was not great. There were even fewer failures and broken pledges among the large cities and in states with strong library associations and commissions. Communities in such strong library states (as, for instance, California and Indiana) did well in all respects. They received the most building grants, had the fewest grant request failures, and were represented by the most communities obtaining Carnegie funds.

Obviously, the provision of more than $40,000,000 for Carnegie buildings all over the United States had a great impact on public library development. In terms of 1968 purchasing power, Carnegie's public library building benefactions would probably be equal to more than $150,000,000.[14] Public libraries in the United States are currently going through a similar wave of building expansion under the Library Services and Construction Act.

The importance of Carnegie library philanthropy lies in its perfect timing. It came in the best possible period—during the height of library expansion in the United States. Beginning in the 1890's, states began to play active roles in organizing public libraries in each community. The need for library buildings was desperate, and Carnegie's gifts helped to fill the void. The provision of new buildings created an avid interest in and enthusiasm for libraries in their early, crucial years of development.

An important factor in further stimulating public library development was the publicity and advertising resulting from these beneficences. Although the public library, by the beginning of the twentieth century, was generally accepted and approved as a worthy agency, it was, nevertheless, often confronted with lack of understanding, little appreciation, and even with indifference. Carnegie dramatized the value of libraries. Here was a famous millionaire who believed that libraries were important and who gave millions for their support. Carnegie and the Carnegie Corporation provided the incentive for each community to obtain a library for its populace. The rivalry among some towns to outdo each other was still another factor. In the long run Carnegie made more libraries and books available to more people and helped speed the momentum of the public library movement.

Carnegie's initiative also stimulated other library benefactions. During the 1890's, more than

$10,000,000 were donated for libraries by philanthropists. From 1900 to 1906, 3099 individual contributions were made to libraries totaling more than $24,000,000. Almost half of this amount was expended for buildings and sites.[15]

But, more importantly, Carnegie's philanthropy widened the acceptance of the principle of local government responsibility for the public library. The method of giving was not perfect. Poor sites were often selected. The 10 percent support pledge was sometimes broken or more often not surpassed. Nevertheless, it was a wise provision. It placed indirect pressure on government bodies and the public to accept the organization and maintenance of the public library as a governmental service.

In library architecture, too, Carnegie provided a stimulus. Derogatory comments are often heard about Carnegie library architecture. These remarks, however, usually refer to the older libraries built before Carnegie and the Corporation became involved in architectural control. The short architectural memorandum in simplified spelling, issued by James Bertram in 1911, was composed of the best library opinion of the time on the subject. It decried architectural elaboration and offered basic principles and outline sketches, all of which led to a more open, flexible, and less expensive structure. But it still left every community with a great deal of freedom to plan its own library interior as it liked, within these few reasonable bounds, and to design the exterior as it pleased, as long as it refrained from expensive columns, portals, stairways, and domes. The memorandum was the beginning of modern library architecture, and many of the principles are still in effect.

But one must be careful not to give Carnegie philanthropy all the credit for the growth of the public library. At times some commentators imply that Carnegie practically founded the entire public library movement, or that it would long have rested on a plateau with little further development. On the contrary, the public library system of the United States was expanding under its own power before Carnegie's generosity started on a "wholesale" basis in 1898. In just twenty years the number of public libraries had grown from 188 in 1876 to 971 with 1000 volumes or more in 1896.[16]

By 1923, 3873 towns with populations of 1000 or more had public libraries serving a total population of 56,782,000 (or 53.5 percent of the entire United States population, then listed as

105,710,000). Of these 1408 Carnegie library towns were serving 32,956,500 people (31 percent), and 2462 communities with non-Carnegie libraries were serving 23,823,500 (22 percent). Two additional facts must immediately be presented as further interpretation: (1) a few Carnegie libraries were located in towns with less than 1000 population, and (2) almost all the larger cities were represented on the Carnegie library listing of 1408 towns, but many of these had buildings in their library systems which were not built with Carnegie funds.[17]

William Learned intimates that not all the 1408 Carnegie library communities had organized their libraries as a result of the Carnegie offer, but he gives no breakdown of the number not doing so. This is unfortunate since the usual implication is that every Carnegie gift was a newly established library. A careful analysis of the microfilmed Carnegie Library Correspondence files and the questionnaires which were sent to libraries for which the files lacked sufficient information revealed that about two thirds of these communities already had a free public library or were in the process of organizing one when the Carnegie gift was made. To be sure, many had just been organized or were being organized as a result of the stimulation of Carnegie benefactions and with the hope of obtaining new buildings. Table 1 gives a detailed breakdown and analysis of the Learned and Carnegie Library Correspondence files findings.

It is interesting to observe that only in the southern and southwestern states did Carnegie's benefactions actually bring about more newly established public libraries and not just new buildings for already established libraries. All 14 of the Carnegie grants in Alabama were newly established libraries, as were 19 out of 20 in Georgia. On the other hand, all 35 of the Carnegie grants in Massachusetts were to already established public libraries, as were 57 out of 60 in Wisconsin. It can be seen that the incentive of Carnegie's gifts was enough to accelerate the library movement to a stampede. Some 188 public libraries in 1876 jumped to 3873 by 1923. By 1967, according to the *American Library Directory*, the total had reached almost 7000.

Recognition must also be given to James Bertram and Alvin Johnson as two important figures in Carnegie library history and in American public library development. Bertram was the real power behind Carnegie public library building grants. Alvin Johnson's sagacious and pene-

TABLE 1

Analysis of United States Public Libraries, 1896-1923*

I: Communities possessing public libraries of 1000 volumes or more in 1896.
II: Communities obtaining one or more Carnegie library buildings by 1923.
IIA: Number already having (or organizing) a public library before the Carnegie grant.
IIB: Number not having a public library at time of Carnegie grant.
III: Communities of 1000 population or more in 1923 possessing public libraries unaided by Carnegie funds.

ANALYSIS BY STATE

STATE	I	II	IIA	IIB	III
Alabama	0	14	0	14	13
Arizona	1	4	2	2	6
Arkansas	0	4	0	4	22
California	28	121	91	30	50
Colorado	6	27	19	8	18
Connecticut	61	8	7	1	135
Delaware	2	0	0	0	10
District of Columbia	0	1	1	0	0
Florida	2	10	1	9	27
Georgia	1	20	1	19	20
Idaho	0	10	6	4	12
Illinois	62	105	81	24	110
Indiana	23	155	100	55	37
Iowa	23	99	61	38	51
Kansas	10	58	31	27	56
Kentucky	1	15	4	11	28
Louisiana	1	4	2	2	6
Maine	31	17	14	3	131
Maryland	3	1	1	0	20
Massachusetts	271	35	35	0	257
Michigan	40	53	33	20	116
Minnesota	14	58	41	17	54
Mississippi	1	10	1	9	11
Missouri	6	26	7	19	30
Montana	7	17	12	5	21
Nebraska	11	68	42	26	42
Nevada	0	1	0	1	1
New Hampshire	76	9	6	3	75
New Jersey	19	29	24	5	150
New Mexico	0	3	0	3	8
New York	106	41	35	6	218
North Carolina	2	9	2	7	42
North Dakota	1	8	6	2	22
Ohio	29	77	53	24	80
Oklahoma	0	24	12	12	44
Oregon	0	25	17	8	16
Pennsylvania	23	26	10	16	137
Rhode Island	41	0	0	0	43
South Carolina	2	14	7	7	9
South Dakota	1	25	12	13	17
Tennessee	2	10	1	9	6
Texas	1	30	7	23	61
Utah	0	23	16	7	15
Vermont	24	4	4	0	106
Virginia	0	2	2	0	27
Washington	3	33	19	14	20
West Virginia	1	3	1	2	10
Wisconsin	34	60	57	3	74
Wyoming	1	16	7	9	1
Total	971	1,412	891	521	2,465

ANALYSIS BY REGION

REGION	I	II	IIA	IIB	III
Northeast	658	173	137	36	1,292
Southeast	12	112	21	91	211
Midwest	231	633	433	200	552
Southwest	2	61	21	40	119
Northwest	37	252	151	101	204
Far West	31	180	127	53	87
District of Columbia	0	1	1	0	0
Total	971	1,412	891	521	2,465

*Sources: William S. Learned, *The American Public Library and the Diffusion of Knowledge* (New York: Harcourt, 1924), p. 84, citing the U. S. Bureau of Education, *Statistics of Libraries and Library Legislation in the United States, 1895-1896* (Washington, D. C.: Govt. Print. Off., 1897) for Column I; Carnegie Library Microfilmed Correspondence for Column II, II A, II B; and William S. Learned, p. 84, citing the *American Library Directory, 1923* (New York: Bowker, 1923) for Column III.

trating report on Carnegie libraries led to broader support by the Carnegie Corporation to public libraries in the United States.

CONTINUING ACTIVITIES OF THE CARNEGIE CORPORATION IN PUBLIC LIBRARY DEVELOPMENT

The Carnegie Corporation, it will be recalled, was organized in 1911 by Andrew Carnegie in order to ". . . promote the advancement and diffusion of knowledge and understanding among the people of the United States." It was to accomplish this purpose through grants to schools, libraries, research, and publications. Carnegie had personally distributed $29,452,853 for library buildings up to 1911. Then the public library giving was turned over to the Corporation, which distributed $11,781,000 for this purpose up to 1917. After that time the Carnegie Corporation did not consider any new requests for buildings, but it did make grants as late as 1919 for requests which had been made before 1917.

The Corporation has never ceased receiving requests for library buildings, although the tempo of such appeals has diminished. At the end of 1924, James Bertram reported that 1500 meritorious applications were on file for library buildings.[18] An accurate record kept from 1923 to 1953 reveals a total number of 1631 requests for funds by libraries of all kinds for establishment, buildings, books, equipment, renovation, and expansion, with the following breakdown:[19]

1923-45	1149	1950	92
1946	16	1951	41
1947	77	1952	57
1948	81	1953	40
1949	78		

The secretary of the Corporation reported in 1965 that requests were still being received for library buildings, as well as for repairs and expansion of old libraries and for information regarding the disposal of old structures that had been or were being replaced.[20]

Andrew Carnegie's philanthropy continued to benefit public libraries long after the formal termination of building grants. This extended library philanthropy is still in evidence to this day, and in many ways is even more important than the original bequest of Carnegie buildings. Indeed, the Carnegie Corporation, which took over Carnegie's philanthropy program, has been so identified with libraries that many people have assumed it was operating solely for the benefit and control of libraries and librarians.

During the Corporation's first fifty years of operation, from 1911 to 1961, it spent $33,457,142 to improve library service. Although this expenditure represents only about 11 percent of the total of all its grants during the first fifty years, the Corporation has been associated with every major development in library service in the United States. A brief review of these library involvements will show their importance and also demonstrate that the Carnegie Corporation did follow through on many of Alvin Johnson's recommendations. The Corporation has given support to all types of libraries, but only those grants involving or greatly affecting public libraries are noted here.[21]

Following World War I, Corporation trustees did not resume gifts of money for buildings. Instead, during the period 1917-25, they organized a series of conferences to determine the manner and means by which the Corporation might be of assistance in improving library services and training.

In 1918 the Corporation asked Charles C. Williamson to make a study of library training. His report[22] recommended that librarians should receive their education in a university rather than in a training school sponsored by a public library. Williamson also recommended the establishment of a graduate library school for advanced study, a national accrediting and certification system for library schools, and numerous fellowships. His study was a monumental work which resulted in a complete revision of the curriculum in library schools.

A Carnegie Corporation-sponsored study in 1924 by William S. Learned[23] centered on the role of the library as a medium for spreading information. It called for expanded services to be provided by the American Library Association, and for local and regional experiments and demonstrations leading to better ways of getting books to the people.

In 1926 the Corporation embarked on a ten-year "Library Service Program" for which the trustees approved $5,000,000 in financial support. The aim of this program was to strengthen the library profession by supporting the activities of the American Library Association, by improving training opportunities, and by support for certain centralized library services and projects.

Andrew Carnegie had already provided $100,000 in endowment funds to the American Library Association in 1902, and the Corporation gave $549,500 for the general support of the Association from 1924 to 1926. In 1926 it added $2,000,000 in endowment funds. During this period the Corporation also provided financial assistance to the Library of Congress and to bibliographic centers and regional catalogs, such as those at the Denver and Philadelphia public libraries.

Gifts for the endowment and support of library schools and the establishment of the first graduate library school at the University of Chicago totaled $3,359,550. Fellowships for library training and the sponsorship of conferences, studies, and publications were also provided. Among the latter was a book on public library architecture by Joseph L. Wheeler and Alfred M. Githens.[24] This volume came to be the indispensable handbook for the planning and design of public libraries.

The Corporation provided funds for several demonstrations of methods and techniques for bringing books to people of all ages who were living in rural areas far from the major population centers. In 1925 the first of these was started in Louisiana with a grant to the League of Library Commissioners. A central lending library was begun, several parishes (counties) were encouraged to establish libraries with initial book collections provided by the commission, and summer library training courses were provided for the first time by a university in the state. Shortly after the demonstration began, the Louisiana state legislature voted money to supplement the funds of the commission during the demonstration period, and later continued its financial support of state-wide library service. Other such experiments and demonstrations were to follow throughout the United States.

Following World War II, during which the Corporation's library philanthropy was for the most part in a state of suspension, the trustees and officers evolved a new Corporation grant program in which library interests no longer had a major emphasis, although library grants were not excluded. In fact, although the number of grants and the amount expended may have decreased, those which were made were of great importance.

The Corporation provided $212,170 to the Social Science Research Council for the Public Library Inquiry. The idea of a study of the library's actual and potential contribution to American society was suggested by the American Library Association. The appraisal was made in sociological, cultural, and human terms with the investigators asking and answering such questions as:

> Who uses the library and why?
> Who are the librarians and how well qualified are they for the job?
> Where does the money come from and is it adequate?
> What services does and should the library perform?

The overall report was published in 1950.[25] Specific studies were issued in twelve volumes between 1949 and 1951. The most significant finding was the poor status of the American public library outside the major cities. There was a superabundance of small, poorly financed, independent local libraries with inadequate book stocks and reference services. The Public Library Inquiry discovered that 65 percent of all libraries were in small towns of less than 5000 and spent less than $4000 per year. The survey suggested the organization of larger library systems and the concentration of state and federal library aid for the encouragement of such systems. The small libraries could and should continue to serve the communities that organized them. But they should also be related to other surrounding libraries in order to form regional systems with common pools of books and other materials, specialized personnel available for guidance, and centralized reference and processing services.

Again, financial assistance from the Carnegie Corporation helped the American Library Association, in 1956, to formulate and publish what popularly became known as the Public Library Standards.[26] The Public Library Inquiry discovered the failings of the public libraries, and the Standards presented what they should be doing by setting up minimum guidelines of good service. Public libraries were urged to cooperate, federate, or consolidate into library systems for better library service.

In 1956 a grant of $50,000 was made to the School of Library Science at Western Reserve University for the study of a new curriculum in library training in the light of modern cultural and technological developments. A statement was to be formulated on the nature of librarianship and on the kinds of knowledge librarians should have in order to fulfill their professional functions.

The Corporation's financial support of demonstration centers for extension of library service in rural areas, of the Public Library Inquiry, and of the Standards was an important factor in bringing about federal aid for public libraries. The Library Services Act (P. L. 597, 84th Congress), signed into law in 1956, was designed as a five-year program to demonstrate improved public library services in areas of less than 10,000 people which had nonexistent or inadequate library service. The Act was extended in 1960 for five additional years. In 1964 the Library Services Act was amended and renamed the Library Services and Construction Act (P. L. 88-269). Benefits were extended to urban as well as to rural areas, and for the first time these funds were not limited to operation and maintenance but could be expended for construction. An amendment in 1966 included money for strengthening cooperation among libraries. Federal aid has always been based on matching funds from states and in many cases from local government.

In signing the Library Services and Construction Act on February 11, 1964, President Johnson declared:

. . . chances are that the public libraries are among the oldest buildings in any community. Only four per cent of our public libraries have been built since 1940. Many of them were built through the wise generosity of Andrew Carnegie forty years ago.

This Nation needs a larger and more diversified collection of books. We need better housing for these books. We sorely need libraries closer to the people, whether through more centrally located libraries or through bookmobiles and branch locations. The central fact of our times is this: Books and ideas are the most effective weapons against intolerance and ignorance.[27]

Thus, the rural areas which were somewhat neglected by the original Carnegie library benefactions were the first to receive federal aid. More recently, all kinds of public libraries—rural, suburban, and urban—have found a new library benefactor on the scale of Andrew Carnegie.

Building on the foundation laid by the social libraries, public libraries in the United States have had four important phases of growth. The public library enabling laws, beginning in the 1850's, were the first stimulus. Carnegie's gifts to public libraries were the second. A third major stimulus could well be attributed to the library activities of the Carnegie Corporation. We are now experiencing the fourth—that of the stimulus of federal support. This latest development has come about, to some extent at least; as the result of the influence of Andrew Carnegie and the Carnegie Corporation's library activities. Carnegie's benefactions have, in truth, played a major role in American public library development.

FOOTNOTES

[1] Burton J. Hendrick, *The Benefactions of Andrew Carnegie* (New York: Carnegie Corp., 1935), p. 13-15.

[2] Samuel Eliot Morison and Henry Steele Commager, *The Growth of the American Republic* (New York: Oxford Univ. Pr., 1950), II: 312-13.

[3] Harold Underwood Faulkner, *The Quest for Social Justice, 1898-1914* (New York: Macmillan, 1931), p. 279.

[4] Sidney Ditzion, *Arsenals of a Democratic Culture* (Chicago: American Library Assn., 1947), p. 150.

[5] William Munthe, *American Librarianship from a European Angle* (Chicago: American Library Assn., 1939), p. 18.

[6] Dwight L. Dumond, *America in Our Time, 1896-1946* (New York: Holt, 1947), p. 19-20.

[7] Stuart P. Sherman, *Americans* (New York: Scribner, 1922), p. 254-55.

[8] Mark Sullivan, *Our Times: The United States*, 1900-1925 (6 vols.; New York: Scribner, 1932), IV:159, 163.

[9] Ralph Munn, "Hindsight on the Gifts of Carnegie," *Library Journal*, 76: 1967-70 (Dec. 1, 1951).

[10] James Truslow Adams, *The Epic of America* (Boston: Little, 1931), p. 345.

[11] Henry T. Drennan, "The Public Library Service Gap," in *National Inventory of Library Needs* (Chicago: American Library Assn., 1965), p. 40-41.

[12] *Bowker Annual of Library and Book Trade Information*, 1968 (New York: Bowker, 1968), p. 6.

[13] Hagerstown, Md., Carnegie Library Correspondence, Microfilm Reel No. 13.

[14] Based on the U. S. Dept. of Labor, Bureau of Labor Statistics, *Consumer Price Index*, with 1957-59 = 100: 1900 = 29.3, 1910 = 33.3, July, 1968 = 121.5.

[15] "Gifts to Libraries," *Library Journal*, Vols. 15-31 (1890-1906).

[16] Samuel S. Green, *The Public Library Movement in the United States*, 1853-1893 (Boston: Boston Book Co., 1913), p. 152-53; U. S. Bureau of Education, *Statistics of Libraries and Library Legislation in the United States, 1895-1896*

(Washington, D. C.: Govt. Print. Off., 1897); William S. Learned, *The American Public Library and the Diffusion of Knowledge* (New York: Harcourt, 1924), p. 73.

[17] William S. Learned, *op. cit.,* p. 71-73. (Learned listed 1408 communities receiving Carnegie grants; later listings by the Carnegie Corporation reveal 1412).

[18] James Bertram to Mrs. Charles Scheuber, librarian, Dec. 30, 1924 (Fort Worth, Texas, Carnegie Library Correspondence, Microfilm Reel No. 11).

[19] Information obtained from Carnegie Corporation files in New York City.

[20] Letter from Miss Florence Anderson, secretary of the Carnegie Corporation, to the author, Oct. 12, 1965.

[21] Most of the following review was obtained from the Carnegie Corporation of New York, *Carnegie Corporation Library Program*, 1911-1961 (New York: Carnegie Corp., 1963), p. 3-24.

[22] Charles C. Williamson, *Training for Library Service* (New York: Carnegie Corp., 1923).

[23] William S. Learned, *op. cit.*

[24] Joseph L. Wheeler, and Alfred M. Githens, *The American Public Library Building: Its Planning and Design with Special Reference to Its Administration and Service* (New York: Scribner, 1941).

[25] Robert D. Leigh, *The Public Library in the United States: The General Report of the Public Library Inquiry* (New York: Columbia Univ. Pr., 1950).

[26] American Library Association, *Public Library Service: A Guide to Evaluation, with Minimum Standards* (Chicago: A.L.A., 1956).

[27] Germaine Krettek and Eileen D. Cooke, "Federal Legislation," *Bowker Annual of Library and Book Trade Information*, 1965 (New York: Bowker, 1965), p. 155.

ADDITIONAL READINGS

Carrier, Esther Jane, *Fiction in Public Libraries, 1876-1900* (New York: Scarecrow Press, 1965).

Kalisch, Philip Arthur, *The Enoch Pratt Free Library: A Social History* (Metuchen, N. J.: Scarecrow Press, 1969).

Leigh, Robert, "Changing Concepts of the Public Library's Role," *Library Quarterly* 27 (October, 1957), pp. 223-34.

Long, Harriet Geneva, *Public Library Service to Children: Foundation and Development* (Metuchen, N. J.: Scarecrow Press, 1969).

Lydenburg, Henry Miller, *History of the New York Public Library* (New York: The Public Library, 1923).

Monroe, Margaret, *Library Adult Education: The Biography of an Idea* (New York: Scarecrow Press, 1963).

Spencer, Gwladys S., *The Chicago Public Library: Origins and Backgrounds* (Chicago: University of Chicago Press, 1943).

Williamson, William, *William Frederick Poole and the Modern Library Movement* (New York: Columbia University Press, 1963).

Whitehill, Walter Muir, *Boston Public Library: A Centenial History* (Cambridge: Harvard University Press, 1956).

Woodford, Frank B., *Parnassus on Main Street: A History of the Detroit Public Library* (Detroit: Wayne State University Press, 1965).

V

DEWEY, THE AMERICAN LIBRARY ASSOCIATION, AND EDUCATION FOR LIBRARIANSHIP

1876 was a momentous year in the United States, for it marked the centennial of American independence, and confirmed the people's faith in their country's strength and security. This important national anniversary also stands out as an extremely significant year in the history of the library profession in the United States. In 1876 the young librarian of Amherst College, Melvil Dewey, was instrumental in launching the American Library Association, the *Library Journal,* and his famous decimal classification. A few years later, Dewey established the first library school in this country. From that time on, his name was synonymous with library education.

Today the American Library Association is a thriving organization of over 30,000 members, the *Library Journal* prospers in New York, the Dewey Decimal System remains the world's most popular classification scheme, and schools similar to Dewey's library school have been established from coast to coast. The essays that follow explain how it all began, and capture for a fleeting moment the character of the man who exerted enormous influence over every phase of American librarianship during the last quarter of the nineteenth century.

Raking the Historic Coals: The American Library Association Beginnings

Edward Holley

In the following paper, Edward Holley, winner of the Scarecrow Press Award for his biography of Charles Evans, presents a history of the events that led up to the establishment of the American Library Association, and discusses the controversy over who was primarily responsible for the organization's founding. The history of the ALA in the twentieth century remains to be written, but there are now underway several projects planned for 1976, the centennial year of its founding.

In his book, *The Emerging of Modern America,* Allan Nevins names 1876 as one of "two memorable years" in post-Civil War America. The nation had gone through a civil war, experienced a mire of scandals and political corruption perhaps not equaled in its history, and survived a debilitating financial panic. Moreover, the Hayes-Tilden election with its cliff-hanging results late in the year sorely tested the political faith of the country. Yet from all these stresses the nation had emerged with moderation and restraint, a remarkable testimonial, Nevins thinks, to the "steadfastness and orderliness of the American people."[1]

That same year, so significant as a time of testing for the United States, also saw the nation celebrate its centennial in a huge exhibition in Philadelphia. The emphasis was upon American achievement, and there was a new spirit in the air, an optimistic and courageous outlook for the future. Above all, educational activity at all levels beyond the elementary school was then receiving renewed attention. It was a time ripe for new ventures to match an expanding country.

From the viewpoint of the librarian, the year 1876 has further importance: it marked a turning point for American librarianship and the birth of the modern library profession. Despite the fact that public libraries had already expanded rapidly in the previous quarter of a century, librarians as yet had no professional organization through which they could communicate with each other. In October, 1876, the practitioners of the craft met in Philadelphia for "mutual consultation and practical co-operation," to promote "efficiency and economy in library work," and to present

"plans for a permanent organization."[2] In looking back upon the year's work, an older librarian, with a hint of prophecy, remarked to Melvil Dewey, "Through all coming time 1876 will be looked upon as the most eventful year in the history of libraries—the year in which the librarian farily claimed and received at the hands of the public his place among the recognized professions."[3]

Others echoed a similar sentiment, from the *Publishers' Weekly*, tireless advocate of library causes, to the journals of more general interest such as *Harper's* and *The Nation.* From across the Atlantic, Henry R. Tedder, Librarian of the Athenaeum Club (London), speaking at the first International Conference of Librarians (1877), said that the year 1876 almost marked a "new period in the history of bibliothecal science"; and at the same conference, John Winter Jones of the British Museum acknowledged American librarianship's major contribution: "The idea of holding a Conference of Librarians originated in America—in that country of energy and activity which has set the world so many good examples, and of which a conference of Librarians is not the least valuable . . . ."[4]

In the perspective of history, 1876 was indeed a landmark year for the American librarian. Not only was his professional association organized, but the U. S. Bureau of Education published its massive survey, *Public Libraries in the United States of America*[5] (including the first edition of Cutter's *Rules for a Printed Dictionary Catalogue* as a separate part); and the *American Library Journal* began publication as the first professional

SOURCE: Reprinted from Edward Holley, *Raking the Historic Coals; The ALA Scrapbook of 1876* (Chicago: Beta Phi Mu, 1967), pp. 3-22, by permission of the author and publisher. Copyright ©1967 by Beta Phi Mu, International Library Science Honor Society.

library magazine. As if this were not enough, the year also saw the appearance of the first edition of Melvil Dewey's decimal classification and subject index, which was to sweep the field of classification and within the next two decades supersede most of the classification schemes then in existence. Never before or since have American librarians been able to claim as much fruition within a single twelve-month period.

In retrospect, it is a bit startling to realize that the name which was to become synonymous with librarianship, that of the energetic Melvil Dewey, held no magic power in 1876. One of the youngest men in the profession, Dewey had graduated only the year before from Amherst College and was virtually unknown among the practitioners of the period. The acknowledged Nestor of the profession, William Frederick Poole (then 55), is said to have been indignant at the presumption of this young man.[6] In later years Dewey liked to recall that he had started the American Library Association despite the opposition of one of the chief librarians of the period. He should not have limited himself to Poole. Another prominent librarian, Ainsworth Rand Spofford, Librarian of Congress, declined to lend his name to the project, "because I have always entertained insuperable objections to figuring in conventions (usually mere wordy outlets for impracticables and pretenders)."[7] He added that he looked "with distrust upon mixing the methods of the bibliographer, which are those of patient and accurate research, with the methods of the stump, which are conspicuously the reverse."[8] Dewey himself admitted, in a communication closer to the conference date, that "most of the leading librarians were doubtful of the possibility of accomplishing much," and that only Charles Ammi Cutter, of the Boston Athenaeum, was pre-eminent among the hopeful.[9] All the same he had to add that the doubtful had become enthusiatic and worked side by side with the more confident. The singling out of Poole for special criticism came later.

This, however, is to jump ahead of the story. The point to be made here is that Melvil Dewey, despite his indisputable contributions later, was not a well-known figure at the beginning of the conference in 1876. This fact, initially, caused serious difficulties in securing the necessary backing of some leading librarians.

The 1876 library conference was not the first to be held in America. That distinction belongs to the conference of 1853, a gathering whose organization bears strong similarities to its successor twenty-three years later. Charles B. Norton, publisher of *Norton's Literary Gazette,* in the spring of 1853 began urging a library conference which his two editors, Seth Hastings Grant and Daniel Coit Gilman, had first publicized the year before.[10] Grant was then serving as Librarian of the New York Mercantile Library; and Gilman, later to make his mark as President of Johns Hopkins, had just graduated from Yale. Just which of the three—Norton, Grant or Gilman—actually wrote the editorial is unknown. At any rate, Norton's various editorials stimulated considerable interest; and an official call, signed by twenty-six librarians and bibliographers, was mailed in May.[11]

Eighty-two persons attended the conference in September, 1853, in New York City. The proceedings were dominated by Charles Coffin Jewett, then Assistant Secretary and Librarian of the Smithsonian Institution. At the time, Jewett was waging a losing battle with Dr. Joseph Henry, Secretary of the Smithsonian, over the proper way to disburse the institution's funds. He was a leading figure in the library world, and later served as Superintendent of the Boston Public Library from 1858 to 1868. Poole, who was a member of both conferences, said that "the Convention of 1853 made a lasting impression on the minds of all the librarians who were present and that it must be regarded as an era in American bibliography."[12]

From other accounts, too, the 1853 conference appears to have been highly successful. On the second day, Reuben A. Guild, Librarian of Brown University and another member of both conferences, introduced a resolution urging a permanent library organization with annual meetings.[13] The resolution was unanimously adopted, and many of the delegates confidently assumed, as they left for home, that a conference would be held the following year. Yet almost a quarter of a century intervened before another library conference was held. The reasons are probably varied, including the outbreak of the Civil War; but certainly among the chief reasons was the fact that Jewett was forced out of his position at the Smithsonian the following year. Too, Norton, the chief backer, met with financial reverses, and there was no one else to take the helm.

At this point it is pertinent to look at the development of other professions and their organizations during the nineteenth century. Perhaps the librarians had been premature in 1853. While it is true that the teachers had organized the National Education Association in 1851 and the American Association for the Advancement of Science had preceded the N.E.A. by three years, most professional associations came into existence after the Civil War. Furthermore, one might note that both the N.E.A. and A.A.A.S. were broad discipline groups, with a rather inclusive patronage. More specialized groups such as the American Chemical Society (1876), the Modern Language Association (1883), the American Historical Association (1884), the American Economic Association (1885), and the Geological Society of America (1888) all date from the last quarter of the nineteenth century. In fact, a veritable flood of professional and scholarly associations came into being in the twenty-year period between 1876 and 1895. Both Arthur M. Schlesinger and Arthur E. Bestor, Jr., have discussed the formation of these associations in terms of the transformation of American scholarship and the expansion of learning in the post-Civil War period.[14] The impact of these currents on libraries was profound; and, given the rise of public libraries with the need for increased staffing and services, it would have been unusual for librarians not to have organized professionally during this period.

The idea of forming a library association, or at least the calling of a conference of librarians, did not spring full-blown from the head of Melvin Dewey in the spring of 1876 as has sometimes been asserted. Dewey's own hindsight in making such a claim is confusing. In response to an article on the origin of the Association which Bowker had published in January, 1896, Dewey stated that he had been at work on the idea of library development, including a plan for a national association, a library journal, and a library bureau, at least four years before he began his relationship with Bowker and Leypoldt at the *Publishers' Weekly* office in May, 1876. Even further down the road, in 1917, Dewey stated that the evolution of his plan occurred in 1875. Whatever the truth of the matter, Bowker's response to Dewey's claims in 1896 was that "on some of these points my remembrance is confirmatory of Mr. Dewey's and on others he speaks for himself,"[15] but he added that he did not want in any sense to deny Dewey due credit for the largest share in general library development.

As early as August, 1875, Thomas Hale

Williams, Librarian of the Minneapolis Athenaeum, had written to John Eaton, U. S. Commissioner of Education, suggesting the importance of a library convention and proposing a list of topics to be discussed. While the exact date of the Williams letter is uncertain, John Eaton did not reply until the following February.[16] He expressed regret at not having responded sooner and sent along letters from several chief librarians who had commented upon Williams' proposal. Unfortunately these letters have been lost. Why Williams, who was a member of the 1853 Conference, did not participate in the 1876 Conference is unknown, but he was having difficulties at home defending his policies at the Athenaeum at about that time.

Among those named by Eaton as responding to the Williams proposal were Justin Winsor of the Boston Public Library, the foremost librarian of the country, William F. Poole of the Chicago Public Library, Henry A. Homes, of the New York State Library, and Lloyd P. Smith of the Library Company of Philadelphia. In his solicitation Commissioner Eaton had not overlooked the Librarian of Congress, A. R. Spofford, who did not "seem sanguine that a Convention of librarians would accomplish much practical good."[17]

Nothing really came of Williams' letter, despite the implication of the government report that he somehow had a direct connection with the preparations for the 1876 conference.[18] He did not attend the Philadelphia conference nor do letters exist indicating that he made suggestions about its program. However, he should be given credit for stimulating thought about a library conference in the months preceding the actual conference preparations. John Eaton himself suggested the logic of librarians meeting during the centennial, since other educational and scientific bodies would undoubtedly do the same.[19] Other extant letters also suggest that the idea of a library meeting was much in the air early in 1876, and some prominent librarians had already reacted favorably to such proposals.

According to traditional library history, the 1876 conference wheels were set in motion at a meeting in New York on May 17-18, 1876, in the offices of Frederick Leypoldt, editor and publisher of *Publishers' Weekly*.[20] Leypoldt, an indefatigable promotor of bibliographical work, had begun publishing notes on libraries in the first number of his journal in 1872, had published a special "Library Number" in October of the same year, and in January, 1876, had begun a regular department called "Library and Bibliographical Notes." An idealist infected with the same sort of enthusiasm as Dewey, Leypoldt saw libraries as important agencies in book distribution. In his perusal of foreign journals, he had noted the suggestion of an anonymous correspondent of the London *Academy,* for March 18, 1876, that an international congress of librarians would be very productive. Almost a month later, in the April 22 issue of *Publishers' Weekly,* Leypoldt published the *Academy* letter in its entirety. At the same time the Boston Athenaeum librarian, Charles Ammi Cutter, noted the suggestion with approval in the April 20 issue of *The Nation.*

During late April and early May, Leypoldt and his partner, Richard Rodgers Bowker, apparently discussed various methods of library co-operation and Bowker turned his attention to writing an editorial on the subject for the May 20 issue of *Publishers' Weekly.* Just as the issue was about ready to go to press, Melvil Dewey, "a library enthusiast from the Amherst College Library," to use Leypoldt's phrase, appeared in New York to discuss his proposed *American Library Journal.* Since he had already entertained the thought of establishing a separate library periodical, Leypoldt immediately became interested in the new journal which Dewey had already planned with the Ginn brothers of Boston. He and Bowker discussed with Dewey how they could merge their interests in such an undertaking. Leypoldt told Dewey that they had been preparing an editorial urging a library conference for their library number, which was now ready for the press. Dewey heartily seconded the idea of a conference and said he had already talked with Justin Winsor and other Boston librarians concerning such co-operation. He thought they would be happy to assist.[21]

Somewhat peculiarly in view of Dewey's later assertions that he had been thinking about a library conference for from one to three years, there is no evidence in the transcription of the Dewey diaries from January 1, 1875, through June 11, 1876, indicating any concern with such a conference before this May 17 meeting with Bowker and Leypoldt. Admittedly this is an argument from silence, though one wonders why, if the conference idea were such a major part of Dewey's thinking, it was absent from his record of personal activities. Certainly other

Dewey proposals such as metric reform, simplified spelling, the library journal, and classification, all received attention. Dewey did hold numerous discussions with Boston librarians in April and May, 1876, and the conference idea may have been included in their conversations. The question which has to be asked is whether or not the idea was expressed in more than general terms prior to the meeting with Bowker and Leypoldt. I personally think not. Bowker later stated that the conference idea came partly from the 1853 Conference and partly from the favorable response to the recently formed American Book Trade Association in which Leypoldt was actively engaged. The editorial in the first issue of the *American Library Journal* also gives credit for the conference idea to the May meeting and the 1853 Conference. Since this is the document closest to the actual date, its statement should be given the highest consideration.

Neither Leypoldt nor Bowker has received as much credit for the origin of the Conference as they are due. They were essentially modest men, who provided the quiet background support necessary for the success of any new venture, while Dewey was never reluctant to claim his full share of the credit for 1876. The only point which would bring Bowker charging to the defense was the thought that the *Library Journal* was the product of the Conference and the Association. As he so rightly insisted, it was the other way around. Neither was he willing to give Dewey all the credit for the *Journal,* which he maintained was an older idea discussed by him and Leypoldt. When Bowker was having difficulty with Dewey over the publication of the *Library Journal* a year and a half later, he wrote Cutter, "As to ed. relations, I have opposed not at all his equality but the supremacy he claims, on the ground that D. alone originated the *Journal.* He deserves full credit for the Conf., the Conv. the splendid advances made in library arrangements—much, but not *all,* for the *Journal,* wh. was an old idea of Mr. L. and myself, too."[22] If Bowker felt especially sensitive on this point, he had a right to be; Bowker and Leypoldt insured the *Library Journal's* success by subsidizing its deficits for the first ten years of its existence. Still, his courtesy was always apparent, even when he felt he must disagree; and he was frequently willing to forego his own share of the credit.

Except for the massive Bureau of Education report, which cites Williams' letter, all subsequent published literature refers to this May 17-18 meeting as the beginning step in the formation of the American Library Association. In a very real sense this is true, although it is not the whole story. In addition to the background already described above, there were other significant influences which played their part.

Having decided to join forces, the three individuals, two from the book trade and one from the library world, drew up the proof of a call for a library conference which they sent to several eastern librarians, while telegrams were dispatched to W. F. Poole at Chicago, Charles Evans at Indianapolis, and Thomas Vickers at Cincinnati.[23] This preliminary document asked approval of various chief librarians for the calling of a meeting in Philadelphia on August 15, 1876, or on such other date as might be generally acceptable. This "proof" was signed by Leypoldt, Dewey, W. I. Fletcher of the Watkinson Library (unauthorized), and L. E. Jones.

On May 19, Dewey journeyed to Philadelphia, where he saw Commissioner of Education John Eaton, who agreed to participate in the venture and placed the facilities of the Bureau at Dewey's disposal in sending out the official call. Strong initial reaction to such a document might well have been anticipated. There were many librarians who were immediately enthusiastic. Among these were the youngsters such as Charles Evans at Indianapolis (then 25) and William T. Peoples of the New York Mercantile Library (then 33), although one of the oldest, Lloyd P. Smith of Philadelphia, came quickly into the camp.

Yet the response of the library leaders, those with influence and power, could at best be described as lukewarm. Justin Winsor, later to be president of the American Library Association for its first ten years, noted that he was willing to do anything helpful for the library cause; but he did not think that he could make it to Philadelphia in a centennial August. Spofford's attitude as Librarian of Congress has already been made clear; and Poole, who had never heard of Dewey, wrote Winsor, "It won't pay for you and me to attend that barbecue."[24] In short, the real leaders were not going to be hoodwinked by a wild-eyed young radical and a couple of tradesmen from the publishers' association.

Youth and age have traditionally been at odds with each other, and the library profession is no exception. In a report on the second library conference held in New York City in 1877, *The World* (New York), published the following:

As in all conventions, a slight division is apparent.

The party of young librarians was eager for the adoption of Continental methods, for decapitalization in the French style, and uniformity of labels, indexes and calendars, to which the conservative majority gave guarded encouragemе .t. To hear the frank, mirthful Dewey, editor o ᵗhe *Librarian's Monthly* [sic] or the earnest, enthusι. ᵗic young Tyler, who has stepped from the Astor Library to the head of the rich and growing Johns Hopkins at Baltimore, enlarging on the advantages of omitting all capitals possible in a catalogue of books, one was fain to look upon it as a chief earthly interest, while the emphatic Spofford, who has charge of the Congressional Library, or the deprecatory Homes of Albany, and Poole of Chicago protest against any such neo republicanism of letters and beheading of capitals.[25]

That this situation had also occurred a year earlier was confirmed by William E. Foster, next to Dewey the youngest man at the 1876 Conference. According to Foster the spirit of innovation was not generally acceptable in 1876, and the librarians in convention assembled were certainly not the vanguard.[26]

It was as obvious to Dewey as to anyone else that support from the leaders was essential; but it was equally clear, later, that the conference would not have succeeded without Dewey's youth, energy, and enthusiasm, a fact which Winsor, Poole, and Cutter all acknowledged publicly.[27]

Since Poole subsequently fought Dewey's proposals on a number of occasions, there has arisen the pleasant fiction that Poole was the strongest and possibly the only strong opponent of the convention idea. Such a conception may not be unrelated to Poole's argumentative nature and his vigor in debate on controversial issues. He and Dewey were alike in the certainty that their own view of a problem was the right view. While it is true that Poole was leery of endorsing a conference whose originators he did not know, his opposition has been much overstressed, as his biographer, W. L. Williamson, has pointed out.[28] Not only was he joined by others in the sentiment that librarians should not proceed blindly on such matters, but his postcard of May 31, to Winsor, may well have saved the day for the conference and the association. Poole insisted that he would not sign an official call unless Winsor personally started the whole business anew and promised to attend. His ultimatum had its effect. Once Winsor so promised, Poole sailed into the fray and became one of the most valuable members of the conference planning committee. Years after Poole's death, even while acknowledging his contribution, Dewey related that Poole had a feeling "the movement had one foot in the grave and the other foot on a banana peel."[29] The statement is much too strong. Although Poole did not hesitate to be blunt in his letters, his advice was usually worth heeding; and, once convinced, he was sincerely interested in making the conference a success.[30]

By mid-June enough of the leading librarians had signed the call to warrant its printing and general distribution. Among those who signed were Justin Winsor, Charles Ammi Cutter, John Langdon Sibley of Harvard, S. F. Haven of the American Antiquarian Society, Addison VanName of Yale, Lloyd P. Smith, Henry A. Homes of the New York State Library, and, of course, Poole and Dewey. Leypoldt and L. E. Jones discreetly left their names off the list; and Fletcher's was not included because his boss, J. H. Trumbull, was opposed to the whole idea.[31] This first printed call was forwarded to librarians all over the country, and their responses immediately began to come into the New York office of *Publishers' Weekly*.

Librarians from all types of libraries—private, society, law, medical, theological, free public, the large and the small, and the geographically dispersed—responded to the initial call. Some of the best suggestions came from librarians of the smaller libraries who had looked to the Boston Public Library's *Bulletin* or to correspondence with the major librarians for their guidance. Indicative of the status of these libraries is the fact that they had to contain only 300 volumes to be listed in the government report. Mrs. Emily F. Carnes of Galveston, Texas, of whom practically nothing is known, gave an excellent overview of the problems of the small library. As librarian in a small community (albeit an important one in its region), she was not only isolated from the mainstream of library development but had to battle against the natural inertia of the public. She was not alone. There are other names, such as that of Mrs. H. L. Patterson, librarian of the year-old Muncie, Ind., Public Library, who felt it essential that she attend the conference, but somehow did not make it. Daniel W. Fink, State Law Librarian of Rhode Island, was disappointed that he did not see the names of more law librarians on the printed call, since he thought that they needed cooperation as much as any other group. One wonders if this isn't still true of this group of separatists.

These librarians wanted many topics discussed, but they especially wanted to know what to do about cataloging and classification, indexing magazines, creating other bibliographical tools, and the mutilation and pilfering of library materials.

Classification was far from narrowing down to two basic schemes nor was there anything like general agreement on cataloging rules. With free public libraries springing up all over the country and with academic libraries soon to receive the full impact of the Germanic research emphasis, no topics were to receive more time, thought, and discussion than the classification system or the cataloging rules to be adopted. Both Dewey's classification and Cutter's rules, which appeared later that year,[32] were seminal publications with far-reaching impact upon the profession. Time and again in their plans to attend the conference, the letter writers also urged that the proceedings be published. Those who sent regrets were especially eager to see the data they hoped would be forthcoming.

Soon a conference planning committee was formed with Justin Winsor as chariman, assisted by Lloyd P. Smith and William F. Poole, with Melvil Dewey serving as Conference Secretary. The reason for Poole's insistence upon Winsor as chairman is not difficult to reconstruct. He was unquestionably the leading American librarian in 1876. The vigorous growth of the Boston Public Library and its innovations in library methodology provided inspiration for struggling librarians in less favored circumstances. Moreover, Winsor's scholarly mind thoroughly investigated every situation before he formulated his own principles. His annual reports, with their mass of comparative data on libraries abroad as well as those in America, foreshadowed the report from the Bureau of Education. Indeed when John Eaton decided to investigate the library situation in the country he turned to Winsor for advice and the final product owed much to Winsor's suggestions. Libraries as far away as Tokyo sought his annual reports and bulletins.[33] Winsor was frequently consulted by new library boards. Hence, his name on the conference call was an assurance to most librarians that such a conference would be well worth attending.

In 1876 Winsor was in the prime of life (age 45); a man of dignity and mild manners, he seemed destined to preside over scholarly meetings.[34] When he spoke, his low-pitched voice carried to all corners of the room, and nothing escaped his tireless eyes. Meetings over which he presided were always under complete control. He and Poole were long-time friends and frequently in agreement on the main points at issue. They were *conservatives,* in the best sense of that term, respecting rules but not fearing them. Both had broad knowledge of the management of all types of libraries, but they preferred their own solutions to problems in a given situation and cared little for a rigid conformity among libraries. In his presidential address of 1879, Winsor clearly enunciated the dangers of cooperation as well as its virtues.[35]   Although he was not so argumentative as his older colleague, Poole, he was not a stuffy man either. A subtle sense of humor is revealed in his "A Word to Starters of Libraries," in the first issue of the *American Library Journal* as well as in some of his other writings.[36] Winsor's was a steadying influence and he was always able to maintain a sense of balance in discussions; the fledgling association was fortunate to have him to steer its course for the first ten years.

The local chairman of the committee, Lloyd Pearsall Smith, had followed his father as librarian of the Library Company of Philadelphia. Smith was, as Poole said, "a conservative, and he had a right to be one,"[37] for he headed the oldest continuing library not connected with a college in the country. Since he was a Philadelphia resident and a member of the 1853 Conference, he was the obvious choice for local arrangements. Charles Evans noted that he was "jolly, companionable, and *at home.* "[38] Witty and gracious, Smith impressed all who came into contact with him by his charm. Another member of the conference said of Smith: "His cordial greetings, his kindly interest in everybody and his natural politeness in listening quietly and amiably to all views expressed, including those which his conservative nature and education could not approve, made him a very valuable member of the conference and the Association."[39]

In a period of rapidly expanding public libraries, heavily used by the people, Smith reportedly never accepted their necessity. Dewey related that he had once visited Smith in the recently completed Ridgway Branch in Philadelphia. Expecting to see two or three hundred people, he was surprised to see only three or four and asked Smith if this were the average attendance. Smith responded, "Dewey, there is scarcely a day that *somebody* doesn't come into this library."[40]

Of Poole, perhaps enough has been said to indicate that he was a giant of a man, both physically and mentally. A towering six-footer, like Winsor he wore a beard; but unlike Winsor he had side whiskers which gave him the appearance of the "old rat," an expression Dewey facetiously used to describe him to Bowker.[41] His gruff,

Western manner made him a vigorous opponent in debate, and "plain talk" was his trade-mark.

However, his exterior concealed a kindly spirit; and his genius for friendship among his subordinates made them loyal to him for life. When he read a paper, he had a most benignant manner, and he would pause occasionally to ad lib with the impression of taking the audience into his confidence. Poole had successively been librarian of the Boston Mercantile, Boston Athenaeum, Cincinnati Public, and the Chicago Public libraries. He had trained many apprentices who worked in libraries throughout the country and his periodical index was widely known and appreciated. As Dewey said of him, perhaps in a calculating manner but nonetheless truly, "We can't do without you and feel satisfied. Your name is always mentioned among the very first, and it would look all wrong not to see it in the list we now have."[42]

Few librarians have ever been neutral about the Conference Secretary, Melvil Dewey. The man arouses the strongest emotions pro and con. In the late nineteenth century he had numerous disciples who went forth to spread the missionary word about "securing the best reading for the largest number at the least expense."[43] Through his subsequent editorship of the *Library Journal* and his position as Secretary of the American Library Association, Dewey soon became known as the foremost exponent of modern librarianship. Many of his ideas were subsequently accepted unquestioningly by his disciples. He also aroused annoyance, and sometimes antagonism, among a smaller number. One of Poole's protégés described the uncritical proponents of Dewey's methods as "Dewey-worshippers," while another noted that he had "been so long on the Publishing Board with Mr. Dewey that I have got thoroughly in the habit, when he gets through, of saying something on the other side . . . ."[44] Dewey's son has stated that his father was rarely without a harrassing number of enemies, partly because of his business integrity, but more probably from his occasional failures in tact and patience.[45]

Because of hero-worship, Dewey's position has been somewhat obscured "as it was in the beginning." At the time of the conference Dewey was not quite 25 and apparently the youngest conference member. Like Poole, he was a six-footer, but with a wiry, loose-knit frame and no beard— only sideburns.[46] Alert on his feet, he had a head full of ideas which poured forth rapidly in a high-pitched voice. He had come to Boston, the acknowledged "hub" of the library world, to found a library periodical, a metric bureau, and an organization to reform spelling, all at the same time. Along with this tremendous energy, there was a streak of stubbornness in Dewey; and, if he found his way blocked in one direction, he merely achieved his goal by going another route. He had a strong sense of his own righteousness and could be irritatingly prudish about smoking and other vices of which he disapproved. At the conference during a committee meeting, Smith and Poole stepped out for a smoke. Dewey took the opportunity to ram through his proposals. When Poole subsequently protested the final report, Dewey noted it had been voted on when a minority retired "shall I say it—to smoke."[47]

Yet Dewey's skill and persistence in the office of Conference Secretary represented major contributions to its success. Most of the detailed work of the meeting preparations fell on him; and he performed them well, jotting down his shorthand notes on letters, sending items off to Winsor for concurrence, and prodding the conference committee for decisions. Nor can one fault Dewey on his bold conceptions and his creative vision. With the metric system, spelling reform, and a library conference and journal all teeming in his brain at the same time, only an essentially likeable young man could have succeded in arousing so little antagonism among the naturally conservative leaders of the emerging profession.

Writing to Bowker after the conference, Poole commented, "It is cruel to put so much work upon one person, even if he is a good fellow. Dewey is a remarkable man, and I have become much interested in him."[48] When they had first met at Lloyd P. Smith's house prior to the conference, Poole had come across the parlor, drawn himself up to his full height, and said laughingly, "Well, Dewey, you are a better looking man than I thought you were."[49] As Foster perceptively notes, "both by correspondence and by personal interviews and appeals he succeeded in overcoming the natural inertia of the men most influential in this connection, and in bringing together a representative gathering in October."[50] Despite some exaggerated claims about the conference origin, Melvil Dewey deserves full credit for bringing to fruition an idea which had not gone beyond the discussion stage among his colleagues.

In line with various suggestions, the conference committee changed the date from August 15 to October 4-6 to take advantage of the cooler weather. They accepted an offer from the Historical Society of Pennsylvania to provide meeting rooms without charge. In late July the U. S. Bureau of Education mailed a second printed circular, giving the new date and place of meeting. Some 2,000 copies were sent to librarians in this country and abroad. Meanwhile, Dewey was writing prospective speakers; and, in mid-September, he distributed the program in the form of advance proofs from the first number of the *American Library Journal.* He urged the centennial exhibition as an added attraction for librarians from a distance to make the effort to go to Philadelphia.

The rest is history, and that fairly well reported. On Wednesday morning, October 4, 1876, the Librarians' Conference opened in the halls of the Historical Society of Pennsylvania. The society's president, John William Wallace, gave the opening address; and behind him, seated in a semicircular recess of a bay window, sat the librarians of Philadelphia. Wallace's speech of welcome summarized well the major problems confronting librarians of the day: the need to cope bibliographically with the flood of books, the kind of building to erect, the kind of classification and the direction of the printed catalog, specialized collections, and the need for developing a new science—"BIBLIOTHE-CAL SCIENCE." The conference then proceeded to organize itself, promptly electing Justin Winsor president, and A. R. Spofford, James Yates, William F. Poole, and Lloyd P. Smith vice-presidents. Winsor moved quickly to the appointment of committees and the organization of the conference. Dewey, Evans, and Guild were elected secretaries, an especially important election since Poole had refused to let Dewey hire a stenographer because of the expense.[51] Dewey then asked every librarian to register and reported that he had received a telegram from Samuel R. Warren of the Bureau of Education stating that he had started from Washington for the conference with copies of the government report.

The initial organization took most of the morning; but when the conference reassembled at 3 p.m., it began a furious pace which "horrified the reporters" and later horrified the secretaries, who had to prepare the proceedings for issuance as a double number of the *American Library Journal.*

Dewey called attention to the burden this put upon the secretaries in his report: "The absence of a stenographer encouraged freedom of debate, but it put upon the secretaries and editors a Herculean task in the after-gathering of the *disjecta membra.* Most of the speakers have been furnished with a minute of the details in which they took part, and requested to write out their remarks; the results have been worked, revised, and reworked into shape, in consultation with several officers. This method approximates accuracy, but it has caused great delay . . . . " That the secretaries were highly successful is apparent from "The Proceedings."[52] Eleven formal papers were delivered, beginning with that of Poole on "Some Popular Objections to Libraries." Following each paper there was lengthy discussion which called forth diverse opinions as well as the testimony of personal experience.

Of the 103 who registered, 90 were men and 13 were women, a ratio of the sexes which was later almost to reverse itself. Seventeen states were represented, although the largest attendance was from the East Coast, with the South not being represented at all. Among the non-librarians present were Dr. Daniel Read, retired president of the University of Missouri, and Henry Barnard, educator, of Hartford, Connecticut. Although most of the leading librarians were there, several distinguished names were missing. None of the Harvard librarians attended, nor did anyone from St. Louis. Both Haven of the American Antiquarian Society and John Shaw Billings of the Surgeon-General's Library could not be present but they did send personal representatives.

There were a variety of libraries represented, including 13 from academic libraries, 43 from private, subscription or special libraries, and 24 from free public libraries.[53] However, even though the public librarians were in the minority, it was they who controlled the convention and who notably advanced the Association which came out of it. Moreover, as Boromé has pointed out, while there were conservatives and liberals, visionaries and standpatters, the librarians at Philadelphia were "positive individuals who had entered upon their calling by choice."[54] They were not school teachers who couldn't teach, lawyers incapable of practicing, nor clergymen whose only merit was "that bronchitis was a demerit in their original

calling."[55]   In short, they were professionals, with a strong sense of professional responsibility, who wanted their place in the educational sun.

One cannot resist noting that—whether the profession has advanced so little in the past 90 years or whether basic problems tend to persist from generation to generation—the Association is still debating some of the same issues raised by the conference. Indeed, the beginning librarian might well be given the excellent address of John William Wallace as an admirable summary of contemporary problems. Perhaps it is true that the more things change the more they remain the same.

On the third day of the conference came the call to form a permanent organization. All of those who wanted to join the new Association were urged to sign the register. The irrepressible Dewey, with characteristic flourish, took the book and wrote, "Number one, Melvil Dewey."[56] He then passed it to Charles Evans who signed as number two. Before the end of the year a total of 41 persons had joined the fledgling Association. The following year saw the membership rise to 110, and by the end of 1878 it had reached 197.[57] Although it was at least a decade before the Association could be said to be on a sound footing, the profession never lost that initial momentum. Unlike the 1853 conference, the Library Conference of 1876 really sparked a movement.

According to the latest report, membership in the American Library Association reached 34,754 at the end of 1966. As Mr. Dewey prophesied so well in the *American Library Journal:*

> Of the permanent results of the Conference, the organization of the American Library Association must be put first, because this means the frequent repetition of the Conference; a recognized authority which may promote or endorse desirable improvements, and furnish decisions on the many points at issue in which prospective general usage is the sufficient criterion; and otherwise a chance to reap the benefits of organized co-operation.[58]

FOOTNOTES

Editors note. The following abbreviations are used in the footnotes for this article:

AAS	American Antiquarian Society
AL	Autograph letter
ALA	American Library Association
ALJ	*American Library Journal*
ALS	Autograph letter signed
BPL	Boston Public Library
CUL	Columbia University Libraries
IUL	University of Illinois Library
Lbk	Letterbook

LJ   *Library Journal*
LS   Letter signed
NYPL New York Public Library
PW   *Publishers' Weekly*
TD   Typed document

[1] *Allan Nevins*, The Emerging of Modern America, 1865-1876 *("History of American Life," Vol. VIII), (New York: Macmillan, 1927), ch. xi, "Two Memorable Years: 1873 and 1876," esp. p. 317.*

[2] *The phrases come from the first and second printed calls* "For a Library Conference" *printed in 1876.*

[3] *As quoted by Dewey, "The American Library Association," ALJ, 1 (March 31, 1877), [245]-246. The first volume was called* American Library Journal, *but at the end of the year "American" was dropped from the title to reflect its international scope.*

[4] *Henry R. Tedder, "Introduction," p. [ix] and John Winter Jones, "Inaugural Address," p. [1], Conference of Librarians, London, 1877,* Transactions and Proceedings *(London: Chiswick Press, 1878).*

[5] *U. S. Department of the Interior, Bureau of Education,* Public Libraries in the United States of America; Their History, Condition, and Management, *Special Report, pts. 1 and 2 (Washington: Government Printing Office, 1876), cited hereafter as* Public Libraries in the U. S., *1876.*

[6] *Richard R. Bowker, "Seed Time and Harvest—The Story of the A.L.A.,"* A.L.A. Bulletin, *20 (Oct., 1926), 304.*

[7] *Spofford to Leypoldt,* ALS, *May 29, 1876.*

[8] Ibid.

[9] *Dewey, "Past, Present, and Future of the A.L.A.,"* LJ, *5 (Sept.-Oct., 1880) 274.*

[10] *George B. Utley*, The Librarian's Conference of 1853; A Chapter in American Library History *(Chicago: American Library Association, 1951), pp. 10-15.*

[11] Ibid., *pp. 131-132, reproduces the printed call.*

[12] *Poole, "Address of the President,"* LJ, *II (July, 1886), 199-200.*

[13] *Utley, op, cit., pp. 84, 99-101.*

[14] *Arthur M. Schlesinger*, The Rise of the City, 1878-1898 *("A History of American Life," Vol. X), (New York: Macmillan, 1933), ch. vii, "Increasing the World's Knowledge," esp. pp. 220-222. Arthur E. Bestor, Jr., "The Transformation of American Scholarship, 1875-1917,"* Library Quarterly, *23 (July, 1953), 173-174.*

[15] *Bowker, "A Postscript,"* LJ, *21 (Feb., 1896), 52. For Dewey's later comments see Dewey, "What the* A.L.A. Was Meant to Be and to Do," *Wisconsin Library Bulletin, 13 (Feb., 1917), 41-42.*

[16] *Williams to Eaton, copy of letter dated incorrectly Aug. 3, 1876, Minneapolis Athenaeum. Eaton to Williams, Lbk, Feb. 7, 1876, National Archives.*

[17] *Eaton to Williams, Lbk, Feb. 7, 1876, National Archives.*

[18] Public Libraries in the U. S., *1876, p. xxvii.*

[19] *Eaton to Winsor, LS, July 2, 1875, Superintendent's File, BPL.*

[20] *This fairly standard story can be found in numerous articles by Bowker and is well summarized in Jay W. Beswick,* The Work of Frederick Leypoldt, Bibliographer and Publisher *(New York: R. R. Bowker Co., 1942), pp. 51-58. See also Frederic M. Melcher, "Among the Founders," LJ, 76 (Dec. 1, 1951), 1960; and E. McClung Fleming,* R. R. Bowker: Militant Liberal *(Norman: University of Oklahoma Press, 1952), pp. 57-58.*

[21] *Dewey, "Dairy," no. 5, May 18, 1876, Dewey Papers, CUL.*

[22] *Bowker to Cutter, Lbk, Jan. 3, 1878, Bowker Papers, NYPL.*

[23] *Bowker stated that he wrote the circular letter and the telegrams sent to the leading librarians. Bowker, "The* Library Journal *and Library Organizations: A Twenty Years' Retrospect," LJ, 21 (Jan., 1896), 5.*

[24] *Poole to Winsor, postcard, signed, May 31, 1876, Superintendent's File, BPL.*

[25] *The Librarians' Convention," The World (New York), Sept. 7, 1877, p. 5, col. I.*

[26] *Foster, "Five Men of '76,"* A.L.A. Bulletin, *20 (Oct., 1926), 320.*

[27] *Winsor, "The President's Address,"* LJ, *2 (Sept., 1877), 6; Poole, "Address of the President," LJ, 11 (July, 1886), 201; Cutter "Cooperation Committee," LJ, 4 (July-Aug., 1879), 287.*

[28] *William L. Williamson*, William Frederick Poole and the Modern Library Movement *("Columbia University Studies in Library Service," no. 13), (New York: Columbia University Press, 1963), ch vii.*

[29] *Dewey, "Our Next Half-Century,"* A.L.A. Bulletin, *20 (Oct., 1926), 309-310.*

[30] *Poole's own defense is summed up in his letter to Dewey, ALS, Dec. 28, 1883, Dewey Papers, CUL.*

[31] *Poole to Winsor, ALS, Sept. 18, 1876, Superintendent's File, BPL.*

[32] *[Dewey]*, A Classification and Subject Index for Cataloguing and Arranging the Books and Pamphlets of a Library *(Amherst, Mass., 1876), 42 pp. Dewey's preface is dated June 10, 1876. Charles Ammi Cutter,* Rules for a Printed Dictionary Catalogue *(Washington: Government Printing Office, 1876), 89 pp., pt. II of* Public Libraries in the U. S., *1876.*

[33] *Joseph A. Boromé, "The Life and Letters of Justin Winsor," (Unpublished Ph.D. dissertation, Columbia University, 1950), pp. 218-224.*

[34] *Description of Winsor is from Boromé, "Life and Letters of Justin Winsor," passim; Foster, "Five Men of '76," A.L.A. Bulletin, 20 (Oct., 1926), 313-314; Samuel Swett Green,* The Public Library Movement in the United States, 1853-1893 *... (Boston: The Boston Book Company, 1913), pp. 25-30; and "The Librarian's Convention," The World (New York), Sept. 7, 1877, p. 5, col. 1.*

[35] *Winsor, "The President's Address,"* LJ, *2 (Sept., 1877), [5]-7.*

[36] Winsor, "A Word to Starters of Libraries," ALJ, 1 (Sept. 30, 1876), 1-3.

[37] Poole, "Address of the President," LJ, 11 (July, 1886), 204.

[38] Evans to Dewey, postcard, signed, June 24, 1876.

[39] Green, Public Library Movement, p. 39. The description of Smith is largely from Green's book.

[40] Dewey, "Our Next Half-Century," A.L.A. Bulletin, 20 (Oct., 1926), 309.

[41] Dewey to Bowker, LS, Oct. 24, 1876, Bowker Papers, NYPL. The description of Poole is from Williamson, William Frederick Poole, passim; Green, Public Library Movement, pp. 30-34; his letters and the early proceedings of the American Library Association.

[42] Dewey to Poole, June 5, 1876, as quoted in Poole to Dewey, ALS, Dec. 28, 1883, Dewey Papers, CUL.

[43] Dewey, "The American Library Association," ALJ, 1 (March 31, 1877), 247.

[44] Mary Abbie Bean to Charles Evans, ALS, Aug. 10, 1890, Evans Papers, IUL. W. I. Fletcher, "Proceedings," LJ, 26 (1901), c139.

[45] Godfrey Dewey, "Dewey, 1851-1951," LJ, 76 (Dec. 1, 1951), 1964.

[46] Descriptions of Dewey from a variety of sources including Foster, "Five Men of '76," A.L.A. Bulletin, 20 (Oct., 1926), 318-320; Fremont Rider, Melvil Dewey (Chicago: A.L.A., 1944), passim, as well as his diaries, letters, and published materials in the early LJ.

[47] ALJ, 1 (Nov. 30, 1876), 140.

[48] Poole to Bowker, ALS, Nov. 14, 1876, Bowker Papers, NYPL.

[49] Dewey at the Lake Placid Conference, LJ, 19 (Dec., 1894), 170.

[50] Foster, "Five Men of '76," A.L.A. Bulletin, 20 (Oct., 1926), 319.

[51] Poole to Dewey, postcard, signed, Sept. 18, 1876.

[52] "The Proceedings," ALJ, 1 (Nov. 30, 1876), 91-45.

[53] Williamson, "William Frederick Poole and the Modern Library Movement," (Unpublished dissertation, University of Chicago, 1959), pp. 363-365, is the source of this analysis.

[54] Boromé, "Life and Letters of Justin Winsor," p. 241.

[55] Winsor, "Free Libraries and Readers," ALJ, 1 (Nov. 30, 1876), 67.

[56] William Stetson Merrill, "Early Days at the Newberry Library: Reminiscences of Persons and Events, 1889 to 1894," typewritten MS, Oconomowoc, Wis., March 15, 1954, p. 23 verso, in Newberry Library, Chicago.

[57] American Library Association, "Membership List, Including Register of Members Present at Boston and Other Conferences," printed list bound with LJ, 4 (1879), but probably published separately.

[58] [Dewey, "Editorial"], ALJ, 1 (Nov. 30, 1876), 90-91.

Historical Development of Education for Librarianship in the United States

Louis R. Wilson

Formal education for librarianship is a product of the last decade of the nineteenth century. Before that librarians had gained their training in an apprentice system. Nineteenth century America spawned a complex of social, economic and intellectual forces which contributed to the rise of the professional schools. The rapid development of public and academic libraries with their concomitant need for trained staffs, the rise of the university, and the growth of professional schools in allied fields signaled the end of apprenticeship training for librarianship.

In the following essay, Louis R. Wilson outlines the pivotal developments in American library education. Dr. Wilson was dean of the University of Chicago Library School, and a principal actor in the unfolding drama of which he writes.

Education for librarianship has maintained a prominent place in the thought of American librarians from the first meeting of the American Library Association in 1876. It took concrete form in 1883 when Melvil Dewey outlined his proposal for a school of library economy at Columbia. A committee was appointed to consider the subject of education for librarianship in general as well as the specific proposal made by Dewey.

From that date to the present, the American Library Association has not been without a committee on library training. At first it was a special committee. In 1903 it became a standing committee and was required to submit a report annually. In 1923, upon the recommendation of this committee, a Temporary Library Training Board was appointed. The Temporary Training Board was succeeded in 1924 by the Board of Education for Librarianship, which was charged with the responsibility of considering all problems incident to the professional training of the men and women who were to administer the libraries of the nation. That Board still operates today on the major concerns of library education.

During 1947-48 the subject of "Education for Librarianship" has been considered at conferences held on the Pacific Coast, in the South, in the Midwest, and in the East. Now the Graduate Library School renews consideration of this topic. My assignment in this discussion is to comment upon what I consider the most important movements, events, and influences that have characterized the development of this field. I have selected ten of these factors for consideration here.

THE FIRST SCHOOL AT COLUMBIA

The first important step in this development was the establishment of a School of Library Economy at Columbia in 1887. Melvil Dewey presented the proposal for such a school at the meeting of the American Library Association in 1883, and spent four years in developing the plan for it and in overcoming the opposition of the faculty and trustees of Columbia to it.

Two significant decisions were involved in the establishment of this first school. American librarians, after full and careful consideration, decided in favor of educating librarians through a professional school in preference to apprenticeship in libraries; and they approved a thoroughly practical curriculum embodying best practice, with little consideration of theoretical studies.

Both of these decisions have had important consequences, the effects of which are still evident. As a result of the first decision, the foundation for the present system of library schools was firmly established, as contrasted with the English system of apprenticeship which continued unbroken until 1919 and is still preferred by many English librar-

SOURCE: Reprinted from Louis R. Wilson, "Historical Development of Education for Librarianship in the United States," in Bernard Berelson, ed., *Education for Librarianship* (Chicago: American Library Association, 1949), pp. 44-59, by permission of the author and publisher. Copyright ©1949 by the American Library Association.

ians. Even though the curriculum was severely practical and limited, it was developed systematically, and afforded the student an opportunity of mastering in a minimum of time the various subjects embraced in the curriculum and of seeing them through an over-all and unified perspective impossible through apprenticeship in a single library. To this decision, more than to any other one thing, may be attributed America's acknowledged leadership in the field of modern library procedures.

This Conference, like the conferences at Berkeley, Urbana, Atlanta, Chicago, and New York during the past year, is concerned with the second decision. It is confronted with the problem of developing curricula not conceived of in the framework of the scheme adopted by Dewey, and largely followed until the late 1920's. It is attempting to formulate, outside that framework, programs of study that will be truly professional and will nicely articulated in their entire structure, from undergraduate and preprofessional studies through the strictly professional and graduate levels.

THE ASSOCIATION OF AMERICAN LIBRARY SCHOOLS

The second important step was the establishment in 1915 of the Association of American Library Schools. This organization, following the example of similar professional schools in other fields, was set up with the expectation of shaping educational policy in librarianship. It deepened the professional consciousness of those engaged in the administration of the schools and it established certain standards which other schools were expected to meet and to maintain in order to become members. Its effectiveness, however, was severely limited, and continues to be limited, although its membership now includes all schools accredited by the American Library Association, some of whose faculties are demonstrating marked ability in the development of significant programs of study.

The importance of the organization derives from its potentialities rather than its past accomplishments. What it may accomplish in the future will depend upon whether it will bring its collective thinking to bear seriously upon its problems, work out appropriate solutions, and adopt new procedures which will insure a sound program of professional training. Failure to do this in the past may be largely attributed to lack of funds to insure

meetings of the Association and its committees apart from the meetings of the American Library Association; absorption of the interest of the directors (who were also directors of libraries) in the programs of the American Library Association; lack of familiarity of the faculties, particularly in the early period, with the procedures of other faculties and of other professional educational associations in dealing with the problems of formulating and enforcing standards; and, since 1926, the automatic admission of all schools accredited by the Board of Education for Librarianship to membership in the Association without the stimulating experience of re-examining standards and applying them in the accreditation of new schools and of assuming responsibility for constantly exploring the field. The Association has also been a closed organization and has lacked the infiltration of points of view which stem from contacts with other bodies and individuals. For these reasons, the Association has been largely unable to exercise influence in the development of professional objectives and standards with anything like the comparable results secured by other professional associations such as those in the fields of medicine, law, engineering, commerce, and social work. Perhaps the future will witness a strengthening of its role in library education.

NEXT STEPS IN THE 1920's

Education for librarianship underwent extensive professional reorganization and experienced a new degree of financial support in the 1920's. Several movements contributed to this end. Three stand out as particularly important and constitute the third, fourth, and fifth events to which attention will now be directed.

The first grew out of a paper read by C. C. Williamson at the Asbury Park meeting of the American Library Association in 1919 on "Some Present-Day Aspects of Library Training." In this paper Williamson proposed a better-organized system of library training agencies under the supervision of a library training board which would adopt standards and regulate the certification of librarians. This was the central idea which he carried into his studies of all types of library training for the Carnegie Corporation from 1919 to 1921, and elaborated in September, 1923, in his famous report on "Training for Library Service."[1]

The second grew out of two related actions taken by the American Library Association in 1920 and 1923 before the Williamson Report was published. In fact, they largely prepared the way for the discussion and acceptance of his report. They were the appointment in 1920 of a National Board of Certification for Librarians and the discussion of its studies and reports during the next two years; and the adoption of a recommendation of the Committee on Library Training in April 1923 that a Temporary Board on Library Training be appointed "to investigate the field of library training, to formulate tentative standards for all forms of library training agencies, to devise a plan for accrediting such agencies, and to report to the Council."

The third movement grew out of the decision made in the first half of the 1920's by the Carnegie Corporation of New York to project a comprehensive program of library development, including education for librarianship, which assumed the form of what came to be known as the "Ten-Year Program of Library Service," and which resulted in the expenditure of approximately five million dollars, much of which was for the support of various aspects of education for librarianship.

These three movements were so far reaching in their influence that they merit separate consideration.

THE WILLIAMSON REPORT

The Williamson Report was the first to make itself felt. Williamson spent considerable time visiting the existing library schools and carefully studying all aspects of education for librarianship. Trained in the field of political science, and experienced as a municipal reference librarian and director of the information service of the Rockefeller Foundation, he was able to view the schools objectively and critically. His analysis of the status of library school faculties, budgets, curricula, and students revealed a situation wholly unflattering. His prescription for the improvement of the condition of the schools included recommendations that they become integral parts of universities; that their staffs contain a high percentage of full-time instructors chosen for distinction in ability and training; that the first year of study be general and basic; that there be a sharp differentiation between professional and clerical studies, with the latter largely eliminated; that specialization be reserved for the second and third years; that financial support be substantially increased; and that a national examining board be created to formulate requirements concerning library training in general and to pass upon the credentials of library school graduates.

Here was a bold, penetrating analysis that defined the professional field, described the serious limitations within it, pointed out the possibilities of improvement through advanced study and investigation, and, in a very real sense, charted the possible course for a sound development within the field. The report was widely discussed, and, as a result in part of the preceding studies and discussions by the American Library Association of certification and training, many of the recommendations were carried out later at Columbia, under Dr. Williamson's direction, and at many other library schools.

THE BOARD OF EDUCATION FOR LIBRARIANSHIP

The importance of the work of the Temporary Library Training Board and its successor, the Board of Education for Librarianship, from 1923 to 1933, is probably less generally recognized and understood by the present generation of librarians than that of the Board during the past fifteen years. In this recent period, due to reduced personnel and more limited funds, the Board has concerned itself largely with routine; only occasionally has it undertaken special studies or large-scale operations like those carried on during its first decade. Among the accomplishments of the Board were: the visiting of each school by several of its members, with an over-all discussion of the school's administrative organization, staff, financial support, and curriculum; the preparation of minimum standards for different types of schools and their accreditation; the publication of textbooks prepared under its direction for the use of library school students and librarians generally; the encouragement of the establishment of schools in certain areas and the discouragement of others that seemed ill-advised; the allocation of funds made available by the Carnegie Corporation for the support of existing schools; the recommendation of endowment for new schools; the establishment of the American Library School in Paris; the provision of fellowships for librarians and prospective librarians; and, in 1933, the changing of its standards from a quantitative to a qualitative basis.

In this work the Board brought the schools face to face with the meeting of standards imposed by an outside agency. It discussed conditions affecting the schools with administrative officers of the universities with which the schools were connected. It recommended budgets to be provided by institutions contemplating the establishment of schools. It conferred with the Association of American Universities concerning degrees to be awarded upon the completion of the various curricula. And in 1933 it changed its standards from a quantitative to a qualitative basis in order to give greater flexibility to the schools in setting up special objectives and engaging more generally in experimental programs.

Naturally this kind of activity evoked criticism and opposition. The Second Activities Committee in 1930 reported that the work of the Board had elicited more criticism, mostly adverse, than any other organization within the Association. The Board responded spiritedly. It stated that the inspection and the accreditation or nonaccreditation of schools was a difficult task to perform; and that measuring the effectiveness of the schools and classifying them accordingly naturally led to differences of opinion and, in some instances, to pointed resentment. In general, the profession rallied to the Board's support, some of the critics reversing themselves to the extent of suggesting that greater financial support be given the Board in order that it might carry on its work more effectively.

This kind of activity involved the Board in certain mistakes. At the beginning, it lacked some of the familiarity that present library school faculties have with admission requirements; university organization and procedures; undergraduate, graduate, and professional curricula; and the attitude of graduate faculties concerning professional studies and degrees. A case in point is to be noted in the Board's dealing with the Association of American Universities concerning the degree to be awarded upon the completion of the fifth year, devoted to professional study. The Board accepted the ruling of the Association that a certificate or a second Bachelor's degree be awarded instead of a professional or Master's degree. Acceptance of this ruling in 1926 has been responsible for much of the confusion concerning the proper content of the preprofessional, professional, and graduate-professional curriculum and for salary discrimination against holders of second Bachelor's degrees, since it was not clear what the degree stood for. Nevertheless, the Board set up a program to the effectiveness of which the Williamson Report and the grants of the Carnegie Corporation greatly contributed. In fact, it largely provided the framework within which the schools have carried on for the past quarter century.

THE TEN-YEAR PROGRAM OF LIBRARY SERVICE OF THE CARNEGIE CORPORATION

The Ten-Year Program of the Carnegie Corporation helped make possible the implementation of the recommendations of Williamson and of the Board of Education for Librarianship. The Corporation provided funds for the Williamson study and it financed in large measure the program of the Board of Education for Librarianship during its most active period. It aided in merging the library schools of the New York State and the New York Public libraries at Columbia in 1925, and contributed $25,000 annually to the support of that school from 1925 to 1935. During the same period it contributed a similar amount annually to other then-established schools upon recommendations made by the Board, and at the end of the ten-year period it distributed the million-dollar principal among them in the form of endowments. It likewise provided for the establishment of the library school for Negroes at Hampton Institute and the School of Library Science at the University of North Carolina. And in 1926, upon the recommendation of the Board and the Chicago Library Club, it made available funds for the establishment and endowment of the Graduate Library School at the University of Chicago. In 1929, after the re-establishment of the School of Library Service at Columbia and the provision for advanced study there, at Chicago, and at the universities of California, Illinois, and Michigan, it established a number of fellowships from which in the following decade 93 librarians benefited.

THE ESTABLISHMENT OF THE GRADUATE LIBRARY SCHOOL

The establishment of the Graduate Library School at the University of Chicago may be considered as the sixth event in the historical sequence. In 1925 the Carnegie Corporation issued its famous Office Memo called the "Ten-Year Program in Library Service." This memorandum followed the report of Williamson, the report of the Temporary Library Training Board, the appointment of the Board of Education for Librarianship, and the publication of Larned's *The American Public Library and the Diffusion of Knowledge* in 1924. This program involved the expenditure of $5,000,000. One of the items included in it was, as President Keppel phrased it, "an allotment of one million dollars to make possible a graduate library school of a new type which could occupy for the librarian's profession a position analogous to that of the Harvard Law School or the Johns Hopkins Medical School."

Wheeler, in his *Progress and Problems in Education for Librarianship*, says: "The foundling of the Graduate Library School . . . may well turn out to be of greater influence on library training and on librarianship than the publishing of the Williamson Report in 1923 or the establishment of the Board of Education for Librarianship in 1924." Miss Howe, in her *Two Decades of Education for Librarianship*, remarks that the School fully met the criterion that it was to be "an integral part of a university which meets the standards for graduate study laid down by the Association of American Universities."

Whether the statements made in the Office Memo by President Keppel or these statements by Mr. Wheeler or Miss Howe have been realized, it is probably too soon to say. Nevertheless, its establishment stands out as one of the most significant developments in the history of education for librarianship in America and may be commented on at some length, since the conclusion of the twentieth year of its operation is being celebrated at this meeting.

This significance is to be seen in several facts. The first was the composition of its initial faculty. Contrary to the expectation of the profession, it was drawn in large measure from disciplines other than that of librarianship. Its head was drawn from the fields of higher and rural education. His principal contact with libraries had come through a survey of college and university libraries. A second member was an expert educational investigator, with a special penchant for investigation of the sociological and psychological aspects of reading. A third was a historian with a brilliant record in the field of medieval scholarship, one of whose major works deals with medieval libraries. A fourth, with a special interest in Arabic manuscripts, had grown up in the University of Michigan library, had taken his Doctor's degree in a theological seminary, and had come to the School via service in the reorganization of the Vatican Library and the study of American college libraries for the Carnegie Corporation. Of the three other members of the staff prior to 1932, one had come from library school and extensive graduate training, another had long and varied library experience, and another held a Doctor's degree from a theological seminary and had served as an expert on rare books in the Newberry Library. When I came to the headship of the School in 1932, only one member of the then existing staff had come up through the regular channels of library schools and work in a public library. The "irregularity" of the groups was seemingly so glaring to the strictly library-minded members of the profession that it was not until the Board of Education had changed from quantitative to qualitative standards in 1933 that I dared submit the application of the School to it for inspection and accreditation!

The value inherent in this unusual situation was fourfold. Here was a staff, several of whose members were familiar with the curricula and procedures of professional schools in other fields; it was untrammeled by the crystallized form of the prevailing curriculum of education for librarianship; it was acquainted with the fields of bibliography, history, education, psychology, and sociology upon which librarianship could and must draw for its enrichment; and it was extensively trained in scientific methods of graduate study and research. The effect produced upon the library profession was similar to that of shock which is sometimes essential in bringing back to reality the sufferer from amnesia and other mental disorders. In this instance, the shock was desirable to jar the profession out of its prolonged devotion to the practical techniques set up by Dewey and at no time thereafter wholly satisfactorily departed from.

A second value was the separation of the head of the School from the administration of the university library. A program of advanced study, investigation, and publication had to be set up. An effective staff had to be organized, and leadership and guidance had to be provided for graduate students in a new and undeveloped field. This called for the full time, energy, and thought of the head, and for freedom from the innumerable decisions which the administrator of a large university library must make daily. Freedom from such interruptions was essential in order that the dean could devote such time as was necessary to the consideration of the "changing needs of librarianship" and to the formulation of a program suitable to meet them.

These were initial values. Others have accrued throughout the years. At the head of the latter may be placed the development of a critical, scientific attitude in the School's students. They have been taught to challenge unproven assumptions, to devise experimental techniques for the solution of unsolved problems, and to reach conclusions only after thorough examination and testing.

The School has also developed an extended series of important library publications. Its series, *Studies in Library Science*, now contains more than thirty volumes, many of which have been notable in the advancement of various phases of librarianship. *The Library Quarterly* has regularly published the results of extensive investigations and its reviews have critically appraised the important literature of librarianship and related subjects.

Through its teaching and publications the School has likewise contributed to the development of a philosophy of librarianship, the lack of which had long been decried. Munthe, in writing of Butler's *An Introduction to Library Science,* published in 1933,[2] said "Dr. Butler employs a universally valid process of philosophical reasoning in an attempt to show it is impossible to understand a social institution like the library without scientific investigation of the social, psychological, and historical problems that attach themselves to it . . . Butler's little book is the first attempt at a scientific synthesis of library science in its various aspects, and a step on the road toward a philosophy of librarianship. Some day it may rank among the classics of the library profession."

This was a first step in the formulation of a philosophy of librarianship. J. H. Wellard, in his *Book Selection, Its Principles and Practice*[3] and *The Public Library Comes of Age,*[4] has taken a second step. He set the library in its relation to the history, literature, bibliography, psychology, and sociology. He gathered up the results of many of the studies of the School and worked them into a sustained synthesis that may well be studied by all students who would understand the bases upon which the public library movement in America and England rests.

The School's publications have contributed another factor of importance to the acceptance of librarianship as a scholarly professional discipline. They have clarified the field of librarianship and have made it understandable to scholars in other fields. Munthe, in writing of Joeckel's *The Government of the American Public Library,*[5] said: "One might be tempted to say this treatise alone is sufficient documentary evidence in justifying the existence of the School." *A Metropolitan Library in Action*, by Joeckel and Carnovsky,[6] and *The Chicago Public Library, Origins and Background,* by Spencer,[7] evoked the interest and commendation of the historian and political scientist as well as of the student of American social institutions. Illustrations might be drawn of the impact of other publications and studies upon

other fields, particularly of the publications growing out of previous conferences like this one, but these are sufficient for the purpose of showing how librarianship has been enriched, and how other disciplines have profited from this activity of the School.

Skepticism as to the value of the Doctorate in librarianship has also been reduced, certainly in university and research libraries if not in public libraries, owing to the leadership and accomplishments of graduates of the School. Wheeler bears testimony to this fact; and Munn, who in his *Conditions and Trends in Education for Librarianship* (1936)[8] maintained that library schools were not training for leadership and that comparatively few librarians with advanced training were required in cities like Pittsburgh, somewhat modified this statement in his American Library Association presidential address, "Fact versus Folklore," in 1940.[9] There he stressed the point that if libraries were to respond effectively to changing needs, they must have objective studies of every kind, particularly concerning the reading interests and abilities of their patrons. Through its graduates who hold Ph.D. degrees, the School has demonstrated that extended training in advanced studies and research not only tends to insure such competence, but that it does so more quickly than prolonged experience.

These influences may be thought of as having been tangential to education for librarianship. Three that have affected the subject directly will now be pointed out.

The first is the contribution the School has made to the upbuilding of the staffs of other schools. At the very outset the School held conferences for the training of teachers in library schools. In the two decades since its establishment, it has steadily supplied directors and staff members to the faculties of other schools. The number of holders of advanced degrees in faculties of other schools has steadily increased since 1929, and several schools which began offering work leading to the Master's degree and the Doctorate in librarianship in 1948 or have strengthened their work at the graduate level, will be staffed in considerable measure from the School's graduates with higher degrees.

The second direct contribution has been the example the School has set in formulating a professional curriculum that proceeds logically through the various stages of general, preprofessional, professional, and graduate-professional education. It first undertook this step in 1941-42. That it was able to do this was due in part to the organization of the School as an integral part of the University of Chicago. Without reference to a general graduate school, it has been able to work out a program in keeping with the spirit and structure of the University that breaks away from the excessive techniques of the Dewey tradition and that prescribes the nature of the preprofessional and professional fields. It has done this not in the old framework, but in a new framework in close cooperation with other departments and schools. This development holds promise of the highest order.

The third direct contribution has been the steady provision during the past two decades of fellowships, scholarships, grants-in-aid, and research assistantships for graduate students in librarianship, from which a hundred or more librarians have benefited. Many of the beneficiaries have been employed in surveys and studies conducted by the School, have published the results of their investigations in the *Library Quarterly* and the series of *Studies in Library Science*, and have gained experience in attacking library problems from which the profession generally has profited.

This activity has by no means been limited to the School. On the contrary, the Carnegie Corporation provided a series of generous fellowships from 1929 to 1942 in which 93 librarians participated, and library schools in general have offered scholarships, fellowships, and assistantships to a growing number of students throughout the nation. This activity has emphasized, however, the fundamental importance of such assistance for graduate study and the enrichment of library service.

THE CONTRIBUTION OF PRACTICING LIBRARIANS

The influence exerted by practicing librarians constitutes the seventh aspect of the development of education for librarianship. This has been in the main of a conservative nature. However, there have been notable exceptions. Perhaps the two most notable have been the approval by the leaders of the American Library Association in 1883 of a library school as preferable to apprenticeship for the training of librarians, and the constructive work of the Temporary Library Training Board and the Board of Education for Librarianship from 1923 through 1933.

Against these significant developments is the tendency for many practicing librarians to insist that graduates of library schools joining their staffs should be able to render the kind of service normally expected of apprentices in their own library systems. Placement of advanced students at higher than beginning levels, particularly by public libraries, has been fairly difficult; and opportunities provided by libraries for leaves of absence with pay for advanced study and for assignments to tasks involving extensive specialization, experimentation, and research, have been comparatively few. Part-time positions have been more generously provided, particularly by the New York Public Library and the libraries of universities whose library schools have formerly awarded the Master's degree.

THE ROLE OF CERTIFICATION AGENCIES

Education for librarianship has likewise felt the impact of accrediting agencies within and outside the field of librarianship. The adverse effect of the ruling of the Association of American Universities upon the degree awarded for the completion of the one-year professional program has already been noted. The role of graduate faculties in determining the conditions under which graduate programs of the schools are to be carried out has also been suggested. The part played by school accrediting agencies and state certification boards has also been extremely important.

The point does not require elaboration. The example in the states served by the Southern Association of Colleges and Secondary Schools will suffice to show the extent of this influence. Before the Southern Association adopted its standards for the training of high school librarians in 1927, there were only two library schools in the area. The establishment of the standards stimulated the organization of schools at William and Mary, the University of North Carolina, George Peabody College, and Louisiana State University; and of departments of library science for the training of school librarians in a score of additional institutions. State aid for public libraries has likewise made it possible for state library agencies to set up definite professional requirements to be met by county and regional librarians. All these requirements have had to be considered by the schools and have been reflected in the programs of study offered by them.

STUDIES OF THE PAST DECADE

The ninth influence to be considered in the development of education for librarianship has been that of related studies which have proliferated during the past decade. I shall not undertake to single these out by name. Some of them were related to the fiftieth anniversaries of the Schools at Columbia and Illinois. Others have been undertaken for the Carnegie Corporation. Still others have been developed by members of library school staffs. All have dealt with various phases of the subject. They have analyzed conditions, pointed out limitations, and prescribed remedies. Fortunately they have been projected against the background of from fifteen to twenty-five years of experience of library school as parts of American universities. They reflect the influences described in the foregoing sections of this paper, and provide in large measure the foundation of the new curricula recently put into effect. This new development will be looked back to in the future as marking a significant advance in education for librarianship.

NEW CURRICULA

Finally, passing consideration must be given to the new curricula that are emerging from these studies. They represent something more than individual opinions. They are the outgrowth of studies which have preceded them and they embrace programs of action which will markedly affect the future of education for librarianship.

The most obvious change in the new programs is the change in the degree to be awarded at the conclusion of what has usually been considered the fifth year of undergraduate and professional study. The second Bachelor's degree is to be dropped by a number of schools and the A. M. or the M. S. is to be awarded.

The change in the degree, however, is not the most fundamental change. It is only superficial. The most significant change is to be found in the nature of the curricula leading to the new Master's degree. Requirements for this degree have been restated and represent an attempt at placing pre-professional, professional, and graduate-profes-

sional studies in a logical order and in keeping with the spirit of professional and graduate study. The pressures exerted by undergraduate colleges and graduate schools have been relaxed to such an extent that a more realistic approach to the professional requirements of librarianship has been made possible.

The content of the curricula also exhibits extensive change. A glance at the courses offered at Chicago, Illinois, and Columbia, for example, reveals a sharp break from the titles of courses contained in the minimum standards adopted by the American Library Association upon the recommendation of the Board of Education in 1926. A core curriculum introduced at the undergraduate level replaces much of the former curriculum. New courses such as The Library and Society, Books and Libraries in the Cultural Process, Communication and Libraries, Readers and Reading Interests, The Resources of Libraries, The History of Scholarship, and Methods of Investigation are combined with other professional courses and seminars as well as graduate courses from other disciplines. In two new instances they are continued beyond the fifth-year level with advanced courses and seminars leading to the Doctorate. Closer integration with other schools and departments has been effected, with consequent enrichment throughout the entire professional curriculum. The total result is the provision of a program of professional and intellectual content that should go far in giving the future librarian the background, competence, and scholarly understandings that will better fit him for the exacting demands of American librarianship.

It is upon this kind of foundation that education for librarianship is being placed today. After sixty years, the framework established by Dewey and only partly modified by Williamson and the Board of Education for Librarianship has, in considerable measure, given place to the framework fashioned by the needs of modern librarianship. From these changes, generally long overdue, librarianship stands to profit greatly.

FOOTNOTES

[1]Carnegie Corporation of New York, *Training for Library Service* (New York: Updike, 1923).
[2]University of Chicago Press.
[3]London: Grafton, 1937.
[4]*Ibid*, 1940.
[5]University of Chicago Press, 1935.
[6]*Ibid.*, 1940.
[7]*Ibid.*, 1943.
[8]Carnegie Corporation of New York.
[9]In *A.L.A. Bulletin*, 34 (1940) 38-84, 402.

ADDITIONAL READINGS

Downs, Robert B., "Education for Librarianship in the United States and Canada," In *Library Education: An International Survey* edited by Larry Earl Bone (Champaign: University of Illinois Press, 1968), pp. 1-20.

Elliot, Clark A., "The U. S. Bureau of Education: Its Role in Library History, 1876," In Library History Seminar Number 3, *Proceedings* edited by Martha Jane Zachert (Tallahasse, Florida: *Journal of* Library History, 1968), pp. 98-111.

Grotzinger, Laurel A., *The Power and the Dignity: Librarianship and Katharine Sharp* (New York: Scarecrow Press, 1966).

Havlik, Robert J., "The Library Services Branch of the U. S. Office of Education: Its Creation, Growth, and Transformation," In Library History Seminar Number 3, *Proceedings* edited by Martha Jane Zachert (Tallahassee, Florida: Journal of Library History, 1968), pp. 112-123.

Rayward, W. Boyd, "Melvil Dewey and Education for Librarianship," *Journal of Library History* 3 (1968), pp. 297-312.

Rider, Fremont, *Melvil Dewey* (Chicago: American Library Association, 1944).

Tauber, Maurice F., *Louis Round Wilson, Librarian and Administrator* (New York: Columbia University Press, 1967).

Utley, George Burwell, *The Librarians' Conference of 1853* (Chicago: The American Library Association, 1951).

Vann, Sarah K., *Training for Librarianship Before 1923* (Chicago: American Library Association, 1961).

VI

THE GROWTH OF SPECIALIZATION—INTO THE TWENTIETH CENTURY

The period covering the latter half of the nineteenth century and the first half of the twentieth represents a time of rapid growth and increasing specialization in American libraries. We have already seen how the public library idea, with its small beginnings in New England, spread and gained wide acceptance throughout the country. Other types of libraries were growing with equal rapidity. To adequately discuss that growth in all of its diversity would require several book-length studies.

The essays that follow focus on a number of major developments in American library history from 1850 to 1950. Many others might have been included. However, since several areas of modern librarianship are still in the process of developing, and since significant developments in many of the sub-fields of librarianship—such as school and special librarianship—are really products of the last twenty years, we have been forced to cover a number of important topics only sparingly. For this reason, the list of additional readings for this section has been enlarged and should serve to guide readers to the extensive literature available on American libraries during this period.

The Context for Reference Service: The Rise of Research and Research Libraries, 1850–1900

Samuel Rothstein

Literary nationalism, the rise of universities, increased wealth, specialization and professionalism were among the factors which contributed to the development of research libraries in this country. Samuel Rothstein, the author of the most comprehensive study of the history of reference services in American libraries, discusses the rise of research and research libraries in the context of these factors, and analyzes the implications these developments had for reference services.

Arthur Bestor has called the changes that took place in the organization of American intellectual life in the latter half of the nineteenth century a "fundamental transformation" and an "intellectual revolution."[1] At the mid-century these changes were hardly yet apparent. The universities remained still faithful to the traditional prescribed curriculum of liberal arts and religion inherited from the colonial era and to the stultifying textbook-cum-recitation method of instruction.[2]

The study of natural science, which promised a more liberal approach to scholarly investigation, had not yet been able to make its influence felt in the university. Under pressure to bring under their aegis the growing body of scientific knowledge, the universities had finally permitted the sciences entry but only through the back door. Unwilling to accord to the newer disciplines the prestige of a full-fledged partnership with the traditional subjects, the colleges adopted the expedient of admitting the natural sciences as separate "schools." The Lawrence Scientific School (established in 1842) and the Sheffield Scientific School (founded in 1847), attached to Harvard and Yale respectively, had only the minimal and most grudgingly accorded connection with their parent institutions.[3]

Under these discouraging circumstances natural science studies could not aspire to high levels of scholarship. Where instruction was offered it was elementary in character; graduate work and laboratories were still all but unknown.[4]

If the university environment of the mid-century proved bleak for the nurture of scholarship, the non-academic world offered equally meager sustenance. Though the general scientific societies inherited from the eighteenth century continued to maintain their existence, their activities demonstrated little more than a continued interest in the promotion of learning in the polite tradition of the Enlightenment.

The historical societies were more numerous and active; Dunlap has listed sixty-five founded before 1860.[5] However, as Dunlap points out, the motives for the establishment of the historical societies were by no means all related to the cultivation of scholarly interests. Patriotism, civic and state pride, respect for ancestors, the self-interest of founders, and the desire to emulate the example of societies already in existence all played their part.[6] An undiscriminating zeal for collection diverted many societies into the profitless piling up of relics, minerals, natural history specimens and curiosities of dubious value.[7] Even where the attention remained firmly centered on the authentic materials of historical scholarship, few societies were able to advance from the collection of materials to the active exploitation of them in publications of significance.[8]

The federal government could offer little more in the way of encouragement for the organization of research. Though the censuses and such scientific bureaus as the Coast and Geodetic Survey had made a beginning in the collection of scientific data, attention and support remained limited to the severely practical, with little regard for the long-range utility of basic research. A more significant venture was the establishment of the

SOURCE: Reprinted from Samuel Rothstein, *The Development of Reference Services Through Academic Traditions, Public Library Practice and Special Librarianship* (Chicago: American Library Association, 1955), Chapter 1, "The Context for Reference Service: The Rise of Research and Research Libraries, 1850-1900," pp. 6-19, by permission of the author and publisher. Copyright © 1955 by the American Library Association.

Smithsonian Institution in 1846, but this indeed was something of a lucky stroke, prompted by the unexpected bequest of the Englishman, James Smithson. It was hardly a conclusive demonstration of any national interest in scientific investigation.

From this review of American scholarship at the mid-century there emerge two central and related facts. The first is that research activity— the extension of knowledge by scholarly inquiry— was insignificant in quantity and character, and the ideal of research all but unknown. The second is that the structure of American intellectual life did not yet provide organized arrangements for the promotion, training, and support of scholarship. What scholarship existed at the mid-century was the scholarship of the gifted amateur. Bestor points out that in the field of history, for example, the most prominent writers, such as Prescott, Bancroft, Motley, and Parkman, had practically no institutional connections.[9] Their training was the product of independent reading and study abroad. While engaged in scholarly investigations they supported themselves out of private funds. They themselves gathered the bulk of the materials needed or paid for the trips necessary to consult them. The mid-century scholar functioned largely in independence from his colleagues, doing for himself the spadework which his chosen theme required. And when he published his results, these made their appearance through the channels of the regular commercial publication agencies, unassisted by special subsidies. Research was still an avocation—if occasionally a full-time one—and not yet a profession.

THE TRANSFORMATION OF AMERICAN SCHOLARSHIP, 1850–1900

Though no particular significance can be attached to the dates 1850 and 1900, which themselves mark only convenient lines of demarcation, it seems clear that the period defined by these limits witnessed a fundamental change in the structure of American scholarship. The introduction of the natural sciences, even as subjects of low prestige, heralded the break-up of the tightly-closed and narrowly circumscribed curricula that had kept the universities hostile to the spirit of free investigation. The needs of a national economy that was becoming rapidly industrialized gave scientific studies an obvious importance which was soon reflected in their rapid rise in the academic hierarchy. The federal govern-

ment recognized and encouraged the new status of scientific studies by the passage of the Morrill Land Grant Act in 1862, which provided federal subsidies for higher education in science, technology and agriculture.

Other subjects were also successful in winning academic acceptance. Chairs in history were created at Columbia and at Michigan in 1857. Modern languages, first established as an elective subject at Harvard through the efforts of Ticknor, began to vie in prestige with the classical languages. Cornell University was founded in 1868 with the avowed purpose of teaching any subject that seemed desirable to the faculty and students. With the inauguration of the free elective system at Harvard under President Eliot, the way became open for a hitherto unprecedented degree of specialization in studies.

A potent influence for change came from without in the form of ideas and methods imported from the German university. The nineteenth century had seen the German universities become centers for advanced scholarship. Their high prestige and elaborate facilities, especially laboratories, attracted many foreign students, amongst them Americans who wanted something more than their own modest institutions could offer.

From Germany the returning scholars brought back the use of the lecture and the seminar as teaching devices more appropriate for the pursuit of higher education than the cramping textbook and recitation method hitherto enthroned by tradition. More important, they brought back the idea that the pursuit of truth per se and the extension of knowledge through research were the highest functions and responsibilities of the university.[10]

The ideas imported from the German university found their fullest realization in Johns Hopkins University, founded in 1876. Without attempting an exact adherence to the German model, Daniel Coit Gilman and his associates were able to incorporate its ruling ideas into their new institution. As Gilman's biographer described it, "the graduate work was carried on in its main lines upon the model of the German universities; . . . the keynote of the German system was also the keynote of Mr. Gilman's conception of the university that was to be."[11] This "keynote" was research, for Johns Hopkins University was to be " a university permeated by the spirit of the universities of Germany, with research as the center, the heart, of the whole organism."[12]

The example of Johns Hopkins University was,

in its turn, a magistral influence in turning the course of the American university toward graduate work and research, and in making their symbols—the graduate school and the Ph. D. degree—characteristic features of American higher education. At the 1902 ceremonies celebrating the twenty-fifth anniversary of the founding of Johns Hopkins University, the nation's leading educators joined in acknowledging its leadership in the university research movement.[13]

Actually, however, Johns Hopkins University was more important in the development of American research for what it represented than for what it directly brought about. As the first American university to give full-fledged and deliberate recognition to research as a dominant concern of higher education, its contribution was distinctive and conspicuous. But the trend was already apparent before the opening of Johns Hopkins University in 1876. Yale and Harvard established graduate schools as early as 1847 and 1872 respectively. Harvard granted its first Ph. D. degree in 1873, and the University of Michigan did likewise in 1876.

Similar reservations must apply to any attempt to equate the development of American graduate education with deliberate adaptation to another setting of the ruling ideas of the German university. W. Stull Holt's study of the correspondence of Herbert B. Adams has shown that the German influence on American scholarship was not as intimate nor as far-reaching as has been commonly supposed.[14]

All this suggests that the transformation of American scholarship in this period resulted from no simple acceptance of any single idea but was the complex product of a number of elements, indigenous and foreign. Bestor has characterized it as "a far larger process of assimilation."[15] The broadening of the curriculum to include scientific, technical and professional education, the introduction of the graduate school as the agency for the training of scholars, the acceptance of research as a university function on a coordinate basis with teaching—all these were elements in the process. The new university of 1875 brought them together into one institution.[16]

In fact, the very essence of the movement was that scholarship became institutionalized.[17] Where the earlier scholars had worked independently, relying only on their own resources, the new university provided a center of concentration. It offered scholars the means of training, a subsidy for their investigations, the association of colleagues and media for the dissemination of their researches. The American college of the mid-century gave room only to teachers; the new American university made a place for the scholar and, in so doing, made of scholarship a profession.

With the professionalization of scholarship came the customary results of professionalization—the disappearance of the amateur and the increase of specialization. The professional scholars controlled the channels of training and the major means of communication. Only the properly trained student with the requisite set of academic credentials could hope to win the university position that assured support for his research; only the professors had effective access to the learned journals published by their institutions and edited by their associates. "Research," concluded Robert Binkley, "ceased to be an honored sport and became an exclusive profession."[18]

The rise of the university, which made possible a career in scholarship, also led to a sharp increase in the number of research workers. Inevitably there followed a splintering of learning into smaller segments and an attendant specialization in scholarship. Its effects were visible in the formation of national societies dedicated to the advancement of particular subjects. The American Philological Association (founded in 1869), the Archaeological Institute of America (1879), The Modern Language Association (1883), the American Historical Association (1884), the American Economic Association (1885) were typical examples of the many learned societies, representing smaller divisions of knowledge, which in this period came to supersede in prominence the older general scholarly associations.[19]

A by-product of specialization was a change in the characteristic form of publication, most easily visible in the field of history. Where the mid-century historians—a Bancroft or a Parkman—had taken whole centuries and continents for their themes and brought forth their results as multi-volume histories, the newer specialists carefully exploited their smaller areas in monographs and articles. The sub-division of topics in turn made for a greater emphasis on documentation. The monograph did not afford room for large-scale generalizations. It was meant primarily as an exploration in depth, an objective ascertainment of all the facts on a particular small topic, in which every statement had to be supported by relevant documents.

None of these processes of professionalization and specialization of research achieved full development overnight, but their progress was surprisingly rapid. In 1875 the very word "research" was, according to Daniel Coit Gilman, a new term in the academic vocabulary. Since that time, he noted graphically, "the conception of 'research' . . . spread throughout our land from peak to peak like the signal fires described by the Greek dramatists."[20]

The sharp increase of interest in research helped carry the conception outside the academic walls. For the first time research began to be an active factor in the operation of industrial enterprises. Hitherto, industrialists had relied on the abundance of natural resources and the protection of the tariff as the chief means of maintaining profits. With growing competition and the depletion of natural resources facing it, industry began to question the efficiency of its processes and to look to applied science research for new approaches to its problems.[21]

The same realization that research could have important practical value gave impetus to the expansion of the work of scientific investigation sponsored by the federal government. The Department of Agriculture, from its establishment in 1864, quickly became an important producer and sponsor of research in a wide variety of fields. The Smithsonian Institution under Joseph Henry and Samuel Langley achieved a position of leadership in basic research. New agencies for research such as the Bureau of Mines, the National Bureau of Standards and the National Institutes of Health added significant contributions in applied science.

However, the research activities of industry and government represented emergent tendencies rather than fully-realized movements. Up to the end of the nineteenth century research continued to find its chief base in the universities, where it was recognized as one of their primary responsibilities. Daniel Coit Gilman described this sense of obligation with dramatic emphasis:

> The third function of a university is to extend the bounds of human knowledge. Call it research, call it investigation, call it scientific inquiry, call it the seeking for truth—never has the obligation been so strong as it is now to penetrate the arcana of the world in which we dwell, to discover new facts, to measure old phenomena, and to educe principles and laws that were written in the beginning, but have never yet been read by mortal eye.[22]

By accepting research as one of its basic functions, the university assured the means of support for the productive scholar and made possible the emergence of a new class—the professional scholar

working within an institution and dependent upon institutional arrangements for the prosecution of his studies.

THE DEMANDS OF THE NEW SCHOLARSHIP UPON THE LIBRARY

The nineteenth century converted scholarship from an amateur's avocation to a full-time profession. Inevitably the needs and working habits of professionalized and institution-centered scholarship differed vastly from those of the independent investigators of the earlier period. With the change in methods there came also a basic reorientation of scholars' attitudes to the library.

A principal feature of the change in attitude was vastly increased regard for the importance of libraries to the progress of scholarship. The roots of the change probably went back as far as American students' first contact with the impressive collections of the German university libraries. George Ticknor, a pioneer in the establishment of the idea of research in America, wrote to his friend Stephen Higginson from Göttingen in May, 1816:

> I cannot, however, shut my eyes on the fact, that one very important and principal cause of the difference between our University [i.e. Harvard] and the one here is the different value we affix to a good library, and the different ideas we have of what a good library is . . . what is worse than the absolute poverty of our collections of books is the relative inconsequence in which we keep them. We found new professorships and build new colleges in abundance, but we buy no books; and yet it is to me the most obvious thing in the world that it would promote the cause of learning and the reputation of the University ten times more to give six thousand dollars a year to the Library than to found three professorships, . . . We have not yet learnt that the Library is not only the first convenience of the University, but that it is the very first necessity,—that it is the light and spirit,—and that all other considerations must yield to the prevalent one of increasing and opening it on the most liberal terms to *all* who are disposed to make use of it.[23]

Ticknor's contemporaries and successors in attendance at the German universities echoed his appreciation of the worth of the library in university studies. Of the first generation of American scholars in Germany, Edward Everett, George Bancroft, and Joseph Green Cogswell all were influential builders or donors of libraries. In the next generation, Henry Philip Tappan was an energetic promoter of library interests at the University of Michigan. He personally solicited funds for the University's library from the citizens of Ann Arbor; his son John became the University's first regular librarian.[24] At about the same time, Francis Lieber, a German émigré and first occupant of the chair of history at Columbia College, was writing to his friend General Halleck: "We cannot do in our days without large public libraries, and libraries are quite as necessary as hospitals or armies. Libraries are the bridges over which Civilization travels from generation to generation and from country to country."[25]

Herbert Baxter Adams typified the group of German-trained historians who helped establish the idea of scientific historical research in the generation after 1875. For him "the most important factor in the constitution of an historical department is the proper adjustment of relations with the college or university library. . . . The promotion of historical study in any college or university is absolutely dependent upon the use of books."[26]

However, like the research movement itself, the appreciation of libraries was not confined to the German-trained scholars. Yale University was relatively remote from German influence in the nineteenth century, yet the reports of President Dwight came to echo the same sentiment. "The Library is, in a most important sense, the center of the University life," he wrote in 1893; "The place where it is located is the place towards which teachers and students alike must turn, in order to find the means of pursuing their investigations."[27]

By the end of the century such assertions were so numerous as to make the statements "the library is the heart of the university" and "the library is the center of the university" only commonplaces. When President Benjamin Ide Wheeler announced on his accession to office at the University of California, "Give me a library and I'll build a university about it,"[28] he could claim credit only for the forcefulness of the expression; the idea was already in the public domain.

A realistic appraisal of all these encomiums about the importance of the library would conclude that they reflected not so much foreign influence or philosophical appreciation of the place of books in the progress of scholarship as the increasing dependence of the scholar upon the library. The amateur scholar of the earlier era worked more or less completely on his own so far as book resources were concerned. It was taken for granted that the accumulation of a large private library was the necessary and cus-

tomary procedure of the scholar. At best he could expect that the materials he required, if already collected, would be scattered among numerous institutions, with perhaps the most important of them reposing in libraries and archives abroad.

The biographical accounts of the amateur scholars offer ample evidence as to their all but complete independence of institutional libraries. Ticknor's *History of Spanish Literature* was based on his own collection of some thirteen thousand volumes. Hubert Howe Bancroft's autobiography is largely the story of the formation of his outstanding private library.[29] George Bancroft estimated that his "expenses of various kinds in collecting materials, MSS, and books, in journeys, time employed in researches, writing, copyists, money paid for examination, etc., etc., might be put without exaggeration at fifty or even seventy-five thousand dollars."[30]

Wealth was then the normal pre-requisite of scholarship in the days of the amateur. The men of the new professional group usually had no such private resources to draw upon. If they were able to consult and utilize the materials necessary for their research, it was because of the existence of the institutional library. A number of other factors joined in increasing the dependence of the scholar upon the library. The mounting flood of publications attendant upon the increase of knowledge was rapidly making even the largest of private libraries insufficient for thorough research. At the same time a more rigorous conception of research was demanding a more exhaustive investigation of sources. Thus, in the field of history, the idea of "scientific history" popularized by Von Ranke emphasized the careful collection of facts—facts which could be taken as established only when supported by an imposing array of documentary evidence.[31]

If all these factors made the scholars much more dependent upon the library, a reciprocal influence made the library in its turn subject to a whole series of demands from the scholars. Of these the first, the strongest, and the most common was the pressure for more materials. The cry for more books ran through the whole period of the transformation of scholarship. Struik has noted the demand of the European-trained scientists of the 1860 decade for the specialized journals with which they had become familiar abroad.[32] Herbert Baxter Adams attributed the growth of the University of Michigan's collections to "the intelligent demands made by the faculties, by the students, and by the administration."[33] The reports of President Eliot at Harvard and President Dwight at Yale persistently hammered at the need for greater library resources. At the end of the century the demand had lost none of its urgency. Charles Mills Gayley pressed for the acquisition by the University of California of the Bancroft Library in the full confidence that he and his fellow scholars had and would continue to have "no greater need than that of materials and sources with which to develop investigation and first-hand scholarship."[34]

Closely related to the demand for increased resources was the desire for easier access to the materials. If the institutional library was to serve him in place of a private collection, the professional scholar wanted the same unrestricted approach to the books he needed that his amateur predecessor had enjoyed in his personal library. This claim was reinforced by the exigencies of the newer teaching methods. The distinctive feature of the seminar was the first-hand investigation of the original materials by the students under the close supervision of the professor. Preferably this process would take place in the library itself, where the group could discuss the students' work within easy reach of the materials cited. Thus Henry Adams, in casting aside the textbook method in favor of having his students go directly to the original sources, criticized the existing library policy at Harvard of keeping books all but locked up in the alcoves, and demanded greater accessibility to materials for his students.[35]

President Gilman took up the same theme in many of his annual reports. For example, he expressed his satisfaction at the growing tendency of the Johns Hopkins library system to develop in the direction of departmental collections, for he thought no measure likely to be of more assistance to the research men than "placing those books which are most likely to be needed, or which specially bear upon the work, within easy reach of the worker's hand."[36]

With repetition the idea of easier access to materials became crystallized in the catchphrase that the library should be the "laboratory" of the humanist and social scientist, usually uttered with a corollary statement that the library should no longer be a "store-house of books."[37] The concept of the library as a laboratory implied its use as a tool for investigations. As a tool it could be most effective when it furnished not only the required materials but also the means of obtaining

a subject approach to the particular topics of interest. The need of a subject approach to library materials gained added intensity from the very growth of collections so vigorously advocated by the scholars. A small collection required only the broad classification appropriate to a personal library; with a many-fold expansion of resources a more minutely organized arrangement of the books was needed, if the much desired free access to materials was to produce anything other than confusion. In the same way, the catalog had to become more than a simple record of holdings, for it became increasingly apparent that no scholar could hope to know all the literature of potential value, especially on subjects outside his immediate specialty.

These circumstances motivated the scholars to press for some form of subject approach to knowledge. Herbert Adams' review of the facilities for the study of history in American colleges led him to complain that in many college libraries searching for material on a given topic was like looking for a needle in a haystack. By way of contrast he held up for commendation Melvil Dewey's newly re-organized library at Columbia, where the object was to "organize so thoroughly its literary resources in any given field like history or political science that they can be speedily massed upon a given point with the precision and certainty of a Prussian army corps in the execution of a military manoeuvre."[38] Hubert Howe Bancroft had a subject index compiled for his large personal library at a cost of $35,000; "by this or other similar means alone can the contents of any large library be utilized; and the larger the collection the more necessity for such an index," he maintained.[39]

Such statements were, however, fewer in number and much less explicit than the demands for more materials and easier access to them. There was evidently some feeling that the library had to be organized so as to provide a subject approach to knowledge, but the details of organization do not seem to have concerned the scholars. Evidence on this point is lacking, but it may be plausibly surmised that the research men considered matters of classification and subject cataloging technical problems that could be safely left to the librarians.

Evidently for most scholars, the overwhelming preoccupation with the accumulation of materials cast a shadow of indifference over all library matters other than the acquisitions function. Certainly this was true for problems of library staffing and service. In general the scholars, if one may judge by the absence of comments in memoirs and biographies, felt relatively little need or concern for reference services. Such statements as did appear came only late in the century.

A related theme—teaching the use of books and libraries—did arouse some considerable interest. President Barnard of Columbia devoted considerable attention to the topic, arguing that instruction in the use of library materials was a task as important as that performed by the professors in the regular academic departments. He concluded with some fervor that "it has seemed more and more important to careful observers to give such instruction and aid to undergraduates as shall enable them in all their after lives to do their individual work more readily and more successfully."[40] Herbert Baxter Adams, who was familiar with the instruction given at Columbia and at Cornell, thought that "such a course of general bibliographical information, given to students by the librarian of their college or university, cannot be too highly commended."[41]

The same two scholars were those most explicit in voicing a demand for reference work proper. In the same report in which he advocated a program of instruction in "practical bibliography," Barnard argued that in the interest of educational progress the Columbia library "must be put in charge of a librarian, himself well acquainted with books and their uses, and experienced in guiding inquirers in bibliographical researches."[42] Adams thought that a "great public library, like a great railway station, must have a bureau of information, . . . "[43]

Both Adams and Barnard seem to have had in mind assistance for the undergraduate and the neophyte in learning rather than aid for the mature scholar. Adams did indeed have words of commendation for the more specialized assistance that George Baker was providing in the library of the School of Political Science at Columbia, but even here he was probably thinking of the seminar students rather than of their instructors.[44]

In the absence of explicit statements from the scholars themselves, it is impossible to define precisely their attitude toward the idea of personal assistance by the librarian in their own researches, but a statement from Hubert Howe Bancroft affords a good clue to their reasoning.

> Often have I heard authors say that beyond keeping the books in order, and bringing such as were required, with some copying, or possibly some searching now and then, no one could render them any assistance.

> They would not feel safe in trusting any one with the manipulation of facts on which was to rest their reputation for veracity and accuracy.[45]

The scholar of the late nineteenth century was familiar with the idea of reference work and some, at least, approved of such library assistance for their students. Few yet thought of it as important for their own researches.

THE RISE OF THE RESEARCH LIBRARY

By definition the research library is a service agency for scholarship. Its establishment and development have therefore, not surprisingly, followed closely along the lines marked out by the development of learning in America.

At the mid-century the research library could hardly have been said to exist. Some efforts in purposeful collection had already been made by the historical societies, notably by the American Antiquarian Society and the New York Historical Society, but such zeal was by no means the rule. Most historical societies' collecting was as lukewarm and as haphazard as their other contributions to learning. As late as 1876 the government report on *Public Libraries in the United States of America* credited only thirteen of the then extant societies with collections numbering more than 10,000 volumes.[46]

The small achievement of the historical societies in the development of libraries was matched by the general paucity of American library resources at this time, both in turn reflecting the low level of scholarship in the country as a whole. William Fletcher alleged that in 1850 the entire library resources of the United States aggregated only a million volumes.[47] In the same year an article in the *North American Review* gave the following illuminating table of holdings for the largest libraries in the United States:[48]

Harvard College, including the Law and Divinity Schools	72,000 volumes
Philadelphia and Loganian Library	60,000 volumes
Boston Athenaeum	50,000 volumes
Library of Congress	50,000 volumes
New York Society Library	32,000 volumes
Mercantile Library (New York)	32,000 volumes
Georgetown College (D. C.)	25,000 volumes

Brown University	24,000 volumes
New York State Library	24,000 volumes
Yale College	21,000 volumes

Provisions for use were equally negligible. W. N. Carlton has collected some examples, now amusing, of the way in which narrowly conceived and rigorously applied regulations made college book collections all but unusable.[49] Thus the Amherst College Library up to 1852 was open only once a week for the withdrawal of books and provided no facilities for reading on the premises. At Brown in 1843 no undergraduate could take a book off the shelves without the special permission of the librarian. A Maryland college did not permit any lending at all—the practice had indeed formerly existed, but it was discontinued because of abuse of the privilege!

It would be unfair to see in such regulations mere ineptitude; in part at least they reflected only a prudent concern for the protection of books at a time when these were few and esteemed precious. But they also reflected the well-nigh complete divorce of the college library from the ordinary process of scholarship. The student used his textbooks; the professor, if anything more than a teacher, his personal collection. President Hadley of Yale recalled a conversation which seemed to typify the attitude which imposed a separation between the scholar and the college library:

> One of the professors of the old school—and, I might add, one of the more enlightened professors of the old school— said to me only a few years ago, "I conceive that the chief educational use of a university library is to lend an occasional book to a professor who does not happen to have the book in his own library." He regarded the university library as a sort of museum; the actual laboratories where the work was done were the special libraries of the professors.[50]

An even more revealing glimpse of the college library in the old order is offered by the exchange of correspondence between Gilman, then librarian at Yale, and President Woolsey. When Gilman complained at the administration's lack of support for the library—he was paying his sole assistant out of his own salary and had himself to stoke the small stove that was the single source of heat for the building—Woolsey sent this astonishing reply: "In regard to your leaving your place my thoughts have shaped themselves thus: the place does not possess that importance which a man of active mind would naturally seek; and the college cannot, now or hereafter, while its circumstances remain as they are, give it greater prominence."[51]

While restrictive regulations and the grip of tradition were keeping university libraries all but moribund, a new tool for scholarship was being forged outside the academic community—the public library. The public library in its present form may be said to date from the founding of the Boston Public Library in 1852. As with most social institutions, the motivation behind its establishment and development was complex. The detailed studies of Ditzion and Thompson indicate that the desire for popular education, a naive faith in the efficacy of "good" reading in the preservation of virtue, civic pride, and sheer imitation all played their part in the creation of the public library.[52]

But, as Shera makes clear, the interest of scholars, especially the historians, in finding a viable basis for the preservation and servicing of the materials of research was a compelling and perhaps decisive motive.[53] Certainly, in the larger cities at least, the public library collections from the outset included material of a character manifestly intended only for scholarly use. The Everett collection of documents in the Boston Public Library, the "Green Library" in the Worcester Free Library, and the comprehensive collection of bibliographies brought together by Joseph Green Cogswell for the Astor Library were cases in point.

Evidence for the belief that at this time the public library was more quick to respond to the needs of scholarship than the university library is given in the statistics of library holdings compiled by Rhees. His figures for 1857-1858 showed that less than a decade after their founding the Astor Library and the Boston Public Library had accumulated 80,000 and 70,000 volumes respectively. The comparison with the college library holdings of the same date is illuminating. After more than two centuries of operation, the Harvard College Library had brought together only 74,000 volumes, and Yale, after a century and a half of existence, only 36,000 volumes. Other academic institutions had fared even worse. Rhees credited the Brown University Library with only 29,500 volumes, Columbia with 18,000, Princeton with 1,000, and Pennsylvaina with 5,000![54]

As the research movement gathered strength, its impact on the library began to make itself more clearly and widely felt. Library reports from the seventies on indicated a clear recognition of responsibility for service to research. Librarian Homes described the New York State Library as "one for historical and scientific research chiefly."[55] The Lenox Library proclaimed in 1883 that the use of the library "will be hereafter enlarged and extended, to promote research."[56] Raymond Davis of the University of Michigan Library claimed that "the especial purpose for which the University Library exists is *the increase of knowledge*."[57] Daniel Coit Gilman, speaking at the opening of the new Princeton University Library building in 1898, summed up the progress of a half-century: "Finally, libraries are now recognized as places of research, ... This marks a great advance quite in accord with the dominant spirit in inquiry and investigation."[58]

In thus aligning themselves with the research movement, the university and reference libraries undertook, more or less consciously, to fulfill the demands of the scholars. The most urgent of these demands, as previously noted, was for larger book resources, and the librarians gave to the work of acquisitions the first claim on their attention and energy. Almost every librarian of the period felt that his library's major responsibility and hope for distinction lay in the large-scale amassment of materials. Justin Winsor, librarian at Harvard, thought that no single American library had yet come close to satisfying the book requirements of the specialist in any given field, and that the only hope that any would ever do so lay in broad, almost indiscriminate collecting.[59] Of Joseph Rowell, librarian of the University of California,

his biographer wrote: "He had always vastly preferred an increase in accessions to an increase in staff assistance. He had repeatedly doubled his own tasks in order repeatedly to double the accessions."[60] Raymond Davis summed up his career at the University of Michigan Library in a single revealing sentence. "If I were asked to characterize in a few words my work as librarian my answer would be ready: *A struggle for books*."[61]

The result of this conjunction of scholars' demands and librarians' activity was a pronounced increase in the dimensions of American library resources. At the outset of the period American library holdings appeared insignificant in comparison with the riches of European libraries. A generation later the New World could almost rival the Old, if not yet in the intrinsic value of its resources, at least in the number of volumes held. Table I sets forth the record of book holdings for a number of prominent libraries in 1876 and in 1891.

The theme of collection and its corollary theme of building needs indisputably dominated the attention of the librarians. They relegated to the background all but a few pressing problems of internal administration. Of these easily the most important were those connected with cataloging and

TABLE 1

Research Library Holdings in 1875 and in 1891

LIBRARY	NUMBER OF VOLUMES 1876[a]	NUMBER OF VOLUMES 1891[b]
Brown University Library	45,000	71,000
California University Library	13,600	42,287
Cornell University Library	10,000	111,007
Columbia University Library	33,590	135,000
Harvard University Library	227,650	292,000
Michigan University Library	28,400	77,705
Pennsylvania University Library	25,573	100,000
Princeton University Library	41,500	84,221
Yale University Library	114,200	185,000
Astor Library	152,446	238,946
Detroit Public Library	22,882	108,720
Cleveland Public Library	24,000	66,920
Boston Public Library	299,869	556,283
Grosvenor Library	18,000	35,000
Library of Congress	300,000	659,843
Surgeon-General's Library	40,000	104,300

[a]Source: U. S. Bureau of Education, *Public Libraries in the United States of America: Their History, Condition and Management,* Special Report, Part I (Washington: Government Printing Office, 1876), pp. 762-773

[b]Source: U. S. Bureau of Education, *Statistics of Public Libraries in the United States and Canada,* by Weston Flint, statistician of the Bureau of Education ("Circular of Information," No. 7; [Washington: Government Printing Office, 1893]), pp. 22-203. The basis of computation was not the same as in the 1876 statistics, so the two sets of data are not wholly comparable. However, the general impression conveyed by the comparison—that of rapid growth in library holdings—is undoubtedly reliable enough.

classification, and the "use of books," both in turn reflecting the larger aim of converting the library from a "storehouse of books" into a "laboratory for scholarship."

Neither problem was entirely new or peculiarly the product of the research movement pressures. Librarians since the day of Callimachus had recognized that the arrangement, display, and use of the materials in their charge were responsibilities inherent in their professional position, regardless of the type of library. But the demands of the scholars for a subject approach to knowledge lent a certain added urgency to these responsibilities for the managers of libraries that presumed to exist for the prosecution of research. For example, John Burgess, a leader in the research movement at Columbia, recalled how he pressed the college administration for the appointment of a librarian who could make the literature of his subject more readily available through subject cataloging and close classification.[62]

As a result of such pressures, when Dewey came to Columbia, a principal feature of his "revolution" in the library's administration was the reorganization of the cataloging and classification procedures. A similar absorption with the catalog was evident in Winsor's reports at Harvard, in Billings' administration of the Surgeon-General's Library, in Rowell's management of the University of California Library. The work of cataloging was customarily the first to receive the recognition of formal departmental status. A safe guess would be that insofar as a librarian was then recognized as a professional worker, such recognition was based primarily on his technical qualifications in cataloging.

The proper form for the required guide to the library's resources was a matter of lively controversy. By the end of the century, however, the arguments over printed versus card catalog, classed versus dictionary arrangement, broad versus close classification, had been more or less decided. Only the card catalog could keep abreast of a rapidly growing collection, while specific subject headings and close classification seemed to provide the best approach to the minute subjects wanted by the specialist scholars. Though nothing like uniformity or full satisfaction on these matters was achieved then (or even yet), the task of constructing the technical apparatus of the research library had been accomplished in its essentials by 1900.

The other great problem of internal administration—the "use of the library"—was solved with less controversy. The increased dependence of the scholar upon the institutional library clearly called for longer hours of opening and easy access to materials. Though independent reference libraries such as the Astor, the Lenox and the Reynolds continued to oppose circulation of their books on the grounds that such service dispersed materials and increased costs, the university libraries, with the scholars actually on their doorstep, could not and did not resist. Harvard, which had provided forty-eight hours of service per week in 1876, was open eighty-two hours a week in 1896; Yale increased its hours of service from thirty-six to seventy-two in the same period.[63] Columbia changed even more radically. The library gave twelve hours of weekly service in 1876; in 1888 Dewey offered prospective library school students the inducement that "for 14 hours daily there is opportunity for work."[64]

The same liberal policy of "service" was bringing the university library user much freer access to his materials than he had heretofore enjoyed. When Justin Winsor came to Harvard in 1877, Henry Adams had already been petitioning for permission to have his seminar students given direct access to the shelves.[65] Winsor thoroughly approved of the seminar method and its library implication—use not storage. In his first report he proclaimed his advocacy of a liberal lending policy:

> Books may be accumulated and guarded, and the result is sometimes called a library; but if books are made to help and spur men on in their own daily work, the library becomes a vital influence; the prison is turned into a workshop.[66]

In subsequent reports and articles Winsor expanded his idea into a full-fledged "doctrine of use," summed up in the dictum "A book is never so valuable as when it is in use." In his own institution he admitted advanced students to the stacks, extended the reserve book collections and threw open the reference collection to all comers.[67]

The new doctrine rapidly gained adherents. It became generally accepted that reference books should be available on open shelves.[68] Even the conservative reference libraries, which clung to the policy that their books ought not to leave the building, assiduously collected statistics of within-the-building circulation that would demonstrate "the use of the library." The Lenox Library, for example, which had been heretofore quite content to be a museum of typographical rarities, hopefully noted in its 1884 report an increasing use of its materials by scholars and promised measures for its encouragement.[69]

The ideas of service had important implications for reference service as well, but these were not fully realized in most research libraries in the nineteenth century. The detailed account of the genesis of the concept of reference service and of its development as a research library function is reserved for the next chapter. It may, however, be said at this time that reference service was never seen as more than a secondary responsibility in the nineteenth century research library.

The development of research and the professionalization of scholarship made the research library a necessity. They also brought to it demands for a large-scale expansion of holdings, for improved physical facilities, for freer access to books, and for an apparatus that would provide a subject approach to materials. The librarians in their turn put these first things first and gave their chief attention to the problems of acquisitions, cataloging and classification, and circulation. Their achievement was considerable. At the mid-century, roughly speaking, America was practically without research libraries. Fifty years later its libraries could claim collections of some magnitude, a well-developed system of catalogs and shelf arrangements, and a policy of administration that sought to make them indispensable tools for scholarship. The foundations had been laid for the organization of an expert personal service.

FOOTNOTES

[1] Arthur B. Bestor, Jr., "The Transformation of American Scholarship, 1875-1917," *Library Quarterly,* XXIII (July, 1953), 165.

[2] Cf. Andrew Dickson White, *Autobiography of Andrew Dickson White* (New York: The Century Co., 1905), 1, 26, 28, 255. White, later president of Cornell University, recalled that in his student years at Yale (1850-54), all independent investigation was stifled in the interest of rote recitation of prescribed subject matter.

[3] Andrew Dickson White, "Scientific and Industrial Education in the United States," *Popular Science Monthly,* V (June, 1874), 171.

[4] U. S. National Resources Committee, Science Committee, *Research—a National Resource* (Washington: Government Printing Office, 1938-41), II, 20.

[5] Leslie Whittaker Dunlap, *American Historical Societies, 1790-1860* (Madison, Wisconsin: Privately Printed, 1944), p. vil.

[6] *Ibid.,* pp. 10-13.

[7] *Ibid.,* pp. 73-76.

[8] U. S. Bureau of Education, *Public Libraries in the United States of America: Their History, Condition and Management,* Special Report, Part I (Washington: Government Printing Office, 1876), p. 313.

[9] Bestor, *op. cit.,* p. 166.

[10] Charles Franklin Thwing, *The American and the German University; One Hundred Years of History* (New York: The Macmillan Company, 1928), pp. 19, 130.

[11] Fabian Franklin, *The Life of Daniel Coit Gilman* (New York: Dodd, Mead and Company, 1910), p. 196.

[12] *Ibid.,* p. 227.

[13] Johns Hopkins University, . . . *Celebration of the Twenty-fifth Anniversary of the Founding of the University and Inauguration of Ira Remsen, L. L. D. as President of the University, February Twenty-first, and Twenty-second, 1902* (Baltimore: The Johns Hopkins Press, 1902), pp. 39-40, 62. Woodrow Wilson called Johns Hopkins "the first . . . in which the efficiency and value of research as an educational instrument were exemplified in the training of many investigators . . . ." (p. 39).

[14] Though Adams was a graduate of a German university and was teaching at Johns Hopkins, the most important intermediary of German influence, he maintained very little correspondence with German fellow-historians, and his admiration for German scholarship was by no means unqualified. Herbert Baxter Adams, *Historical Scholarship in the United States, 1876-1901; as Revealed in the Correspondence of Herbert Baxter Adams,* edited by W. Stull Holt ("The Johns Hopkins Studies in Historical and Political Science," Series LVI, Number 4. [Baltimore: The Johns Hopkins Press, 1938], p. 11.

[15] Bestor, *op. cit.,* p. 169.

[16] *Ibid.,* pp. 169-70.

[17] *Ibid.*

[18] Robert C. Binkley, "New Tools for Men of Letters," in *Selected Papers of Robert C. Binkley,* edited with a biographical sketch by Max H. Fisch (Cambridge: Harvard University Press, 1948), p. 191.

[19] Merle Curti, *The Growth of American Thought* (2d ed.; New York: Harper and Brothers Publishers, 1951), pp. 580-93.

[20] Daniel Coit Gilman, "Research—a Speech Delivered at the Convocation of the University of Chicago, June, 1903," in his *The Launching of a University* (New York: Dodd, Mead and Company, 1906), pp. 242-43.

[21] U. S. National Resources Committee, Science Committee, *op. cit.,* II, 24-28.

[22] Daniel Coit Gilman, "Higher Education in the United States," in his *University Problems in the United States* (New York: The Century Company, 1898), p. 296.

[23] As quoted by Thomas Wentworth Higginson, "Göttingen and Harvard Eighty Years Ago," *Harvard Graduates Magazine,* VI (September, 1897), 6.

[24] Charles M. Perry, *Henry Philip Tappan, Philosopher and University President* (Ann Arbor: University of Michigan Press, 1933), pp. 232-34.

[25] Francis Lieber, *The Life and Letters of Francis Lieber,* edited by Thomas Sergeant Perry (Boston: James R. Osgood and Company, 1882), p. 361.

[26] Herbert Baxter Adams, *The Study of History in American Colleges and Universities* (U. S. Bureau of Education "Circulars of Information," No. 2; [Washington: Government Printing Office, 1887], p. 43.

[27] Yale University, *Report of the President . . . for the Year Ending December 31, 1893,* p. 80.

[28] Quoted by Benjamin Kurtz, *Joseph Cummings Rowell, 1853-1938* (Berkeley: Printed by the University of California Press, 1940), p. 42.

[29] Hubert Howe Bancroft, *Literary Industries,* Vol XXXIX, *The Works of Hubert Howe Bancroft* (San Francisco: The History Company, Publishers, 1890), *passim.*

[30] M. A. DeWolfe Howe, *The Life and Letters of George Bancroft* (New York: Charles Scribner's Sons, 1908), II, 261.

[31] W. Stull Holt, "The Idea of Scientific History in America," *Journal of the History of Ideas,* I (June, 1940), 358-62. For a description of the "scientific historian" as "slave to documentation," see Dixon Ryan Fox's account of the working methods of Herbert Osgood. (Dixon Ryan Fox, *Herbert Levi Osgood, an American Scholar* [New York: Columbia University Press, 1924], p. 47.

[32] Dirk J. Struik, *Yankee Science in the Making* (Boston: Little, Brown and Company, 1948), p. 342.

[33] Adams, *The Study of History . . . . op. cit.,* p. 120.

[34] Manuscript letter of December 1, 1898, in the Bancroft Library, quoted by John Walton Caughey, *Hubert Howe Bancroft, Historian of the West* (Berkeley: University of California Press, 1946), p. 357.

[35] In a letter of 1875, addressed to the Harvard Corporation; quoted by Robert W. Lovett, "The Undergraduate and the Harvard Library, 1877-1937," *Harvard Library Bulletin,* I (Spring, 1947), 223.

[36] Johns Hopkins University, *Seventh Annual Report of the President . . . 1882,* pp. 56-57. See also in this connection Johns Hopkins University, *Fourth Annual Report of the President . . . 1879,* p. 18.

[37] Adams, *The Study of History . . .,* *op. cit.,* p. 46.

[38] *Ibid.,* p. 84.

[39] Bancroft, *op. cit.,* pp. 241, 243.

[40] Columbia College, *Annual Report of the President . . . May 7, 1883,* p. 45.

[41] Adams, *The Study of History . . .,* *op. cit.,* pp. 167-68.

[42] Columbia College, *op. cit.,* p. 44.

[43] Herbert Baxter Adams, *Public Libraries and Popular Education* ("Home Education Bulletin," No. 31; [Albany: University of the State of New York, 1900]), p. 89.

[44] Adams, *The Study of History . . . ,* *op. cit.,* pp. 82-83.

[45] Bancroft, *op. cit.,* p. 565.

[46] U. S. Bureau of Education, *op. cit.,* pp. 375-77.

[47] William Isaac Fletcher, *Public Libraries in America* (Boston: Roberts Brothers, 1894), p. 115.

[48] [George Livermore], *Remarks on Public Libraries;* reprinted from the *North American Review,* July, 1850 (Cambridge: Printed by Boiles and Houghton, 1850), p. 17.

[49] W. N. Carlton, "College Libraries in the Mid-Nineteenth Century," *Library Journal,* XXXII (November, 1907), 483-84.

[50] Arthur Twining Hadley, "The Library in the University," *Public Libraries,* XIV (April, 1909), 116.

[51] Quoted in Franklin, *op. cit.,* p. 78.

[52] Sidney Herbert Ditzion, *Arsenals of a Democratic Culture; a Social History of the American Public Library Movement in New England and the Middle States from 1850 to 1900* (Chicago: American Library Association, 1947), pp. 190-93; C. Seymour Thompson, *The Evolution of the American Public Library* (Washington: Scarecrow Press, 1952), *passim.*

[53] Jesse Hauk Shera, *Foundations of the Public Library; the Origins of the Public Library Movement in New England, 1629-1855* (Chicago: University of Chicago Press, 1949), pp. 206-13.

[54] William J. Rhees, *Manual of Public Libraries, Institutions and Societies in the United States and British Provinces of North America* (Philadelphia: J. B. Lippincott and Co., 1859), pp. 585-651.

[55] New York State Library, *Sixty-first Annual Report . . . for the Year 1878,* p. 23.

[56] Lenox Library, *Fourteenth Annual Report . . . for the Year 1883,* p. 5.

[57] University of Michigan Library, *Librarian's Report for the Year Ending Sept. 30, 1888,* p. 6.

[58] Daniel Coit Gilman, "Books and Politics," in his *The Launching of a University, op. cit.,* p. 197.

[59] Justin Winsor, "An Address," in *Public Exercises on the Completion of the Library Building of the University of Michigan, December 12, 1883* (Ann Arbor: Published by the University, 1884), pp. 30-36.

[60] Kurtz, *op. cit.,* p. 52.

[61] University of Michigan Library, *Annual Report of the Librarian for 1905-1906,* p. 55.

[62] John William Burgess, *Reminiscences of an American Scholar: the Beginnings of Columbia University* (New York; Columbia University Press, 1934), pp. 216-19.

[63] Kenneth J. Brough, *Scholar's Workshop; Evolving Conceptions of Library Service* (Urbana; University of Illinois Press, 1953), p. 112.

[64] Columbia University, School of Library Service, *School of Library Economy, Columbia College, 1887-1889; Documents for a History* (New York: School of Library Service, Columbia University, 1937), p. 109.

[65] *Supra,* pp. 12-13.

[66] Harvard College Library, ["Report of the Library"] in *Fifty-second Annual Report of the President . . . 1876-77,* p. 109.

[67] Lovett, *op. cit.,* pp. 223-227.

[68] Louis Kaplan, *The Growth of Reference Service in the United States from 1876 to 1893* ("ACRL Monographs," No. 2; Chicago: Association of College and Reference Libraries, 1952), p. 5.

[69] Lenox Library, *Fifteenth Annual Report . . . for the Year 1884,* p. 5.

The Heart of the University

Kenneth Brough

*In the preceding essay Samuel Rothstein documented the ways in which the develop-
ment of research and the professionalism of scholarship made the research library a
necessity. In addition to creating a need for greatly increased resources, these factors
also forced librarians, faculty members, and administrators to alter their conception of
the academic library's role in light of the changing needs of the university. In the following essay Kenneth Brough shows how this conception of the library's function
evolved at four trend-setting universities: Harvard, Yale, Columbia and the University
of Chicago; Brough also outlines the effects of this evolution on modern university libraries.*

The importance of the library—its significance and related values—is bound up at least in part with aims and with functions: The aims of the university membership and the functions of the library in helping to achieve these aims. Presumably an object so complex as a university library may have many shades of significance and value to its clients; it may be symbolic of the entire tradition of learning or it may have special meaning as a convenient place to work.

Evolving Conceptions of the Library's Purpose

The conception of the library as a central and vitalizing force in the university developed steadily in the latter part of the nineteenth century. Governing boards, presidents, deans, professors, librarians, and alumni worked together in the accumulation of books. In their efforts to increase the resources and usefulness of the library, they emphasized constantly its importance to the university. With almost no exception these spokesmen agreed that the library should become the focal point of the institution's intellectual life. As demands for research and new methods of instruction made it imperative to extend the book collections and to provide better facilities for their use, the university world began to refer to the library as the "first necessity" of the institution.

Christopher Columbus Langdell, dean of the Harvard Law School, in his 1872-73 report to President Eliot described the library as the "most essential feature" of the School. Langdell emphasized not the fact that the School had a large col-

lection of books but rather the manner in which the library entered into all teaching and research activities. He summed up his belief in this statement: "Everything else will admit of a substitute, or may be dispensed with; but without the library the School would lose its most important characteristic, and indeed its identity."[1]

The conception of the library as the symbolic center of the intellectual life of the university apparently became firmly rooted first at Harvard. Commenting on proposals for the renovation of the library building, President Eliot in 1871 drew attention to the desirability of its location in the college yard.[2] It was where it belonged, in the center of the university. By 1876 the central position of the library had become for President Eliot not only a physical actuality but also a symbol of its importance in the institution. Justifying the expense of enlarging Gore Hall, he affirmed that the Corporation had taken into consideration that "the Library is the centre of the University, and that it would be easier to carry on the University without productive funds than without books and reasonable facilities for their use."[3]

At Yale, President Timothy Dwight in his inaugural address in 1886 declared that the library must be a "central thing" in that institution.[4] His conception of the library as the pivotal point of university life appears in several later addresses and reports. The significance of the library as a radial point of university activity was emphasized at Columbia and at Chicago at the turn of the century.

In the twentieth century an even stronger meta-

SOURCE: Reprinted from Kenneth Brough, *The Scholar's Workshop: Evolving Conceptions of Library Service* (Urbana: University of Illinois Press, 1953), Chapter 2, "The Heart of the University," pp. 23–36, by permission of the author and publisher. Copyright © 1953 by the Board of Trustees, University of Illinois.

phor superseded the "center" and the "core." This phrase preserved the idea of centrality, and, in addition, it included the conception of the library as the vital organ of the university. As the "heart of the university," the library became in the thinking of the academic world not only a central point of intellectual life but also a living source of energy. The phrase was not new to the twentieth century; President Eliot had used it in 1873 to emphasize the importance of the library in the work of the Harvard Law School.[5] However, the conception did not gain wide acceptance until about 1900; James Hulme Canfield, who became librarian at Columbia in 1899, probably did most to popularize it.

Librarians and presidents alike have found it convenient to describe the library as the pulsing heart of a great organism. The comparison served well as an introduction to their comments on the condition of the library, to justify expenditures for books and administration, and to reinforce pleas for additional financial support. The phrase often served as a slogan in campaigns for new buildings. "No need of the University is greater today than that of the central Library," proclaimed President Harper of Chicago, in 1903. "The Library is, or should be, the very heart of the institution."[6]

But these phrases—"essential feature," "center," "core," and "heart of the university"—are more than campaign slogans or the conventional furniture of academic writing. The evolving conceptions they reflect have permeated library practice and have shaped the functions of the modern university library.

THE FUNCTIONS OF THE UNIVERSITY LIBRARY

In the broadest sense, the university library has two basic functions: it must preserve recorded knowledge, and it must make this knowledge available for use. The two functions inevitably result in conflict. The measures necessary to assure complete protection of library materials would preclude any use of them whatever. Absolute freedom in the use of materials, on the other hand, would soon bring about the loss or destruction of many of them. Moreover, if an institution should devote a disproportionate share of its resources to the acquisition and preservation of books, provisions for their effective use would suffer; and the converse is equally true.

Because of the conflict between these two basic functions, preservation and use, any discussion of the purposes of the university library must revolve in large part around the degree of emphasis given to each. Earlier writers emphasized the importance of preservation or the importance of use, or they discussed the balance which must exist between the two. As the structures of the university and of its library have become more complex, however, secondary instrumental functions have emerged and have been made explicit. Formal elaborations of the purposes of the university library are, nevertheless, largely a product of recent years.

The "Storehouse of Knowledge"

The historic role of the academic library is that of a storehouse, a treasury in which a heritage of accumulated knowledge is kept safe for future generations of scholars. By collecting and preserving the written and printed records of the past, the library has shared with the museum one of the principal responsibilities of the university—the conservation of knowledge. Museums have gathered together an endless variety of artifacts; libraries have concentrated their efforts chiefly on books and manuscripts. Although modified by the increasing importance given to other functions, the conception of the library as an agency for the conservation of knowledge has by no means faded to insignificance. Let no one believe that, in these later years, the university has lost all concern for the safety of its books!

The storehouse conception of the library has appeared frequently, and it has persisted until the present day. Librarian George Hall Baker of Columbia in his report for 1893 alluded to the library as a "storehouse and workshop for the prosecution of the whole body of sciences embraced in a university curriculum."[7] Discussing the library as an agency of the university, President Angell of Yale in 1924 called it "a rich storehouse of knowledge . . . . Yale's greatest offering to scholars."[8] In 1931 Librarian Roger Howson of Columbia mixed old and new metaphors when he termed the library a "repository of accumulated wisdom" and compared it to a storage battery "charged with the knowledge of all times and all countries."[9] At the dedication of Columbia's South Hall in 1934, John Buchan spoke of that new structure as "a repository of the varied wisdom of the ages."[10] On the same occasion, President Nicholas Murray Butler quoted words used a few days before by the King of England at the opening of the new library at Cambridge University: " 'It is a workshop of new knowledge and a storehouse of seasoned wisdom.' "[11]

At Harvard, where the sense of trusteeship seems particularly strong, the importance of the conservation function of the library has been emphasized repeatedly. In the preface to his 1830-31 *Catalogue of the Library of Harvard University,* Benjamin Peirce affirmed that "a fund, from which so many minds are constantly drawing their chief supplies . . . should be as rich, as munificence and zeal for the promotion of learning can render it."[12] A special committee, appointed in 1866 by the Board of Overseers to consider the progress of the library, maintained that "it is the reservoir from which the teacher and the pupil of to-day are to draw the accumulations of the past . . . and to which they, in turn, are to add the fruits of their labors for the teacher and the pupil of the future."[13] In 1876, President Eliot declared that "the libraries and other collections of a university are storehouses of the knowledge already acquired by mankind, from which further invention and improvement proceed."[14] In an address delivered at the University of Chicago in 1891, he set forth teaching, investigation, and the accumulation of "great stores of acquired knowledge in the form of books and collections" as the three principal functions of a university.[15] Pleading for a new building and increased financial support, Librarian William Coolidge Lane in 1904 referred to the Harvard Library's honorable history as "the chief depository of the tools of scholarship in America."[16] In his annual report for 1939-40, President James Bryant Conant made this statement: "To maintain and preserve the eternal values, a university among its other functions must 'perpetuate learning to posterity.' To this end the support of our libraries is one of the first responsibilities of the Governing Boards."[17] At the dedication of the Houghton Library in 1942, he again emphasized the conservation purpose of the university library, avowing that "one of the functions of a university is to act as a guardian of the cultural riches of the past."[18]

Justin Winsor and the Doctrine of Making Books Useful

In merely hoarding knowledge, however, the library of the modern university meets only a part of its responsibilities. During the latter half of the nineteenth century a movement to make the library a center of present usefulness—as well as a storehouse against future need—steadily gathered

force. Books came to be considered primarily as tools rather than as treasures. Professors needed materials for their investigations and for their teaching, and some of them required students to consult original sources. Eager to make the library responsive to this increased demand, librarians of the new school emphasized the importance of making books readily available. Justin Winsor, appointed librarian of Harvard College in 1877, became the chief apostle of the new doctrine. In his first report, he laid down the basic principle which was to govern his administration: "Books may be accumulated and guarded, and the result is sometimes called a library; but if books are made to help and spur men on in their own daily work, the library becomes a vital influence; the prison is turned into a workshop."[19]

Winsor's background and earlier work fitted him especially well for his new responsibilities at Harvard. He had served for nine years as head of the Boston Public Library, then the largest institution of its kind in the country. His work had gained for him considerable prestige among his fellows, and in 1876 they had elected him first president of the American Library Association. In the following year he had attended the international Convention of Librarians in London where he had taken a prominent part in the proceedings. A scholar in his own right, he commanded the respect of the Harvard faculty. Furthermore, the lifelong friendship of President Eliot provided a secure basis for administrative cooperation in the development of the library.

Opinion slowly gathering over a long period of years had prepared the way for Winsor's leadership. A special committee appointed in 1866 by the Harvard Board of Overseers to study the reports of the visiting committees of former years included the following statement in its recommendations: "The usefulness of books largely depends upon facility of access and the conveniences attending them. A building which is merely a place for their deposit and safe keeping has no claim to be called a library; and, unless it be amply provided and furnished with every convenience for their use, the most valuable works are sleeping, and are not living teachers of men . . . ."[20]

Such opinion concerning the functions of the library was not confined to Harvard. In his chapter on college library administration in *Public Libraries in the United States* (1876), Librarian Otis H. Robinson of the University of Rochester discussed the increased emphasis placed on the use of books. In his judgment the preservation of materials had dropped to a position of secondary importance. Books worn out in service, he declared, provided the best possible evidence of the value of the library.[21]

"I try never to forget that the prime purpose of a book is to be much read," Winsor stated in 1878.[22] "It is with me a fundamental principle that books should be used to the largest extent possible and with the least trouble," he reiterated in 1879. "There should be no bar to the use of books but the rights of others . . . ."[23] Throughout the period of his administration he consistently adopted library practices which made books more accessible to readers, emphasizing always that accumulation and preservation constitute only the first steps in library management.

In February, 1878, Winsor began to keep a record of the numbers of books for home loan or for use within the building delivered to readers over the loan desk of the Harvard College Library. From that time on, statistics of the use of the library consistently appeared in his annual reports to the president. Winsor announced with satisfaction each gain toward the attainment of his ideal of extensive utilization of library resources. In 1879 he could state with obvious pleasure that the overnight use of reserved books and periodicals had doubled in a single year. Moreover, he was eager to attract an increasing proportion of the students to the library as well as to bring about multiplication of the numbers of books lent. Thomas J. Kiernan, to whom Winsor had given the title of Superintendent of Circulation in 1877, made a study of book use in the period from 1875 to 1880. On the basis of this study Winsor reported that the percentage of students using the library had increased from 57 per cent in 1874-75 to 77 per cent in 1879-80. Summarizing the first ten years of his work as librarian of Harvard, Winsor made this statement in 1877: "There has been no more gratifying symptom of progress for these ten years than the large increase in the proportion of students using the Library. In 1876 not over half were users of the Library; in 1887 nine in every ten were more or less frequent visitors at Gore Hall."[24] President Eliot in a memorial address made this comment on Winsor's delight at the evidence of the growing usefulness of the Harvard Library: "he worked steadily to increase the home use of the books in his charge, and to facilitate the use of them within the Library. He liked to record year by year the accessions to a collection, but he was far more interested in the statistics of circulation and use . . . . In 1893 he men-

tions that out of 1,449 undergraduates only 41 made no recorded use of the Library. In all his annual reports he presents statistics on the use of the Library, and nothing gave him so much satisfaction as a demonstration of increasing use."[25]

Gradually other institutions adopted the practice of recording the use made of the library. In 1884 Melvil Dewey initiated at Columbia detailed statistics of the circulation of books. Zella Allen Dixson, associate librarian of the University of Chicago, published records of circulation in her report for 1898-99. Even Addison Van Name of Yale, one of the last of the old school of librarians, in 1900 included in his report a paragraph concerning the number of books borrowed and the use of materials within the building. His statement carries a suspicious tone of vagueness suggesting that it might be based largely on conjecture, but the very fact that Van Name had come to believe it desirable to make any declaration about the utilization of library resources testifies to the widespread acceptance of the doctrine that books should be used as well as collected and preserved.

That the prime purpose of a book is to be read—a principle revolutionary in the early days of Justin Winsor's career—has become a truism of library administration echoed again and again by university officials of later decades. "No grandeur of buildings, no mere vastness or variety of collections, no ostentation of any sort whatever, can atone for the loss of opportunity or for unnecessary restrictions in the use of the volumes themselves," proclaimed Canfield of Columbia in 1900.[26] His successor, William Dawson Johnston, affirmed in 1911 that "the aim of the library is not the collection of books, but the distribution of them . . . ."[27] President Butler in 1926 declared that "the aim of the trained library administrator is not merely to collect books, but to make books useful."[28] "A book, regardless of its intrinsic soundness, is worthless as a social document unless it is read," maintained Professor Leon Carnovsky of the University of Chicago Graduate Library School in 1933.[29] "Books not used are sterile," avowed Wallace Brett Donham, dean of Harvard's Graduate School of Business Administration, in 1937.[30] Closely allied to the idea of the book as an object of utility another conception had developed: the university library is essentially a laboratory, a workshop for the scholar.

Making books more useful had at least two implications for Winsor: barriers which hindered or prevented easy access to the collections must be removed, and books must serve new purposes. A book was not a capsule to be swallowed whole but instead a book was a tool, one of many with which the student could forge ideas for himself. In such a scheme the library must become a workshop in which professors and students alike could carry on their labors with the tools necessary for their purposes conveniently at hand. Winsor in his first report alluded to the library as a workshop; and in the following year (1878) he revealed this conception of the library more fully: "a great library should be a workshop as well as a repository. It should teach the methods of thorough research, and cultivate in readers the habit of seeking the original sources of learning."[31]

The physical sciences had led the way in emphasizing original investigation; and the thought of the scientist in his laboratory with students grouped about him learning at first hand the methods of research, and with necessary apparatus immediately available, soon enriched the workshop conception of the library. In an address to the American Social Science Association in 1879 Winsor developed the following elaboration: "The library will become the important factor in our higher education that it should be. Laboratory work will not be confined to the natural sciences; workshops will not belong solely to the technological schools. The library will become, not only the storehouse of the humanities, but the arena of all intellectual exercise."[32]

The conception of the library as a laboratory quickly became popular. Dean Langdell of the Harvard Law School in 1886 described the conception of the library in that School:

> My associates and myself, therefore, have constantly acted upon the view that law is a science, and that it must be learned from books. . . .
>
> . . . .
>
> We have also constantly inculcated the idea that the library is the proper workshop of professors and students alike; that it is to us all that the laboratories of the university are to the chemists and physicists, all that the museum of natural history is to the zoölogists, all that the botanical garden is to the botanists.[33]

In the same year Librarian Dewey of Columbia declared that the library must serve graduate students not in the physical sciences in the way that the chemical laboratory served the chemists.[34] Ephraim Emerton, Winn Professor of Ecclesiastical History at Harvard, in 1899 complained that, because of an inadequate building, Harvard fell far short of the ideal in library service. The following passage indicates his conception of the proper relationship of the library to the university:

It would seem to be superfluous at this day to emphasize anew the importance of the Library in the University scheme. "The laboratory of the Humanities," "the heart of the university," "the brain of the academic body:" these are some of the phrases which have become common in utterances official and nonofficial. Especially the laboratory figure has been worked with effect to show that the Library is no longer a mere storehouse of books, but a great workshop, wherein scholars of all grades, teachers and learners alike, have their places. The common phrase, "laboratory method," as applied to the "moral sciences," implies that the very existence of effective instruction along these lines depends upon a suitable provision for the daily practice of all concerned. As the chemical laboratory demands ample supply of chemical materials, ample space for each student, and liberal opportunity for the teacher to pursue his own researches in close association with the students whose work he directs, so the effective use of the Library makes precisely the same demands. . . .[35]

The laboratory figure had become the most popular metaphor used to describe the library. President Harper of Chicago in 1902 affirmed that the library "is, in fact, a laboratory; for here now the students, likewise the professors . . . spend the longer portion of their lives."[36] In his first annual report (1908-09), President Abbott Lawrence Lowell of Harvard stated that "the library has been called the laboratory for the humanities, and it is in fact the principal workshop of the University."[37] Librarian Schwab of Yale declared in 1910 that the library was "primarily the general laboratory of the University, the central workshop where students and instructors in every line expect to find the tools necessary to carry on their work."[38] At Chicago in 1930, Dean Gordon Jennings Laing of the Graduate School of Arts and Literature maintained that to the School "books and proper facilities for their use are what laboratories and laboratory equipment are to a graduate school of science."[39] In 1931 President Butler of Columbia, discussing the Edward S. Harkness gift which made possible the construction of South Hall, referred to the projected building as "the new laboratory-library."[40]

President Eliot's Emphasis on Balance Between Conservation and Use

The university library must serve as a storehouse for the conservation of books and the other records of man's thoughts and deeds, and it must also provide a laboratory for the use of these materials. The achievement of both of these purposes requires a sense of balance in administration.

Probably better than any other chief administrator of his time, President Eliot of Harvard grasped the significance of this central problem. During his long period of service, the storage of the rapidly expanding book collections presented increasing difficulties. Sucessive enlargements and alterations of Gore Hall provided only temporary relief. Furthermore, changing methods of instruction and new emphasis on research demanded better facilities for the convenient use of books. The accelerated growth of the faculty and student body intensified the predicament. Eliot's vigorous and continued efforts to reach a solution gave him an intimate understanding of the problem of balance in library functions.

In a series of lectures delivered at Northwestern University in 1908, Eliot twice emphasized the need for maintaining a right proportion between preservation and utilization. In discussing the responsibilities of trustees, he dealt with the need for laying down rules which would make possible both the conservation of books for the future and their use by the present membership of the university:

> The general rules under which libraries and scientific collections are to be used are subjects for careful consideration on the part of university trustees. On the one hand these expensive collections can have but one justification, namely, that they are constantly and effectively used; on the other hand, they need to be preserved in good condition for the benefit of future generations of students. The problem of the trustees is to lay down rules which will provide a safe middle way between use which tends toward destruction and security which is inconsistent with use. The tendency at the present time among trustees is to divide the collections into two parts, one part to be preserved at the risk of not being so serviceable to the present generation as it might be, the other to be made as serviceable as possible to the present generation, even at the risk of destruction.[41]

Eliot's treatment of the duties of librarians in a subsequent lecture clearly reflects a point of view built up during a sharp controversy which had arisen at Harvard several years before in connection with the size of the book collections and the manner of their storage. The dispute had spread to include most of the Harvard faculty and the librarians of other large universities. Eliot had addressed two conventions of librarians on the subject. Here it is sufficient to note that Eliot had come to consider professors and librarians unreasonable in their refusal to give up any books—no matter how seldom they might be used—or to consent to storing those volumes less in demand in an inexpensive building remote from the main library.

Eliot warned that librarians must set up workable policies to govern the relationship of the bulk of their collections to the space available for display, for work, and for storage. Otherwise, even though they might perform valuable services for scholars of the future, they would very likely find it impossible to make the library an effective help to the present generation. In planning expenditures librarians must make suitable provision for the use of the library as well as for adding to the book collection. In concluding, Eliot cautioned that "there is danger that if utilization lags behind collection, much of the cost of collecting will be lost."[42]

Louis Round Wilson and the Functions of the Modern University Library

Louis Round Wilson, dean of the University of Chicago Graduate Library School from 1932 until 1942, has discussed the functions of the university library more frequently and at greater length than any other individual in recent years. In his statements he reaffirmed the basic importance of both conservation and utilization. In addition, he elaborated these two basic purposes into subsidiary functions which define more explicitly the major responsibilities of the librarian and his staff.

In an address delivered at Vanderbilt University in 1938 Wilson made this summary:

> . . . the modern university library has consciously or otherwise redefined its functions in recent years. It knows that: (1) it must aid the university in conserving materials; (2) it must acquire all materials essential to the extension of knowledge in the special fields of instruction and investigation supported by the university; (3) it must provide bibliographical apparatus to make available its own materials and those in other libraries; (4) it must provide suitable quarters in which the student, instructor and investigator may utilize library materials; and (5) it must promote the work of the teacher, student and the public through a competent staff. . . .[43]

In collaboration with Maurice Falcolm Tauber of the Columbia University Library staff, Wilson in 1945 published a major work on the university library. In a chapter on "The Functions of the University and Its Library," the authors listed six functions of the university: "(1) conservation of knowledge and ideas, (2) teaching, (3) research, (4) publication, (5) extension and service, and (6) interpretation."[44] Four of these functions require no explanation, but the fifth and sixth need clarification.

Under "extension and service" Wilson and Tauber grouped the more commonly understood extension activities—extension and correspondence courses, agricultural extension and experimentation, adult education programs, and the like—and the less directly utilitarian contributions which the university makes to the general welfare through participation by its staff in research, consultation work, and public affairs. The sixth named function, "interpretation," has to do with the dissemination of new knowledge, and thus it overlaps three of the other five—teaching, publication, and extension and service.

Instead of describing independent functions of the library, Wilson and Tauber named eight "essentials" of a university library program properly organized to assist in the attainment of the broader objectives of the university as a whole. These essentials are: "(1) resources for instruction, research, and extension; (2) a competent library staff; (3) organization of materials for use; (4) adequate space and equipment; (5) integration of the library with administrative and educational policies; (6) integration of the library with community, state, national, and international library resources; (7) adequate financial support; and (8) a workable policy of library government."[45] Since later chapters treat in detail the development of conceptions of library service which they represent, no attempt will be made here to discuss these eight elements of a university library program.

SUMMARY

As the university world grasped the importance of the extensive use of books in the new program of instruction and research, the library became a necessity rather than a treasure only. Its central location on the campus grew to be symbolic of its meaning in the university scheme. This thought of centrality evolved into the conception of the library as the pulsing heart of the institution, providing a vital element for all intellectual activity.

The conception of the library as a depository has been modified rather than abandoned. The library has become a more extensive and more elaborate storehouse with each succeeding generation. Librarians have redoubled their efforts to collect and preserve the records of man's thought and achievement. Books are tiered by the hundred thousand in fireproof, air-conditioned stacks. Original documents and costly first editions receive a measure of protection which rivals that bestowed by banks upon their money and securities.

But the depository function no longer is allowed to preclude effective utilization of this accumulated wealth by students and investigators of the present. Increased production of books and more money with which to buy them have enabled the library to treat many volumes as objects to be worn out through intensive use. Furthermore, adequate provision of study-space within the library building and an expanded and improved administrative organization have made it possible for contemporary readers to use costly and even unique materials in their daily work. The "heart of the university" has become a laboratory as well as a storehouse.

FOOTNOTES

[1] Harvard University, *The Annual Report of the President . . .* (1872-73), p. 63. (Hereafter cited as HRP.)

[2] HRP, 1870-71, pp. 41-42.

[3] HRP, 1875-76, pp. 26-27.

[4] Yale University, *Addresses at the Induction of Professor Timothy Dwight, As President of Yale College, Thursday, July 1, 1886* (New Haven, 1886), p. 38.

[5] HRP, 1872-73, p. 17.

[6] University of Chicago, *The President's Report: Administration*, Decennial Publications, First Series, I (Chicago: University of Chicago Press, 1904), cxxv-cxxvi.

[7] Columbia University, *Annual Report of the President . . .* (1893), p. 151. (Hereafter cited as CoRP.)

[8] YRP, 1923-1924, p. 17.

[9] CoRP, 1931, p. 452.

[10] John Buchan, "The University, the Library, and the Common Weal," *Columbia University Quarterly*, XXVI (December, 1934), 310.

[11] N. M. Butler, "The Libraries of Columbia: Address at the Dedication of South Hall," *Columbia University Quarterly*, XXVII (September, 1935), sup. 5.

[12] Harvard University, *A Catalogue of the Library of Harvard University in Cambridge, Massachusetts . . .* (Cambridge: E. W. Metcalf & Co., 1830-31), I, xvi.

[13] Harvard University, *Proceedings of the Board of Overseers of Harvard College in Relation to the College Library, 1866-1867* (Boston: Press of Geo. C. Rand & Avery, 1867), p. 7.

[14] C. W. Eliot, *Educational Reform: Essays and Addresses* (New York: Century Co., 1909), pp. 43-44.

[15] *Ibid.*, p. 225.

[16] HRP, 1903-04, p. 210.

[17] HRP, 1939-40, p. 11.

[18]"Dedication of the Houghton Library," *Harvard Library Notes,* IV (March, 1942), 63.

[19]HRP, 1876-77, p. 109.

[20]Harvard University, *Proceedings of the Board of Overseers of Harvard College in Relation to the College Library, 1866-1867,* p. 5.

[21]O. H. Robinson, "College Library Administration," in U. S. Bureau of Education, *Public Libraries in the United States . . .* (Washington: Government Printing Office, 1876), p. 516.

[22]HRP, 1877-78, p. 111.

[23]HRP, 1878-79, pp. 109, 111.

[24]HRP, 1886-87, p. 121.

[25]Massachusetts Historical Society, *Proceedings,* Second Series, XII (1897-99), 32.

[26]CoRP, 1900, p. 356.

[27]CoRP, 1911, p. 255.

[28]CoRP, 1926, pp. 39-40.

[29]Leon Carnovsky, "Reading in College Residence Halls for Men," in F. W. Reeves and J. D. Russell, *Some University Student Problems,* The University of Chicago Survey, X (Chicago: University of Chicago Press, 1933), 153.

[30]HRP, 1936-37, p. 241.

[31]HRP, 1877-78, p. 105.

[32]Justin Winsor, "College and the Other Higher Libraries," *Library Journal,* IV (November, 1879), 402.

[33]Harvard University, *A Record of the Commemoration, November Fifth to Eighth, 1886, on the Two Hundred and Fiftieth Anniversary of the Founding of Harvard College* (Cambridge: John Wilson & Son, University Press, 1887), pp. 86-87.

[34]CoRP, 1885-86, p. 148.

[35]Ephraim Emerton, "A Blot in the Scutcheon," *Harvard Graduates' Magazine,* VII (June, 1899), 509.

[36]W. R. Harper, "The Trend of University and College Education in the United States," *North American Review,* CLXXIV (April, 1902), 457.

[37]HRP, 1908-09, p. 28.

[38]YRP, 1909-1910, pp. 262-63.

[39]University of Chicago, *President's Report . . .* (1929-1930), p. 7. (Hereafter cited as ChPR.)

[40]CoRP, 1931, p. 40.

[41]C. W. Eliot, *University Administration* (Boston: Houghton Mifflin Co., 1908), pp. 36-37.

[42]*Ibid.,* p. 253.

[43]L. R. Wilson, "The Role of the Library in Higher Education," *School and Society,* XLVII (May 7, 1938), 587.

[44]L. R. Wilson and M. F. Tauber, *The University Library: Its Organization, Administration, and Functions* (Chicago: University of Chicago Press, 1945), p. 9.

[45]*Ibid.,* p. 12.

The Beginning of Public Library Service to Children

Harriet Long

The founders of America's first public libraries viewed them as extensions of the local school systems to be of service to people after they finished school. As a result, librarians directed their services exclusively to adults, and usually did not provide services to children. In time, however, a number of innovative and concerned public librarians began to pioneer in services directed at young people. Harriet Long, a leading authority on the subject, has written the first in-depth history of this movement. In the following paper, she portrays the struggle to introduce public library services to children, which at the turn of the century culminated with the widespread acceptance of children as a legitimate and significant part of the public library's clientele.

THE BEGINNING OF PUBLIC LIBRARY SERVICE TO CHILDREN

The year 1876 is a memorable one in the library movement in the United States. At the Conference of Librarians, held in Philadelphia, the permanent society of the American Library Association was formed. Toward the close of the year, the first issue of *Library Journal* was published, the only representation of library interests in periodical literature. From this unique position, *Library Journal* ably helped to formulate and communicate wise methods of conducting libraries. Finally, a valuable report on *Public Libraries in the United States of America* gave great impetus to the library movement.[1]

According to the statistics gleaned from this report there were 188 free municipal libraries organized under state laws and supported by general taxation. The majority, 156, were in the eastern states, but Ohio had nine, Wisconsin four, Indiana three, Illinois fourteen, and Iowa and Texas had one each.

Accompanying the statistics are articles by eminent librarians of that day, on the history, economy and administration of public libraries. Among these is the first expressed concern over the needs of the younger readers, by William I. Fletcher, then Assistant Librarian, Watkinson Library of Reference, Hartford, Connecticut, and soon to become Librarian of Amherst College. It is entitled "Public Libraries and the Young,"[2] and raises the question "What shall the public library do for the young, and how?"

Mr. Fletcher expresses regret that most libraries had fixed a certain age, commonly twelve or fourteen, below which youthful patrons were not privileged to use public libraries, in spite of the growth in output of juvenile literature. He says:

> The lack of appreciation of youthful demands for culture is one of the saddest chapters in the history of the world's comprehending not the light which comes into it. Our public libraries will fail in an important part of their mission if they shut out from their treasures minds craving the best, and for the best purposes, because, forsooth, the child is too young to read good books.[3]

He asserts that if the public library claimed to be an educational institution, then it should exert its influence upon the young as early as possible. Fletcher voiced approval of the practice adopted by a few recently established libraries, of making no restriction whatever as to age. However, if the doors of the public library were open to the young, he said, then wholesome mental food had to be provided, books which were not merely amusing or entertaining or harmless, but which were instructive and stimulating, and likely to appeal to the better nature of youthful readers. The schools, too, said Fletcher, should work together with the library in directing the reading of pupils, the teacher sending them to the library for information on subjects in the curriculum, thereby in-

SOURCE: Reprinted from Harriet Long, *Public Library Service to Children: Foundation and Development* (Metuchen, N.J.: The Scarecrow Press, 1969), Chapter 7, "The Beginning of Public Library Service to Children," pp. 80-94, by permission of author and publisher. Copyright © 1969 by Scarecrow Press.

troducing them to classes of books to which otherwise they would be indifferent.

It is impossible to measure the influence of Fletcher's article. Whether or not his plea for cooperation between the public libraries and the public schools in providing books and guiding the reading of the young was the motivating force, the period from 1876 to 1900 was marked by a growing relationship between the two educational institutions. The majority of librarians believed that rather than abolish all age restrictions, young readers could be better served through loans of books to the schools, where the teacher, in constant association with the pupils, could guide their reading. Furthermore, as librarians of an educational institution their responsibility was to those who had completed the free common school, and who, unable to afford the purchase of books, might wish to continue their education through access to free books. The public library thus would serve as a "capstone" to the public school system. Consequently, the many public library buildings erected following the Civil War provided no facilities for children.

Many local libraries were erected as memorials to citizens who had made good. Men in this country had not acquired wealth through hereditary fortune but had risen from a lower class and were self-made, and they were often desirous of helping those who were members of the class from which they had come. Philanthropy to educational and cultural purposes was generous and public libraries attracted many a philanthropist who found it desirable to perpetuate his memory in so popular and worthy an institution.

The general pattern of the public library building typical of that period was a delivery room where the public might consult a printed list of books, or, later on, a card catalog; having found the author and title of the book desired, they applied at a window in the grill or at a desk in the center of an open arch, behind which were the stacks of books. Open shelves, which are common practice today, were unknown. In the delivery room there might be chairs and a table or two, with magazines and newspapers, thus serving as a kind of reading-room. Larger libraries had a separate reading-room, and in some a reference room was provided as well.

An occasional one of these libraries opened its doors to children. Mary Root describes her use of the Providence, Rhode Island Library:

> I found myself in a strange country where few books were visible. Instead, there were innumerable little drawers with cards which I could push back and forth on rods in a delightful, diverting way, until an intriguing name popped up: *Wide, Wide World, The Diamond Necklace, Vanity Fair.* Standing on tip-toe, I would grasp a pencil on a huge chain and write the numbers on a slip to be handed to a lady with a green shade over her eyes. Little quivers of excitement and fear always ran down my spine, as sitting on a too-tall chair I awaited the prize drawn. The 'fear' was due to the moment my name would be called aloud to the listening world—plus that 'green shade' which must again be approached.[4]

Since children were barred from most libraries, however, cooperation with the public schools was emphasized and various patterns of cooperation were presented and discussed. As early as 1879, Samuel S. Green, Librarian of the Worcester, Massachusetts, Public Library, had pioneered in working out a plan with the Superintendent of Schools, whereby the school studies would be made more interesting and profitable by the aid of special loan privileges to teachers. In 1891, at the San Francisco Conference, in a paper on *Libraries and Schools,* he reported:

> A few years ago no aid was afforded systematically by public libraries to schools. Now, on the contrary, in a very large number of towns and cities libraries are closely connected with the schools. I should say that almost all public libraries are trying in one way and another to be of assistance to schools.[5]

Most of the early cooperation was with the so-called grammer school (7th-9th grades) and the high school. The first step was the issuing of special cards to teachers enabling them to draw extra books, six in number, to use in the classroom. Then, in libraries that had sufficient book stock or the funds to buy books for the purpose, this privilege was extended to permit a teacher to borrow from twenty to fifty volumes, to be circulated to the pupils, the teacher acting as librarian. The loan period varied, but the entire collection could, at some stated time, be exchanged. Teachers were held responsible, although in some instances pupils were required to have public library cards so as to relieve the teacher of responsibility for books out on loan. A further development, experimented with in an occasional community, was to have all the books which were sent to a school kept in one place, usually the school office, to which the pupils came by class on certain appointed days of the week to select the books to take home, using the usual borrower's card of the public library. These collections of books borrowed by the schools were sometimes selected by the libraries, sometimes by the teacher, the latter often being aided by lists compiled by the librarian. Generally speaking, not many books were provided for the wants of young children in the lower grades at first, although the teachers might borrow on a special card books which would be useful to them in their teaching, and some which might benefit the pupils.

The fundamental idea in this cooperation was that if young people of school age could be taught how to use and appreciate good books, they might guide themselves to profitable reading after they graduated. In families where parents could give this direction, no other help was needed, but in many families the parents were unable or unwilling to do so. Hence the only possible advisers were the teachers who had a constant opportunity to lead their pupils to the reading of good books, and to teach them how to get and use the treasures of the public library. Thus the teacher was the guide, and the librarian the intelligent provider of material.

The success of these various patterns of cooperation was great in some communities, the only drawback being the lack of enough books to meet the demand. However, a few libraries reported that the system of distributing books through the schools did not grow as rapidly as had been hoped, because the heavy burden of regular work left the teacher little time or strength to take on an added responsibility. Other reports mentioned the indifference of some teachers, and their lack of knowledge of books for the young and inability to appreciate the usefulness and importance of books in education. To remedy these problems, librarians urged that a course in children's literature and the use of books be included in the training of teachers. When the Library Department of the National Education Association was formed in 1896, librarians had a greater opportunity to urge its inclusion.

In an 1895 issue of *Library Journal,* the editorial page was given over to the relations of the library and the school, referring to it as "the most vital branch of a library's administration," for "it is through this medium that the children may be reached most easily, most directly, and most effectively." The editorial recognized that the aid of the teacher was essential but recognized also that the teacher was the unknown quantity, whose sympathy and cooperation must be sought through personal contact and through talks at teachers' meetings.[6]

Since, with few exceptions, public libraries

barred children below the ages of twelve or fourteen, children turned to the libraries established by other agencies, wherever they existed. It must not be forgotten that Sunday School libraries still existed in large numbers; by 1880 practically every Sunday School in any village in the United States had its library. However, there was no longer an American Sunday School Union or an American Tract Society publishing the moral tales which had formerly filled the shelves. Instead there was a flood of children's books, and Sunday School librarians were not competent to select wisely from the good, bad, or indifferent publications available. A few of the religious denominations sought to remedy the situation by issuing approved buying lists, but Sunday School librarians, even so, were easy prey. Some of them, indeed, would simply send an order for so many dollars' worth of books to some leading publisher, leaving the selection to his judgment or interest. Book collections were often augmented by gifts when families weeded out their home libraries. And yet, the Sunday School library continued to have its advocates who argued that such a library could concentrate more carefully than the public library on a narrower range of reading. Its clientele, too, was a more homogeneous group, whereas the public library must provide for all classes. Since the number served was more limited, a friendly and intimate relationship could be created which would help in putting good reading into the hands of the young.

During the last decade of the 1800's there was some discussion at meetings of public librarians as to what should be done about the Sunday School libraries. In an occasional locality the public library loaned books to the Sunday School on the same basis as to the public schools. It was also suggested that these libraries might well be managed as branches of the public library. Finally, the consensus seemed to be that with good public libraries available the Sunday School library, as it presently existed, was no longer necessary, but should function as a church library or religious material and lesson aids. Its disappearance was a gradual process, however, with the availability of a public library being a factor in that process.

Miss Emily Hanaway, principal of the primary department of grammar schools in New York City, found that many of the children in her school were either without access to suitable books or were reading books of an injurious kind. In 1885 she gathered together remnants of an old school library, sought donations of books from publishers and others, and set up a library in a day nursery opposite the school. Miss Hanaway believed that the most suitable time in a child's life to lay a proper foundation for taste in reading was in the years before twelve. Thus this library, and others she hoped to establish, would supplement the benefits of the New York Free Circulating Library which did not serve children under twelve. In order to carry out plans for other libraries she enlisted the aid of clergymen and other representatives of the community to form the Children's Library Association, which was incorporated in 1890. Members paid one dollar a year, associate members from five to twenty dollars, and this constituted the only source of regular income.

Lack of resources prevented the establishment of more than the one library. In April, 1890, there were 762 patrons, often standing in line on the sidewalk awaiting a turn to enter the small room. Melvil Dewey was interested in the project and urged the New York Free Circulating Library to provide quarters for the library in its new George Bruce Branch. This was done, but the children disturbed other readers as they went up and down the stairway to the third floor where the room was located, and the experiment was abandoned. After a precarious existence, moving from place to place, the library was finally dissolved.

The humanitarian movement, which found one avenue of expression in the social welfare of children, now became aware of the child's need for books. In 1888, the Children's Aid Society in Boston started the first home library and urged that philanthropic-minded people start them elsewhere. Set up in the homes of poor children, largely those who had little or no opportunity to attend the public schools, each library consisted of a bookcase filled with fifteen books and a supply of juvenile magazines. In a household willing to accept such a library, the bookcase was fastened to the wall of the living-room, a trustworthy boy or girl in the family served as librarian, and a group of readers consisting of ten boys and girls from the neighborhood, ages seven to sixteen, had access to the library. Each child who wished to join recorded that fact on a card, and the parents signed, or more likely, made a cross, indicating their willingness to have their child join.

For each home library there was a volunteer visitor who met with the children weekly when books were exchanged, became acquainted with them, encouraged good reading by discussing the books and reading aloud, arranged pleasant outings, and in other ways entered into the lives of the youth-ful readers. Students from Harvard College often volunteered as visitors. By 1891 there were thirty-seven such libraries in Boston, and by 1894, sixty-nine in different parts of the city and the immediate suburbs. The movement began to spread; other cities in which they were organized were Lynn, Massachusetts, Chicago, Providence, Philadelphia, Baltimore, and Albany, New York.

Settlement houses in foreign neighborhoods opened reading rooms for old and young. In New York City in 1893, the Neighborhood Guild, had a reading-room and circulating library for men, women and children. It was open every evening except Saturday, and borrowers could take books home by paying twenty-five cents a year, unless they were under sixteen, in which case the cost was five cents per year. In the same city, in 1899, the University Settlement moved to new quarters opposite one of the largest public schools and reported its reading-room crowded with Russian, Polish and Jewish children. The librarian describes her clientele as follows:

> It is easy to speak lightly about these children's errors, and to seem to amuse one's self at their expense, but the limitations of their childhood never impressed us more deeply, nor have we ever realized more the important part which the library and clubs play in their lives. These children depend almost wholly upon what they receive from books for moral and mental stimulus. They have no athletics, no real games, no music, no art. The changing seasons mean little more to them than the transition from winter's cold to the sweltering heat of summer. They know nothing of nature. Wild flowers! they rarely see them. They never see the stars, though the sky is above them—the street lamps blind their eyes. From their teachers in the public schools, from the club associations, and from their books they must often get all they are to know of the good and beauty of life. Their hours are divided into those spent at home in a hot, crowded, unsanitary tenement, those spent in the street or candy saloon, and those spent in the dark, overcrowded school. Their home life few can know; it is often destroyed by privation and ignorance; their street life, he who has eyes and a heart may read.[7]

The first librarian of a public library to express concern for the children roaming the streets was Mrs. Minerva Sanders of Pawtucket, Rhode Island. Because Pawtucket was the community where Samuel Slater set up the first textile mill, it early became a manufacturing center. Mrs. Sanders adapted her library to local conditions, inaugurating open shelves contrary to accepted practice, and making the public library a friendly, welcoming place. It was not only a center of culture, but a place where the workingman, too, could find books of value to him on the open shelves. But to Mrs. Sanders, children were always the greater responsibility. Considering the character of the community, and of Mrs. Sanders herself, it was appropriate for her to present a paper at the Thousand Islands Conference on "The Possibilities of Public Libraries in Manufacturing Communities."[8] In it she says:

> The greater responsibilities, however, are with our children, the future parents and guardians of our commonwealth. What are we doing for them as public libraries, as educators? Working hand in hand with the schools faithfully and well, as shown by the valuable and interesting reports published in the *Library Journal* . . .
>
> Does our responsibility rest here? What of the multitudes of waifs worse than homeless, without restraining or guiding influence, to be thrown into the community to swell the numbers of paupers and criminals . . .
>
> We may say this is the work of charitable institutions and humane societies; not so; this is essentially our work. We call ourselves educators, and have the honor to be recognized as such; the work of a public library is to teach, to elevate, to ennoble; there is no limit to its possible influence. Must we wait, then, until our children (for they are all ours as a community) are fourteen years of age or upwards . . .
>
> We maintain that we cannot begin too early, and that this is a part of library work from which we get the greatest percentage of reward. Again I ask, what are we doing for these children, the future pride or dishonor of our communites?[9]

Mrs. Sanders not only expressed concern, she welcomed children to the reading-room. Four tables and chairs, lowered by having the legs sawed off, seated seventy children in a corner of the room, while nearby were shelves of appropriate books. The boys and girls responded by calling her "Auntie Sanders."

The outstanding pioneer in public library work with children was Caroline M. Hewins, who left Boston for Hartford, Connecticut, to become librarian of the Young Men's Institute, a subscription library, in 1875. In this city of 50,000 people, some 600 men and women were members, paying three dollars yearly for the use of one book at a time, or five dollars for the use of two. In 1893, the library, much enlarged in volume, became free and changed its name to the Hartford Public Library.

As was common then, nothing was being done for children; but Miss Hewins, remembering the great value and joy of her own childhood reading, had them in mind from the beginning, and throughout her librarianship in that community she steadily developed a service for them. At the Young Men's Institute, upon her own initiative, whe separated the book collection to see what was there for those children whose families were members. Finding that the books by Andersen, Grimm, Hawthorne, Scott and Dickens showed little use as compared with those by Horatio Alger, Harry Castlemon, Martha Findlay and Oliver Optic, she immediately began to raise and publicize the question of better books and better reading for children.

As she retired the poorer books and replaced them with better ones, she compiled lists, and by 1878 the Young Men's Institute was issuing a quarterly bulletin which regularly included suggestions for children's reading. At a time when published lists for the young were non-existent, Miss Hewins compiled *Books for the Young; a Guide for Parents and Children.*[10] A notice in *Library Journal* describes it as follows:

> The result of years spent not only in trying to guide the reading of children, but in actually reading with them. The list is preceded by a suggestive preface, followed by hints, 'how to teach the right use of books,' a course of 'English and American history for children,' and 'a symposium on books for children.' As a guide through the mass of the best existing juvenile literature, the value of this little book to parents can hardly be overstated.[11]

Miss Hewins provided a large and steadily increasing service to the children of Hartford in a building which had only a corner for their use. She initiated many of the methods to be followed by others in the years to come. Stories were read aloud to assembled groups of children, and an occasional story told; an Agassiz Club was formed, with nature walks on Saturday mornings; and the public schools were visited. However, it was not until 1904 that an adjacent private home was purchased and a children's library opened. The acquisition of this building for the use of the young was no doubt hastened by the development of Hartford as a manufacturing center and its resulting increase in population, including large numbers of children.

As valuable as her contribution was to the children of Hartford, Miss Hewins began to ask challenging questions, and stimulated others to ask questions about public libraries and their service to children, in a series of reports at the Conference of Librarians over a period of twelve years. The first report[12] Miss Hewins presented was at the Conference in Cincinnati in 1882. To prepare it she sent, to librarians of twenty-five leading libraries in ten different states, cards bearing the question, "What are you doing to encourage a love of reading in boys and girls?" Her conclusions were: (1) the number of parents who supervise their children's reading is small; (2) the number of teachers who read and appreciate the best books is also small; (3) much may be and has been done by promoting cooperation between libraries and schools, and by sending books into the schools; (4) in the public libraries direct personal intercourse is the best way of gaining influence over boys and girls.

By 1893, in her "Report on the Reading of the Young,"[13] Miss Hewins presented the answers to another leading question, "Have you an age limit?" Among the 146 public libraries which responded, seventy-four, or exactly one-half, set the age limit at twelve or fourteen; sixteen set the age limit even higher, at fifteen or sixteen; while thirty-six, or one-fourth, had no age limit at all. Most reported that they had no method of directing the reading of children but acknowledged some personal supervision. Five libraries had, or were about to have, a special assistant for children.

The very fact that Miss Hewins also raised, for the first time, the question, "Have you a children's room?" is evidence of some progress in the development of service to children, even though only five reported special rooms, present or prospective. Three wished that they had such a room, while others believed that the use of a room in common with adult readers taught the young to be courteous and considerate of others. Most reported the adult reading-rooms open to children, who sometimes had a table of their own. Miss Hewins expressed her own opinion that books for children should be kept separate, thus making it easier for the librarian or assistant to find a book for a child; and she approved of a separate catalog, thus relieving the crowd at the card catalog.

Miss Lutie E. Stearns, of the Milwaukee Public Library, gave the "Report on the Reading of the Young" at the Lake Placid Conference in 1894.[14] This is a famous and detailed report, far-reaching in its influence. One hundred and forty-five libraries sent full and complete replies. Progress had been made in the previous year, for now thirty percent had no age limit as against twenty-five percent then. The other seventy percent varied the age limit from eight to sixteen years. Reason for age restrictions were advanced such as, "We must preserve our books," the oft-repeated "We must draw the line somewhere," and "Our books are not suited to young people."

In answer to the question, "Do you have special lists or catalogs?" the majority answered that they designated children's books by some sign in the main catalog. Only four had special card catalogs, free or for sale at a nominal sum. Cooperation with the schools continued to be favored according to the pattern described earlier in this chapter.

There is no doubt but that the pertinent questions directed to public librarians in these reports by Miss Hewins, and by others under her instigation, stirred the library profession. Brookline, Massachusetts, in 1890, opened the first reading-room especially for children in the basement of the public library, a room which seated forty in all. Pictorial newspapers and juvenile magazines were put in the room, together with bound volumes of *Harper's Weekly* and the *Youth's Companion,* and a supply of books was sent down from time to time. The Minneapolis Public Library, in 1893, was the first to open a children's room in a corridor in the basement, a room for both reading and the circulation of the children's books that were kept there on open shelves. In 1894, the Denver Public Library took a room which had been a ladies reading-room, separated from the delivery room by an open arch, fitted it with chairs and tables of suitable height, and put the children's books on low shelves. Without doubt Denver acted thus so that the children would not annoy the adults. John Cotton Dana, the Librarian, wrote:

> What to do with children in the free public library is one of the unsettled problems of library economy. For the comfort of the elder readers it is certainly desirable that children should not come in large numbers into the main part of the library in which the public is given access to the shelves.[15]

A problem was created, as soon as the age limit was abolished and the doors of public libraries were open to the young. They did not come in one by one in a decorous manner; they poured in. Their very numbers forced the doors to open wider and wider, and demanded separate provision for service.

The first general discussion of library work with children at an American Library Association Meeting was in 1897. Linda A. Eastman[16] speaks of the occasion as follows:

> 'It is in the air,' whispered a gentleman sitting next to me at the Philadelphia Conference during an ani-

mated discussion of methods of work with children, and referring to the wide-spread interest in the subject which is marking a new phase of library progress. The facts which substantiate his remark would indicate the time is ripe for the development of this phase: a full conception of the public library carries with it a necessary emphasis on the work with the young, for if the public, the great mass of the common people, is to profit greatly by its public library, it must be trained into the use of books—trained from childhool. [17]

The same year, Mary Wright Plummer reported on "The Work for Children in Free Libraries," [18] before the New York Library Club. From replies to questions she had sent out it was clear that a large number of libraries still had an age limit for borrowers. However, she could also report that an increasing number of public libraries had opened either circulating libraries or reading-rooms for children. A number reported crowding, with children often sent home because the room was too full, and most of them mentioned many foreigners among the children. Indeed, service to children had progressed to the point where a consideration of staff to work with them was being given some thought. Mrs. Plummer, in the same article, said:

If there is on the library staff an assistant well read and well educated, broad-minded, tactful, with common sense and judgment, attractive to children in manner and person, possessed, in short, of all desirable qualities, she should be taken from wherever she is, put into the children's library, and paid enough to keep her there. [19]

By the turn of the century, then, public library service to children had made a promising beginning. It was even being argued that in a few of the larger cities where branch libraries were being built, these branches should be located near public schools and should contain a separate room, or part of one large room, for the use of children. No longer would children be served solely by sending collections of books into the schools. They were now being recognized as part of the public, needing their own quarters, their own book collection, and a staff to serve them. Whether or not the tendency of the period to emphasize the welfare of children had the effect of compelling public libraries to include children as part of their clientele cannot be answered affirmatively without more evidence than is available. And yet it is difficult to believe that the one had no effect upon the other.

FOOTNOTES

[1] U. S. Bureau of Education *Public Libraries in the United States of America* (1876).

[2] *Ibid.*, p. 412-18.

[3] *Ibid.*, p. 413.

[4] Root, Mary E. *"American Past in Children's Work,"* Library Journal, LXXI (April 15, 1946), 548.

[5] Green, Samuel S. "Libraries and Schools," *Library Journal*, XVI (San Francisco Conference 1891), 22.

[6] Editorial *Library Journal* XX (April 1895), 113.

[7] Moore, Helen "City Children and the Library," *Library Journal*, XXV (April 1900), 170.

[8] Sanders, Minerva A. "The Possibilities of Public Libraries in Manufacturing Communities," *Library Journal*, XII (Thousand Islands Conference 1887) 395-400.

[9] *Ibid.*, p. 398.

[10] Hewins, Miss C. M. (comp.), *Books for the Young; a Guide for Parents and Children* (New York: F. Leypoldt, 1883).

[11] *Library Journal* VIII, (May 1883), 79.

[12] Hewins, Caroline M. "Yearly Report on Boys' and Girls' Reading," *Library Journal*, VII (Cincinnati Conference 1882), 182-90.

[13] Hewins, Caroline M. "Report on Reading of the Young," *Library Journal*, XVIII (July 1893), 251-3.

[14] Stearns, Lutie E. "Report on Reading of the Young," *Library Journal* XIX (Lake Placid Conference 1894), 81-87.

[15] Dana, John Cotton "The Children in the Public Library," *Outlook*, LIV (1896), 555.

[16] Eastman, Linda A. "Methods of Work for Children," *Library Journal*, XX (November 1897), 686-88.

[17] *Ibid.*, p. 686.

[18] Plummer, Mary Wright "The Work for Children in Free Libraries," *Library Journal*, XXII (November 1897), 679-686.

[19] *Ibid.*, p. 681.

The Changing Character of the Catalog in America

David C. Weber

For those charged with organizing the growing library collections in America, the increasing size and diversity of these collections made their job far more complicated. In the following review of cataloging practice in America, David Weber outlines the ways in which the growth of library collections influenced the character of the catalog, and shows that economic and not philosophic considerations have often been responsible for changes in catalog production.

Librarianship is a sociological art. It uses many techniques and faces many intellectual problems found in many other professions. The fundamental responsibility of librarianship is the systematic provision and effective utility of graphic records. Its basic technique for achieving this goal is bibliography, the major instrument of library services.

"Bibliographic control" is the organization of individual works in an order for effective retrieval. The resultant "bibliographic organization" may take the form of shelf arrangement or classification, but the term is generally used with reference to a bibliography or catalog in printed or card form. "Individual works," as used above, may mean word compositions, paintings, vases, and so forth; and "word compositions" refers to any unit whether one poem, a letter, an article, technical report, or a lengthier work. In one method or another libraries must provide bibliographic control over all graphic records in their custody.

One other distinction should be made. Bibliographic control means providing content accessibility as well as physical accessibility. Contents are made accessible by means of indexing and abstracting services and by individual lists and formal bibliographies. Physical access is provided through catalogs of the holdings of a particular library with book numbers by which to locate each item. Analytics in a library catalog serve both these forms of bibliographic control.

ORIGIN OF CATALOGS

Techniques for bibliographic control have progressed over the years. A detailed title page, a table of contents, and an index to a single book were the first steps in improving access. When books were few in number, a reader or librarian could know what was in each and where each was shelved. (It has been said that as a rule of thumb any individual can know well 10,000 documents). A list of holdings was useful for inventory purposes, and as collections grew the inventory would also be used to assist in locating volumes. The great libraries of several hundred thousand scrolls in such places as Alexandria and Pergamum must have had finding lists; however, the only known specimen is the "list of cases containing the books on great rolls of skins" graven on the House of Papyrus walls at Edfu, not far below the Aswan Dam. An early union list of holdings in English monastic libraries was compiled to improve access toward the end of the thirteenth century. During the nineteenth century, when the publications of journals and magazines increased markedly, libraries had the added problem of achieving subject indexing of articles. As individual American libraries tried to control this sudden increase in individual works, several lists were published, notably the comprehensive general indexes compiled by William F. Poole in 1848, 1853, and 1882. Analysis followed of volumes of essays and other compilations, resulting in *The A.L.A. Index* of 1893. Then five libraries prepared for some 250 learned journals analytics which the American Library Association began publishing on cards in January, 1898. The H. W. Wilson Company later took over these activities for its series of indexes. Similarly each year we find libraries, individuals, or firms compiling such works as an index to *Articles on American Literature, 1900-1950* (Duke University Press, 1954), an index to *Articles on Antiquity in Festschriften* (Harvard University Press, 1962),

SOURCE: Reprinted from David C. Weber, "The Changing Character of the Catalog in America," *Library Quarterly*, 34 (1964): 20–29, by permission of the author and publisher. Copyright © by the University of Chicago Press.

and the *Meteorological and Geoastrophysical Abstracts* (American Meteorological Society, 1950———). In this fashion libraries have been increasingly relieved of much of their work on content accessibility.

The analysis of content has always been a concern of libraries, though rarely have individual budgets permitted much to be accomplished. Reliance can be placed on published analysis by others wherever it exists. The control of physical accessibility, on the other hand, must remain a dominant local concern as long as libraries seem impelled to cater to local nuances of classification or have material not part of a national control program.

A catalog should be designed to answer questions as to what books are in the library—questions of physical accessibility. The best catalog answers the greatest variety of questions with the greatest ease for the least expense. For reasons of economy a library may refuse to answer certain types of inquiries and may today rely on published lists, indexes, abstracting services, and bibliographies for considerable support.

The physical form taken by catalogs has varied over the years. before reviewing the major forms that have been used, it may be well to suggest the objectives which have generally controlled these forms.

The overriding influence has been the desire to provide ease of access for one of more of several requirements:

1. The local need to find books in the collection by author, title, subject, or form
2. The need to have the catalog available in several local locations
3. The need to add or change records frequently to keep the listing up to date
4. The belief that scholars will welcome widespread availability of the catalog as facilitating their work.

A secondary influence is financial. This seems to control most decisions. It may dictate a brief-entry typed on sheets, or it may permit a handsome publication by virtue of a subsidy. Some local requirements can be met together with national interests if the production can be a union list or can otherwise be a sound commercial venture. Library catalogs will have a wide variety of combinations of access requirements and financial strictures.

Lacking regular funds for purchasing books, libraries often relied on gifts for the majority of their acquisitions.[1] It seems evident that catalogs made for inventory purposes were early seen as an effective means of acknowledging and soliciting gifts. In the Colonial period these motivations were dominant; however, as time progressed, the need for an index to the collections came to be the primary motive for catalog preparation.[2]

PATTERN OF EARLY CATALOGS

In order to understand the use made of the catalog in its two major forms, in books and on cards, we shall review the catalogs of the oldest American university library because its records are clear and its method of library administration was quite typical of the best thought of the day.

In 1667, the Overseers of Harvard College drew up laws for the young library providing for a library keeper and for three catalogs: (1) books as they are placed, (2) alphabetical author list, and (3) lists by donors. Here we seem to find motivations of inventory, access, and appreciation. The first printed catalog appeared fifty-six years later. This octavo catalog was compiled by Joshua Gee in 106 pages and published in 300 copies: *Catalogus librorum Bibliothecae Collegij Harvardini quod est Cantabrigiae in Nova Anglia. Bostoni Nov-Anglorum, MDCCXXIII.* Two years later a ten-page supplement was published and, in 1735, another ten-page supplement appeared.

The reason for publication of the first American library catalog seems clearly to have been the opportunity to solicit additional gifts. The Harvard Corporation "Upon the Intimation lately made by Mr. Hollis, and formerly by Mr. Neal, that it may be of great Advantage to the College Library, that a Catalogue of the Books in the s̄d Library be printed and Sent abroad, Voted, that forthwith the Library-keepr take an exact Catalogue of the Books in the Library, and that the same be printed in Order to transmitt to friends abroad . . ."[3]

The Harvard laws of 1667 are confirmed in almost identical language by those of 1736, and there is evidence that a manuscript catalog by donors continued to exist. One and possibly two manuscript catalogs of the collection arranged by size were later prepared before the fire of 1764. In November, 1765, the corporation voted that the librarian "be allowed for reducing the Books of the new Library into alphabetic Order, and transcribing several copies of them."[4] In December of 1765, new laws were adopted in which the third regulation for the library read: "A written catalogue of all the Books in each Alcove, shall be hung up therein; And an alphabetical Catalogue of the whole Library, divided into Chapters, according to the Diversity of Subjects, shall be printed and a Copy chain'd in each Window of the Library. There shall also be an Account of the Donors, open to every Ones inspection, to begin with the Donors to the former Library."[5] (The count in June, 1766, was 4,350 volumes.)

The 1765 catalog was folio manuscript, and an early supplement was quarto. In addition, the Librarian "apparently made copies of donations and arranged them in a docket file as a donors' catalogue."[6] Another catalog was begun in 1770 and dropped; another was completed during 1771. In 1781, the library was using the 1779 folio alphabetical manuscript catalog for its books and a separate alphabetical folio manuscript catalog of 1781 for its pamphlets which had not previously been cataloged.

Meanwhile in 1773 a second printed catalog had been published as a result of the 1767 laws, which quoted a still earlier regulation. This stated that certain duplicates should be set aside and cataloged "for the more common use of the College . . . & the Librarian shall prepare a Catalogue of such Books."[7] The 1773 catalog had a Latin title page which may be translated as *Catalogue of the Books in the Cambridge Library selected for the more frequent Use of Harvard men who have not yet been invested with the Degree of Bachelor in Arts.* An explanatory note following the title page has been translated as follows:

> Inasmuch as the Catalogue of Books in the College Library is very long, and not to be completely unrolled, when Occasion demands, save at very great expense of time, embracing Books in almost all Tongues and about all Sciences and Arts, most of which are above the Comprehension of Younger Students, it has seemed wise to put together a briefer Catalogue, to wit, of Books which are better adapted to their use . . .[8]

The full manuscript catalogs of 1779 and 1781 lasted until 1789 when two men were employed to prepare a new folio manuscript of the 12,000 volumes in alcove (shelf) arrangement and subject divisions. This became the third printed catalog in 1790, *Catalogus Bibliothecae Harvardianae Cantabrigiae Nov-Anglorum,* in 362 pages. And doubtless there then was "a Copy chain'd in each Window of the Library." This became crowded in turn and a 1795 manuscript catalog of the alcoves was prepared.

THE NINETEENTH CENTURY

Another alcove catalog was begun in 1817 in twenty-one folios but never finished. During 1821-22, the reclassified collection was listed by Librarian Cogswell in a new alcove catalog of eighteen folios. In the year following, Cogswell introduced an early form of the card catalog as had existed since the turn of the century in various German and Scandinavian libraries.[9] This alphabetical "sheet catalogue" was composed of "seventeen boxes," and books would there be listed by author. A separate subject catalog and a shelf-list (or alcove) catalog remained. However, in 1823, Cogswell's successor copied the "sheet catalogue" into five volumes and tradition was restored.

The next printed catalog at Harvard was the author list published for the Law School Library in 1826, supplemented four times from 1833 to 1846. A fifth catalog, the third general catalog of the University, was issued as *Catalogue of the library of Harvard university* appearing in 1830, an alphabetical author list with a subject index. These two volumes listed nearly 35,000 books, and the "systematic index" was in a small third volume which also included a catalog of maps and charts. In 1834, a supplement of 260 pages was published; in 1835-36, a second was planned but never printed. Meanwhile the 1781 pamphlet catalog was replaced in 1833 by a manuscript which occupied eight large folio volumes at its termination in 1850.

A new manuscript catalog was proposed in 1840. This one foretold a remarkable change in the physical form of the library catalog and was a "slip catalogue" which would list holdings on cards 1½ inches tall and 6½ inches long. By 1847, this alphabetical catalog of additions had been adopted and existed on cards measuring 2 by 9½ inches, an outgrowth of Cogswell's sheet catalog and of the experience with interfiling entries cut from the 1790 printed catalog together with written additions to make copy for the 1830 publication.

Since the creation of this card catalog, the only printed catalogs of substantial portions of the Harvard Library have been the following:

Catalogue of Scientific Serials of All Countries . . . 1699-1876. 1 volume, 1879.

A Classified Catalog of Chinese Books. 3 volumes, 1938-1940.

The Kress Library of Business and Economics: Catalog. 2 volumes, 1940-56.

Catalogue of the Lamont Library. 1 volume, 1953.

Author and Subject Catalogues of the Library of the Peabody Museum of Archeology and Ethnology. 53 volumes, 1963.

Let us now turn to one major and early innovation of public libraries which deserves special note. A catalog of different character was proposed in the middle of the nineteenth century: a catalog published in parts, as were many popular novels of the day. Mr. Cogswell, who was then at the Astor Library, proposed "to take up the library by departments, and prepare a classed catalogue, to be printed as each department is completed."[10] The Astor Library issued in 1854 a *Catalogue of Books . . . Relating to the Languages and Literature of Asia, Africa, and the Oceanic Islands.* The Boston Public Library adopted this plan and in 1866 issued three brief subject lists followed by several others in later years. Each of these was reprinted repeatedly.

This method of spreading costs was used for a slightly different purpose by the Boston Library when it began issuing its very popular quarterly bulletin of recent additions in 1867. The bulletin was the "current-awareness" service of its day. This practice was initiated by other libraries such as the Chicago Public (in its *Temporary Finding Lists . . .* which were an immediate success when first issued in 1874). Harvard began its *Bulletin* in 1875 and continued it for a slightly different purpose in its distinguished series of *Bibliographical Contributions*, 1878-1911. Many libraries now issue these bulletins in one form or another. These bulletins lent themselves to being cut and pasted on cards to improve the card catalog appearance, as was reported in 1872 by the Boston Public and the St. Louis Public School Library. (The Harvard Library issued printed catalog cards from 1888-1931, as did various other libraries.)

THE OCCASIONAL BOOK CATALOG

As the above summary indicates, the manuscript catalog was the basic form, with the printed edition a rarity. From 1636 until 1840 the wealthiest university had only three general printed catalogs with three supplements—a total of six times when the printed list was relatively up to date. Meanwhile, at least fourteen fresh manuscript versions were begun, and one or more was used to keep up-to-date the record of the collection. Yale College had issued five catalogs, between 1743 and 1823, with the largest only 122 pages. Ranz has noted that "it would be unfortunate if the impression were left that the usual practice for libraries was to print catalogs of their collections. Indeed, quite the opposite was true, for the great majority of libraries printed no catalogs during this period."[11]

It is correct to state, therefore, that the issuance of a printed book catalog was always an unusual event. One copy of the Harvard 1790 catalog was annotated with new acquisitions, and perhaps the other book catalogs were as well; yet these were in fact single "manuscript" copies. In nearly all libraries, manuscript records were the rule although many of them published one or two catalogs in the middle half of the nineteenth century. Typical of these were the catalogs of the Eastport, Maine, Athenaeum in 1836; of the Portland Athenaeum in 1839 and 1849; of Colby College in 1845; and of Bowdoin College in 1821 and 1863, with a medical list in 1830. (In fact Bowdoin's 1863 catalog with 16,000 volumes was far above average in size.) Library catalogs, with only four or five exceptions, listed less than 40,000 volumes. A few libraries put out annual supplements.

It was natural that the social library and public library felt a particular urgency for issuing printed catalogs because the publication served to attract new members as well as to encourage use and support. The general availability of a catalog increased the circulation of books and is even said at the Boston Public to have "had a marked effect in elevating the character of the circulation."[12]

The only large libraries which were consistent publishers of catalogs were such wealthy institutions as the Astor Library, Boston Athenaeum, the Boston Public Library, the Library of Congress, the New York Mercantile Library, the New York State Library, the Library Company of Philadelphia, and later the United States Surgeon-General's Office. The most universal user of the printed catalog during the period 1850-75 was the state library; the academic library had all but abandoned them.[13]

THE MODERN CARD CATALOG

The use of the manuscript catalog was reserved for librarians. It was apparently never available to the public, yet few justifications of printed catalogs appear to have been based on the resultant saving of librarians' time. One of these is the comment of the Brookline Public Library that the printed catalog "meets an urgent demand from the public, as well as a need *within* the library, and facilitates all the routine work of the circulating department beyond measure."[14]

The historic significance of Harvard's 1862 card catalog seems to have been not only its format but also its open availability to readers. In the summer of 1862, the new catalogs of authors and subjects were first made accessible to all students and "all literary gentlemen" who were "freely admitted."[15] Just one hundred years ago, Ezra Abbot wrote his famed "Statement Respecting the New Catalogues of the College Library."[16] These catalogs set the pattern followed ever since, so some description of this change may be appropriate.

The "slip catalogue" of the 1840's included all additions filed by author on 2 × 9½ cards. These cards were particularly designed for the chief librarian's use. They recorded author, title, classification, binding condition, date of receipt, name and residence of donor, if a gift, and cost and fund if a purchase. The new "Indexes," begun October 11, 1861, on 2 × 5 cards, were particularly designed for use by readers; and they recorded subject, full name of author, title, place and date of publication, size, illustrations, and classification. Included in the catalog were cards for analytics and cross-references. The cards were kept in four cases each holding twenty-eight drawers, 15¼ inches long, in seven tiers. The only major difference from modern card catalog cases was that each drawer was double width to hold two rows of cards, a notable economy before later standards increased the card size and weight by 50 per cent.

These improvements and innovations in the catalog were recognized by the Harvard Overseers. The Committee To Visit the Library reported its satisfaction:

> The new Catalogue on cards . . . has been making such progress and has been so constantly in use, during the past year, that experience has dissipated all doubts as to its intrinsic *practical* value. The theoretical soundness and the beauty of its method have never been questioned; and it would seem that the Librarians and the frequenters of the Library must now be congratulated on the possession of the best mode yet devised of summarily answering the questions, 1. "Is the book I want in the Library?" 2. "What books in the Library treat of the subject on which I am seeking information?"[17]

The new Harvard form for the library catalog was adopted almost universally within the United States during the next decade. Only four or five of the very largest libraries had the financial resources to hope to continue printing a general catalog. Aside from those wealthy libraries, only the small libraries had printed catalogs; very few of those holding above 20,000 volumes had printed lists. The card catalog more nearly met their requirements. The beauty and permanency of library card catalogs seemed assured when the Library of Congress began issuing its printed catalog cards in November, 1901.

With the increased cost of issuing printed catalogs, with the greatly increased size of public libraries of all types, and with the growth in book publishing and book availability, the urge to print catalogs declined rapidly during the 1880's and 1890's. Further, the growing desire to reveal the subject content of public and academic libraries increased the bulk of catalogs in a way which hastened abandonment of printing plans.[18]

In those years of transition when the published catalog could no longer be the constant goal, there was a clear understanding of the advantages and the disadvantages of the card and book forms, nowhere better summarized than by Charles A. Cutter.[19] Suffice it to point out the obvious currency and economy of the card file and the wide availability and ease of use of the book. The comparative advantages could only be altered as mechanical techniques invalidated the early assumptions of cost and time.

Attempts have occasionally been made to combine the card advantages with the book form. The Rudolph Indexer was widely discussed and tried in a few locations in the mid-1890's.[20] Visible file drawers have found usefulness in such areas as the control of current serial records. The upright visible record is widely used to present cards in a book format.

One other departure was investigated in a card catalog mechanization study undertaken in 1958 by the Operations Research Department of the University of Michigan. This project analyzed the feasibility and costs of using closed-circuit television and a card manipulating device to permit access to a card catalog from a remote location. No application was found where the costs could be justified.[21]

THE NEW ERA

Between the 1870's and the 1950's the growth of library catalogs was not matched by printing techniques economically equal to the reproduction task although photo-offset had helped. Single volumes for special collections continued to be issued. National libraries dutifully obtained funds to continue publishing. Yet when one tries to find an early indication that techniques existed which once again permitted a library to publish a general catalog, it seems to occur in 1951 when the branch catalogs of the King County Public Library in Seattle, Washington, were issued in tabulating-machine format. The author, title, adult subject, and juvenile subject catalogs were updated by fortnightly changes arranged in shelflist order, and the entire catalog was replaced every six weeks. These innovations were forced on Librarian Ella R. McDowell because there were 38 branches and a typical branch annually exchanged 69% of its books with the central collection. The use of rented tabulating equipment provided the King County Public Library with an ideal control of physical accessibility for a rapidly changing deployment of its books.[22]

With 114 service outlets and only 25 of these equipped with card catalogs, the Los Angeles County Library adopted the King County system in modified form in 1952 by publishing its *Children's Catalog.* This was followed two years later by the first edition of the *Adult Catalog.* In 1956-60 the New York State Library published three *Checklists* of its books and pamphlets in three large subject areas, a return to the printing of catalogs-in-parts now made possible by the tabulating machine.

In 1958, the twelve-volume *Catalog of The Avery Memorial Architectural Library,* Columbia University, was the first of many G. K. Hall publications employing xerography for reproduction. And a second major new technique had appeared. In 1959, the National Library of Medicine began using the Listomatic camera for production of the *Current List of Medical Literature.* This machine was one of the sequential card cameras—a third major new technique. High-speed computers have qualified as the fourth major new technique which can be exploited in the preparation of library catalogs.

These samples may serve to indicate that printing techniques of the 1950's had brought costs down to a reasonable level. The Avery catalog has long been a major scholarly tool in the arts, and its publication helped the library staff as well as the scholarly world; and the National Library of Medicine could expand its indexing coverage considerably by use of a superb new mechanical technique. Further, the growing complexity of li-

brary organization was a strong reason for using these methods. King County had a fluid collection to serve a wide area with a small staff; record-changing had to be minimized if not eliminated. Los Angeles County had a comparable problem of providing access to its collection with minimized records. The New York State Library was striving to make it as easy to find books as to find telephone numbers, and the state-wide interlibrary lending process was greatly simplified by the issuance of the book catalog.

The quantity of library catalogs published in the past few years constitutes a major event in library history. It is welcomed for its liberating effect, but appreciation is cautious because of the purchase costs and the possible lack of suitable standards in these publications. One result has been the preparation by the ALA Book Catalogs Committee of a statement on "Preferred Practices in the Publication of Book Catalogs."[23] The technological achievements are certainly most heartening to librarians. They are the result of mathematical and chemical advances earlier in this century applied in newly designed machines. Significant improvements are constantly being made.[24]

The access motivations for printing a library catalog referred to earlier in this paper still pertain while the economic controls are not so restricting. The regional and national interdependence among libraries strengthens the old arguments. One new motive is evident: concern over the great space now occupied by card catalogs in the largest libraries.

As far back as 1904, William C. Lane saw this space problem approaching since the catalog "occupies much floor space . . . . Its bulk gives some cause for uneasiness . . . . The question of space must be seriously reckoned with by the architect. . . ."[25]   Lane's successor fifty-two years later reported "these catalogues . . . are becoming more and more enormous and complex jungles of cards . . . and they outgrow the space that is readily available for housing them."[26] There seems to be no library which yet has printed its catalog in order to reduce space. Nevertheless, though it may not be a prime reason, the great saving of space through conversion to book form will provide a substantial dividend and one which the larger libraries may have to achieve later in this century.

It is too early to see what will result from the publication of the huge catalogs of the University of California, Berkeley and Los Angeles. Their printing was prompted by the need to have records for these collections available on the other campuses of the University; and, from the experience of the past century, it seems most doubtful that the card file will soon be discarded at either Berkeley or Los Angeles.[27] Libraries which can afford these sets will simply have two more exceedingly useful catalogs on their shelves for purposes of bibliographic sleuthing, inter-library borrowing, and photocopy orders.

FOOTNOTES

[1] Louis Shores, *Origins of the American College Library 1638-1800* (Nashville, Tenn.: George Peabody College, 1934), p. 109; the point also seems clear in Jesse Shera, *Foundations of the Public Library* (Chicago: University of Chicago Press, 1949), p. 201.

[2] James Ranz found in his study of early printed catalogs that this motive became dominant as soon as libraries grew to even a modest size ("The History of the Printed Book Catalogue in the United States" [unpublished Ph.D. dissertation, University of Illinois, 1960], pp. 62-63).

[3] Colonial Society of Massachusetts, *Publications*, XVI (1925), 467. In addition, Ranz has noted that "the promotional character of Colonial catalogs was quite evident in their handsome physical appearance" (*op. cit.*, p. 76). On the other hand, Yale's first catalog, in 1742, seems to have been motivated by the need to improve access: President Thomas Clap noted that "before this Time there never had been any perfect Catalogue of the Books in the Library; for want of which the Students were deprived of much of the Benefit and Advantage of them" (*The Annals or History of Yale-College* . . . [New Haven, Conn., 1766], p. 43).

[4] Clarence E. Walton, *The Three-Hundredth Anniversary of the Harvard College Library* (Cambridge, 1939), p. 18.

[5] *Ibid.*, p. 25.

[6] *Ibid.*, p. 19.

[7] "The Laws of Harvard College 1767," Chapter vii, Regulation V, The Colonial Society of Massachusetts, *Publications*, XXXI (1935), 369.

[8] Keyes D. Metcalf, "The Undergraduate and the Harvard Library, 1765-1877," *Harvard Library Bulletin*, I (1947), 30.

[9] Ruth French Strout found the first mention of card catalogs in the 1791 "French Instructions"; see "The Development of the Catalog and Cataloging Codes," *Library Quarterly*, XXVI (1956), 30.

[10] Astor Library, *Annual Report of the Trustees . . . 1854* (New York, 1855), p. 30.

[11] *Op. cit.*, p. 81.

[12] U.S. Department of the Interior, Bureau of Education, *Public Libraries in the United States of America* (Washington, D.C., 1876), p. 572.

[13] Ranz, *op. cit.*, p. 145.

[14] U.S. Department of the Interior, *op. cit.*, p. 572.

[15] *Report of the Committee of the Overseers of Harvard College Appointed To Visit the Library for the Year 1863* (Boston, 1864), pp. 11, 31.

[16] *Ibid.*, pp. 35-76.

[17] *Ibid.*, pp. 6-7.

[18] This point is well developed by Ranz, *op. cit.*, p. 146, who also gives a useful discussion of catalog costs from Colonial times through the nineteenth century.

[19] U.S. Department of the Interior, *op. cit.*, pp. 552-54. See also James A. Whitney, "Considerations as to a Printed Catalogue in Book Form," in Boston Public Library, *47th Annual Report* (1898), pp. 49-59.

[20] Editorial, *Library Journal*, XVIII (1893), 277.

[21] University of Michigan Engineering Research Institute, *Final Report: Application of a Telereference System to Divisional Library Card Catalogs—a Feasibility Analysis* (Washington, D.C.: Council on Library Resources, 1958).

[22] Dorothy Alvord, "King County Public Library Does It with IBM," *PNLA Quarterly*, XVI (1952), 123-32.

[23] *ALA Bulletin*, LVI (1962), 836-37.

[24] Among many recent descriptions, Richard H. Shoemaker, "Some American 20th Century Book Catalogs: Their Purposes, Format and Production Techniques," *Library Resources and Technical Services*, IV (1960), 195-207; C. D. Gull, "Mechanization: Implications for the Medium-sized Medical Library," *Bulletin of the Medical Library Association*, LI (1963), 197-210; *The MEDLARS Story at the National Library of Medicine* (1963), esp. chap. iv; and Samuel N. Alexander, *The Current Status of Graphic Storage Techniques: Their Potential Application to Library Mechanization* (Washington, D.C.: Library of Congress for the Conference on Libraries and Automation, 1963).

[25] "Present Tendencies of Catalog Practice," *Library Journal*, XXIX (1904), 140.

[26] Harvard University Library, *Annual Report for the Year 1955-56* (Cambridge, Mass., 1956), p. 6.

[27] For a brief discussion of attendant problems see David C. Weber, "Book Catalogs: Prospects in the Decade Ahead," *College and Research Libraries*, XXIII (1962), 307.

The Library of Congress under Putnam

David Mearns

In 1899, Herbert Putnam (1861-1955) accepted the position of Librarian of Congress. For the next forty years he was to direct the national library with vigor and imagination. He instituted the sale of Library of Congress catalog cards, encouraged the development of the Library's classification scheme, started the National Union catalog, established programs for the nation's blind, and stimulated the growth of the outstanding documents and reference divisions at the Library. All of these projects increased the influence of the Library of Congress until it held a position of unrivaled leadership in library affairs in this country.

In the following tribute to Putnam, David Mearns captures the character of this fascinating man, and in doing so illuminates the history of the Library of Congress during the first half of the twentieth century.

An appraisal of the Putnam legacy must begin with two characteristics of it borne clearly, constantly in mind. The first is this: The Library of Congress, as it exists today, is in its outward seeming the Library as he left it. True, in the interval, the administrative structure has sustained some innovation; the collections have grown apace; strange figures bend over the desks and walk along the corridors. But the services and their purpose; the duties that animate the institution; the direction of its progress: these remain substantially the same.

The second characteristic is of comparable significance: When Herbert Putnam took the oath of office on that April morning of 1899, and mailed the attestation to the Secretary of State,[1] he was already a professional, experienced in the executive practices of his calling, recommended for new exertions by his colleagues throughout the land, and appointed on the basis of a firmly established reputation for distinguished capacities. He believed, as he said, "in library work as a useful division of public service,"[2] and succinctly enumerated his previous career in these terms:

Librarian, Minneapolis (Minn.) Athenaeum; 1884-1887.
Librarian, Minneapolis (Minn.) Public Library; 1887-1891.
Librarian, Boston (Mass.) Public Library; 1895-1899.
President, Mass. Library Club; '96-'97.
President, American Library Association, '98; filling out the term of Justin Winsor.
Delegate (representing the United States) at the International Library Conference held at London; 1897.

Has written no monographs, but is the author of various articles in magazines, periodicals and in professional journals.[3]

But if the measure of Herbert Putnam's achievement as Librarian of Congress is to be taken, it is necessary to understand the conditions prevailing when first he "viewed them with a responsible eye,"[4] and to record his impressions, insofar as may be possible, in his own words. The main "building stood as planned: the outside quadrangle, the octagonal reading room centered within it, and the three main book stacks radiating from it—north, east and south—to the quadrangle itself."[5] It had been opened for more than a year and, perhaps, some of its more lamentable features had been detected. Generally speaking, Herbert Putnam considered it "a poor economy to build your building first and select afterwards the man who will have to operate it." It were "better to pay him a full salary for a couple of years for doing nothing more than observing, investigating and preparing to give advice than to put him in only when the machine has been constructed."[6] In the case of Mr. Putnam himself that had been impossible. But to a member of the House Committee on Appropriations he once privately confided:

"The *present* expenditure is a large one. It is in my opinion larger than the present service justifies. Until the Library of Congress be equipped for really efficient service to Congress on the one hand, and to

SOURCE: Reprinted from David C. Mearns, "Herbert Putnam and His Responsible Eye," in *Herbert Putnam, 1861-1955, A Memorial Tribute* (Washington: Library of Congress, 1956), excerpted.

scholarship at large on the other, it is little more than a reference library for the District of Columbia.

"I do not see how Congress is justified in spending $300,000 a year in maintaining a reference library for the District of Columbia. Nor does such a library justify a seven million dollar plant."[7]

The situation was altogether deplorable. Mr. Putnam was emphatic when, on January 26, 1900, he described the Library of Congress as "a mass of material not yet equipped with the official records which are requisite for its safety, or with the catalogues and other paraphernalia which are necessary for its effective use."[8]

Small wonder that he, a little ruefully, had expressed to a journalist on the *New York Tribune* a "hope that the profession and the public generally, while anticipating much in the future, will be content to see the much emerge slowly. I doubt if anything would appear above the surface for a long time to come."[9] Or that, in a different mood, he had complained to R. R. Bowker: "We have plenty of authority; all that we need is the money."[10] The absence of apparatus caused him grave misgivings; it was difficult to dramatize the implications. And then something happened that played into his hands. A Washington paper for Sunday, March 25, 1900, announced that "A number of rare and costly books forming a part of one of the most valuable collections of the Congressional Library, were stolen on Thursday night from the Library reading room." The report went on to say that "thefts of books are becoming more and more frequent, and . . . hardly a week passes without several volumes being stolen."[11]

Mr. Putnam made the most of it. Early the next day he dispatched what was, for him, an unusually long letter to the Members of the Joint Committee on the Library:

"It is not my practice to attempt in the Press corrections of misstatements or exaggerations. Where, however, the subject matter is one necessarily of concern to Congress, it is only proper that the Committee on the Library should have in its possession the exact information. I, therefore, communicate to the Committee that information in the present instance:—

"*One* book has apparently been stolen from the Library. It was issued to a reader on Thursday evening. It was not a book of extreme rarity, but it has sold for as much as $55. I know of no other recent theft. It is the first one reported to me since I took office. I know of no justification of the statement that there has been a series of thefts since the Library moved into the new building.

"Every library suffers from occasional theft, and the Library of Congress cannot hope to be entirely an exception,—nor has it been in times past; though its chief losses have been from employees. Under present conditions, however, it is peculiarly liable to loss, from several causes avoided elsewhere:

"(1) There is no '*shelf-list*' of the Library. This is the record customarily kept of the books as they stand on the shelves. Lacking this record it is impossible to check up the contents of any particular shelf and ascertain promptly whether any books be 'missing.'

"(2) There is no *subject catalogue* of the printed books. Yet the large part of the applications are for the 'best books' on this or that subject. The attendants may suggest from their own memory, but are frequently obliged to supplement this by an examination of the shelves, where the books are roughly grouped by subject. In consequence some of them are constantly absent from their posts in the Reading Room.

"(3) There is at present no provision by which rare books may be examined under special supervision. There is no special room; there is no force of special attendants. A book of extremest rarity would now be examined only in the Librarian's office. But this is an administrative office. The arrangement has inconveniencies by day; and the office is closed in the evening. In the evening the only room open for readers is the main rotunda. This is used by the general public. It is in constant movement, from scores of readers entering and leaving. The attendants are busied with hundreds of demands, absorbing and distracting them. A single reader can be differentiated from the rest only by assigning him a particularly prominent desk;—a single book, only by noting the issue in a special record. Both these precautions were taken in the present instance: both failed,—as they are likely to fail when the special reader is only one of a group of special readers, and the attendants as a whole are busied with other routine, and no single attendant can be detailed to watch a single reader, even if under suspicion.

"Under the circumstances the book of extremest rarity would not be issued—nor is it. Such books are for the most part in locked cases in the exhibit hall or in safes elsewhere. But the book stolen was an ordinary printed book, whose high value is not intrinsic but due to its rarity. It was Haywood's 'History of Tennessee.' It was not a merely curious book. It was a *useful* book, which could not well be refused to a reader. It was not on the open shelves, nevertheless. It was kept in a locked room. But this room had no special attendant, to supervise its use there; and the book was sent for and issued in the main reading room—under the special precautions, which, however, proved insufficient.

"(4) The Reading Room has not its full complement of attendants, even for the ordinary service. The exigency of work in other divisions of the Library—particularly in the Copyright Office—has necessitated the detail to them from the Reading Room force of over a dozen persons. With the force thus depleted it is not possible to cope properly with the routine demands,—still less to arrange for special supervision of special use.

"Owing to a similar defect the four existing divisions of the Library handling special material—the Manuscript, Map, Music, and Print Divisions—are closed at four o'clock. Yet the demand for the material they contain by no means terminates at this hour. They should be open until ten. Until this be done, and until, in addition, provision be made for the accommodation of the 'special collections' in a special room, where their use by the proper persons may be specially facilitated and yet specially guarded, the Library cannot be said to be affording adequate service to the public; nor taking adequate precautions for its own safety.

"As I have explained in connection with my Estimates, the shelf list of a library is the stock book. Without it no inventory can be taken. Without an inventory it is impossible at any one time to state positively what books, if any, are 'missing.' The statement that but one book has recently been stolen must, therefore, be qualified as I have qualified it above:—but one book has recently been stolen to my knowledge. The conditions which force the administration of the Library to this qualification,—the absence of the proper records which would enable such statements to be unqualified, has been and is a source of anxiety and constant apprehension. The apprehension of loss and of the mortification of an inability to state positively whether or not there has been loss, will not abate until the Library be equipped with those records and receive its proper complement of attendants; in other words, until the work which my Estimates propose shall be begun next year, shall have been completed."[12]

Herbert Putnam, a man of confident patience, would have to wait nearly three decades for his rare book room; but, on the whole, the immediate results of the *affaire* were not too (shall we say?) unsatisfactory. A lesson in first principles was

vividly imparted. The erroneous news story was corrected.[13] Acting upon the theory "that this was only one of the cases frequently occurring in a library where a book missing and actually taken away without leave has, nevertheless, been taken without particular criminal intent." Haywood's *Tennessee* was recovered in a matter of hours.[14] And what was infinitely more to the point, the Library was voted substantially the total of the funds requested in the Estimates. The organization (or, better, perhaps in the case of a century-old institution, the reorganization) of the Library could be effected.

Outwardly, Mr. Putnam was unmoved. Impassively suppressing an impulse to gloat, he admonished Helen E. Haines, editor of the *Library Journal*:

> "There is one suggestion, or rather caution, perhaps, that you will let me make with regard to your editorial reference (if you make one) on the appropriation granted. The Committee granted what they did because as compared with the work to be done, my estimate seemed to them reasonable.
>
> "Now, it would not do to be enthusiastic as to the amount of the Appropriation, as if it were a matter of surprise. The Committee must not be made to feel that they have been lavish. They have only done that an expert would say, I think, was necessary; but they have done no more, and ought not to be made to fell that they have done more, for it is their duty not to be lavish. So that the gratification should not be that Congress has been generous to the Library, but only that Congress has been able to take an intelligent view of the real needs, and to grant what was reasonable and necessary to meet them."[15]

For the ancient in these purlieus, reading those lines evokes the image of a little, red-headed man, in a high-backed chair, pipe in mouth, feet on hassock, brows arched, brown eyes flashing, mustachios bristling, and hands—those graceful, sophisticate, constantly moving hands—waving as he dictates to his secretary, Allen Boyd, whom he had engaged with the "understanding" that the employment is "absolutely to terminate" in three months "*unless* a new arrangement be made for its continuance."[16] (It was. It lasted for nearly forty years.)

The Library's classification, as he found it, did not favorably impress Mr. Putnam. It had been designed by the first Baron Verulam and Viscount St. Albans, adapted by Thomas Jefferson, and modified by Ainsworth Spofford. It seemed to lack the exactness, the precision, required by the modern world. He determined to replace it. Accordingly, with this in view, he addressed an enquiry to the ingenious Melvil Dewey:

> "I have heard it said that you were engaged upon a revision of the Decimal Classification. Is this true? If so, when will the revision, or any part of it be ready for use?
>
> "I ask not from any mere abstract interest, but because we are about to reclassify. If by any possibility I can justify the use of D.C. I shall prefer to use it. In its present form, the arguments against its use in this Library seem insuperable. Our work of reclassification will, however, extend over several years, and it may be that your revision will proceed fast enough to keep pace with us.
>
> "You can understand one obvious necessity in the case of this Library: the disproportionate provision for Americana.
>
> "I understand that while you have not patented the Classification, you stipulate against its use in part; or rather, the assignment of any part of the notation to classes or sub-classes varying from those for which it stands in your scheme. Would you feel stringent about this stipulation in case we should find it possible to use here the notation in the main, but should find it impracticable to use it precisely in some of the sub-divisions?"[17]

But after months of intensive study, Mr. Putnam reached the reluctant conclusion that "we cannot use, without modification, any one [scheme] now in the field, and to modify may be less satisfactory than to devise newly for ourselves."[18] He determined to "devise newly" and from that decision there emerged the classification "which has since been recognised as the best for a large library."[19]

• • • •

Ohio State University's President, James H. Canfield, on the eve of his abandoning education in favor of librarianship, June 9, 1899, marked "private" a half-apologetic letter to Mr. Putnam:

> "I presume there is no question as to your receiving all manner of advice from all sorts of cranks covering everything that you have yourself thought of and found feasible, and much that nobody ever ought to think of at all. I want to add my quota to either one or the other of these classifications.
>
> "It has long seemed both desirable and possible to have all books deposited at the Congressional Library carefully catalogued on most approved methods by expert cataloguers—and cards printed in quantities sufficient to supply the various libraries of the country. In other words—the great bulk of card cataloguing could be done in a more satisfactory way and a more complete way, if it were done at one point: and that point, naturally, is the Congressional Library. . . .
>
> "Having made the suggestion—or having stated my point, I leave the matter with you."[20]

It is unlikely that Herbert Purnam was struck by the novelty of Dr. Canfield's idea; it is more probable that he knew then, as he certainly knew shortly thereafter, that

> "It was suggested a half century ago by the Federal Government through the Smithsonian Institution. Professor [Charles Coffin] Jewett's proposal then was a central bureau to compile, print and distribute cards which might serve to local libraries as a catalog of their own collections."[21]

But clearly, Mr. Putnam felt that the time had come to do something about it. In replying to Dr. Canfield, he wrote:

> "So far from regarding your suggestion as in any way or manner eccentric I should consider the project proposed essentially within the proper function of this Library' Since July 1st 1898 fifty copies have been printed of each author card representing an accession by copyright. This number represents, of course, no greater multiplication than may be necessary for our own catalogues, including reserves. But if fifty card copies can be printed there is no reason why five hundred should not be, and I see no reason why these additional copies should not be made available to other libraries at a cost which will cover actual outlay.
>
> "The cards being used for the recent accessions are of the standard LB postal size, a departure from that in our old catalogue and one step further in the direction of cooperative service.
>
> "The Library of Congress should be undertaking such a service on a large scale. It can do so adequately and conveniently only with a printing plant of its own. At present delays in the Government Printing Office cause an uncertainty as to the receipt of cards which would defeat any project which involves a dependence on us of other libraries."[22]

By the following Spring, Herbert Purnam was corresponding with the Public Printer concerning the establishment of a Branch Printing Office and a Branch Bindery in the Library of Congress.[23] But it was not until October 15, 1901, following his return to his office after an absence of several weeks, that he made an interesting disclosure to a reporter of *The Evening Star:*

> "The trip that I have just taken," said Mr. Putnam, "was primarily to attend in behalf of the Library conferences of certain state library associations. I attended one of the association of New York state, held at Lake Placid; one of the association of Ohio, held at Sandusky, and one of the association of Iowa, held at Burlington. I attended also a meeting representing the library interests of Chicago and vicinity, and incidentally visited the University of Illinois, at Champaign, where there is the largest school for library training west of Philadelphia, and one of the largest and most efficient in the United States. There is an association representing the library interests of the country as a whole. That is the American Library Association. That holds an annual meeting. It was

this year at Waukesha, Wis. This has not proved sufficient to provide for all the necessary discussions of problems in library economy and practical projects in library work, especially cooperative work, so that associations have been formed in each of many states, and even within these in each of several of the largest cities."

He expatiated on the theme for several minutes, and then explained:

"At each meeting there are always some projects under consideration for cooperation among libraries as a whole in processes of cataloging, etc., and for the promotion of greater efficiency in the effort to advance the higher research. It is to these particularly that the Library of Congress owes a duty and in these it must necessarily be interested. It has the largest collection of books in the western hemisphere, increasing more rapidly than any other single collection; it is organizing within its walls bibliographic apparatus and an expert bibliographic service of high efficiency; it has an opportunity absolutely unique to render its bibliographic work of general utility. I say absolutely unique because it receives without any cost to itself every book entered under the copyright law and a large mass of other material through exchange and the exchanges of the Smithsonian Institution and a very large amount of material through deliberate purchase. It has now a corps of cataloguers who are experts, who are engaged in classifying and cataloguing this material and in reclassifying and cataloguing the material on hand. It has within its walls a printing office, a branch of the government printing office, to print the product of this work. These products can be multiplied in such a way as to be available to other libraries at a cost which is only the cost of the least cost factors; for instance, in the case of catalogue cards, the additional stock and the presswork. Libraries securing the benefit of this work through the additional copies will, of course, reimburse to the government the expense of producing them, but the expense will be but a small fraction of the far greater expense which they have been incurring in an attempt to do the whole work individually.

"As among national libraries, the opportunity of the Library of Congress is unique in another respect, in that it is the national library of a country whose library interests are enthusiastic and active in cooperative undertakings which will increase the efficiency of the material they hold and eliminate wasteful duplication of effort and expense.

"Practically all American libraries today have card catalogues. In these every book appears under its author, under the subjects of which it treats, and sometimes under its title, if the title differs from the subject. Some books have to appear in, perhaps, only two places, others in forty or fifty, where there are many authors and many subjects treated by them. On an average a book appears in from three to five different places. Now, the cards that libraries have used were in the first instance written; they then came to be typewritten, and in recent years they have in some libraries come to be printed. Printing is pos-

sible, of course, only for the larger libraries which are handling a large number of books and making elaborate catalogues— the New York public library prints, the Boston public library, the Harvard College library, the John Crerar of Chicago and even the Carnegie at Pittsburgh.

"The Library of Congress has for some time been printing. It has now within its walls a branch from the Government Printing Office.

"Now, the cost of getting any particular book into the card catalogue is far greater than the public has any notion of. There are various elements of cost; there is the work of the cataloguer, who is an expert; then there is the work of the transcriber, if you multiply copies of the card by transcription or by the typewriter. If you print there is the cost of composition and presswork. The stock would cost the same whether you transcribe or print. But the two most costly factors are the work of the cataloguer, the expert, and the work of the compositor or transcriber. It has been estimated that on the average the total cost of getting a book into a library catalogue is from 25 to 35 cents. Not a single volume, of course. A book may be in a hundred volumes, and yet represent only one title to be handled; but on the average the cost is from 25 to 35 cents for each book, or what the libraries refer to as a 'title'.

"Now, the interesting thing is that until now libraries have been if effect duplicating this entire expense; multiplying it, in fact, by each one undertaking to do the whole work individually for itself. There are thousands of books which are acquired by hundreds of libraries—exactly the same books, having the same titles, the same authors and contents and subject to the same processes. But each library has been doing individually the whole work of cataloguing the copies received by it, putting out the whole expense. . . .

"There have been distributions of printed cards on a small scale or covering special subjects. The United States Department of Agriculture distributes its card indexes to subscribers paying the cost of the extra copies privided for the purpose, and is thus making generally available in convenient form, at nominal cost, information of great value to investigators. The American Library Association (not as a scheme for profit, since it is not a commercial body, but merely as a measure of professional cooperation) has issued cards indexing certain scientific serials, and even cards cataloguing certain current books. But the association has no library nor any corps of expert cataloguers. For the material to be catalogued it had to depend upon voluntary gift or loan from the publishers. The cards issued did not cover enough titles to interest a large library; they covered too many to interest a small one. Yet a subscription had to be required for the entire series. There were never more than a hundred subscribers.

"Since the Library of Congress moved into the new building expectation has turned to it. . . . It receives these copyright deposit copies, on or before the date of publication—and thus in advance of any other library. . . . It is classifying and cataloging this material on its own account. It is printing the results in the form of cards. It is reclassifying and recataloging its existing collection (excluding duplicates, over 700,000 books and pamphlets), and is printing these results also on cards. These cards are of the standard form, size, type and method of entry (the library has been in consultation for over a year past with a committee of the American Library Association—a committee of experts—in order to arrive at standards in all these respects). What it prints is an author card. It prints by way of memorandum on the card the subject headings that it will use on the copies destined for subject cards. The cost to it of the first author card, including the work of the cataloguer, is doubtless over 30 cents for each book. But a second copy of the card can be run off for a fraction of a cent.

"Now it is receiving this urgent appeal: To permit other libraries to order extra copies of the cards which will cover books that they are acquiring: just as they are permitted to secure extra copies of the card indexes of the Agricultural Department, or, indeed, of any government publication, paying the cost plus 10 per cent.

"The Library of Congress would be putting out no greater expert labor than before; the government would be fully reimbursed for the additional mechanical work and material; and the other libraries of this country would be saved an expense, which in the aggregate is now an enormous expense, of duplicating, indeed of multiplying many times over, the outlay on the two factors of cost which are the large factors . . . Between 1891 and 1896 there were 7,000,000 volumes added to the 4,000 libraries in the United States. These may represented 500,000 different 'books' or 'titles'. The cost to catalogue these once, at 35 cents a title, would have been but $175,000. They were catalogued many times over; how many times can only be guessed, for, of course, some books were acquired by only one library, others by hundreds of libraries. Assuming that on the average each book was catalogued only six times, the total cost to the 4,000 libraries was $1,050,000. Could they have acted as a unit, having the books catalogued and the cards printed at some central bureau and multiplying copies to supply the need of each, the total cost would certainly have been kept within $300,000. The saving effected during this short period alone would, therefore, have been two-thirds of the total; on the basis assumed, over $700,000.

"American instinct and habit revolt against multiplication of brain effort and outlay where a multiplication of results can be achieved by a machine. This appears to be a case where it may. Not every result, but results so great as to effect a prodigious saving to the libraries of this country. The Library of Congress cannot ignore the opportunity and the appeal. . . .

"The distribution of cards for current publications may begin very shortly. Very likely it will cover also the publications of the present calendar year, so that the undertaking will be coeval with the century. The cards first issued will doubtless be those for the current American copyrighted books. . . .

"The possible and actual use of the printed cards is not confined to the main catalogues, nor, indeed, to the catalogues at all. They can be used in catalogues of special subjects in the 'shelf list' of the library, and in various different records. Indeed, over a dozen different uses have been planned out of them for libraries, or in part adopted.

"What will become of the cataloguers?

"The cataloguers are perhaps the most enthusiastic for the project. Cataloguing is a work of many processes. The centralization will eliminate only two, and these the initial. It will free some human energy. In the smaller, more popular libraries this will be available for direct service to readers, of which these can never be sufficient. In the libraries for research the service freed will be available for advanced cataloguing and analytical work, and for other bibliographic work indispensable to the full efficiency of the library, but which now can little be afforded, owing to the necessary expense upon these two elementary processes."[24]

The announcement of the new service was sent to 400 libraries and 17 State library commissions on October 26th.[25] The "much" was emerging.

At his domed office on Capitol Hill and in his rooms at the Albany on H Street[26]—Mrs. Putnam and their daughters being then in Europe—newcomer Putnam was, he insisted, "busily engaged in the practical administration of a particular Library," with "little time in which to meditate upon general problems."[27] But the plans, forming in his mind, were broad; they depended, for their execution, largely on the extent of his own powers.

Upon one subject his mind was made up: The American people were properly entitled to the freest access to the national resource over which he presided. To Charles Harris Hastings, later a member of his own staff, then President of the Bibliographical Society of Chicago, he wrote:

"I think students with a purpose should receive at the hands of the librarians not merely advice as to consulting the catalogues; but counsel as to the authoritative works on special subjects; and guidance as to unexpected sources of information. I do not see how it is possible to fix 'to what point the expenses of such service may be legitimately charged to the public.' I think that students who are engaged upon work tending to public improvement should receive the utmost assistance; and the cost of such assistance is very properly a 'charge on the public'; particularly is this of force in municipal and government libraries."[28]

• • • •

In those first years, a principal preoccupation of Herbert Putnam was the gathering of his forces. Applications were received by the hundreds. Each was civilly, but noncommittally, acknowledged. To demands for patronage, he would replay that unfortunately the only existing openings were for posts requiring special training and experience: qualifications which the particular constituent appeared to lack; he would, however, be happy to receive recommendations in behalf of more eligible candidates. Actually, he gave personal attention to the recruitment and selection of the staff. The letterbooks are filled with messages to the deans of library schools asking for the names and aptitudes of outstanding students. He was in constant correspondence with other librarians concerning, in minute detail, the demonstrated abilities, personality traits, and supposed capacities of those ambitious men and women who sought to transfer their careers to the Seat of Government, and to join in what appeared to them to be a great emprise. When, after the approval of the appropriations for the fiscal year 1901, he had settled upon the many new appointments, he sent a list of all their names, together with their qualifications, to the professional journals and to organizations concerned with the advancement of library science.

He was fashioning an élite corps. Some of its members were willing, even eager, to accept compensation at a rate of less than a dollar a day; others (astonishingly many) blithely begged (and for a time were permitted) to present their services absolutely free in exchange for training and experience. But where positions were of critical significance to the development of the Library, Mr. Putnam disdainfully rejected the niggardly salaries attaching to them. Thus, in submitting his estimates for the fiscal year 1902, he informed the Secretary of the Treasury:

> "This position [Chief of the Division of Manuscripts] became vacant September 1st [1901]. I am holding it vacant until the salary shall be placed at a sum which will enable me to secure for it a thoroughly adequate person. This division deals with the material which forms one of the two greater divisions in a national library.... The interests involved are altogether too important to be entrusted to a second-rate man."[29]

The staff or, to use his own term for it, the "force" with which Herbert Putnam surrounded himself was composed of extremely able men and women, infused with a sense of mission, dedication, and their almost limitless opportunities for patriotic endeavor. They were competent, conscientious, devoted; their lives governed not by the length of the work-day but by the work on hand. For this, there would always be too few. Mr. Putnam, at the close of the first six months of his administration, drew attention to the fact that

> "During the past year nearly every regular employee of the [Copyright] Office has without extra compen-

sation worked over time. The total of over time for that year (excluding the personal over time of the Register whose working day rarely ends until 10 o'clock) has amounted to 9,789 hours: the equivalent of 7½ clerks for an entire working year."[30]

Much the same could have been claimed for other units of the Library—and for himself. He was slow to delegate powers; meanwhile there were countless interviews to conduct, callers to receive, letters to compose in that idiom that was so inimitably his own, recommendations to approve or to reject, vouchers to sign, instructions to transmit, and inflexible decisions to reach. And, in addition to the immeasurable, the appalling complexities, interventions, exasperations of administrative routine, there was the necessity of determining the destination of his Library, the dimensions to which it would aspire, the objects which it would be designed to serve, the purpose for which it would exist and steadily move forward. Herbert Putnam was called upon to act as architect for a structure which would grow and grow and never quite complete. For him those first years were the years of planning. There was nothing tentative in the plans that emerged. They were final, complete; the task thereafter would be the task of execution.

Theodore Roosevelt's first Annual Message, dated December 3, 1901, contained two paragraphs on "an activity of the Federal Government which" had "not yet received mention" in such a document[31]; they read:

> "Perhaps the most characteristic educational movement of the past fifty years is that which has created the modern public library and developed it into broad and active service. There are now over five thousand public libraries in the United States, the product of this period. In addition to accumulating material, they are also striving by organization, by improvement in method, and by co-operation, to give greater efficiency to the material they hold, to make it more widely useful, and by avoidance of unnecessary duplication in process to reduce the cost of its administration.
>
> "In these efforts they naturally look for assistance to the Federal library, which, though still the Library of Congress, is the one national library of the United States. Already the largest single collection of books on the Western Hemisphere, and certain to increase more rapidly than any other through purchase, exchange, and the operation of the copyright law, this library has a unique opportunity to render to the libraries of this country—to American scholarship—service of the highest importance. It is housed in a building which is the largest and most magnificent yet erected for library uses. Resources are now being provided which will develop the collection properly, equip it with

the apparatus and service necessary for its effective use, render its bibliographic work widely available, and enable it to become, not merely a center of research, but the chief factor in great co-operative efforts for the diffusion of knowledge and the advancement of learning."[32]

It should not imperil the national security, pain the fastidious and the credulous, or create convulsive surprise to announce to a candid world that these passages were based upon an *aide-mem-oire* submitted by the Librarian of Congress himself.

• • • •

The Putnam epoch extended from 1899 to 1939 and its annals are set forth in those forty volumes which contain his reports to the Speaker of the House and the President of the Senate. The narrative is progressive, the style is rarely dull (and then only when another hand than his composed it); it is the story of an institution responding to a natural force known as "Putnam's law." The honors, the new dignities, that came to the Library were sometimes matters for "gratulation"—a favored word—but they never reached the fever-point of being rapturously unexpected. Indeed, to the seeker of the Putnam secret there comes a realization that among the subtleties and in-definables one formidable element can be isolated: consistency.

When, in 1936, members of his staff were preparing an exhibit for the Dallas exposition in observance of the centennial of the independence of Texas, Mr. Putnam was asked to compose a slogan which might be hung in large letters above the display, and which would express the distinguishing features of the Library of Congress. He thought for a moment and then, taking a slip of paper, wrote: "Universal in scope; national in service." It was apt, of course, and memorable. But it was no sudden improvisation; it had been forming on his tongue and shaping on his pen for more than three decades.[33]

• • • •

Herbert Putnam felt a sense of close kinship with his appointees. One who was closer to him, perhaps, than any other has written of "the long rich years" given by "his beloved Library family," and has told how he "used to come home always heartened by his hours at the Library, buoyed with appreciation of the accomplishments of each and all."[34] Such assurances are indisputable; but,

more than this, they expose a quality of his nature not always quite transparent.

For to the staff, Herbert Putnam bore a relationship not unlike the relationship of the Great White Father to the aborigines of North America. He was venerated. He was endowed with extraordinary gifts. He was changeless and timeless. He was a spirit cast in the image of other men but too carefully socked and booted ever to suggest affliction with ceramic feet. For his mistakes—they were rarely discoverable—he was readily, quickly absolved. His actions were sometimes inexplicable, incredible, inscrutable, but there was confidence in his wisdom, in his judgment, in his foresightedness.

He was stern. He exacted the highest standards of professional and personal conduct. He could mete out reprimand with waspish elegance and laceration. He had his Siberias to which to condemn the exiles. For the "good of the service" he was not restrained by any "practical" or mundane consideration from the instant exercise of his dismissal powers. He was patient with less than perfect competence; intolerant only of disloyalty to usage and the canon. But he was not unjust, not easily provoked, not recklessly, impetuously, incensed. So far from being a martinet, he was so calm, precise, equitable, informed a disciplinarian that the transgressor (unless a hopeless dullard) found the charge unanswerable and himself incapable of rebuttal.

It would be true to say that he was not prodigal in praise, holding, as he did, a certain excellence to be a proper, natural, even requisite, expectation. His approval was usually tacitly expressed. But when the public, the press, or the politically puissant unfairly impugned, impeached, or inveighed against, his blameless cohorts, he was promptly their outraged, withering, formidable defender. He could utterly destroy a churl, humble a poltroon, and repudiate a bare imposture. When champion, protector, or advocate, Herbert Putnam was unassailable. He knew himself to be as inseparable from the staff as he was from the Library itself. He once wrote:

"The development [of the Library] is not, of course, just *my* story of my own . . . past . . . is so merged in it as to be insignificant apart from it. In the interest of it I have avoided association with outside enterprises not directly contributory to it, and have reduced merely social relations to a minimum."[35]

Of course, the staff's pride in him was inordinate: pride in his urbanity, suavity, courage, understanding, prescience. There was pride in his wit; in his intellectual gaiety and exuberance. There was pride in his attraction for the learned men who sat at his Round Table in the Library's attic, or who hovered about his place in the Cosmos Club. There was pride in his eloquence, his idiom, the faultless style of his compositions. There was pride in his ethos, his equity, his moral hardihood. There was pride in his punctilio, in his sense of fitness and unfitness, in a tradition which first he made and then he served. And more than pride, there was gratitude for his honor, which was never humbled, never compromised, never diminished. The Putnam legacy is a wisp o grandeur.

Twice he was called upon to make what he termed an "exemplary exit."[36] He made the first on October 1, 1939, when he acceded to the post of Librarian of Congress Emeritus. It was then that he withdrew to new chambers in the northwest pavilion, where he, unobtrusive and unobtruding, might watch the Library as it was maneuvered by other hands than his. If he was pained by what he say, the hurt drew from him no cry of anguish, no measured protest, no demurrer of whatever kind. Scrupulously, he avoided any show of concern. He never injected himself into any situation, never interposed objection, never volunteered an opinion, never overtly expressed a doubt or audibly sounded an alarm. Herbert Putnam and his unparalleled experience were accessible. There, he was available for consultation, for counsel, for collaboration. He would have been, for the newcomers, a magnificent ally. But he could not have been wholly insensitive to his isolation. There were times, then, when his thoughts turned to Mr. Spofford, whom *he* had superseded more than half a century before. Once he uttered them, saying:

"Very few executives have had the fortune to live with their posterity and to be welcomed with a eulogy instead of an elegy. But if you are summoning shades of the past, you must not fail to summon one shade and keep *him* contemporary – the valiant, persistent (I was seeking for the other word) and it is 'forecasting,' 'foretelling,' 'prophesying' – shade . . . Ainsworth Spofford."[37]

At least there was continuity, movement, generation. There was permanence and strength and animation.

Occasionally he seemed frail, but he had always seemed frail. Some there were who said his step was not quite so agile as once it was. Word came that forming cataracts obscured his vision. But Herbert Putnam was imperishable. He had lived so long. He had survived so many. Surely he *would* go on, *must* go on, indefinitely. . . . His mind was keen, his memory clear, his resolution indomitable. Herbert Putnam was still impeccable. It was folly to suppose that mortality – mere mortality – would be his undoing. Even to his family he seemed "almost invulnerable – as though he could live forever."[38]

But on August 1, 1955, while vacationing, he sustained a fractured hip when he tripped on the street. The summer had been one of his happiest and most invigorating. The break was set with a "pin and plate," at the Hyannis Hospital, by a noted Boston Surgeon, Dr. Gerald L. Doherty. It mended so rapidly that he could be moved on the 13th to a comfortable rest home on a hill at Falmouth, near Woods Hole. There he appeared happy and more relaxed, but his gallant old heart was tired. At nine-thirty on Sunday evening, August 14, just after his daughters had bade him goodnight, Herbert Putnam "died peacefully in bed."[39] Doctors gave as the cause a coronary thrombosis. Herbert Putnam, for a second time, had made an "exemplary exit." Across the sea, an English colleague noted that "with Herbert Putnam . . . there passes away the Panizzi of the Twentieth century, one of the two great formative lives of the library profession."[40]

• • • •

FOOTNOTES

[1] To John Hay, April 5, 1899. Librarian's Letterbook No. 1, f.3.
[2] To Walter H. Russell, April 24, 1900. Librarian's Letterbook No. 4, f. 489.
[3] Librarian's Letterbook No. 2, f. 540.
[4] Putnam, Herbert. The national library: some recent developments. *In* American Library Association, *Bulletin,* v. 22, Sept. 1928: 346.
[5] Ibid.
[6] To S. F. Smith, October 11, 1900. Librarian's Letterbook No. 7, f. 73.

[7] To General Henry H. Bingham, March 31, 1900. Librarian's Letterbook No. 4, f. 260.

[8] U.S. *Congress. House.. Committee on Appropriations.* Legislative, executive and judicial appropriation bill, 1901. Hearings conducted by the subcommittee [Washington, Govt. Print. Off., 1900] p. 7-8.

[9] To George F. Bowerman, April 10, 1899. Letterbook No. 1, f. 39.

[10] To R. R. Bowker, December 7, 1899. Letterbook No. 2, p. 661.

[11] Washington post, Mar. 25, 1900, p. 2, col. [4]

[12] To the Members of the Joint Committee on the Library, March 26, 1900. Librarian's Letterbook No. 4, p. 206-209.

[13] Evening star (Washington) Mar. 26, 1900, p. 2, col. [6]

[14] To the City Editor of *The Evening Star,* March 27, 1900. Librarian's Letterbook No. 4, f. 222.

[15] To Helen E. Haines, April 29, 1900. Librarian's Letterbook, No. 4, f. 547. See also, letter to Emory R. Johnson, April 18, 1900. Librarian's Letterbook No. 4, f. 422.

[16] To Allen R. Boyd, June 1, 1899. Librarian's Letterbook No. 1, ff. 382-383.

[17] To Melvil Dewey, April 6, 1900. Librarian's Letterbook No. 4, f. 312.

[18] To W. I. Fletcher, October 19, 1900. Librarian's Letterbook, No. 7, f. 178.

[19] Esdaile, Arundell J. National libraries of the world. London, Grafton, 1934. p. 113.

[20] James H. Canfield to Herbert Putnam, June 9, 1899. Secretary's Office File.

[21] Putnam, Herbert. What may be done for libraries by the nation. *In* American Library Association. Papers and proceedings, 23d meeting; 1901. [n.p.] p. 13.

[22] To James H. Canfield, June 12, 1899. Librarian's Letterbook No. 1, ff. 468-469.

[23] To the Public Printer, May 8, 1900. Librarian's Letterbook No. 4, ff. 673-677.

[24] Evening star (Washington) Oct. 15, 1901, p. 3, col. [5]; p. 7, col. [3].

[25] MacLeish, Archibald. Introduction. A catalog of books, represented by Library of Congress printed cards. v. 1. Ann Arbor, Mich. Edwards Bros., 1942. p. vi.

[26] To Simon Wolf, April 25, 1899. Librarian's Letterbook No. 1, f. 128.

[27] To J. Y. W. MacAlister, editor of *The Library,* London, May 22, 1899. Librarian's Letterbook No. 1, f. 339.

[28] To Charles Harris Hastings, December 4, 1899. Librarian's Letterbook No. 2, f. 650.

[29] To the Honorable the Secretary of the Treasury, October 1, 1900. Librarian's Letterbook No. 7, f. 6.

[30] To the Honorable the Secretary of the Treasury, October 10, 1899. Librarian's Letterbook No. 2, ff. 305-306.

[31] Herbert Putnam to the President, October 15, 1901. Theodore Roosevelt Papers.

[32] Roosevelt, Theodore. First annual message, White House, December 3, 1901.

[33] Such phrases as "a collection of books universal in scope," "a collection universal in scope," "universality in scope," "the service of the national authority," appeared in Herbert Putnam's "What May Be Done For Libraries By the Nation" in American Library Association's *Papers and Proceedings of the Twenty-third General Meeting . . . Held at Waukesha, Wisconsin, July 4-10, 1901,* p. 9-15. In his letter of October 15th, 1901, to President Roosevelt (Theodore Roosevelt Papers) he wrote: "The new building, the new provision of space, equipment, and expert service denote a purpose to elevate the Library into one national in scope and service."

[34] Shirley Purnam O'Hara to David C. Mearns, August 18th, 1955.

[35] Harvard University. Class of 1883. Report No. [7] Fiftieth anniversary. Cambridge, 1933. p. 278.

[36] Herbert Putnam: "Remarks on Receiving a Gift of Recordings, April 1, 1953." Typescript in dossier, Librarians of Congress, in the Manuscripts Division.

[37] Remarks of Herbert Putnam at a Dinner Held at the Mayflower Hotel, Washington, D.C., December 12, 1950, To Honor the One Hundred and Fiftieth Anniversary of the Library of Congress. Transcript in the Manuscripts Division.

[38] Brenda Putnam to Milton E. Lord, August 28, 1955. Copy in the possession of D.C.M.

[39] Shirley Putnam O'Hara to David C. Mearns, August 18, 1955.

[40] Esdaile, Arundell. Library association record, v. 57, Oct. 1955: 420.

ADDITIONAL READINGS

Brodman, Estelle, "The Special Library, the Mirror of its Society," in *Approaches to Library History* edited by John David Marshall (Tallahassee, Florida: Journal of Library History, April, 1966), pp. 32-48.

Clemons, Harry, *The University of Virginia Library, 1825-1950* (Charlottesville: University of Virginia Library, 1954).

Kruzas, Anthony Thomas, *Business and Industrial Libraries in the United States, 1820-1940* (New York: Special Libraries Association, 1965).

La Montagne, Leo E., *American Library Classification: with Special Reference to the Library of Congress* (Hamden, Connecticut: Shoestring Press, 1961).

McMullen, Haynes, "Administration of the University of Chicago Libraries, 1892-1928," *Library Quarterly* 22 (October, 1952), pp. 325-334; 23 (January, 1953), pp. 23-32.

Mearns, David C., *The Story Up to Now; The Library of Congress 1800-1946* (Washington: Government Printing Office, 1947).

_____, "Herbert Putnam: Librarian of the United States," *D. C. Libraries* 26 (January, 1955), pp. 1-24.

Oliphant, Orin J., *The Library of Bucknell University* (Lewisburg, Pa.: Bucknell University Press, 1962).

Peterson, Kenneth G., *The University of California Library at Berkeley, 1900-1945* (Berkeley: University of California Press, 1970).

Pomfret, John E., *The Henry E. Huntington Library and Art Gallery, From its Beginnings to 1969* (San Marino: Huntington Library, 1969).

Powell, Lawrence Clark, *Fortune and Friendship: An Autobiography* (New York: R. R. Bowker, 1968).

Roseberry, Cecil R., *A History of the New York State Library* (Albany: New York State Library, 1970).

Thompson, Lawrence S., "Historical Background of Departmental and Collegiate Libraries," *Library Quarterly* 12 (January, 1942), pp. 49-74.